A CITY IN FRAGMENTS

A CITY IN FRAGMENTS

Urban Text in Modern Jerusalem

Yair Wallach

STANFORD UNIVERSITY PRESS
Stanford, California

STANFORD UNIVERSITY PRESS
Stanford, California

Printed in the United States of America on acid-free, archival-quality paper

Library of Congress Cataloging-in-Publication Data
Names: Wallach, Yair, 1973– author.
Title: A city in fragments : urban text in modern Jerusalem / Yair Wallach.
Description: Stanford, California : Stanford University Press, 2020. | Includes bibliographical references and index.
Identifiers: LCCN 2019037473 (print) | LCCN 2019037474 (ebook) | ISBN 9781503610033 (cloth) | ISBN 9781503611139 (paperback) | ISBN 9781503611146 (epub)
Subjects: LCSH: Written communication—Jerusalem. | Language and history—Jerusalem. | Jerusalem—Description and travel. | Jerusalem—History—19th century. | Jerusalem—History—20th century.
Classification: LCC DS109.15 .W35 2020 (print) | LCC DS109.15 (ebook) | DDC 956.94/42—dc23
LC record available at https://lccn.loc.gov/2019037473
LC ebook record available at https://lccn.loc.gov/2019037474

Cover photo: British Palestine police outside the Palestine Royal Commission, Jerusalem, 1936. Library of Congress

Cover design: Rob Ehle

Typeset by Kevin Barrett Kane in 10.5/14.4 Brill

Contents

Maps and Figures

Note on Transliteration and Translation

THIS BOOK FOLLOWS MODIFIED VERSIONS OF THE ARABIC AND Hebrew transliteration systems specified by the *International Journal of Middle Eastern Studies* (*IJMES*) and the Library of Congress, respectively. All diacriticals and long-vowel markers have been removed except for the *ayin/ayn* (ʿ in both languages) and *aleph/alif* with *hamza* (ʾ). For the definitive forms "the" I have used a hyphenated "al-/ha-," except for individual names in Hebrew that are familiar in different forms, such as Hamenahem or Hacohen. Individual names or terms with an established English spelling were preserved as such (for example, Sultan Suleiman).

When available, I have used existing English translations of non-English quotations. All other quotations from Arabic, Hebrew, and French are my translations.

A CITY IN FRAGMENTS

INTRODUCTION

IT WAS IN THE EARLY HOURS OF A SPRING EVENING. I WALKED behind the supermarket, climbed down a low stone wall, and slipped through a large hole in the wire fence. Before me stretched the railway lines, overgrown with weeds, leading to Jerusalem's old train station. It had stood empty and unused since the line to Tel Aviv finally shut down in 1998. I approached the main building, walked through the rubble of smashed glass, broken roof tiles, and pieces of wood beams, and entered the ticket office. Looking from inside the counter, the Perspex window shield was perforated with the Israeli railway logo; light rays shot through the holes of its Star of David. On the floor were scattered freight-train log sheets, a dirty thermos, and mangled plastic chairs. I walked down the corridor, past a corner, amid graffiti and painted walls. The half-dismantled stairway led upward, to the upper story. There I edged carefully next to the wall, as much of the floor had collapsed. Finally I was outside, on the station roof. I looked at the large stone sign on the station wall, above the door. In worn-out greyish white, with the letters plastered over but still readable, it said JERUSALEM in French, and "Kudüs-i-Sherif" in Ottoman Turkish. Below this original 1892 sign was the Hebrew stone sign emplaced shortly after the establishment of the British Mandate. In a brighter shade of white, and in somewhat antiquated serifed Hebrew, was written "Yerushalayim." That trilingual, two-phased sign was the reason for my trespass. I stared at it, trying to make sense of it, trying to make sense of that place.

I was aware of the history of the station. The Ottoman Jaffa-Jerusalem railway was a project spearheaded by the entrepreneur Yosef Navon, an Ottoman Sephardic Jew, in partnership with the Ottoman district engineer George Franjiah, an Orthodox Christian Arab, and the Swiss Protestant banker Johannes Frutiger. The line and the station were constructed and operated by a French company. Their 1892 inauguration was celebrated by local intellectuals as a triumph of progress and enlightenment.[1] The railway survived much of the twentieth century's upheavals, wars, and atrocities. The line was targeted by Palestinian insurgents during the Arab Revolt (1936–1939) and the station itself was bombed by the Jewish Irgun militia in 1946. After the 1948 war the line operated as part of Israeli railways, in increasingly limited capacity, until its 1998 closure. Since then the station had stood deserted and quickly fallen into a dilapidated state, as it was reclaimed by teenagers, homeless, and junkies. The trilingual name of the station used to welcome those arriving in the city and bid farewell to those leaving it, whoever they

FIGURE 1. Roof of railway station, with the name of the city in French, Ottoman Turkish, and Hebrew (2006).
Source: Yair Wallach.

FIGURE 2. The Jerusalem Railway Station, [1892–1914].
Source: Library of Congress, Matson Collection, American Colony photographers.

were and whatever Jerusalem meant to them. The sign stood for the city. It stood for its bright modern future. Now it was plastered over, decaying, half obliterated. And that seemed to say something about Jerusalem, about signs, about text and modernity.

For many years I walked the streets of Jerusalem in a real and metaphoric sense, searching for writings on its walls. I was especially attracted to the little-noticed, half-erased texts: worn-out stone inscriptions; lettering on sewage covers; mysterious acronyms on gates and facades; faded ceramic street nameplates. Here, in the old train station, I encountered such textual debris in abundance: turn-of-the-century French red roof tiles, proclaiming "St. Henry—Marseille"; a broken metal piece of the railway, embossed with "WDS and co, 1917"; a Hebrew sign "25 kg sack of round rice" hanging strangely from the ceiling; and plentiful graffiti in Hebrew, English, Russian, and Arabic. A blue-and-white commemorative sign on the facade, on the street side, paid tribute not to the builders of the railway but rather to its 1946 Irgun bombers, as if the attempt to destroy the station was more significant, in civic and national terms, than its original construction.

I looked for text in the city, in any form that one could encounter in public or semi-public contexts, in Arabic, Hebrew, and other languages: graffiti, logos, inscriptions, official signs, ephemera. The period that interested me was the century that saw the emergence of modern Jerusalem, under Ottoman and British rule: from the middle of the nineteenth century to the 1948 war that partitioned the city. The texts of the city during this turbulent century registered the dramatic changes and violent ruptures in the modern history of the city: they were chronicles of construction and destruction, heritage preservation and modern development, occupation and displacement. But rather than seeing these texts as passive records, documenting social and political transformation, I was interested in the role they played in facilitating these very transformations.[2] I asked myself what they meant to the people who emplaced them, and the people who encountered them. And I wondered what could be learned, by looking at these texts and signs, about the relationship between modernity and textuality in a place like this one. Jerusalem: a city overwhelmed by its religious and symbolic significance; a place of encounter and disjuncture, of ethnic and linguistic diversity; a battleground for imperialism, colonialism, and nationalism. In its complicated, multilingual, painfully contested, and violent history, Jerusalem provided a rich site for a study of the modern transformation of urban textuality.

My quest for Jerusalem's forgotten textual artifacts was guided by Walter Benjamin's notion of writing history from refuse. Benjamin's investigations of nineteenth-century modernity searched for meaning in marginal aspects of urban life.[3] Modernity was best understood not through grand political narratives but through fashion, street lighting, lithographs, prostitutes, and defunct shopping arcades. The logic of historical development was written into these seemingly insignificant and haphazard practices and artifacts. These fragments of everyday modernity, when placed together in a collage, had the power to call into question narratives of history as progress. By assembling together the random, fragmented, and half-obliterated traces of the mundane, the deep configuration of modernity could be grasped, as if in a panoramic vision. Benjamin's model of the materialist historian was the rag-picker: the scavenger in the trash of history, who searches for discarded objects and obsolete techniques, reassembles them for a radical reusing: a fresh understanding of past and present.[4]

The rags that I set out collecting were the urban texts of modern Jerusalem. They included stone inscriptions, signs on buildings, text on money, graffiti, embroidered banners, protest placards, visiting cards, and identity papers. These "urban texts" were a broad array of media and artifacts that were inscribed and encountered in civic and congregational space in Jerusalem under late-Ottoman and British rule.[5] They consisted of fragments of sentences, words, and numbers, in Arabic, Hebrew, and other languages. While many of these artifacts were not necessarily unique to an urban setting, their instances outside the city were far less common. The city was a site of condensed textuality, where textual interaction was far more frequent and played a key role in constructing the urban experience. Many of the inscribed artifacts and sites formed the backdrop of the city's most dramatic events, but the texts themselves attracted limited or no interest from many scholars who wrote about Jerusalem.

The product of my textual-rag-picking is this book, a collage of inscriptions. It brings together texts that were inscribed in stone, painted on wood signs, struck in gold, printed on paper banknotes and visiting cards, glazed on ceramic tiles, written by hand on walls, and embroidered on cloth banners. When these media and artifacts are placed together as part of a textual field, it becomes possible to see the profound shift that took place in the textual economies of modern Jerusalem in the early twentieth century. The change was manifested not only in terms of format, scripts, material aspects, location, and content of writing, but also in the very meaning of writing and reading. Traditional Arabic and Hebrew urban texts in Jerusalem were invested with divine meaning and strongly embedded within material culture. Struck in precious metals, chiseled deep within lintel stones, and embroidered in golden thread in velvet banners, text had a bodily presence that could not be discarded or abstracted. With modernity, text was stripped of its material skin and was cast as abstract and fragmented signifier. Modern urban text proliferated as external signifier in wood, metal, paper, and cardboard, naming and defining buildings, streets, and people in the service of a wide array of political projects. The operation of textuality was radically redefined. Stone inscriptions, pilgrims' graffiti, and sacred banners, which had been in use for centuries, were displaced and cast as heritage. At the same time, street nameplates, shop signs, identity papers, and visiting cards emerged as key tools for reorganizing population and space.

THEORIES OF TEXT: THE SUPPLEMENT AND THE BLANK PAGE

A starting point for a conceptual investigation of textuality can be found in Jacques Derrida's early work on writing. Derrida played a pivotal role in the poststructuralist "linguistic turn," which placed language at the heart of critical reflection, positing that culture and society are made through language and do not exist outside it. Derrida's early work placed writing, specifically, at the heart of his investigation. *Of Grammatology* (1967) was Derrida's blueprint for a new branch of scholarship, a new "science of writing" which never materialized.[6] In Derrida's broad and ambitious outline, such an interdisciplinary science would pay attention not only to the history and materiality of text but also to its philosophical foundations and psychoanalytical implications. The science of writing would not only investigate the content, techniques, and socioeconomic context of writing; it would also interrogate what writing is in the first place, what are its limits and preconditions. Derrida's own contribution was manifested in his investigation of the metaphysics of writing and its inherent instability. While this "science of writing" remained an unrealized proposition, which he himself abandoned and whose viability he later denied, Derrida's line of inquiry opened up crucial questions about textuality.

Particularly relevant to this book is Derrida's understanding of writing as *supplement*: an external layer which completes the original entity and overdetermines its meaning. Oscillating between an addendum and a substitute, the supplement threatens to corrupt and destabilize the original. According to Derrida, the dichotomy between the original and its appendage is deceptive. If the supplement is able to complete the original object, then that object was lacking in the first place and could never exist by and in itself. Derrida's concept of writing as "the dangerous supplement" refers to the relation between textuality and orality, and the manner in which Western civilization constructs writing as a flawed and corrupt copy of the original speech. Yet this conceptualization opens up important questions about the relationship between text and the material world. The fragmented texts of urban life can be seen as supplementary elements that complete, define, and transform artifacts, buildings, and people. Whether as signs on shops, identity papers defining an individual, or graffiti "defacing" a religious site, text appears as an agency which has the power to organize or disrupt the socio-spatial order of the city. Text is understood as a dematerialized external object that can be attached to things, define them, and alter their meaning.

It is the sweeping, anti-historical nature of Derrida's inquiry which is its most significant limitation. For Derrida suggests that the instability of textuality is not specific to historical and cultural contexts but, instead, stems from the very structure of signification. Crucial here was Derrida's widening of the scope of writing beyond the "narrow" notion of notation. *Of Grammatology* introduced a concept of "arche-writing," which covered all forms of human expression, beyond text or speech. "We say 'writing' for all that gives rise to an inscription in general, whether it is literal or not and even if what it distributes in space is alien to the order of the voice: cinematography, choreography, of course, but also pictorial, musical, sculptural 'writing.'"[7] It is with this "general" sense of writing in mind that Derrida concluded: "*There is nothing outside of the text* . . . in what one calls the real life of these existences 'of flesh and bone' . . . there has never been anything but writing."[8] This proposition opened the tantalizing possibility of reading all forms of human expression as text, simultaneously pushing the discussion away from writing. If the world was text, and could be "deconstructed" as such, there was little reason to limit the investigation to writing in the "narrow" and "colloquial" sense of notation.

The obvious problem with such an approach is that it risks diluting writing to a generalized metaphor. When "text" is expanded to include any form of human signification, the historicity of text is effaced and the cultural and material specificities of its usage are obscured. And yet text in a "narrow" sense is one of the most resilient and adaptable human technologies. Systems of inscribed notations changed remarkably little over centuries or millennia, and yet the application and meaning of textuality has been anything but constant. By ignoring historical considerations, we lose sight of "how, and with what consequences, writing systems are devised, regulated and imposed."[9] But a more serious problem, in my view, is that Derrida's broadened concept of writing was in fact locked within his narrow experience of the contemporary technologies of writing. Derrida's scholarship consisted of interrogative readings of texts from the Western canon, from Plato to Lévi-Strauss. His philosophical interpretation employed visceral and material metaphors such as the hymen, the suture, and the pharmakon (the medicine-poison), but did so with regard to text on paper. While Derrida's concept of "arche-writing" encompassed all forms of signification, he himself said in 1998 that "I have always written, and even spoken, on paper: on the subject of paper, on actual paper, and with paper in mind."[10] The equation of text with tracts on paper implies a notion of reading as a silent, private, and secular operation of deciphering and interpreting, not part of everyday life but rather set against it; not a social praxis but rather an individual, isolated quest for meaning. The problem was not that the widening of the scope of text rendered the term meaningless, but rather that it imposed a limited notion of textuality that was culturally and historically specific, implicitly separating text from everyday life. If this is the case, it is necessary to ask if the crisis of signification, which Derrida analyzed so deftly, is inherent to writing as he suggested or in fact is a historical condition, rooted in modernity.

In contrast, for Michel de Certeau, the historicity of textuality is central to its analysis. De Certeau's "The Scriptural Economy" is an analytical framework that historicizes modern text in a grand epochal narrative.[11] De Certeau argued that premodern writing in medieval Europe was grounded in holy scriptures, whose reading was an embodied practice involving the human voice. The sacred text was the "great cosmological Spoken Word," which believers desired to hear. In early modernity, with secularization, text lost its intimate connection to God and became an instrument of power. Textuality, in its modern sense, was a machinery at the service of capital and colonialism. The logic of capitalism (accumulation) and colonialism (appropriation) reduced people and their environment to a readable text. The emphasis on the colonizing impetus of writing has important implications for analyzing British and Zionist use of text to reshape modern Jerusalem. For de Certeau, the relation between writing and colonialism is epitomized in Daniel Defoe's *Robinson Crusoe*, which he sees as a founding myth of Western modernity. Crusoe, the shipwrecked Englishman, sees the desert island as the empty space which is open to be conquered and civilized through writing. Robinson Crusoe's diary gave him the necessary "blank page" on which he subjugated time, space, and society. Modern writing, argued de Certeau, crucially depends on this "blank page" as an external and autonomous surface which is isolated from the world and has power over it. This exterior position allows for the separation between subject and object, narrator and world, signifier and signified. Upon this autonomous surface a symbolic code and a system of knowledge are formed which produce the world, as text.

De Certeau's analysis of the "blank page" as the founding myth of modern text is particularly insightful. The notion of writing as pure meaning—abstract words that are external to material reality—appears as the basis of the modern understanding of textuality. The text's "ontological referentiality" is a powerful tool which has allowed using words to label, categorize, name, and order. And yet the flaw in de Certeau's analysis lies in subscribing to this mythology. The denial of the materiality of text is an ideological one, for text, in any form, is always part of the material world. Writing and reading are not operations of pure meaning that take place in a void, but rather are embodied social practices. Street nameplates, shop signs, banknotes, and identity cards were encountered and read not in an abstract space but rather in concrete physical circumstances. Rather than accept the myth of the autonomous text, I wish to outline the processes of dematerialization through which text was increasingly understood as external referent and thereby acquired new powers of signification.

As a critic of the Enlightenment, de Certeau viewed modern society as an oppressive techno-structure. Used in the service of capitalist accumulation and colonization, text, in its modern and secular incarnation, reduced everything and everyone to legible terms. De Certeau's pessimistic outlook allowed no escape from this system of inscription, which determines all aspects of life including the human body. This dark view is echoed in other negative approaches to writing which view it as primarily a disciplinary tool. "The state is a recording, registering, and measuring machine," one scholar recently argued.[12] Yet reading texts only as an instrument of overwhelming power is reductive: such a view fails to account for writing's emancipatory potential, its malleability and volatility. To be sure, the modern state has used text as a powerful tool, which manifests itself in urban space in town planning, population registers, and signposting. But the process of inscription is unstable and is threatened by itself, opening space to resist and challenge the established order. In this book I consider the potential of urban texts not only to serve power but also as means to challenge it, by a generation who saw radical rewriting of the self as a form of emancipation.

In Walter Benjamin's writing it is possible to detect an alternative approach to urban textuality, one which identifies emancipatory potential in its radical new form.[13] Benjamin was fascinated by modern textual artifacts, and particularly street texts. He recognized the fragmented and dynamic nature of "leaflets, brochures, articles and placards" as marking a break with the "pretentious gesture of the book." Benjamin's model of writing is not the mythological "blank page" but rather the card index: a collection of observations, quotations, and information, cut and pasted, arranged and rearranged.[14] Modern writing consisted not of coherent long tracts but of fragments, which acquired meaning through connections, juxtapositions, and contrasts. Text was inscribed, printed on, engraved, in material form, and produced through labor. The location of urban texts in the street, "the dwelling place of the collective," created opportunities for counter-appropriation and agitation.[15] Benjamin studied carefully the introduction of house numbers, the logic of street naming, and the changing nature of shop signs, posters, and advertisements, not only as evidence of historical change but also as material technologies that remade the city. He was aware of their employment for the strengthening hold of state and capital over society. But rather than see street texts as mere instruments of power, he believed these were tools that were open for reclaiming. Against the background of the economic and political crisis of the 1930s, Benjamin called on writers to embrace the disruptive, fragmented language of the streets:

> Not to find one's way in a city may well be uninteresting and banal. It requires ignorance—nothing more. But to lose oneself in a city—as one loses oneself in a forest—that calls for quite a different schooling. Then, signboards and street names, passers-by, roofs, kiosks and bars must speak to the wanderer like a twig snapping under his feet in the forest, like the startling call of a bittern in the distance, like the sudden stillness of a clearing with a lily standing erect at its center.[16]

Getting lost was a radical intellectual methodology that allowed an immersion in modernity through its signs. Modern street texts assumed, for Benjamin, a visceral quality, and navigating them was similar to a forest adventure. In that heightened sense of suspense, danger, and excitement hid a promise of emancipation, and a possibility of revolutionary awakening. Signboards and street names could be read against the grain; they could be used to write counter-hegemonic stories for the city and its people.

TEXT, MODERNITY, AND THE CITY

In urban studies, the city is often discussed as "text." As a site of condensed signification, the city is a cosmos of metaphoric textuality, which can be deciphered through semiotic interpretation or "deconstructed" to reveal its inherent instabilities. Such "readings" of the city examine a wide array of "cultural texts" such as photographs, public ceremonies, urban plans, and walking itineraries.[17] Actual texts in the city (inscriptions, signage, graffiti), when they are discussed, are seen as elements of signification alongside myriad other forms of cultural texts. Such interpretive methodology clearly has its strength, as it expands our understanding of the social and cultural construction of the city, but it risks missing the unique traits of urban textuality, its cultural specificities, and its changing nature.

Other scholars, who eschewed the preoccupation with "signs" in favor of urban praxis and social reality, have similarly ignored the texts of the city. The Marxist urban theorist Henri Lefebvre strongly rejected the notion of "reading space": "Social space can in no way be compared to a blank page upon which a specific message has been inscribed," he insisted. "Space was *produced* before being *read*; nor was it produced in order to be read and grasped, but rather in order to be *lived* by people with bodies and lives in their own particular urban context."[18] The "reading" of the city, according to Lefebvre, reduced space to a representation. In so doing it effaced the lived experience of the city, which is created by the urban population as a whole. Lefebvre's work aimed to empower the inhabitants-producers of the city to reclaim space in everyday terms. However, his aversion to the "reading" of the city as a metaphoric "text," and his focus on material urban life, again excluded the actual texts of the city from the field of inquiry. His contrast between representations of the city and its lived reality relied on a problematic distinction between reading and living. Reading was seen as a disembodied operation, occurring outside the real, socially produced space. Urban texts receive a brief and vague mention in Lefebvre's work, despite the fact that, for modern urban dwellers, a significant part of daily encounters with text involve reading signage and ephemera in public, social contexts.

The revolution of digital technology has brought manifold new ways of reading and writing, leading to a reappraisal of the historicity of text. Computers and phone screens cast the book as a historical object, and have led to considerable interest in the history and sociology of writing and reading, including topics such as the history of literacy, printing and publishing, and the use of libraries.[19] These histories of reading have tended to focus on manuscripts, pamphlets, newspapers, and above all, the book as the emblematic form of text, while urban texts are usually ignored. The issue here is not so much a scholarly lacuna; it is rather a series of unspoken assumptions, essentializing reading as an individual, private, and isolated activity.

A more comprehensive approach was put forward by sociolinguists, studying "linguistic landscapes." This field of study examines forms of writing available in public space, such as public road signs, advertising billboards, street names, place-names, commercial shop signs, and public signs on government buildings.[20] Studies of linguistic landscapes investigate hierarchies of power, often in multilingual contexts, and trace the linguistic dimensions of social and political conflicts through signage. In Palestine/Israel, sociolinguists have highlighted Hebrew's hegemony in public space and the erasure and marginalization of Arabic in the urban environment as well as road signs.[21] Cultural geographers have explored the spatial writing of dominant narratives through signage, street names, and place-names.[22] These studies analyze the power dynamics expressed in signage and ask pertinent questions about the presence or absence of languages, their order and status. But they are less likely to ask why the sign was placed there in the first place. The sociolinguist analysis of linguistic landscapes focuses on contemporary dynamics rather than historical development. Such analysis takes for granted text's very presence in the urban realm. This book focuses on similar forms of urban text, but follows a different approach. It takes a step backward to examine the very creation of the modern textual landscape, which we now so often accept as a natural part of our environment. My aim is to return to the moment of the appearance of street nameplates, banknotes, and government signage as standard elements of the urban environment, tracing the very formation of modern urban textuality against traditional forms of writing. My study joins other interdisciplinary investigations into textual technologies, analyzing the shifting meaning of textual signification in specific historical and cultural contexts.[23]

What happened to text in Jerusalem was neither an instance of a generic modern transformation nor a particular product of an idiosyncratic, holy, and ancient city. A small city with regional and global significance, Jerusalem was an entanglement of frames, narratives, and trajectories.[24] The vectors of modernity operate at a variety of scales—local, regional, and global—and their outcome always depends on a specific context. Jerusalem was a condensation of manifold networks: imperial Ottoman governance; relations with the city's hinterland and other urban centers in Palestine and Syria; regional trade in the Levant; commerce and banking with Europe and the rest of the world; the literary circles of the intellectuals of the cultural revival movements in Arabic and in Hebrew; Jewish philanthropy networks from India to North America; the British Empire; and many others. The richness of these networks calls for a historical investigation of urban textuality that is attentive to Jerusalem's particularity while offering wider insights.

LATE-OTTOMAN JERUSALEM

In the 1850s Jerusalem was a provincial town contained within the city walls, with a population of twenty thousand inhabitants.[25] Islamic hegemony was expressed in hundreds of Arabic stone inscriptions, embedded in the city's walls and water fountains, and in dozens of pious institutions. But in the second half of the nineteenth century, the social, political, and textual landscape changed dramatically.

Conventional accounts have often presented Ottoman Jerusalem as an underdeveloped backwater, which was awakened to life by Western intervention and Zionist dynamism. Such accounts portray Jerusalem as a highly segregated city, a mosaic of traditional religious communities, enclosed in their separate quarters. Modernity was said to have arrived in Jerusalem only through European influence and British occupation. The British are credited for bringing progress in the form of urban planning and proper institutions, as they tried to navigate a city divided between Arabs and Jews.[26]

Recent scholarship has thoroughly challenged this narrative and its underlying assumptions. Salim Tamari's work has been invaluable in reconceptualizing late-Ottoman Jerusalem as a modern city undergoing rapid change, driven by the local multi-faith elite in the context of Ottoman reforms and modernization.[27] Tamari has shown that the city was far more mixed and integrated than is usually thought, and that Western portrayals of the walled city's religious "quarters" in guidebooks and maps bore little relation to the socio-spatial reality. Scholars who have followed this direction described turn-of-the-century Jerusalem as a "city in the age of possibilities": an Ottoman city of movement and flow, increasingly connected to the rest of the empire and the world, whose administrators and intellectuals were propelled by a belief in development and modernity.[28]

Ottoman reforms brought a profound reorganization of urban space and political structures. Centralization of governance, for purposes of taxation, conscription, and population control, led to new forms of textual registration of land and imperial subjects. Houses were numbered; censuses collected increasingly detailed information on inhabitants; properties were registered in a new Land Registry. With the gradual transformation of the Ottoman Empire from an Islamic polity to a multinational state promising equal rights to Christians and Jews, new civic institutions were created, such as the local municipality. The city's importance increased in 1874 when the district of Jerusalem, encompassing much of Palestine, became an independent district directly subordinate to the Ottoman government in Istanbul. Urban development projects, led by the municipality, included the upgrading of water systems and roads, a new district headquarters and barracks, and the introduction of civic amenities such as a post and telegraph office, public hospital, municipal gardens, the railway station, and plans for a tram network and electricity provision. By the eve of the First World War, Jerusalem's population had risen to an estimated eighty thousand.[29]

The transformation of Jerusalem was part of wider patterns of urban development throughout the Ottoman Empire. Similar developments, on larger and smaller scales, took place in cities throughout the Arab provinces, from Aleppo to Sanaa.[30] New civic spaces were created, such as parks, promenades, new markets, and city squares, marked with visible clock towers and water fountains. Aggressive urban renewal projects aimed to rationalize street layout and facilitate movement in widened boulevards. Cities were connected to a network of transportation in shipping services, roads, and railways. Postal services were established and a telegraph network allowed rapid communication to the entire world. At the same time, cities in the Arab provinces saw the emergence of an increasingly confident urban middle class, which sought influence in local and imperial politics and championed far-reaching changes in everyday life and social conventions.[31] The movement of revival of Arab identity and language, the Nahda, found an eager urban audience that advocated reforms to rejuvenate Arab culture in the spirit of a liberal and modern age through engagement with Western science and literature.[32] Arabic language stood at the heart of the Nahda, whose primary manifestations were in the revolution of publishing throughout the Levant. Jerusalem was a minor center of the Nahda compared to Beirut, but in Jerusalem as well, local intellectuals opened a public library and were deeply involved in reforms in education. After the 1908 Young Turk constitutional revolution, Jerusalemites launched local newspapers in Arabic and participated keenly in politics in Greater Syria and in the Ottoman Empire.[33]

Studies of Jerusalem typically divide the population in confessional terms into Muslims, Christians, and Jews. Zionist historians have often emphasized that, because of high levels of immigration, Jews already constituted a "majority" in the city in the late nineteenth century. Population estimates for this period are very imprecise and invite methodological questions about the comprehensiveness and reliability of sources.[34] Yet a more fundamental conceptual problem is the anachronistic imposition of demographic anxieties and notions of conflict and segregation.[35] The emphasis on religious difference obliterates other forms of difference, such as class, ethnicity, language, and area of residence. A common Jerusalem identity and Ottoman citizenship were powerful vehicles for cross-confessional alliances. It is even more anachronistic to think of Ottoman Jerusalem as a city already divided between "Arab" and "Jew," as these categories coalesced as antagonistic national identities only during the British Mandate. Inspired by the "relational approach" to the history of Palestine/Israel, I do not assume the existence of two different societies and cultures in early-twentieth-century Jerusalem but instead seek to explain how these two societies came about through interaction with local and global forces.[36] Not many Arabic-speaking Jerusalemites defined themselves primarily as Arab in the late nineteenth century, but by 1920 demonstrators marched in Jerusalem under the slogan "Palestine for the Arabs." In the 1850s, being Jewish meant being part of a Jewish congregation defined by synagogues and rabbinical authority; by the 1930s being Jewish was becoming a national identity. We need to think how these identities were produced, not least through textual practices and artifacts such as population registries, birth certificates, identity papers, and public signage.

The Jewish population of Jerusalem increased considerably in the final decades of Ottoman rule. In the 1850s, there were about five thousand Jews and only a handful of synagogues in the city. By 1914, the Jewish population was estimated at forty-five thousand, and there were more than 220 synagogues and Jewish seminaries in the city, marked with hundreds of memorial tablets in Hebrew.[37] But it is wrong to refer to Jews in Jerusalem as a single, proto-national community, as they are often described. Jews shared Hebrew as a written language of liturgy and congregational affairs and were formally all led by the Ottoman chief rabbi of Jerusalem. However, Jewish communities differed in language of speech, trades, customs, and areas of residence.[38] They maintained separate congregational organizations, schools, synagogues, soup kitchens, cemeteries, and butchers, according to ethnicities. Yiddish-speaking Ashkenazim made up the largest group, estimated at twenty-five thousand in 1914. A further twenty thousand Jews belonged to the Sephardic congregation and to smaller communities from Bukhara, Georgia, Yemen, Morocco, Persia, and Syria, and to several other congregations.[39] The significant Jewish presence in Jerusalem stood out in comparison to other cities in Palestine, and to rural areas, where Jews constituted a very small minority.

Amid this diverse social landscape, in the late nineteenth century a Jewish intelligentsia and a middle class emerged. They cultivated the spirit of the Haskalah, the Jewish Enlightenment, whose center was in Central and Eastern Europe. They sought to promote a modern Jewish identity transcending ethnic congregational boundaries through a vibrant scene of local Hebrew newspapers and in modern schools, established by European Jewish philanthropic networks aiming to reform and modernize Ottoman Jews. Orthodox publishing and notice-posting, often in opposition to the Haskalah, also contributed to making Hebrew highly visible in Jerusalem in the form of commercial notices, rabbinical proclamations, shop signs, and foundation inscriptions on religious institutions.

Ironically, the Zionist movement maintained a highly ambivalent approach to the city which gave it its name. On the one hand, Jerusalem had a large Jewish population, making up half of Palestine's Jews at the beginning of the twentieth century. It was the city mentioned in Jewish prayers and the location of the holiest sites. And yet at the same time, Jewish communities in Jerusalem represented forms of Judaism which were anathema to Zionism as a modernizing movement. In 1910 David Ben-Gurion described these communities as a "lifeless body . . . degenerating in idleness and beggary, drowning in illiteracy, chaotic, splintered, and ruled by a band of hypocrites and cheats, unschooled rabbis and ignorant scholars."[40] Jerusalem's Jewish communities were largely indifferent, if not hostile, to Zionism. Some Zionist institutions, such as the Bezalel Art School, were established in the city, but European Zionist migrants who came to Palestine mostly preferred to settle elsewhere in the country. Local Jewish intelligentsia in Jerusalem were attracted to the Jewish national idea, but their primary focus was on Hebrew cultural revival and recognition for Jewish national rights within the Ottoman Empire—unlike the European doctrine of Political Zionism, which aimed for mass Jewish migration, colonization, and Jewish self-rule.[41]

Alongside these demographic and political developments, late-Ottoman Jerusalem saw a myriad of other changes as an entire way of life was transformed within a mere few decades. The local middle class replaced their dress with European clothes; domed roofs were replaced with sloped tiled roofs; olive-oil lamps were forsaken in favor of kerosene lanterns, and during the war, electric light. Much of this was due to the incorporation of Jerusalem into European circuits of trade, tourism, and influence.

EUROPEAN IMPERIALISM, BRITISH COLONIALISM, AND ZIONISM

Since the early nineteenth century, Western missionaries, scholars, military officers, and travelers were involved in an effort to "recover" biblical Palestine.[42] There was nothing new about Christian visitors experiencing the Holy Land through the Bible. What was new, however, was the "scientific" effort to render the Bible visible in maps, tourist guidebooks, travel accounts, drawings, and photographs—as representations of contemporary Jerusalem. Impressive signage on European mansions and institutions in Jerusalem wrote the Bible into the landscape by invoking Christian events and holy places. Large signs in European languages made English, French, and Russian a striking visual element in the city's landscape. Here was an active process of molding and producing a modern biblical geography.

This effort was not geared toward substantial Western Christian immigration. Although Germans, Swedes, and North Americans settled in Jerusalem and established small colonies, Palestine was never seen as a land suitable for large-scale Christian European settler colonialism. Rather, the biblical rendering of the land provided justification for imperial interest, and later colonial rule. "This country of Palestine belongs to *you* and to *me*," exclaimed the Archbishop of York in the 1865 inauguration of the British Palestine Exploration Fund.[43] In the nineteenth century European powers considerably increased their influence in the Levant, and in Jerusalem their presence was clearly felt. As the "Holy Land," Palestine was an arena of competition between the Great Powers. European consuls in Jerusalem enjoyed far-reaching powers under the Capitulary Treaties: they had the right to try their citizens, who were exempted from local taxes and conscription. These concessions, remaining in force until 1914, facilitated Western economic expansion and incursion into Ottoman sovereignty. Not only did the social landscape change, so did the city's soundscape and built fabric. In the 1850s churches received permission to ring their bells after centuries of prohibition.[44] Rival European powers sponsored the construction of churches, monasteries, schools, hospitals, and pilgrims' hostelries, operated postal services, and facilitated the opening of bank branches. The city outside the walls became replete with monumental examples of European architecture in different national styles, from a replica of a late-medieval Florentine palace (the Italian Hospital) to a German guesthouse built in Gothic Revival style (August Victoria).[45] Jerusalem increasingly relied on European trade, investments, tourism, and pilgrimage. The city's western entrance, leading to Jaffa, now became Jerusalem's civic and commercial center, reflecting the city's incorporation into these networks.

Four centuries of Ottoman rule came to an end in 1917 with the British occupation of the city. British colonial rule continued Ottoman urban development, albeit under a radically different paradigm.[46] The Ottoman discourse of modern progress and development made way for a discourse of conservation and preservation of an ancient holy city. The British imposed on Jerusalem a language of biblical antiquity and religious sectarianism. In 1920 Jerusalem became the capital of British-ruled Palestine, a newly defined political territory created by the League of Nations as a "Mandate," designated for the establishment of a Jewish National Home. Support for Zionism was expressed in the recognition of Hebrew as one of the three official languages, alongside English and Arabic. But in Jerusalem, British officials preferred not to highlight their political commitment to Zionism, instead presenting themselves as custodians of a city of global heritage. In the words of the last High Commissioner to Palestine, Jerusalem was "precious as an emblem of several faiths, a site of spiritual beauty," and "had been in our care as a sacred trust." The primary British mission was to "conserve the old while adding the new in keeping with it."[47] The protection of the "Status Quo" was a cornerstone of British policies in Jerusalem. Originating in an 1852 international agreement regarding the Holy Sepulchre, the principle of the "Status Quo" was extended to other holy places and to the aesthetics of the city more generally.[48] The British imagined the population as segregated along religious lines into hostile communities. They, as enlightened rulers, saw their role as keeping the peace between the sects and protecting the city, which did not belong to its inhabitants but rather to the entire world as a "city of an idea."[49] For British rulers, especially in the early years of the Mandate, textual policies served as tools to promote this preservationist vision. In street nameplates, on banknotes and stamps, Jerusalem was presented as an ancient and holy city.

The city continued its rapid growth under British rule. New neighborhoods were built and villages became integrated into the urban sphere. In 1945, as a result of Jewish immigration from Europe and the Middle East, and Arab migration from Jerusalem's hinterland, the population reached 157,000 people.[50] British encouragement of Jewish immigration and colonization met with staunch Arab opposition and violent resistance. The city became increasingly segregated into Arab and Jewish areas. The escalating conflict led to the incorporation of local Jewish communities into the Zionist project, albeit in a marginalized position. The highly diverse array of Jewish communities coalesced into a Jewish national society—the Hebrew-speaking Yishuv.[51] Yet the hegemonic Zionist elite, made up of recent East European secular migrants, continued to view with suspicion Jerusalem's large population of Middle Eastern Jews and Orthodox Ashkenazim. In 1948 David Ben-Gurion noted in his diary that the Jewish population of Jerusalem consisted of "20% normal people, 20% privileged (university, etc.), 60% strange [*muzarim*] (provincial, medieval, etc.)."[52] The projection of Hebrew onto the streets of Jerusalem, in an attempt to normalize and territorialize the language, was done not only against Arabic but also against existing uses of Hebrew as the sacred language of a religious congregation. Zionist activists disparaged the failure of the city's Jews to adopt the Zionist ethos of radically remaking people and space. At the same time, Zionist efforts to Hebraize Jerusalem were limited by the political conditions of British oversight and Arab control of the municipality. During the Mandate, Zionist textual intervention was largely confined to Jewish businesses and neighborhoods, and the main objective was to encourage and compel Jews to use Hebrew as their everyday language rather than to Hebraize geography. The Hebrew renaming of the landscape on official maps and signs became possible only after the establishment of Israel in 1948.

As the British Mandate was drawing to its end, the 1947 UN partition plan designated Jerusalem as an international enclave under special rule. Days after the plan's adoption, hostilities broke out in the city center. In the ensuing fighting, Jerusalem as the capital of Palestine, shared by Arabs and Jews, gave way to a city divided ethnically and politically. The bourgeois Arab Palestinian neighborhoods in the western part of the city, and much of the city's Arab hinterland, were occupied by Israel. Tens of thousands fled or were expelled.[53] This was part of the Nakba, the devastating destruction of Arab Palestine, which made over seven hundred thousand Palestinians refugees. In Jerusalem the war also created Jewish refugees. Around two thousand Jewish residents of the Old City were driven out after its occupation by Jordan.[54] The 1949 Armistice Agreement divided the city between Israeli West Jerusalem and Jordanian East Jerusalem. The former city center became a borderline and a no-man's-land. This division continues to have profound implications even after the 1967 Israeli occupation of East Jerusalem and its unilateral annexation.

URBAN TEXTS IN JERUSALEM

In the century from the 1850s to 1948, Jerusalem witnessed the dramatic proliferation of new textual artifacts, which were visible in more locations and related to new aspects of life. Public notices, banknotes, street nameplates, visiting cards, commercial signage, government signs, and advertisements made text an ever-present aspect of the city. It is therefore tempting to describe the textual transformation of Jerusalem in terms of growth and diversification, and a shift from orality to textuality. The introduction of new textual media could be seen as an inevitable consequence of growing access to education, rising literacy rates, and a rapidly developing city. As the urban economy became more complex and less personal, the intimacy of close neighborly proximity was lost, and life became increasingly alienated and shifted from face-to-face communication to writing. The cries of market vendors were superseded by commercial signage and printed advertisements in the local press. Official news which had been communicated by city criers in Arabic, Yiddish, and Judeo-Spanish was replaced by printed notices. Commonly used street names were replaced, at least officially, with designated names, fixed in nameplates and marked on maps. Even wedding-invitation customs were changed by the encroachment of textuality. Among Orthodox Christians in Jerusalem, the tradition was to hire an "inviter" (*ʿazama*), a middle-aged woman who visited the invitees one by one as she sang loudly and provided them the details of the occasion. This elaborate custom was replaced in the early twentieth century by letter invitations.[55]

But a narrative of a simple, teleological shift from orality to textuality would be misleading. It is crucial to point out that Jerusalem of the nineteenth century was already a city rich with texts, primarily in Arabic. Hundreds of Arabic inscriptions were visible in the city's landmarks. Colorful Arabic graffiti adorned the houses of residents who returned from the Hajj in Mecca. Arabic could also be seen on Ottoman coins and on holy banners. Hebrew, far less prevalent, was seen in dedication inscriptions in synagogues and schools, printed notices, and pilgrims' graffiti. These traditional textual formats were gradually abandoned with the introduction of modern textual signs: shop signs, monumental signs on new buildings, banknotes, visiting cards, and colonial street nameplates. Not only were there more texts in Jerusalem's streets in the 1940s than in the 1850s, but these were different types of text, indeed a different mode of textuality altogether.

As scholars of literacy have argued in recent decades, the view of a linear transition from orality to literacy, as milestones on a uniform timeline of progress, is simplistic. The sociological fascination with the transition from the voice to writing has often obscured the significant transitions within written culture itself. Each historical and cultural context invests different values and meanings into reading, writing, and textual artifacts. Literacy practices are patterned by social institutions and power relationships; they are fluid, dynamic, and changing.[56] In a period of turbulent change such as in Jerusalem from 1850 to 1948, the issue is not only the increasing percentages of literacy but rather the very meaning of literacy. Reading daily newspapers demanded different skills from reading prayer books; and writing essays and diaries was quite unlike bookkeeping for congregational affairs.[57]

The focus of this book, therefore, is not on the shift from orality to literacy but rather on the transformation of Arabic and Hebrew textual economies. The textual realm not only expanded, it was also reorganized: along with the arrival of new textual artifacts, other forms were removed and repressed. Walter Benjamin's notion of modernity as an assemblage of technologies and practices is useful here: it allows us to resist the perception of a linear chronological development and to search for a structural logic which binds together an array of seemingly disparate objects and practices. Borrowing Michel de Certeau's terms, this configuration could be described as a "textual economy," a field which includes the production, reproduction, and reception of written artifacts. Urban texts such as inscriptions, graffiti, and notices are elements within larger economies of text, alongside printed artifacts such as books and newspapers. By stressing the materiality of these artifacts, and the sociopolitical facts of their production, circulation, and exchange, the notion of textual economy invites us to think of text as a changing and dynamic field rather than a static part of the landscape or unchanging cultural practices. Textual economies are embedded within the political economies and structures of power which frame the production of text, reading, and writing.

Before 1900, traditional urban texts in the sacred scripts of Arabic and Hebrew were written in stone inscriptions, graffiti, holy banners, and coins, and were a material part of the physical environment.[58] Rooted in structures of power, these "traditional texts" inscribed the city with divine cosmologies and the legitimacy of state and congregation. They cut deep into the material fabric to connect sites and objects to ritual and temporal power. But they did not seek to mark territory by naming or to categorize people. They did not aspire to force their nomenclature and worldview upon the entire population. With modernity, however, text shed its material skin and became an external referent, a supplement that could be stamped upon objects, places, and people. Text became a dematerialized signifier, one that had the power to determine the meaning of the signified by naming, labeling, and categorizing. The imposition of order through writing was often understood in gendered terms, as a manifestation of active masculine spirit inscribing itself into the passive feminine environment. The gesture of territorial inscription harbored violence, as it aspired to establish its order as not only hegemonic but also objective, banning other texts, names, and readings. Here was a novel attempt, using textual labels, to stabilize meaning, organize the city into a legible grid, and control its space and population. These new textual technologies gave the reigning authorities unprecedented power in shaping urban space. But they also gave rise to anxieties among officials regarding unregulated counter-writings, which could undermine the logic of signposting.

This book focuses on forms of urban texts that capture this transformation. It does not provide an exhaustive survey of Jerusalem's urban texts. Some textual forms receive limited mention here, such as burial inscriptions, commercial advertisements, political notices, and artistic calligraphy. My aim is not to document the readable landscape but rather to ask what texts meant to their writers and readers. I pay special attention to the liminal quality of text in creating boundaries within the city and facilitating encounter and exchange between different groups. Urban signage often had a threshold quality, producing rites of passage, conflict, and transformation.

Jerusalem under late-Ottoman and British rule was a field of increasingly intense interaction between diverse actors and trajectories, which used textual means to reorganize space, society, and subjectivity. Under British colonial rule, the Zionist project of immigration, colonization, and settlement received state support, against Arab opposition and resistance. These developments pitted Hebrew, as the language of Zionism, against the native Arabic in a battle over the landscape and its meaning. The proliferation of Hebrew as a modern language, used for everyday practices, was heavily encouraged by the Zionist movement as a crucial aspect of the construction of the Jewish National Home and the transformation of Jews into a territorial nation. Through Hebrew, land was claimed and settled, and the Zionist ethos of Return was written onto street corners. During the British Mandate and since, Hebrew was encountered by Arab Palestinians as a colonial language of appropriation and dispossession in what became a zero-sum game between the two languages, heavily focused on naming and renaming. "People are outraged by repeated Hebrew translation, naming Filastin as the Land of Israel," wrote a leading Palestinian intellectual in 1936. "If Filastin is the Land of Israel then we, Arabs, are mere intruders and passersby, and we must leave."[59] After 1948, a mammoth renaming exercise rewrote the country's geography by selecting hundreds of new Hebrew names for mountains, valleys, streets, and habitations. This toponymic effort, which was manifested in maps, books, road signs, and notice boards, facilitated the symbolic and physical erasure of depopulated Arab neighborhoods and villages. French writer Jean Genet, an ardent supporter of the Palestinian cause, abhorred Hebrew when he encountered it on Israeli military signs in Lebanon during the 1982 Israeli invasion. In the abruptness of square Hebrew characters, disjointed and separated from each other, Genet saw "terrifying discontinuity" which stood in contrast to the organic twists and turns of native Arabic script. In Hebrew he saw a violent form of appropriation, conquest, and colonization.[60]

But the view of Hebrew as an instrument of settler colonialism is reductive, and conceals the ambiguities of "Hebrew Revival" as well as the affinities between Arabic and Hebrew. The modern Zionist-Arab conflict hid deep underlying commonalities of the two languages. As ancient Semitic languages, Arabic and Hebrew share a similar logic, system of roots, and vocabulary. For Jews and Muslims, Hebrew and Arabic were laden with sacred meanings that long preceded their use for colonial and national agendas. Both languages are believed to be divine tongues of creation and revelation, and their scripts carry unique sanctity. The aniconic tradition of Islam and Judaism made text a favored textual ornamentation in sacred architecture. While the Zionist impetus to rewrite the landscape of Palestine had a specific colonial urgency, the transformation of language into a tool of signposting and labeling was not unique to Hebrew and had its parallels in Arabic. The nineteenth-century movements promoting the cultural revival of Arabic and Hebrew, the Nahda and the Haskalah, bore striking similarities, and in the Levant generally and Jerusalem specifically, there were links, engagement, and even overlap between the two.[61] In the engagement of Jews and Arabs with new textual forms, we can trace similar dilemmas and a diversity of responses: from Arab Palestinians who seized on modernist reorganization of society through Arabic text, to Jews who were ambivalent about the Zionification of Hebrew and sought to cling to the sacred significance of the language.

These commonalities between Arabic and Hebrew are best exemplified in stone inscriptions, which were the most common form of monumental writing in Jerusalem around 1900. Memorial inscriptions, commemorating the pious commissioners of mosques, synagogues, and religious schools, were an integral and visible part of sacred architecture, consisting of long paragraphs of text in holy script. With modernity, however, these ancient forms of writing faced a crisis; their meaning and relevance were questioned in an age of flow, movement, and radical change. From a living practice of writing, they became a form of heritage to be celebrated and salvaged as the landscape of the city was disrupted by fragmented, succinct, and dazzlingly modern texts.

1 STONE

Arabic in the Age of Ottomanism

IN 1892 THE YOUNG SWISS PHILOLOGIST MAX VAN BERCHEM launched a passionate call to his fellow scholars of the Orient. The thriving discipline of Orientalism had thrust forward the study of Arabic language, literature, and history, he stated, but one field of research had not received its due attention: the study of Arabic inscriptions. "Because of the historical role played by Arabic language in all Muslim lands, Arabic epigraphy left traces from the Atlantic to the Indian Ocean, from Central Asia to Nubia."[1] Scholars who had visited the ruins of the Muslim Orient knew the full significance of the monuments and the inscriptions that one could find there at every step. Islamic inscriptions harbored a "historical value of the highest order." But time was short, and the inscriptions were at risk. These monuments, he warned, were rapidly disintegrating, making the task of creating a "corpus of Arab epigraphy" ever more urgent. Van Berchem called upon his fellow European Orientalists to join this endeavor to produce an exhaustive study of inscriptions in Arabic script in mosques, tombs, caravansaries, madrassas, forts, and bridges from the main urban centers of the lands of Islam. This undertaking by van Berchem, his colleagues, and his students resulted in a series of weighty volumes which laid the foundation of the modern science of Arabic epigraphy.[2]

Many European visitors to Muslim lands saw Islamic inscriptions as indecipherable hieroglyphics whose role was ornamental. These were exotic relics of a monolithic Islamic culture, frozen in its ageless ways. Van Berchem did not see things this way. Rather than decorative Arabesques of a never-changing Orient, he read them as textual and architectural manifestations of a civilization in constant historical change. The inscriptions, in his view, provided a unique "index" to the magnificent past of Islamic civilization.[3] Past, and not present, as the inscriptions had lost their social function and had become relics of a different era. Van Berchem's scholarly mission was propelled by a sense of urgency, as he believed that the contemporary Islamic world was in a terminal state of decline, unable to protect its own heritage let alone rejuvenate its culture. "The Muslim monuments are neglected, their ruins, while still magnificent, will soon become no more than vestiges telling of a bygone artistic glory, their historical inscriptions are disappearing," he wrote. "The destruction of monuments is happening most rapidly in the large [urban] centers. We must therefore start with surveying the cities."[4] The crumbling inscriptions, in danger of disappearance, were a manifestation of this state of decay of the Islamic world. The epigraphic survey was to be conducted by European scholars. Native residents could provide valuable assistance as informants and door openers but should be used "with circumspection," cautioned van Berchem. "They cannot always be trusted to copy [inscriptions] correctly."[5]

Van Berchem's own survey focused on the Levant, documenting inscriptions in Cairo, Damascus, and Jerusalem. While Jerusalem was the smallest and most provincial of the three, van Berchem devoted considerable effort to its survey, which was the height of his career. He visited Jerusalem five times between 1888 and 1914, collecting and analyzing more than three hundred inscriptions. His survey uniquely captures the richness of Islamic inscriptions and their dominance over the urban landscape around the turn of the twentieth century.[6]

Van Berchem was not the first to show interest in Islamic public writing in Jerusalem. Medieval and early modern Muslim scholars had recorded inscriptions and used them as sources in history and geography books.[7] But van Berchem's meticulous research was unprecedented in its rigor, scope, and ambition. His fascination with Palestine's Islamic history was unusual among contemporary European scholars, who focused entirely on the country's biblical and Crusader history. And yet van Berchem's Orientalist characterization of the Ottoman Empire as a civilization in incurable decline stood in contrast to the experience of local inhabitants of Jerusalem. In their eyes Jerusalem was not suffering from decay but undergoing turbulent and dramatic change. Its inscriptions—and indeed the Islamic monuments—were not in danger of imminent disappearance. Quite the contrary, ancient monuments were being restored, reused, and celebrated with pride; new inscriptions were being emplaced. But it was undeniable that Islamic stone inscriptions were becoming a heritage medium of communication, now overshadowed by new textual forms and signage. The crisis of signification was real. A rigorous remaking of the city was underway, marking a break with centuries-old textual traditions and the adoption of new ways of writing public space.

ISLAMIC STONE INSCRIPTIONS IN 1850S JERUSALEM

In 1850s Jerusalem, Arabic inscriptions were by far the most dominant textual form in urban space. As recorded by a British traveler:

> There are many alabaster tablets and friezes let into the walls, over doors, or under oriel windows, or in arched recesses, on which Arabic inscriptions and monograms are elaborately carved in slight relief, and in some cases illuminated in red, blue, and gold; the graceful Oriental characters with their flowing lines, are well adapted for this sort of ornamentation, and are very extensively used in the exterior as well as interior decorations of Moresque buildings.[8]

Van Berchem's survey documented hundreds of such inscriptions in all parts of the city. Mostly carved in stone, they also appeared on ceramic tiles, mosaics, or in rare cases, wood. While other languages and scripts, such as Armenian or Hebrew, could be seen in 1850 Jerusalem, they were contained in specific areas and sites and did not rival the Islamic inscriptions in visibility and monumentality.[9]

Islam's aniconic tradition disapproved of the display of statues and images, making Arabic text the key visual register that expressed the Islamic character of the city and its monuments. The elaborate artistic execution that characterized many of the inscriptions communicated their significance. Appearing inside buildings and outside, on facades and monuments, inscriptions were one of the distinguishing features of Islamic architecture.[10] In Jerusalem they appeared on dozens of pious institutions such as schools, mosques, and holy tombs. Typically placed in prominent positions within the architectural structure, above the lintel, or alongside the entrance, stone inscriptions formed an integral part of the building, merging into the walls.

The choice of the Arabic language for the inscriptions was not obvious. Arabic was the main language spoken in Palestine, but it was not the language of its rulers. The Ottoman Empire, which had ruled Jerusalem since the sixteenth century, used Ottoman Turkish extensively as a language of administration. Yet when it came to public writing in Jerusalem, the Ottomans, like previous non-Arab Islamic rulers, almost exclusively used Arabic.[11] The Ottoman Empire was an Islamic state, and Arabic was the language best suited to express the sultan's claim to be the commander of all believers—especially in an Arabic-speaking area. It was the divine language, in which the Qur'an was revealed; the language of prayer, and the call to prayer; the language of the Hadith, as well as of Islamic scholarship. Writing was viewed as one of God's marvelous gifts to humankind, and the archetypal act of creation. The pen was the first object to be created by God, who used it to inscribe the Qur'an on the heavenly tablet, which is said to have existed before the creation of the world.[12] The Arabic script of the Qur'an was commensurate with the divinity of its content. Its exalted aesthetics was seen as a form of divine presence, akin to the speech of God. The proportions of the letters were designed to reflect inherited notions of the cosmic order. The terseness, simplicity, and geometric harmony of the script held the key not only to aesthetic but also to spiritual development.[13] Calligraphy, whether on manuscript or as inscriptions, placed emphasis on proportion and geometric arrangement, and its development was closely related to the development of Islamic architecture.[14]

Written into the fabric of building, the holy language instilled its aura into the site, incorporating it into an Islamic cosmos. This power stemmed from the popular belief in the divine power of a holy writing, a belief that was shared by Muslims, Jews, and Christians. The clearest expressions of this power of writing were related to issues of life and death. The talismanic power of Arabic script served Muslim mystics in their healing practices when they wrote on patients' foreheads or dispensed amulets of Qur'anic verses.[15] The removal of an inscription was seen as a bad omen which could bring misfortunes.[16] Holy writing could heal and save humans, and it could also help protect buildings and religious enterprises. Some stone inscriptions explicitly warned future generations against diverting the building from its original use: "Whoever changes [the use of the building] or swaps it [for another building] will bear the curse of God, the angels, and the people, all together," threatens one medieval inscription.[17] These threats acknowledged the vulnerability of the text, as inscriptions could be removed, erased, or rewritten.[18] But they expressed a belief that even if the written word could not prevent such misdeeds, at least it had the power to bring divine punishment on those who acted against it.

In total, four hundred historical Islamic inscriptions were recorded in Jerusalem, and they span more than thirteen centuries. The earliest among these dates to the seventh century, shortly after the Arab conquest. Inscriptions were found throughout the entire urban space of Jerusalem, but they were especially concentrated in one area. The rectangular enclosure of Al-Haram al-Sharif, housing the Dome of the Rock and the Al-Aqsa Mosque, was the site of more than half of the Islamic inscriptions.[19] Van Berchem devoted great attention to the site. On his final visit to Jerusalem in 1914, which lasted more than two months, he visited the Haram al-Sharif daily, accompanied by Dominican priests, Ottoman soldiers, and local officials, to record the wealth of inscriptions, resulting in a full volume devoted to the site.[20]

A further sixth of the inscriptions were emplaced on buildings and monuments within a hundred meters of the Haram. Religious schools, pilgrims' hostels, Sufi convents, and princely mausoleums were all clustered on the Haram or nearby, and most displayed inscriptions. In total the Haram and its immediate environs held more than two-thirds of Jerusalem's Islamic inscriptions. A much smaller concentration of inscriptions was found in the Jerusalem Citadel and in the ancient Muslim cemetery.

It comes as no surprise that Islamic inscriptions were heavily concentrated around the holiest Islamic shrine in Jerusalem. But the area of the Haram was not merely a religious center for prayer and study; it was also a locus of political and economic power, and in fact, the hub of the city. Near the Haram was the seat of the governor; adjacent was the Islamic court, which oversaw the running of daily life in the city and was the most influential local institution.[21] Almost all the public baths and water fountains, and some of the city's markets, such as the weavers' markets, were located on routes leading to the Haram.[22] The concentration of inscriptions corresponded to the concentration of power. State, religion, public welfare, and commerce coincided and found expression in a dense textual landscape.

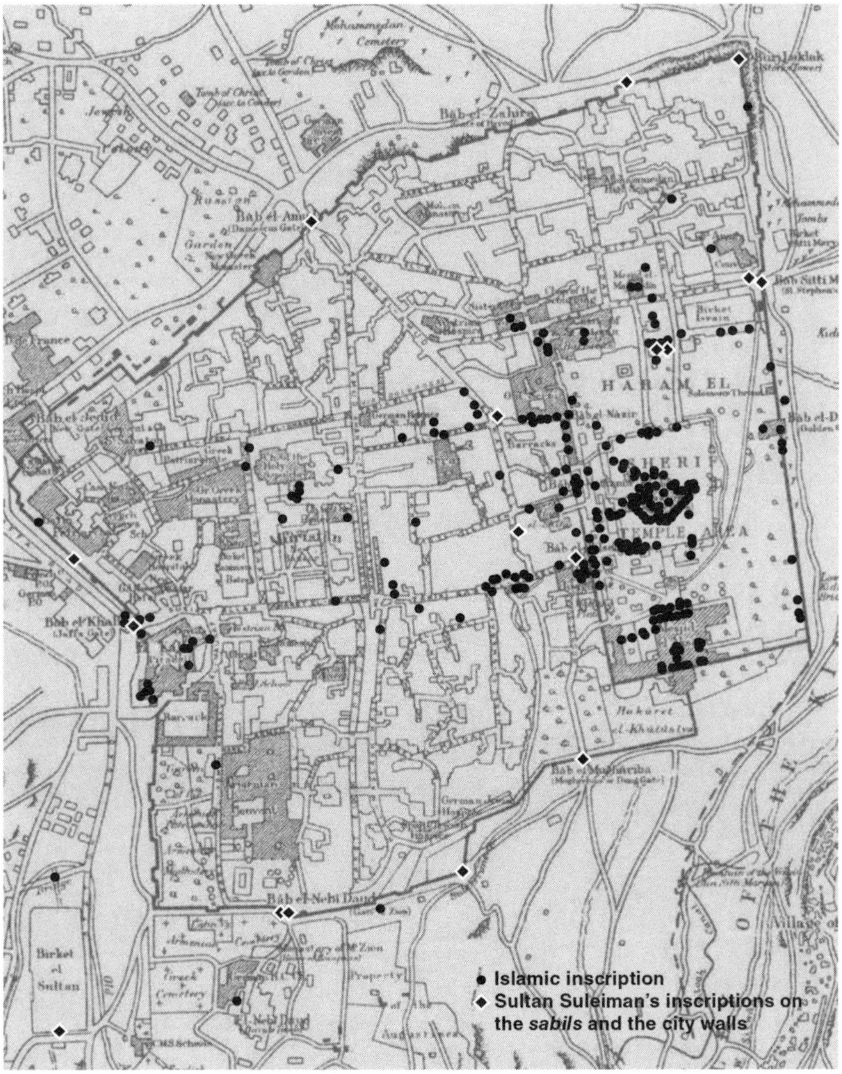

MAP 1. Locations of Islamic inscriptions in Jerusalem, based on Walls and Abul-Hajj, *Arabic Inscriptions*.

Source: Underlying map from Survey of Egypt map of Jerusalem, 1917.

Additions and graphic work: Maya Wallach.

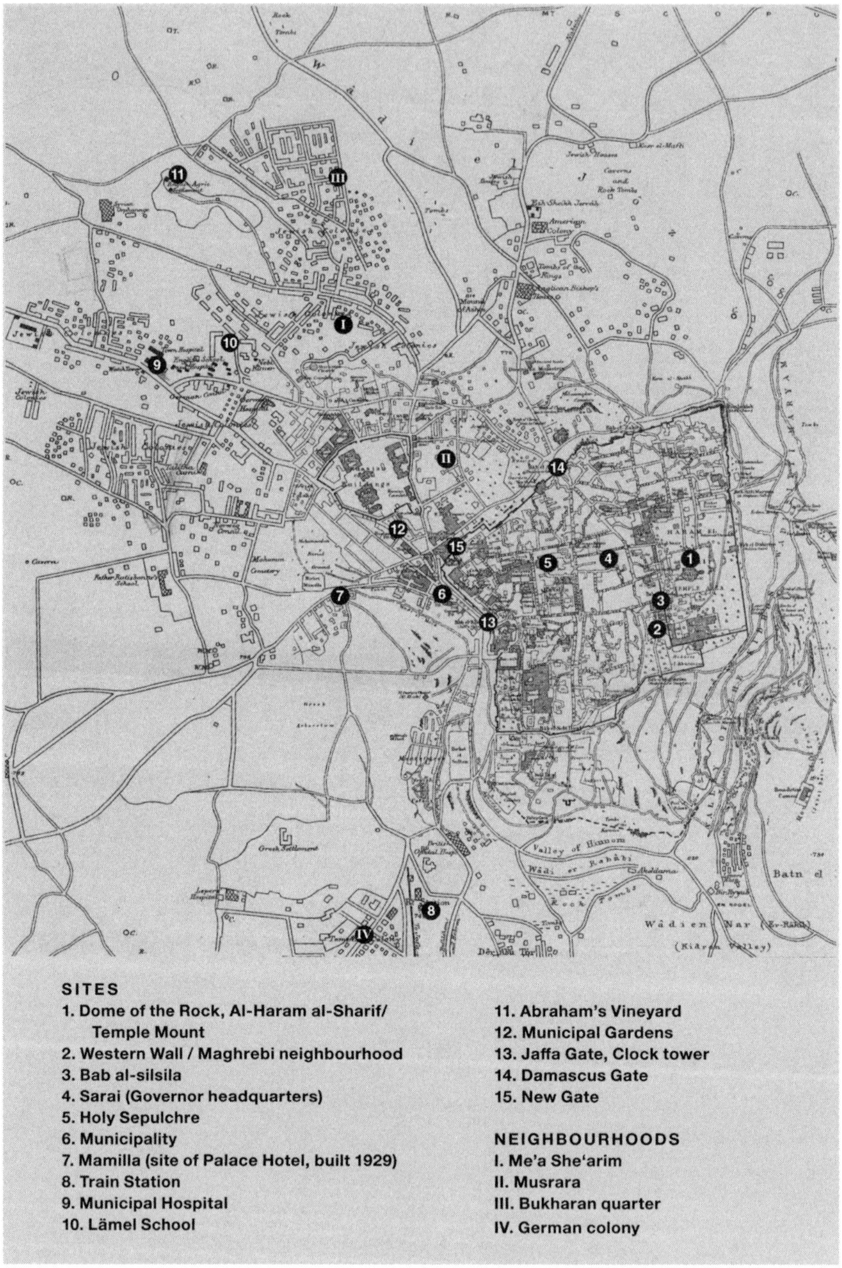

MAP 2. Sites and neighborhoods in early-twentieth-century Jerusalem.
Source: Underlying map from Survey of Egypt map of Jerusalem, 1917.
Graphic work by Maya Wallach.

FOUNDATION INSCRIPTIONS: THE *SABIL* OF BAB AL-SILSILA

The function and rhetoric of Islamic inscriptions can be understood if we examine one example in detail. The elaborate sixteenth-century inscription of the *sabil* (water fountain) of Bab al-Silsila (Gate of the Chain) was located near one of the gates of the Haram.[23] The inscription was engraved on a rectangular slab of white marble, like most stone inscriptions in Jerusalem. In beautiful Ottoman lettering style, the text read:

> This blessed *sabil* was constructed by the order of our master the sultan the great king and the illustrious khan, the holder of the nations' necks, sultan of the Turks [*Rum*], Arabs, and Persians, the glory of Islam and Muslims, the shadow of God in the two worlds, the protector of the two sacred sanctuaries, the sultan Suleiman, son of Sultan Salim Khan may God perpetuate his reign and his sultanate, and make his justice and beneficence endure, on the twenty-second of the sacred month of Rajab, in the year nine hundred and forty-three [4 January 1537][24]

Striking in its absence is the name of the monument and its location. The name Bab al-Silsila appears nowhere here, and this omission was no accident. There were twelve inscriptions at the gate and in its immediate vicinity, of different dates, but none of them mentioned the name Bab al-Silsila.[25] Indeed, out of hundreds of Islamic inscriptions recorded in Jerusalem, only a handful refer to their locations by name.[26] Inscriptions always included the names of patrons and their titles; they often described the type of the monument (school, mausoleum, water fountain), but almost never the name of the site—or, for that matter, the name of the neighborhood, the city, or any other geographical proper names. The omission of names from public display did not mean they were unknown or insignificant. The name Bab al-Silsila appears in medieval chronicles and has been in use at least since the fifteenth century.[27] In Jerusalem as in other cities in the Middle East, many place-names remained unchanged for many centuries despite their total absence from the textual landscape. Or perhaps this absence contributed to their persistence, as it is far more difficult to remove a name from popular consciousness than it is to replace a sign.

But the inscription was not a sign. That is, it was not a title. It was a full, grammatically correct sentence, with clear beginning and end, running over three rows of equal length and height. No word was highlighted: all

FIGURE 3. Residents collecting water from Sabil Bab al-Silsila [1900-1920].
Source: Library of Congress, Matson Collection, American Colony photographers.

FIGURE 4. Inscription marking the building of Sabil Bab al-Silsila under Sultan Suleiman, 1537. The inscription is painted. Photographed in the early twentieth century.
Source: Library of Congress, Matson Collection, American Colony photographers.

were in equal size and spacing. The lettering was in relatively large characters, zigzagging vertically, making use of empty spaces between words, with letters overlapping.[28] Whoever wished to read it had to follow the text in its entirety, as they would struggle to pick out a single line or word. The arrangement of the text may seem awkward, as the transition between the first and second lines cuts through the titles of the sultan. This discontinuity was not uncommon in Islamic inscriptions: the end of the row often breaks grammatical contiguity or separates between a name and an adjective. But this did not seem to matter; the inscription is a coherent and integrated whole. Dedication inscriptions, marking the foundation or renovation of a monument, were the most common and prominent form of Islamic writing. They varied in execution and style yet followed a strict textual formula which was maintained in Jerusalem for thirteen centuries, from the earliest examples of Islamic inscriptions—in the seventh-century Dome of the Rock, the first monument built by a Muslim ruler—to early-twentieth-century Ottoman inscriptions.[29]

The inscription referred to the site as "this blessed *sabil*." The word *this* is key here. It explicitly acknowledged the act of reference between text and architecture, highlighting the text's liminal position: physically embedded in a monument, yet pointing to it and investing it with meaning. The invocation of God's name, the sultan's role as protector of the holy sites, and the Islamic date all pointed to the Islamic cosmology of the text. The inscriptions, set in walls and above entrances, performed their commemorative role by binding socially useful architecture with cultural memory. These edifices—mosques, city gates, *sabil*s, tombs, schools—whether of simple or majestic quality, were, above all, structures for the use of a living society.

And nothing was more useful than an urban water source. Water is a basic requirement, and Suleiman's waterworks benefited the entire population of Jerusalem, including Christians and Jews.[30] Yet the project was planned and described as a primarily Islamic one. Like the other *sabil*s built by Sultan Suleiman, it was constructed within the Haram or near its main entrances, with the explicit purpose of securing a water supply for the ablutions of Muslim believers before their prayer.[31] This inscription was one of thirty-five inscriptions celebrating Suleiman's public works in Jerusalem: the renovation of the

Haram, the construction of the city walls, and the water-supply system. No other Ottoman sultan left such a mark on the urban fabric of Jerusalem, and no other sultan left as many inscriptions. Among these, the inscriptions on the city walls, gates, and water fountains form a distinct group in their similar style, layout, and strikingly beautiful lettering. Their visual and textual similarity made them into an array of almost-interchangeable signs of state power, deployed strategically around the city, marking its outer limits and its center. The inscriptions welcomed pilgrims and traders arriving in the city, worshippers coming for prayer, or residents collecting water from the fountains for their daily needs. The Suleimanic inscriptions created a network of clearly recognizable emblems, investing these sites with imperial patronage and religious meaning.

INSCRIPTIONS IN THE NINETEENTH CENTURY

Scholars of epigraphy have sometimes questioned how often, if at all, inscriptions were read in a proper sense. Some inscriptions are almost illegible; their lettering is cramped and small or their position is too far from potential readers. Such inscriptions appear to have been produced not to be read, but to provide a symbolic affirmation of the presence of the ruler.[32] The Suleimanic inscriptions, however, were executed in large and legible letters and located in plain view, in the busiest places in the city. All the same, they could not be read in a cursory glance; the long sentence demanded a close and careful reading. Many in the city (women, poor, Jews) had limited or no literacy in Arabic. Even among those who could read Arabic inscriptions it is unclear how many did, and for what purpose.

It would be wrong, however, to frame the issue only in terms of proper reading. As long as passersby noticed the inscriptions, recognized them, and had a sense of their meaning, the inscriptions could be said to have a social function. And there is little doubt the Jerusalemites, of all religious groups, were aware of the inscriptions and their content. In 1865 the Ashkenazi newspaper *Ha-Levanon* mentioned "the *sabil*s inscribed by the great Sultan Suleiman, son of Salim, constructed in the year 934 of their [the Muslim] count, as elaborated on the stones of the *sabil*s in Arabic script and language."[33] If the Belarus-born reporter was able to quote the inscription, it is reasonable to assume many more in the city were aware of the inscriptions and their meaning.

Ha-Levanon's story covered the restoration of Suleiman's waterworks after a long period of disrepair. In reusing the sixteenth-century water fountains, the Ottoman authorities were establishing continuity with the past splendor of early Ottoman days at a moment of sweeping administrative and economic reforms. Through renovation and public celebration, imperial piety was constantly inscribed into the city. As already mentioned, inscriptions were routinely painted "in red, blue, and gold", which made them more visible and legible.[34] Regardless of how many properly read them, it is clear that the inscriptions continued to be rewritten.

But something was changing in the Ottoman attitude toward inscriptions. An indication of the change could be found in the renovation of a medieval *sabil* on the Haram. The magnificent Mamluk Qaytbay monument was repaired in 1883 and a new inscription installed on its four sides. Curiously in this case, the Ottoman restoration inscription was written in an ancient Mamluk lettering style, a medieval script which had not been in use for almost five centuries. "A pastiche imitating, not without elegance, the style of the fifteenth century," wrote Max van Berchem approvingly.[35] To write in the style of a long-overthrown dynasty was unprecedented. It was a self-conscious appropriation of a historical style, or in other words, historicism. It showed that the Ottoman authorities were keen to protect Islamic heritage, but also that they saw it as heritage in a modern sense: something which belonged to a different age. Inscriptions were a legacy to be celebrated, one that belonged to a glorious past, not to the present or the future.

The renovation of the *sabil*s was part of Ottoman urban-development efforts—the most wide-ranging civic intervention since Sultan Suleiman. In Jerusalem, as in other cities of the Arab provinces, Ottoman reforms heralded a profound rearrangement of structures and space. These efforts centered on facilitating movement: the flow of light, water, information, capital, tourists, expertise, news, and images. By the 1880s the main gates no longer were kept locked at night. Considerable attention was devoted to the city, and the overriding concern was to open Jerusalem up to development. The governor, district council, and municipality were involved in a series of projects to upgrade infrastructure of transport, water, and communication. Intercity roads to Jaffa, Bethlehem, Hebron, Jericho, and Nablus were upgraded and paved for carriages.[36] The railway line to Jaffa, inaugurated in

1892, was the first railway line in the Levant. Within the city, the authorities invested attention in the regular cleaning of the streets, street lighting in central routes, and clearing market streets from merchandise as well as from street vendors.[37] Roads were paved, cleared, and widened. Blocked and unused gates were reopened; and the city authorities did not hesitate to breach new openings in the sixteenth-century city walls. But the new gate which was opened in 1892 did not display a dedication inscription. Known in popular terms as the "new gate" or "Abdulhamid gate," the name of the sultan was not written above it. Strikingly, monumental inscriptions were also absent from the new civic institutions that were established around that time: the municipality, an Ottoman high school, barracks, municipal hospital, museum, theater, and public gardens. Inscriptions, it appears, were no longer the favored state symbolic medium, nor were they the dominant form of text in the urban landscape.

Ottoman stone inscriptions continued to be emplaced throughout the nineteenth century. They were generally of low artistic quality, with small and pedestrian lettering. One striking feature was the increased use of Turkish, after almost exclusive use of Arabic in Ottoman inscriptions before the nineteenth century.[38] The Turkish-speaking bureaucratic elite asserted the role of Turkish as an official language, even in Arabic-speaking countries such as Palestine, in what is sometimes referred to as Turkification. Arabic was still used for official purposes, and there was no concerted effort to force the population in Jerusalem or elsewhere in the Arab provinces to adopt Turkish as the main language, let alone to define themselves as Turks.[39] But tensions were emerging around language and nationality. Demands for Arab political autonomy and decentralization were accompanied with campaigns for a greater role for the Arabic language—not as the holy language of the Qur'an but as a national language of Arabs, including Christians and Jews. The Ottoman authorities were concerned about the implications of such demands and similar campaigns from other linguistic groups.[40]

Turkish was particularly prominent in new signs that were emplaced on Ottoman institutions and buildings. Made of wood or metal, and not particularly elaborate, these signs were in Ottoman Turkish and sometimes in other languages. One such example can be found in a photograph from the Ottoman prison of Jerusalem (figure 5).[41] Below a medieval stone inscription was a modest sign in Turkish, stating plainly the function of the building: Prison (*Tevkif Hapishanesi*). The sign was an external element, a modern addendum to a medieval building. Through a detached, succinct, and fragmented text—consisting of only two words—a historic building was made into a prison. From part of the structure, text had become a supplement, which claimed to stand for the building, capture its essence, and define it. No longer a long paragraph describing human construction in an Islamic cosmos, text was now an "objective" signifier, without detail, date, or explanation, referring to an architectural signified.

What was the role of this sign? It is doubtful if it had any informative function. A small sign, written in a language not many in Jerusalem could read, could be of little use in this regard. But the sign should be seen as part of an overall architectural and choreographic arrangement, which is captured in this image. Below the sign was a troop of guards, one of them handing a large notebook, most likely a register, to an officer. The soldiers stand at attention in a straight line. The staged photograph asserted structure, discipline, and uniformity. Supervision and control were provided through the officers and facilitated by the register. This was a new order of visibility and readability, ensured by the permanent lamp hanging from the wall, in the written records of the prison, and by the sign hanging on top. The sign of the prison was therefore one element in a profound rearrangement of the Ottoman Empire, pointing toward a rationalized, structured, and legible order.

SIGNS OF OTTOMANISM

"There is nothing in the world more invisible than the monument," wrote the Austrian writer Robert Musil in a 1927 essay mocking engraved plaques, inscriptions, and statues. Memorial inscriptions were "impregnated with something that repels attention, causing the glance to roll right off, like water droplets off an oilcloth, without even pausing for a moment."[42] Monuments were imperceptible because they blended into their surroundings, merged into the squares and walls. In the modern city, characterized by visual stimulation, noise, and movement, pedestrians were unable to notice the monochrome and dull inscriptions. To capture attention, monuments should stand out from their surroundings; they needed to call out, surprise and shock. They should, Musil concluded, adopt the language of slogans and trademarks.

FIGURE 5. Ottoman prison in Jerusalem. The hanging sign above the entrance reads "Prison" in Turkish (*Tawqif Habaskhane*) [1890-1914].
Source: Library of Congress, Matson Collection, American Colony photographers.

The Ottoman authorities seem to have shared these reservations. After more than a millennium in use, monumental Arabic inscriptions lost their status as preferred symbols of state. In the final decades of the empire, it adopted new symbols and signs which corresponded to a new state ideology. Ottomanism (Osmanlilik) was a model of the Ottoman Empire as a family of ethnic and religious groups. All citizens, regardless of their faith or ethnicity, were, in principle if not in reality, equal before the law and held similar rights and obligations. Ottomanism called on all the groups of citizens to unite in the love of the Ottoman homeland and the sultan, and in commitment to reform and modernization. The discourse of progress was central to Ottomanism: economic and technological development were routinely celebrated as heralding a better future. New visual language was required to communicate this ideology, leading to the adoption of abstract, figurative, and emblematic symbols, which, while based on Islamic visual vernacular, became emblems of nonsectarian Ottoman patriotism. These new signs were not part of architecture but rather supplemental elements, interventions in the urban landscape. They were used as national trademarks, which were distributed widely to create an Ottoman scenography.

The most popular of these was the Ottoman red-and-white state flag, featuring a crescent and a five-point star, which became the national flag in the nineteenth century. In Jerusalem, as in other urban centers of the empire, star-and-crescent flags saturated streets, public buildings, parks, and squares, and they transformed these spaces into civic spaces, built on the notion of common citizenship and loyalty. The inauguration of public buildings, state visits, and the sultan's birthday were celebrated with hundreds of Ottoman flags in the streets.[43] While in Europe the star and crescent were perceived as a Muslim symbol, in the Ottoman Empire it was widely used by Christians and Jews as a nondenominational nationalist emblem, appearing as a prominent decorative feature on Jewish wedding documents, and on the school uniform of a secular school in Jerusalem attended by Muslims, Christians, and Jews.[44]

Alongside the flag, the most important state emblem was the *tughra*, a stylized ornamental monogram bearing the name and the titles of the sultan. The *tughra* had been in use by the Ottoman dynasty since the fourteenth century, and its text remained almost unchanged from the sixteenth century.[45] It consisted of the name of the sultan, his father, the titles Shah or Khan, and the suffix *al-Muzaffar Da'iman* ("ever victorious" in Arabic). As its winding form suggests, the *tughra* evolved out of calligraphy, drawn in striking gold, red, and blue inks and organized around three dramatic vertical lines. Some interpreted these lines as horsetails, invoking Ottoman roots as nomadic horsemen of the Central Asian steppe. The *tughra* appeared on the decrees of the sultan and his three closest officials. It was an embodiment of sultanic presence, dispersing his personal authority from the palace throughout the vast empire.[46] The cipher was drawn by a handful of court scribes commanding a special authority; anyone forging it would risk life imprisonment or hand-severing. Its use gradually spread to a variety of artifacts beyond paper and parchment, and coins were among the first of these. But the nineteenth century saw an inflation of the use of the *tughra*. In the explosion of new textual artifacts of administrative reforms, the *tughra* was printed on a range of documents such

FIGURE 6. *Tughra* sign in Nabi Musa celebrations outside Damascus Gate [1909-1914].
Source: Library of Congress, Matson Collection, American Colony photographers.

as title deeds, identity papers, and stamps, bestowing them with the authority of an Ottoman and Islamic tradition. It became a national Ottoman symbol, a "logo," which appeared in Jerusalem and other cities of the empire, carved in stone and painted on public signs.[47]

The reduction of the *tughra* to an abstract motif was brought to an extreme in the Ottoman coat of arms, a symbol designed by an Italian artist and displayed prominently in the public realm in the last decades of the empire.[48] The coat of arms was laden with flags and instruments of war, with a small *tughra* positioned in its center—recognizable but not legible. The coat of arms appeared in the streets on placards and in stone engravings on new civic institutions, such as Jerusalem's Municipal Hospital.

Stone inscriptions were unique artifacts, carved by hand, singular in their content, appearance, and location. The new symbols were of standard and uniform appearance, and therefore could be mass-produced: printed or painted on paper, cardboard, cloth, wood, or metal boards, they could be emplaced everywhere. The *tughra*, coat of arms, and the Ottoman flag were symbols of the industrial age. They were free-floating signifiers of Ottomanism, bearing no specific relation to the sites to which they were attached. Easily recognizable, the new emblems could be discerned from afar, from a moving train or car. They were particularly useful for photographic propaganda, in which the Ottomans showed increased interest. Official Ottoman photographs of inauguration ceremonies presented a formulaic arrangement of officials, audiences, flags, and other state symbols.[49] In such photographs the *tughra* and the coat of arms are easily recognizable, and their display Ottomanized the photograph. Intricate stone inscriptions could never play such a role.

SIGNS OF A CULTURAL AWAKENING

As the Ottoman authorities were turning away from the Arabic language as a privileged register for symbolic inscription, others were embracing it as the language of reform and modernity. In the late nineteenth century, the Arabic language stood at the heart of a project of cultural transformation and "awakening" in Greater Syria. The Nahda was an intellectual movement that sought to reinterpret Arab and Islamic heritage, opening itself up to European intellectual influences.[50] Arabic language was the primary vehicle with which

FIGURE 7. Ottoman Coat of Arms, on the Ottoman Municipal Hospital of Jerusalem (opened 1891).
Source: Mustashfa sultans symbol, by Ranbar, is licensed under CC BY-SA 3.0. https://commons.wikimedia.org/wiki/File:Mustashfa_sultans_symbol.jpg.

the Nahda articulated a modernizing and nonsectarian vision appealing to Muslims, Christians, and Jews alike. This vision initially championed Ottomanist notions of citizenship and development, while toward the late nineteenth century it served to develop notions of Arab national identity within the empire. The emergence of a new middle class, alongside intensifying contact with Western thinking, was the seedbed of this intellectual revolution. Nahda intellectuals agreed with Western Orientalists that Arab civilization was in a state of decay and stagnation. But there was a significant difference. Nahda intellectuals did not content themselves with documenting crumbling monuments of the past: they were engaged in reusing these very monuments for a cultural upheaval. In the reforming Ottoman Empire they identified a critical juncture where Arab culture could be revitalized—not through a return to the ways of the past but rather by adopting and adapting new technologies, and new ways of reading and writing.[51]

In Jerusalem one manifestation of this revival was the Khalidiyya Library. The first Arabic-language public library, established in 1900 by Jerusalem's al-Khalidi aristocracy, the library was located a few steps from the Bab al-Silsila gate of the Haram. This was the age-old center of the city's traditional textual and political economy, densely written in Arabic inscriptions. The library itself was housed in a Mamluk princely mausoleum of the thirteen century.[52] In the photograph of the library's inauguration, a medieval inscription could be seen emplaced above a blocked entrance a few meters to the left of the library entrance.[53] But with the Mamluk lettering barely discernible, the inscription could easily be mistaken for one of the stones of the building. In contrast, the large bilingual library sign could not be missed. The sign was succinct, visible, and far more readable than the traditional Islamic stone inscriptions. Suspended from the wall of the arched niche above the door's lintel, it stood out, literally, hanging diagonally in the air, calling out for attention.

FIGURE 8. The inauguration of the Khalidiyya Library, 1900.
Source: Library of Congress, Matson Collection, American Colony photographers.

The upper line, in Arabic in large letters, read "Truthful books are found within" (*Fiha kutub qayyima*—the Qur'an, 98:3), affirming the Islamic credentials of the library's patrons. In the next line, the Arabic name al-Maktaba al-Khalidiyya (Khalidiyya Library) was outflanked by the French Bibliotheque Haldieh. While Arabic was given priority in the sign, and the Qur'anic quote dominated, the positioning of Arabic side by side with French implied commonalities between the two languages. Both were equivalent modern languages of learning and progress. Such a sign in Arabic, on an Islamic institution, was a marked novelty in Jerusalem. It redefined the relationship between text and architecture, and between Arabic language and urban space. Arabic was now a language that names, defines, and signifies, alongside European languages.

In the photograph, the founders of the library posed for the camera, wearing traditional clothes and headgear of Islamic scholars. The Khalidis were one of the two most influential Arab noble families in Jerusalem and were renowned Islamic scholars and jurists, having served for centuries in the nearby Islamic court. In the second half of the nineteenth century they had become champions of modernization. Members of the family served in the Ottoman Parliament as representatives of Jerusalem and were outspoken supporters of liberal reforms and constitutionalism.[54] They established the library as a "public library," open to the general public and not only to Islamic scholars. Along with their celebrated collection of Islamic manuscripts, the library's holdings also consisted of a large number of works in European languages, including the works of Voltaire, Darwin, Shakespeare, and Milton, as well as a large number of nonreligious printed books and journals in Arabic. The Khalidiyya was an institution of textual reform, marrying the study of classical Islamic texts with modern, scientific, and secular ways of thinking.

The mass introduction of print and publishing in Arabic of newspapers, journals, encyclopedias, and novels was a central aspect of the Nahda. In the second half of the nineteenth century, a modern Arabic textual economy emerged, encompassing new modes of textual production and dissemination. The flow of massive printed output was facilitated through networks of booksellers, mail delivery arrangements, and public reading rooms, such as the Khalidiyya. Arabic speakers' access to books grew substantially, and exposure to journals and newspapers increased even more widely.[55] The new reading public was a print-reading public which was much more accustomed to the clarity of the black-and-white sign than the intricate, rich, and ornate calligraphy of stone inscriptions.

The library sign was one new element in a textual order that sought to define, name, organize, and proscribe—in the name of progress and modernity. The Khalidiyya also had a printed set of rules of conduct which was posted prominently in the reading room, defining various kinds of inappropriate behavior. In its internal organization the library emulated Western libraries: books stood upright on shelves with authors, titles, and catalogue numbers written on a paper label affixed to the spine, making the book titles easily legible and accessible to visitors. In Islamic libraries books were traditionally arranged stacked lying down flat.[56]

The library catalogue was printed by Jurji Hananya Hananya (1864–1920), Jerusalem's leading publishing entrepreneur in Arabic in the early twentieth century. Born to a well-established Arab-Ottoman, Christian family, Hananya started his printing business in 1884.[57] He was the first private publisher in Arabic in Jerusalem, focusing on nonreligious books and pamphlets.[58] He succeeded in obtaining a license from the authorities despite formidable difficulties. Under Sultan Abdülhamid II, the state maintained tight control and heavy censorship over printing. State censorship was relaxed after the 1908 revolution, which reinstated the constitution and the Ottoman Parliament. Hananya then launched a new semiweekly newspaper, named *Al-Quds*. Covering science, literature, and current affairs, the newspaper's masthead displayed the slogan "Freedom, Equality, and Fraternity" in Arabic. *Al-Quds* was the first Arabic-language gazette of wide publication in Palestine. The newspaper became one of the earliest forums for local politics in the district of Jerusalem.[59]

Hananya's printing output symbolized a new textual economy in Arabic that was taking shape in the Levant. He printed dozens of Arabic books, including tracts on language and literature, as well as everyday objects such as receipt books and envelopes.[60] Such artifacts were part of a wide array of textual products whose commercial use had increased in the towns of Greater Syria since the 1870s. Printers in the region advertised their services for the production of notices, circulars, envelopes, notebooks, visiting cards, bank receipts, invitation cards, coupons, and bills of exchange.[61] Text was also employed for political interventions in the form of printed proclamations, used for agitation

من قبل هذا العدد عُدَّ مشتركاً

№ 1 1RE ANNÉE

AL-KOUDS
(JÉRUSALEM)
JOURNAL
BI-HEBDOMADAIRE

PROPRIETAIRE
Georges I. Habib Hanania.

ABONNEMENT
Jérusalem un an 3½ Medjidies
Turquie un an 4 „
Etranger un an 20 francs.

Insertions et annonces
à la 1re page la ligne 3 Pias.
à la 4me page „ 2 „

PAYABLE D'AVANCE.

حرية
اخاء
مساواة

القدس

جريدة علمية ادبية اخبارية
تصدر يومي الثلاثاء والجمعة من كل اسبوع

العدد الاول السنة الاولى

قيمة الاشتراك
في لواء القدس ثلاثة مجيديات ونصف
في البلاد العثمانية اربعة مجيديات
في البلاد الاجنبية ٢٠ فرنكا

صاحب امتياز الجريدة
جرجي حبيب حنانيا

اجرة الاعلان
في الصفحة الاخيرة اجرة السطر غرشان
وللمشتركين ٦٠ باره
في الصفحة الاولى اجرة السطر ٣ غروش
وللمشتركين غرشان
اما الرسائل الخصوصية فالمخابرة بشأنها مع ادارة الجريدة

الدفع سلفاً

القدس الجمعة في ٥ و ١٨ ايلول سنة ١٩٠٨ الموافق ٢٢ شعبان سنة ١٣١٦

FIGURE 9. The masthead of *Al-Quds*, the first independent newspaper in Arabic in Palestine, published in Jerusalem by Jurji Hananya, 1908.
Source: Center for Palestine Studies, Columbia University and Institute of Palestine Studies, Ramallah.

and distributed openly or clandestinely by antigovernment groups in towns of Syria and Lebanon beginning in the 1880s.[62]

The center of gravity of this new textual economy in Jerusalem was not in the age-old Islamic heart of the city, where the Khalidiyya was located, but rather in the new town center that was taking shape around Jaffa Gate. Hananya's print shop and the offices of his newspapers were located in this area, in the bazaar of Suwaykat ʿAlun inside the gate.[63] It was the site of dazzling new forms of texts, for new kinds of readers.

NEW AUTHORS, NEW STORIES: THE JAFFA GATE TOWN CENTER

Jaffa Gate, or in Arabic Hebron Gate (Bab al-Khalil) was the city's gateway to the west and south. As late as the 1870s, travelers approaching the city from this direction were greeted by the solemn-looking fortified gate, which was kept locked at night. There were hardly any buildings outside the walls. "The town appeared closed and sealed," remarked a Jaffa businessman, recalling his first sight of the gate on a visit to Jerusalem as a young boy.[64] The only text in view was in the striking sixteenth-century stone inscriptions in Arabic, commemorating Sultan Suleiman's construction of the walls.

Yet by the 1890s these large, ancient inscriptions were dwarfed by an explosion of new commercial signs, official notices, and advertisements, a cacophony of styles and languages. What had been the city's edge now became its beating heart.[65] As a result of the rapid expansion outside the walls, the urban center of gravity shifted from its historical location in the environs of the Haram to the area around Jaffa Gate. The sprawling center created an organic continuity between the walled city and new developments beyond it. Free access was allowed, as the gate was no longer kept locked at night, and in 1898 the moat was filled to create a large opening for vehicles. This was a new center of flow and movement: it served as the main transport station, with coaches lined up outside the gate. Banks, post offices, shops of imported goods, pharmacies, photographers' studios, hotels, tourists' agents, and souvenir shops were all located in this area. In commercial signage, there was a striking dominance of signs in European languages—English, French, and German—although Arabic, Hebrew, Ottoman Turkish, and Greek were also present.[66]

In the words of the district governor, this was "the most important place in Jerusalem."[67] It was the space most closely identified with civic Ottomanism. For the 1901 Imperial Jubilee, marking twenty-five years of the reign of Sultan Abdülhamid II, a new *sabil* was built next to the gate, adorned with a large *tughra*.[68] Several years later a conspicuous clock tower, crowned with the Ottoman coat of arms, was erected on top of the gate. Both monuments were funded by donations of the local elite and communities, to show their patriotism. Similar clock towers were built in cities in Palestine, and indeed throughout the empire, to mark the Imperial Jubilee, creating a visible language of Ottoman urbanism.[69] The area was frequently draped with Ottoman flags to mark state visits or festivals. Further up Jaffa Road new municipal gardens were built for celebration and recreation. The municipality, which took a leading role in facilitating the transformation of the area, was located here and was preparing more radical changes. A large project was under way to bring electricity to Jerusalem, and to build three tram lines in the city.[70] Their central terminal was planned to be in Jaffa Gate. Large demonstrations, processions, and civic gatherings were held here—for example, during the celebrations of the 1908 constitutional revolution, which were marked with music and speeches about the new age of liberty.

FIGURE 10. Celebrations for the completion of the clock tower, 1907. On the right, the sabil, built in 1901. The sign reads "Long live the Sultan" in Turkish (*Padişahım çok yaşa*). Above the gate is the Ottoman coat of arms.

Source: Israeli National Photograph Collection.

This new center embodied the exciting opportunities involved in the transformation of Jerusalem and the empire. For the emerging middle class, and a new intelligentsia, this was the gateway to modernity's alluring promises. One person who pursued and represented these aspirations was Khalil Sakakini (1878–1954).[71] A prolific writer, freethinker, and progressive pedagogue, Sakakini was an uncompromising modernist for whom the rejuvenated Arabic language was primarily an instrument for the remaking of self and society. Born to an Arabic-speaking Greek Orthodox family in Jerusalem, Sakakini was schooled in Orthodox and British missionary institutions in the city. After a brief and unsuccessful attempt to emigrate to the United States, he returned to Jerusalem in 1908 to open a new secular school which he called the Constitutional National School. It was a radically innovative institution with no physical punishments or exams. Arab culture and identity were celebrated as well as Ottoman patriotism. The school was resolutely secular and nonsectarian; pupils (including Christians and Jews) studied the Qur'an as a foundation for Arabic language and culture.

Sakakini represented a new kind of urban professional who made his living by writing, translating, lecturing, and teaching. The Arabic language was Sakakini's tool of trade, and his products were textual artifacts. He wrote incessantly—articles, books, poems, manifestos, letters, and diaries. He was middle-class in background, education, and attitude but without wealth and property; often penniless and in debt, he spent much of his life without the economic certainty of secure employment. Nevertheless, he was unafraid to cut himself off from traditional support networks of his religious community and to go against the powers that be. He was excommunicated from the church for criticizing the Greek-speaking church establishment and demanding representation for the Arabic-speaking laity in Palestine. During World War I he hid a fugitive American Jew from the Ottoman authorities, and when caught both were exiled to Damascus and imprisoned. In 1920 he resigned from his role in the education department in protest of the appointment of the Zionist Herbert Samuel as High Commissioner. But he embraced these difficulties and challenges, and particularly the freedom of modernity from oppressive structures.

Sakakini's life revolved around the new town center that emerged in Jaffa Gate. He worked as a writer and copy editor for Hananya's newspaper *Al-Quds* as well as for the cultural newspaper *Al-Asmaʿi*, whose offices were in the town center. He gave private lessons in Arabic to foreign students in the hotels in this area; he routinely had his picture taken with family and friends in the photo studios on the street. Above all, he sat in cafés, where he read the newspapers and discussed politics, literature, and philosophy with a circle of students, colleagues, and fellow intellectuals. They nicknamed their favorite café the Vagabonds Café, reflecting their precarious employment. This was the first café for literati in Jerusalem, from which Sakakini managed his writing activities for newspapers in Jerusalem, Beirut, and Cairo while finding time for idle talk and criticism. The manifesto of the "Vagabonds," which Sakakini penned, took pride in their merciless intellectual integrity: "Our party is ruthless in its criticism—we do not favour a friend, nor do we compromise over what is true and just." But the same manifesto also pledged that "idleness is the motto of our party. The working day is made up of two hours."[72]

As an essayist and diarist, Sakakini's modernist style in Arabic was crisp, concise, and novel. It was free of the flowery language typical among contemporary Arab writers. His writing stands out in its pithiness and brevity, as well as in its provocative and nonconformist approach. Sakakini was an embodiment of sociologist Georg Simmel's ideal type of the modern urbanite: "to the point, clear-cut and individual."[73] Perhaps the epitome of this functionalist and rational approach to language was condensed in the telegraph—which Sakakini used frequently for political, professional, and personal purposes. During World War I, when Jerusalem was cut off from the supply of newspapers, Sakakini noted that the only source of information was the telegram news bulletins. These bulletins were displayed at the post offices, where an eager crowd would gather to learn about the developments of the war. Sakakini saw benefits in this new format: "The people have no choice but to get used to the language of the telegram, and they learn to be concise: when they talk or write, they resort to expressing themselves as concisely and succinctly as possible. Perhaps it is one of the benefits of these days."[74] The telegram presented a new form of text: utilitarian, fragmented, and curt. Language was being stripped of its overburdening cultural resonances and turned into a functional and informative tool.

But this celebration of rational, fast-paced modernity did not come without a price. Sakakini was prone to self-doubt and bouts of depression. During his year in New York he frequently recorded his tormented dreams, in which he usually was walking around Jerusalem. These dreams revolved around thresholds, liminal spaces, and moments of transition, such as switching between

FIGURE 11. Residents reading news telegrams in the French post office, before the Ottoman entry into the war, Jaffa Road, 1914.
Source: Library of Congress, Matson Collection, American Colony photographers.

Arab and Western dress. In one such dream, Sakakini found himself walking on a telegraph wire in Jerusalem. After learning that a close friend is dying, he panics: "I could not walk on the wire anymore and I said let me down, let me down."[75] The telegraph appears here as a stage for an unhappy circus performance. Sakakini treads upon the telegraph wire, and upon the confusing, fragmented, and disruptive kind of communication it enabled. It is a language with terrifying and tantalizing promise, one that is a route to modernity but always involves loss and absence. Riven with worry and guilt, far in exile, he is overwhelmed and collapses. This dream captured the electrifying promise and insecurity that modernity meant for Sakakini, who embraced them even when they aroused dread within him.

Toward the end of the First World War, after he was exiled and imprisoned in Damascus by the Ottomans, Sakakini fully embraced Arab nationalism and the revolt against the Ottoman Empire. When he came back to British-occupied Jerusalem, he became the secretary of the Arab Club, one of the two nationalist associations whose offices were located in the city center.[76] Opposition to Zionism and the Balfour Declaration was now galvanizing, and Jaffa Gate was a central site of protest. On one occasion in 1919, members of the Arab Club hung large banners over the street, with slogans proclaiming "We demand full independence!," "Syria shall not be divided," "Syria extends from the Taurus Mountains in the north to the Suez Canal in the south." But British authorities rapidly intervened and ordered these banners to be removed.[77] Jaffa Gate was becoming a contested space, in which bold claims for Arab nationalism were made. In other demonstrations at Jaffa Gate in early 1920, protesters held slogans such as "Stop Zionist immigration," "Palestine is Arab and for the Arabs," "Our country is for us."[78] These banners anchored the Arabic language within a political imagination of territorial sovereignty, as part of an Arab Palestine and Greater Syria. From a language of piety, inscribed in the stones of Jaffa Gate, through the language of Ottoman modernity and the Nahda, Arabic was now becoming the territorialized language of secular Arab nationalism, and the vehicle of mobilization against British colonial rule and the "Jewish National Home." In an anti-Zionist demonstration in March 1920, a Hebrew signboard was vandalized.[79] The Jerusalem-based daily newspaper *Lisan al-ʿArab* complained of commercial Hebrew signage on Jaffa Road, in which Arabic was either entirely absent or written "in ugly script and in humiliating manner." The Arabs of Jerusalem would not keep quiet, warned the newspaper: "Their language is the mark of their nation, their

FIGURE 12. Demonstrators against the Balfour Declaration, marching through the town center from Jaffa Gate, displaying protest signs, 27 February 1920.
Source: Library of Congress, Matson Collection, American Colony photographers.

religion, and their homeland. And this land is first and foremost an Arab land. Any sign that does not display this language in a respectful and aesthetic manner must disappear, and it will disappear."[80]

The direct confrontation between Arab nationalism and Zionism placed Arabic in opposition to Hebrew. But Hebrew was not only the language of Zionism. It was a language of Jewish congregational life—of worship, study, newspapers, commerce, and more—which had become increasingly visible in the streets of Jerusalem since the 1850s. With rapid Jewish immigration, dozens of religious institutions were established, and hundreds of Hebrew stone inscriptions were affixed in their walls and above their entrances. These inscriptions were remarkably similar to Islamic ones, and similarly faced a dramatic challenge. Language was becoming a weapon and a battleground—not only along the new fault lines between Arabs and Jews but also within the Jewish communities themselves.

2 | DOG

The Zionification of Hebrew

IT IS A SUMMER'S DAY AROUND 1910, AND A SIGN MAKER NAMED Isaac Kumer is decorating a marble Hebrew inscription emplaced outside a Jerusalem almshouse. The inscription extols the benefactor—a rich Jewish Bukharan merchant, and proclaims: "The house [is] for the poor and must not be sold or redeemed until the coming of the Redeemer." Kumer carefully paints this text in different colors: "the poor" in black, the words of the ban in red, the name of the donor in gold, "and each of the other words had its own color, until the tablet rejoiced in its hues."[1]

Kumer arrived in Palestine in 1907, escaping military service in Austrian-ruled Poland. His naive dreams of becoming a Zionist pioneer tilling the land did not materialize. Having failed to find his place in the agricultural colonies or the Zionist circles in Jaffa, he moved to Jerusalem, where he became a sign maker and a painter. Rather than building something new, he worked as a decorator.

In Jerusalem, Isaac drifts back to the Orthodox world. He makes much of his living painting Hebrew stone inscriptions on the gates of Jewish institutions like the Bukharan almshouse: religious schools, prayer houses, hospitals, and ritual baths. Adorned with Isaac's paints "that can endure rain and wind and snow," these tablets are found in all the Jewish neighborhoods of Jerusalem.

Suddenly, a dog appears: a stray mutt of brown and yellow colors, with short ears and a sharp nose. Kumer gestures toward the dog with a brush, but the dog does not run away. On the contrary, it curls up against the painter. Kumer starts stroking the dog's skin, "like a clerk stroking the paper before writing." The painter dips the brush in color. Approaching the mutt as if it were an empty page, he writes the letters d-o-g on its back. "From now on, folks won't mistake you, but will know that you're a dog. And you won't forget you're a dog either," he tells the animal. The dog does not go away: it barks at Isaac, as if demanding that he continue writing. "Are you crazy?" asks Isaac. "Do you want me to paint your name in gold?" The dog looks flirtatiously at the brush, and Isaac's hand tingles. "The brush started dripping. The brush didn't dry out until the words Crazy Dog were written on the dog's skin."

This fictional encounter between an immigrant sign maker, a memorial inscription, and a stray dog, in the Bukharan quarter of Jerusalem, is the pivotal scene in S. Y. Agnon's epic novel *Only Yesterday* (1945). Dealing with early-twentieth-century Zionist immigration to Palestine, the novel is structured around two storylines, of the migrant-settler and of the dog-text. The two plots collide again at the end of the book, when the dog—which had become truly mad, that is, rabid—comes back to bite Kumer, leading to the latter's torturous demise. Despite his name, Kumer—"the one who arrives" in Yiddish—never fully arrives anywhere. Instead the failed pioneer becomes Zionism's sacrificial son.

Agnon's enigmatic and tragic tale captures the dislocation of Hebrew in Jerusalem of the early twentieth century and its radical remaking into what could be termed Zionist Hebrew. The novel received a great deal of commentary, much of it focused on the dog and the writing on his back.[2] Yet the memorial inscription received almost no attention, and the contrast between these two forms of writing has been overlooked.[3] The Zionist sign maker who paints the words of pious memorialization uses the same brush and colors to mark the back of a dog. He releases Hebrew from its heavy anchoring in stone and tradition, unleashing the language onto the hills of Jerusalem in the shape of an animated dog-text, only to be destroyed by his own writing. *Only Yesterday* is a powerful and counterintuitive interpretation of the dramatic—and traumatic—transition from a pietistic language of commemoration to a profane text that is used to define, mark, and territorialize.

The growth of Jerusalem's Jewish population in the second half of the nineteenth century led to the sudden proliferation of Hebrew throughout the city, in monumental writing, printed notices, and commercial signage.

FIGURE 13. Endowment inscription of the Haji Adoniya synagogue and almshouse (established 1901), in the Bukharan Quarter.
Source: Tamar Hayardeny.

Perhaps most visible was the appearance of hundreds of stone inscriptions in Jewish institutions of welfare, prayer, and learning. These commemorative inscriptions perpetuated the names of overseas Jewish donors, from Bombay to Newark, who contributed to the upkeep of pious communities in Jerusalem. However, other forms of Hebrew emerged at the same time. Protestant missionaries used Hebrew in their appeals to local Jews; Haskalah-inspired local Jewish intellectuals propagated new ideas about modern Jewish identity; and Zionist activists championed Hebrew Revival and the making of the holy language into a national tongue of everyday speech. By channeling Hebrew's sacred qualities into a project of national salvation, supporters of Hebrew Revival wanted to transform Jews into a "normal," territorialized nation. The Zionification of Hebrew assumed during the British Mandate a clear colonizing zeal. The Zionist use of the language was a challenge not only to Arab Palestinians but also to local Jewish communities and their Hebrew.

FIGURE 14. Endowment inscription of the Mishkenot Sha'ananim almshouses outside Jaffa Gate, 1860, among the earliest Hebrew dedication inscriptions in Jerusalem.
Source: Yair Wallach.

S. Y. Agnon is a particularly interesting commentator on Hebrew's transformation in Palestine. Agnon belonged to the small yet highly influential group of Zionist immigrants to Palestine between 1904 and 1914, known as the Second Aliyah, whom he depicted in *Only Yesterday*.[4] These ideological immigrants, numbering around two thousand, later became the Zionist elite in British-ruled Palestine. But Agnon remained an outsider to this group, despite the great recognition he won. An Orthodox believer among secular Jews, an urban bourgeois among socialist "pioneers," Agnon inhabited a place in between the Jewish Orthodox world of Central Europe that he had left behind and the secular Zionist society, which he never fully joined. *Only Yesterday* condenses the rupture between the two worlds into the violent dislocation of the Hebrew language and its calamitous implications.

Agnon was a member of the Hebrew Language Committee and contributed to the Hebrew Revival as a prolific writer.[5] *Only Yesterday*'s preoccupation with questions of language gives Agnon an opportunity to reflect on a unique historical achievement. On the surface, Agnon's support for Zionism and the Hebrew Revival is wholehearted. *Only Yesterday* won the Jewish National Fund's Ussishkin Prize for Zionist Literature in 1946 and was hailed as the great novel of early Zionism.[6] Yet a closer analysis reveals a deep ambivalence about the rupture of Hebrew and its implications.[7] The nationalization and territorialization of the language constituted a break with Hebrew's divine role and with age-old Jewish writing practices. This remaking of Hebrew involved a cataclysmic crisis of signification, which Agnon locates in a Jerusalem street corner: the collapse of the textual economy of religious memorial tablets and its substitution by a new Hebrew economy of labeling and signposting.

JERUSALEM'S JEWISH COMMUNITIES AND THE HEBREW LANDSCAPE

As with Islamic inscriptions, Hebrew stone inscriptions in early-twentieth-century Jerusalem were the subject of a lengthy and careful survey. This 1920s survey, published under the title *Stones of Memory* (*Sefer Avney Zikaron*) was conducted by local historian Pinhas Ben Tsvi Grayevsky (1873–1941). Like the Orientalist scholars concerned about the disappearance of Islamic inscriptions, Grayevsky was alarmed by the dilapidated state of Hebrew memorial stones. The 1927 earthquake, which destroyed some buildings in Jerusalem, prompted him to launch this exhaustive survey. In his preface Grayevsky explains his motivation and the urgency of the project:

> Because of their antiquity, some of the [stones] are already broken, their letters disappearing. Others have been rendered with lime and plaster so the inscriptions are no longer visible. Yet others I have had to scrub, clean, and wash until I could read them. And some are no longer in their original place. . . . To save them from the ravages of time, and to revive their memory, I have with God's help undertaken this work, to copy them and publish them in a book for eternal memory.[8]

As the tone indicates, Grayevsky was a very different kind of scholar from Max van Berchem. Unlike the Swiss Orientalist, he was an insider to the culture he documented. Born and raised in Jerusalem, Grayevsky was schooled in an Orthodox Ashkenazi yeshiva and never received Western formal education. For his living he worked as a clerk in a Jewish hospital. But he was also an autodidact who read well beyond the scope of traditional rabbinic literature. He was a passionate and prolific writer, publishing 170 booklets on the modern Jewish history and geography of Jerusalem.[9] Self-published, his fourteen-volume *Stones of Memory* series was far from a rigorous scientific enterprise, as he himself acknowledged in his apologetic introduction. Although erratic in its organization, focus, and commentary, the corpus is a rich archive of social history, which, remarkably, received almost no attention in the scholarship of Jerusalem.[10]

In his preface Grayevsky writes about the "antiquity" of Hebrew inscriptions. But in fact, the overwhelming majority of the memorial stones he documented were hardly ancient. Unlike van Berchem's study, *Stones of Memory* does not portray the layered accumulation of inscriptions over centuries but rather the dramatic appearance of Hebrew in the urban space of modern Jerusalem. In a corpus of nearly two thousand Hebrew inscriptions in Jerusalem, only ten dated before 1850. In the early decades of the nineteenth century there were very few Hebrew inscriptions in the city, for the simple reason that there were few Jewish institutions there. In 1830 the local Jewish community numbered two thousand and was dominated by the Sephardic congregation. The only recognized synagogue in Jerusalem was the Sephardic Ben Zakai Synagogue, a complex of four interconnected halls of prayer dating to the sixteenth century.[11] There were a few inscriptions in the Ashkenazi and Karaite synagogues.[12] Beyond these inscriptions, the only other sites in which Hebrew was observable in open space were the Jewish cemetery on the Mount of Olives and holy Jewish sites where pilgrims wrote their names in Hebrew.

In the coming decades, the Jewish presence in the city and the visibility of Hebrew expanded dramatically. Jewish immigration, mostly from Eastern Europe but also from North Africa, Central Asia, and Yemen, transformed the city. Some migrants were driven by religious sentiments. But the main reasons for immigration were more prosaic. Improving global networks of trade and transport made Jerusalem more accessible and easier to reach. Population explosion, economic destitution, and political persecution drove millions of Jews to emigrate from Czarist Russia and Austria-Hungary after 1880. Most went to North America and other destinations. A few tens of thousands arrived in Palestine, and many of these settled in Jerusalem, where half the country's Jewish population lived. Contrary to common perceptions, committed Zionists made up a small minority among Jewish migrants to Palestine until 1914, and those who arrived in the country for Zionist reasons preferred to settle in the colonies or in Jaffa, not in Jerusalem.[13]

Two-thirds of the dated inscriptions in Grayevsky's corpus were emplaced after 1900. By 1908 there were sixty-five Jewish synagogues and seminaries within the city walls, and 160 more outside the walls.[14] On the eve of the First World War, Ashkenazi Jews numbered an estimated twenty-five thousand, making up about a third of the city's population. A further twenty thousand Jews belonged to the Sephardic congregation and to communities from Bukhara, Georgia, Yemen, Morocco, Persia, and Syria, and smaller congregations.[15] These communities were embedded within global networks of philanthropy and commerce whose center of gravity was in Eastern Europe, where most of the world's Jewry lived.[16] In its organized form, the philanthropic system of *haluka* (distribution) was a crucial source of income, especially for the Ashkenazi communities where households received annual subsistence disbursements from the rabbinic authorities.[17] The stone inscriptions were the most visible markers of these networks, announcing the names and hometowns of benefactors. As Agnon puts it in *Only Yesterday*:

> From all over the globe and from distant islands, generous philanthropists establish houses and courtyards, memorials to the holiness of the Lord and His

> Land, to His Torah and those who study it, so that every person with love of Jerusalem in his heart and with means erects a memorial to himself in Jerusalem, builds a house and dedicates it, buys a courtyard and dedicates it.[18]

The act of emplacing the inscription was given great importance. The memorial stone in the entrance to the main Ashkenazi synagogue, Ha-Hurva, built between 1857 and 1864, was emplaced long before the completion of the building. The elders "remembered their promise to the charitable Yehezqel Re'uven, to affix above the synagogue's lintel a large stone in which will be inscribed for eternity his great benevolence toward the Ashkenazi congregation in building this synagogue."[19] Whereas Islamic monumental writing typically memorialized sultans and princes, Jewish institutions depended on more humble benefactors: donors from overseas Jewish communities who wanted their name commemorated in the Holy City. As a result of this system of patronage, Jewish institutions relied on many donors rather than a single patron. When initial funds for the construction of Ha-Hurva did not suffice, fundraisers were sent out to Europe, where they "sold" the windows of the synagogue. When the synagogue was completed, the lintels of the windows were covered with names of donors.[20]

Hebrew memorial inscriptions bore striking similarities to Islamic inscriptions. Written in a holy language and a sacred script, their primary aim was to commemorate patrons. Arabic and Hebrew inscriptions alike consisted of rectangular paragraphs of dense text written in several lines, in a standard format, chiseled in stone and integrated into the fabric of stone buildings.[21] The long sentences were not intended for a cursory look but demanded a close reading. It is impossible to tell how often they were "read" in the proper sense; yet their prominent positioning no doubt made them visible and noticeable. By warning against any future misuse, sale, or exchange, the inscriptions provided the buildings with the protection of the written holy word. The regular repainting of these inscriptions, as in the case of Islamic inscriptions, illustrates that their function did not cease with the affixing of the tablet to the wall. These were not mute and forgotten symbols but rather had enduring significance as architectural elements. The act of inscription—the investment of Hebrew letters into architecture and the binding of religious space with commemoration—was an open-ended and continuous act.

As with Arabic in Islamic inscriptions, the power of Hebrew in monumental writing was derived from its sacred status. As the divine language of creation, according to Jewish tradition, Hebrew was sacred not only in speech and utterance but also in writing. The square Hebrew letters (*Ktav Ashuri*, "Assyrian" script) were the sanctified script.[22] According to Jewish mystical traditions, the Hebrew alphabet and the written Torah existed before the creation of the world and served as a blueprint for its creation. Hebrew words reflected divine structure by virtue of an organic and unbreakable unity of signifier and signified.[23] Writing in square Hebrew letters had to be collected and buried in a religious ceremony known as *Geniza*. According to an 1882 account, in Jerusalem this ceremony took place every three to five years and involved a mass procession, with drumming, singing, and whimsical sword games, as the *Geniza* material was taken out of the city and buried in a cave on Mount Zion. The ceremony was believed to have the power to put an end to a drought.[24]

Illustration of Hebrew's magical power to create and destroy is found in the genre of the Golem legends, which typically involve a learned Jewish scholar who brings to life an inanimate figure of mud by writing sacred Hebrew words. The mythical Golem saves Jews from a predicament but goes out of control and threatens its own creator.[25] A similar folktale appeared in early modern Jewish sources in Jerusalem. The local Jewish community was accused of killing a boy; a local rabbi named Kalonymus brought the dead boy back to life by attaching to his forehead a holy name in Hebrew, written on a piece of paper. The boy pointed to his real murderer, clearing Jerusalem's Jews of any wrongdoing. But the rabbi was punished for writing during the Sabbath—a violation of divine law.[26] Employing the divine power of the language, even for a good cause, carried with it the risk of a destructive backlash. Popular belief in the magical power of Hebrew was widespread in Jerusalem of the early twentieth century, as manifested in amulets and charms that were used as protection against the evil eye. In rooms of mothers and newborn babies, verses from psalms were affixed to the walls and clipped to the net around the bed "inviting the matriarchs and patriarchs and the good angels to come within, and ordering Lilith and her sect to flee and go without." It was "well known" that displaying the names of genies "removes their powers."[27]

Hebrew inscriptions were a medium that highlighted both divisions and commonalities among Jewish communities. In their dealings with the Ottoman authorities or with Diaspora Jewish organizations, Jews in Jerusalem were sometimes addressed as a single community. But in most aspects, Jewish communities acted as separate and distinct communities, differing in congregational structure, cultural praxis, language of speech, and area of residence in the city.[28] Hebrew was a foundation for a pan-Jewish identity as a common language for liturgy and religious scholarship. But in handwriting, for communal affairs, congregations employed different Hebrew cursive scripts. Hebrew's visibility in public space, in memorial tablets inscribed in sacred square letters, created a common Jewish imaginary, and yet virtually all Jewish institutions were identified with one or another ethnic congregation, and this affiliation was often mentioned explicitly in the inscription.[29]

The early twentieth century was the heyday of Hebrew memorial inscriptions in Jerusalem. Hundreds of inscriptions were being emplaced in synagogues, schools, almshouses, and other congregational institutions. But their hegemony over the Jewish social environment of Jerusalem was facing significant challenges. Alternative ideological projects sought to make Hebrew visible in Jerusalem for very different ends. These modern signs were external labels, seeking to name sites and buildings and, by extension, reorganize the city and its population. The earliest example of rewriting geography through Hebrew signage was not a Jewish institution but a British enterprise, set up by a diplomat and an Anglican missionary.

TERRITORIALIZING THE BIBLE: HEBREW IN THE SERVICE OF MISSIONARIES

In 1852 the British consul in Jerusalem, James Finn, purchased a grove northwest of the walled city in order to establish a vocational training farm for poor Jews. Finn was a member of the London Society for the Promotion of Christianity among the Jews, which championed the restoration of Jews to Zion and their conversion to Christianity as vital elements in a divine scheme of salvation.[30] The society regularly used Hebrew in its proselytizing efforts.[31] While unusual among British officials in Jerusalem in his missionary zeal, Finn's interest in Jews fit within a British imperial calculus to win over a local constituency in Palestine. Providing Jews with "protection" from Ottoman "despotism" allowed Britain greater influence and room for intervention.

FIGURE 15. British consul in Jerusalem, James Finn, at the entrance of Abraham's Vineyard 1852.
Source: Library of Congress.

Finn's vocational farm was a complex made up of a farmhouse, workshops, and agricultural land, with an impressive stone gate crowned with the Hebrew inscription Kerem Avraham Avinu (The Vineyard of Our Father Abraham). Below were marked the Jewish year in Hebrew characters (HTRYB, or 5612) and the Christian year 1852. The English name Abraham's Vineyard was marked on the sides of the gate. The name was a translation of the original Arabic name of the grove, Karm al-Khalil, but Arabic did not appear on the sign. The reference to Abraham (in Arabic, Ibrahim al-Khalil) was useful for Finn's grand narrative which connected the ancient patriarch with the Jewish workers he employed on the farm, a narrative that was reinforced in biblical Hebrew verses inscribed in porticoes of the farmhouse. Arabic nomenclature, which gave the site its name, was an intermediary layer that was discarded once it was translated.[32]

Finn's enterprise in Jerusalem was an early example of a European attempt to reclaim biblical Palestine, an approach which anticipated, and to some degree inspired, later Zionist rewriting of Palestine's geography. European missionaries, scholars, and travelers approached Palestine as a familiar landscape, based on their intimate knowledge of the scriptures. In this regard Palestine differed from other colonial contexts where European exploration efforts aimed at incorporating unknown territories into the sphere of Western knowledge and hegemony. Palestine was not unknown: it was understood as the foundation of Christian-European civilization, and therefore had to be "recovered" rather than "discovered."[33] Western archaeologists and cartographers toured Palestine intensively from the middle of the nineteenth century, producing journals, books, and surveys. The most rigorous effort in this vein was the 1870s Ordnance Survey of Western Palestine, launched by the London-based Palestine Exploration Fund. This large-scale survey produced a detailed map of modern Palestine; its primary interest was to bring the ancient Holy Land into visibility. Arabic names of villages, mountains, and valleys were carefully collected because they were considered depositories of historical geography, through which ancient Hebrew names survived.[34]

This biblical geography proliferated primarily in printed form, in European maps, prints, photographs, postcards, and books. But in Jerusalem, it was written onto the landscape in stone and metal signs. Christian Europeans who settled in Jerusalem marked their mansions with biblical names, such as THABOR, referring to the lower-Galilee mountain associated with Jesus's transfiguration; and EBEN=EZER, associated with the biblical battleground named in this way by the prophet Samuel. European welfare institutions similarly used a Christian nomenclature, such as the German school for orphan girls TALITHA KUMI, after the gospel's story of Christ's resurrection of a dead girl.[35] (Among local Jerusalemites the school was called "Sharlota" after its headmistress, Charlotte Pilz—an indication that even the most monumental signage did not necessarily impress itself onto local geographic consciousness.)[36] Like Jewish and Islamic inscriptions, these signs affirmed the pious role of these institutions and their builders by referring to Christian symbolic language. They did so not by describing the institution's sponsors and the act of foundation but rather by affixing names to buildings, giving physical presence to biblical nomenclature.

But Abraham's Vineyard went further than this. Here, long before the emergence of political Zionism, was an attempt to engineer a Jewish "revival" of a modern kind: to make the Jews of Jerusalem into builders and farmers; to remove them from their reliance on commerce and charity and connect them

FIGURE 16. Signs of European institutions in Jerusalem: (top) Talitha Kumi, the German school for orphan girls, built 1868; (bottom) Jesus Hilfe, the lepers hospital in Jerusalem, built 1887.
Source: Yair Wallach.

to the land. The work would instill discipline and turn Jews from fragmented congregations into a cohesive national community. Finn's conscious aim was to undermine local rabbinic structures, which were hostile to his efforts and suspected his motivations. His civilizing mission was imbued with colonial spirit directed toward Palestine and the Jews.

In the coming decades, this message found growing resonance within Jewish modernizing circles. In 1909, Hebrew Revival activist Eliezer Ben Yehuda, a staunch supporter of Jewish nationalism, chronicled his visit to the farm. Outside the estate, the author describes Jewish Jerusalem as dominated by the "rotten and foul-smelling" rabbinic establishment: "empty fields and rutted streets, and bad smell throughout the year, from the running sewage of the [nearby Orthodox] Jewish neighborhoods." But then the author arrives at the gate of the estate and notices its Hebrew sign, pointing to a new order of productivity and solemn unity. Passing underneath the signposted gate, he finds himself in a world transformed: a spotless straight road leading to a house on a hill, with shady trees, fruit orchards, and water wells along both sides. Tanned and lean Jews work diligently to dig further wells. "Jews of all kinds, Poles and Yemenites, Galicians and Moroccans, Syrians, Persians and Sephardim—a small gathering of the exiles, with their dry bones they huddle together, and work in unity and peace, and no one complains."[37] Other Jews in Jerusalem were less impressed with the farm and its missionary patrons. "This was not real work, but charity. To prevent the work from being completed, they would destroy every day what they built the previous day," wrote one Jerusalemite.[38] Among Jews in Jerusalem and elsewhere, Hebrew was undergoing its own dramatic transformation, independently of Finn and his vision.

"HEBREW REVIVAL" AND JEWISH NATIONAL IDENTITY IN JERUSALEM

Throughout the Middle Ages and the early modern period, Hebrew had been used for primarily religious purposes of reading and learning, for prayer, and for communal bookkeeping. In the nineteenth century, East European intellectuals of the Haskalah promoted Jewish cultural renewal in Hebrew, inspired by the Enlightenment. Much like Nahda intellectuals decrying Arab "decline," Jewish scholars lamented the stagnation of Hebrew culture and called for it to emerge from darkness into a new age of light.[39] They employed Hebrew for scholarship beyond liturgy and the rabbinic canon, in areas such as philosophy, science, geography, history, grammar, and literature. One of the

Haskalah's most revolutionary aspects was the development of a belles-lettres writing culture in Hebrew.[40] In contemporary Jewish society in Eastern Europe, literacy consisted of reading skills but not necessarily the ability to write. The foremost Ashkenazi rabbinic authority of Jerusalem, Rabbi Shmuel Salant (1816–1909), never mastered writing and could barely sign his name, preferring to dictate to a professional scribe (*sofer*).[41] Writing was frowned upon, all the more so when it was done for personal, literary, or artistic purposes. The Maskilic embrace of Hebrew as a language of writing stood in contrast to the rabbinic language of reading. In the 1880s the reform of Hebrew acquired a more radical nature, as the movement for Hebrew Revival (*Tehiya*) explicitly aimed to cultivate a Jewish sense of nationhood.

Advocates of Hebrew Revival emerged in Jerusalem as of the 1880s and included both Sephardic and Ashkenazi intellectuals, members of the burgeoning local Jewish middle classes. They found institutional support from European Jewish philanthropy that aimed to modernize Jewish communities in Palestine. Driven by a sense of modern pan-Jewish solidarity, the Rothschilds, the French Alliance Israélite Universelle (AIU), and the German Hilfsverein (Ezra) broke with established patterns of charity which were memorialized in traditional stone inscriptions. They saw local Jews as backward, unproductive, and woefully divided—communities in urgent need of reform. The AIU and Hilfsverein did not want to support existing communal institutions; they approached Jewish communities in Jerusalem with a colonial civilizing mission, seeking to provide them with benefits of European enlightenment and progress through modern education, healthcare, and housing. Jewish cross-ethnic support for Jews in Palestine was by no means a new phenomenon, but it had typically operated in a manner that reaffirmed, rather than challenged, congregational boundaries.[42] Here was something different: powerful pan-Jewish frameworks seeking to transcend and diminish congregational differences and to cultivate a strong, modern Jewish identity based on common heritage and interests—although not yet a national or Zionist one. Hebrew signs that were emplaced on the gates and above the entrances to these institutions, such as the Rothschild Hospital and the Lämel School, addressed a newly imagined community for whom Hebrew was not only a sacred tongue but also a modern language of culture, science, and belles lettres. This was expressed, as in the Khalidiyya Library sign, by the fact that Hebrew featured alongside other languages: German, French, and Ottoman Turkish. Indeed, it was the teaching of "foreign languages" in the Lämel School which provoked the ire of the Ashkenazi Orthodox establishment when the school was established in 1856.[43]

The blossoming Hebrew press played a key role in language reform in the spirit of secularization and nationalization. Hebrew journals which were established in the 1860s in Vilnius, Vienna, Odessa, and Warsaw promoted Jewish unity, enlightenment, and common identity, across borders and territories. By using the Hebrew language, these intellectuals offered a new interpretation of Jewish identity and were able to communicate with congregations that used different languages of speech. To counter these trends, Orthodox circles intensified their publication in Hebrew, not as a "revived" national language but as a means to protect Jewish religious culture from secularism and assimilation.[44] The center of gravity for Hebrew literary production was in Eastern Europe, but Jerusalem became an important hub of Hebrew journalism, with at least five newspapers regularly published in Hebrew on the eve of the war, expressing a variety of ideological standpoints.[45]

№ 28

שנת השלשים וארבע

חבצלת

מְבַשֶּׂרֶת HABAZELETH צִיּוֹן

מכתב עתי יוצא לאור בכל שבוע יבשר וישמיע כל דבר הדרוש להפיץ לבב איש יהודי.

מאת

ישראל דוב פרומקין

ירושלם, ג׳ אב התרס״ד

JERUSALEM 15 Juli 5664.

Monte sur la plus haute montagne, messagère de Sion Élève ta voix avec force, envoyée de Jérusalem! Élève la et ne crains rien. (Isaie XL 9.)

FIGURE 17. *Havatselet*, Hasidic Hebrew newspaper, established by Y. D. Frumkin, 1870. Source: Historical Jewish Press website—www.jpress.org.il—founded by the National Library of Israel and Tel Aviv University.

With the growth of Jewish communities, Hebrew advertisements, commercial notices, and rabbinic proclamations proliferated across the city and became a vibrant, ephemeral medium of communication. "Once upon a time, when a person wanted to inform his peers of something, he would write a notice and post it in the entrance to the synagogue, and that would be it," reported a Hebrew journalist in 1896. "But now the city has expanded, and its neighborhoods are many. The season of printing and posting has arrived, and the competition is fierce. . . . For every novelty, placards are printed immediately, and overnight the entire town learns of a new Matzo baker in Zion."[46] These placards were posted not only outside Jewish institutions but in great numbers in the city center of Jaffa Gate, where, according to early-twentieth-century photographs, Hebrew was the most prevalent language on placards. Rabbinic institutions also used such placards in an intensified manner, often to voice their disapproval of modernizing tendencies. "Notices on municipal administration, on the Ashkenazi council, entire manifestos, and wise advice, rich literature is posted in the streets. And every morning, when you go to town, you spend at least one hour reading notices in the market."[47] The notices, known in Yiddish as *pashkevilim*, were almost entirely in Hebrew rather than in the spoken Jewish languages of Yiddish or Judeo-Spanish.[48] Hebrew's advantage over these spoken languages was not only its cultural and religious significance but also the fact that it was a common language for communities which were otherwise extremely diverse in linguistic terms. "However we think of the Hebrew language—as the language of the rotting past, or also the language of the shining future—in the present we have to consider the fact that the Hebrew language is the only one which unites the branches of Jewish society into a single national race, and only Hebrew, and no other language, is used by the Ashkenazi, the Sephardi, the Yemenite, and the Moroccan," wrote a Zionist Hebrew newspaper in 1907.[49] The use of Hebrew in local newspapers, pamphlets, public notices, signage, and advertising was a natural choice for anyone who wanted to address Jews across congregational boundaries. But some read shop signs as a crucial battleground in the remaking of Hebrew into a living national language. Eliezer Ben Yehuda routinely monitored the use of Hebrew in signage, celebrating the appearance of commercial signs and berating Jewish proprietors for their reluctance to put up signs in Hebrew. In April 1910 Ben Yehuda reported to his newspaper readers that the Sephardic banker Valero had "finally hung a nice large Hebrew sign on the entrance to his bank. Many merchants did the same. Hurrah! Better late than never. . . . Interesting to note that many Christian businesses added Hebrew to their signs. . . . Hebrew is marching ahead, who can stop it?"[50] Jurji Zaydan, the Lebanese Nahda intellectual who visited Palestine in 1914, observed with astonishment Hebrew text in the markets. Shop signs and the names of merchandise often appeared in Hebrew, not in Arabic or in European languages, he noted. In Jewish-owned hotels, wrote Zaydan, rooms were not marked by simple numbers but rather named after "their ancestors and their historical cities."[51] Zaydan read these signs as indications of a looming Jewish takeover of Palestine.

The Hebrew Revival's crowning accomplishment was the transformation of Hebrew into a spoken language. This enterprise, which took shape between 1903 and 1914, was led by educators in Jaffa, Jerusalem, and the Zionist colonies who taught children in kindergartens and schools, cultivating the first generation for whom Hebrew was a primary spoken tongue.[52] The educators behind these initiatives were a mix of Palestine-born Jews and recent immigrants,

FIGURE 18. Orthodox and secular Jews reading Hebrew placards and posted newspaper in Jerusalem, 1930.
Source: Library of Congress, Matson Collection, American Colony photographers.

Zionist colonists and urbanites, Ashkenazim and Sephardim. Hebrew as a spoken tongue bracketed out differences between these different elements and allowed them to think of their project as a national Jewish one. By the eve of the war there were several thousand Hebrew speakers in Palestine: children, teenagers, teachers, and committed enthusiasts. They constituted a small yet highly committed social base that would make possible the postwar Hebraization of Jewish communities in Palestine.

For many Palestine-born Jews, Sephardic as well as Ashkenazi, Hebrew nationalism had a growing appeal, primarily as an urban form of Zionism which focused on cultural autonomy more than it did on Jewish colonization and settlement. The 1908 Constitutional Revolution was a significant catalyst for notions of a Jewish national identity, especially in Palestine. In the new definition of the Ottoman Empire as a family of nations, Jews in Palestine saw political potential for defining themselves as a single national community. In practice, overcoming ethnic, linguistic, cultural, and ideological differences proved impossible, as Jews in Jerusalem failed to establish a common political framework or to secure the election of a local Jewish representative to the Ottoman Parliament. Yet the vision of the "Hebrew nation" in Palestine took shape in those years, inspired by the national "revival" of other ethnic groups in the empire such as Armenians, Arabs, and Greeks.[53]

But for other Zionist factions, Hebrew revitalization was not just about cultural revival. Hebrew was primarily a tool in a project of territorialization and settlement. "Our world rests on three elements: Hebrew land, Hebrew labor, and Hebrew language!" proclaimed the newspaper *Ha-Poʿel ha-Tsaʿir*, the organ of socialist Zionism.[54] These socialist Zionist activists advocated economic and cultural separatism as part of national revival and territorial takeover. "The conquest of language" was a parallel project to the "conquest of land" and the "conquest of labor." These efforts hardened under the British Mandate. A militant Zionist activist group formed, calling itself the Battalion of Hebrew-Language Defenders, to promote the use of Hebrew and clamp down on the use of "foreign languages." The Battalion protested the use of any other languages in Jewish daily life, including in advertising, entertainment, and cafés. Hebrew Defenders in Jerusalem declared "war on foreign signage." In 1927, on the tenth anniversary of the Balfour Declaration, the Battalion warned that "the National Home will not be built without the Hebrew language. . . .

The Land of Israel will not be Hebrew without the Hebrew language." In an allusion to the language of settlement, the Battalion stated that using Hebrew was like using a "mortar trowel" in constructing the national home.[55] This ethos of Hebrew as the modern language of a monolingual nation starkly contrasted with the pietistic language of the memorial tablets, which Pinhas Ben Tsvi Grayevsky set out to survey at exactly the same time. Those stones of memory were anchored in rabbinic tradition and transnational networks and made no territorial claims on the geography of Jerusalem.

THE CHALLENGE OF ZIONISM

Grayevsky's *Stones of Memory* captured the remarkable growth of the Jewish population of Jerusalem and its changing face and character. Within less than half a century, the memorial inscriptions made Hebrew a visible feature of Jerusalem's urban landscape. Yet now their use and meaning were in question. The celebration of piety in stone concealed a cultural crisis. Doubts were growing regarding the very meaning of Hebrew public writing.

At first sight, Grayevsky's compendium appeared to sit within a traditional Jewish textual economy of congregational commemoration. The name *Stones of Memory* recalled books that collected burial inscriptions from Jewish cemeteries. These books aimed to ensure eternal memory for those buried and to allow readers to pray for them.[56] Grayevsky's series included epitaphs in Jewish cemeteries in Jerusalem, Jaffa, and Zionist colonies. The bulk of the corpus focused on Jerusalem, with nearly two thousand foundation and commemoration inscriptions of Jewish institutions. However, Grayevsky also published ancient Hebrew inscriptions that were discovered by Western archaeologists. And in a complete aberration from the Jewish memorial genre, he included in the corpus several non-Jewish inscriptions: translations of ancient Greek and Latin inscriptions excavated in Jerusalem, Islamic inscriptions from Jerusalem and Hebron, and a Samaritan inscription from the synagogue near Nablus. The corpus included letters of endorsement (*haskamot*) from Palestine's chief rabbis, testifying to the religious significance of his enterprise. But Grayevsky also included letters of endorsement from Muslim, Christian, and Samaritan scholars.[57] As a self-fashioned Jerusalem *maskil*, Grayevsky connected the study of Hebrew inscriptions with the scientific study of inscriptions in Greek, Latin, and Arabic, pointing to interfaith respect and a universal, humanistic commitment to the scholarly study of religious heritage.

But Grayevsky's motivation was not only pietistic or pseudo-scientific. His project, as he perceived it, was also a Zionist one. He presented the Hebrew inscriptions as vital historical sources, carrying "important memories" and a "wealth of information" on the early history of Lovers of Zion, "who built Jerusalem from its ruins."[58] The British Mandate recognized the European Zionist movement as the Jewish leadership, marginalizing local Jewish elites in Palestine. Zionist institutions depicted the country's existing Jewish communities as reactionary, diasporic in character, and unproductive. Writing against this outlook, Grayevsky, an Orthodox, Jerusalem-born Jew, attempted to integrate local Jewish communities into the Zionist narrative. The book's hagiographic account of Jewish donors and community leaders portrayed them as a national avant-garde of Jewish revival in Palestine. While he mentioned the 1927 earthquake in Jerusalem as the event that propelled him to record the inscriptions, it appears that the political earthquake of Zionism was more significant in this regard. The emergence of a new kind of Jewish society in Palestine tore through the traditional networks of piety and charity and rendered memorial inscriptions an anachronistic mode of writing.

This earthquake found literary expression in Agnon's *Only Yesterday.* The Bukharan memorial tablet represented a Jewish writing culture which was built on copying and reaffirming holy texts of tradition, in veneration and respect. But this ancestral system of reference was collapsing, and the value of such memorial tablets was called into question.

> And when the Holy-One-Blessed-Be-He remembers His children, He looks first at Jerusalem, sees those houses and courtyards the Children of Israel built in Jerusalem, nods His head affectionately, as it were, and says, This people have I formed for myself, etc., is there a nation in the world I exiled from its land and its eyes and its heart are still on it. And everyone who dedicates a house in Jerusalem puts up a memorial stone, to give him a good place and a name in its walls, and writes his name, and his extravagant generosity is an eternal memory unto the last generation. He who is righteous, his Charity stands and his name is forgotten. He who is not righteous, his name remains and his Charity is enjoyed by those who are unworthy.[59]

As usual with Agnon, what disguises itself as a naive description in a mild pietistic tone is actually sharp criticism. The memorial inscriptions are presented here as an inappropriate obsession with self-commemoration. The name of the benefactor, painted by Isaac Kumer in gold, is an indication of extravagance and excess.[60] The desire to mark one's name in such an ostentatious manner, says Agnon, is the opposite of charity. "He who is not righteous, his name remains." Traditional writing has become hollow and disingenuous, while the dog presents itself to Kumer as a blank page, an opportunity to write the world anew. The crisis of signification is located in Hebrew's transition from a defunct pietistic language to the secular, enticing, and ultimately dangerous language of naming and categorizing.

THE VIOLENCE OF WRITING

Throughout *Only Yesterday*, writing and naming are associated with death and violence. The act of naming, arbitrary as it may seem, carries with it potentially lethal implications; the narrator mentions that in some communities "a man whose sons don't survive doesn't name his son in order to confound the Angel of Death."[61] Isaac's name is registered in the notebook of Reb Alter, the *mohel* who circumcised him as a baby in his Polish hometown. As noted by one critic, the writing of the Hebrew name in the notebook accompanies the violent ritual of the "writing in the flesh," the "inscription of Jewish males into community."[62] The dog's bite undoes the rite of circumcision. When Isaac is close to his horrible death, Reb Alter notices that Isaac's name in his notebook has begun to fade. "One inscription writes out another in a struggle for which [Isaac] is literally the locus."[63]

Many critics interpreted the writing on the dog as an act of violent punishment.[64] In the Jewish context, the abjection of those who defied the law often took the form of excommunication, which was the primary form of congregational sanction. As the dog roams the Jewish neighborhoods of Jerusalem, it is repeatedly stoned and chased away by panicked crowds.[65] Although divided into many communities, Jews are united in fear of the Hebrew-marked danger, running through the city. The symbolic violence of removing a "heretic" from the community through decree, posted in the streets of Jerusalem, was a common and even frequent practice. This textual practice of excommunication notices is exemplified in the novel in the character of the Orthodox zealot Reb Fayesh, the butcher turned rabbi, who "put up his knife and took up his pen."[66] Reb Fayesh encounters the dog-text at night, when he sets out to post notices against Jews who have deviated from the Orthodox way. Startled by the dog, Fayesh's posters fly from his hands, and the scraps of paper hit his face: "Every single note cackles with those words Reb Fayesh wrote on it. In his innocence," adds Agnon with his corrosive irony, "Reb Fayesh believed that the ancestors of the excommunicated rose up from their graves to take vengeance on him, for the notes were white as shrouds of the dead."[67] Soon after the incident Reb Fayesh is struck with paralysis and becomes a living corpse, serving as Agnon's metaphor for the Orthodox world.

The violence of writing is gendered. Writing, as enacted by the *mohel* or Reb Fayesh, is described as a masculine act, and Isaac's encounter with the dog takes on a sexual dimension.[68] Armed with a brush (the Talmudic expression for the male organ), Isaac approaches the "flirtatious" dog with his body "tingling." Isaac's actions are presented as involuntary, as if he is obeying a crude instinct. Immediately after the writing Isaac kicks the dog, scolds it, and chases it away. Toward the end of the book, the erotic violence is reversed. As it prepares to bite Isaac, the dog assumes a male role: its teeth "stood erect and his whole body was taut."[69]

The association of writing with violence, and inscription with erasure, features often in Jacques Derrida's early work, where he suggests that "writing cannot be thought outside of the horizon of intersubjective violence."[70] Writing is the imposition of order, which inevitably builds on erasure and displacement. For Derrida, naming is the archetypal form of violence through language. To give a name is to force uniqueness onto a subject and impose a logic of categorization. Presence is reduced to a sign and put into a straitjacket from which it cannot be released.

> To name, to give names . . . such is the originary violence of language which consists in inscribing within a difference, in classifying, in suspending the vocative absolute. To think the unique *within* the system, to inscribe it there, such is the gesture of the arche-writing, arche-violence, loss of the proper, of absolute proximity, of self-presence . . . incapable of appearing to itself except in its own disappearance.[71]

For Derrida, signification amounts to an unstable chain of violent interventions, starting with the inscription of a name, through its self-effacing and repressive normalization, to a final violence which exposes the tensions created by the act of classification and naming. Isaac's inscription on the dog can be read as the absolute manifestation of writing's "originary violence," the arbitrary aggression that celebrates its potency by marking a being, and through this act condemning it to persecution and misery. Isaac's act reveals the capricious and brutal nature of establishing order through signification: everything can be marked and labeled, but the signifier's connection to the signified is always absent and in doubt. The audacity of this act of excess is then erased and normalized through a backlash of a "second writing"—that of the dog's teeth in Isaac's flesh and the effacement of Isaac's name from the list of circumcised males and from the world of the living. Isaac's horrifying revelation of the godlike power of human writing is once more concealed, if not forgotten, through what appears an act of cruel retribution.

Madness, in Derrida's account, is the dark side of language. Writing imposes a clear divide between right and wrong, true and false, what can and cannot be said. Only through constructing the disorder of madness can language establish itself as an order. Only through crisis can the straight and reasoned path be carved out from the labyrinth of insanity. Isaac's writing is an act of madness that exiles madness onto the dog. Writing separates itself from lunacy through an act of violence, which is later negated, forgotten, and denied—but always harbors within it a potential backlash.[72]

For Derrida, this violence is the part of the "conditions of writing" that exist in all forms of writing, across times and cultures.[73] Derrida's concept of writing refers to all systems of human signification, far broader than the medium of alphabetic notation, which, Derrida argues, is an ethnocentric misconception of writing. As such Derrida denies any significance to the context of writing, its material and political underpinning. This argument is not only trans-historical, it is in fact anti-historical: for history itself appears as the operation of writing par excellence, the attempt to order, establish difference, and reify a sense of civilization.

But Derrida's insight, in its totalizing gesture, seems, in fact, rooted in a specific moment of writing. It is in the twentieth century that the violence of writing reached its apex, and the categorization of people and territories through naming and renaming condemned millions to genocide, deportation, and dispossession. In Jerusalem, the modern obsession with marking and erasing emerges at a particular historical juncture: the moment when the divine order of writing collapses; when the stable place of the Bible, the prayer book, and the endowment inscription is no longer taken for granted; and where textuality is defined through a new grid of street nameplates, population register, and identification papers.

The crisis of signification captured in the writing of Agnon is not a metaphysical or an existential one. Rather, it arrives at a specific historical juncture of modernity. Isaac's inscription on the dog is a rebellion against the congregational writing of the memorial tablet. Integrated into the stone wall, it embedded the house and its benefactor within a cosmos of divine meaning. Hebrew is released into the landscape by the secularization of sacred language, in a political project whose aim was to undo and redo space and population. Zionist Hebrew sought to redeem space and change its nature. What starts as unparalleled freedom and empowerment through writing becomes an obsession with erasure, not only of others—Palestine's Jews and Arabs—but also of the migrant-settler himself. An abyss opens beneath the subject, threatening to drown him as he loses his textual moorings.

TEXT AS SUPPLEMENT

Only Yesterday revolves around the broken relation between marked skin and inner essence, external masks and true meaning, textual signifier and physical signified. To return to Derrida's terms, the words painted on the dog are a supplement, an external element which the dog cannot disassociate himself from. The writing becomes part of him, and he finds himself reduced to this label, which defines him, overwhelms him, and finally destroys him. The dog becomes pure text. In *Only Yesterday* and elsewhere in Agnon's writing, supplements reaffirm their supremacy as the change of outer form corrupts the original meaning within; the skin overdetermines the inner core.[74]

As one critic observed, *Only Yesterday* is a world of writing out of control, in which texts "run amok" and sow disorder and destruction.[75] The dog's wanderings frustrate the attempts of the Orthodox community to retain control over the use of Hebrew text. In one incident, an Orthodox man sets out to collect torn pieces of Hebrew-printed paper thrown away by "heretics," to save them for ritual burial as *Geniza*.[76] The man sees the dog and reaches out to the writing on his back, thinking these are Hebrew letters "lying in the dung"; the dog-text wakes with a start and the man is struck by panic.[77] The encounters of Orthodox rabbis with the unleashed signifier always lead to a loss of speech, which testifies to "their loss of power to nominate, denominate, name, and exclude."[78] Agnon's descriptions make it clear that he considers the Orthodox zealous guarding of Hebrew not as true loyalty to tradition but as perverse attempts to impose order in a world where language is beyond such control. There can be no return to the ancestral way.[79] Orthodox attempts to retain the sacredness of Hebrew are futile and self-defeating. It is their own excessive writing, with copious excommunication notices pasted anonymously on the walls, which destabilizes language further; their words are flat and meaningless papers flying in the streets of Jerusalem.

How, then, to understand the power of language as supplement? Or, in the context of *Only Yesterday*, how to understand the relation between the damning words on the dog's back and its infection with rabies? The novel's ambiguity on this question invites a number of interpretations. The first interpretation connects the dog's infection with Hebrew's sacred powers. The label infected the dog with the deadly disease, in a version of the Golem legend. He is the monster which was brought to life by Hebrew writing and then turns on its creator.[80] The writing on the dog could, alternatively, be seen as divinatory: like the words of the oracle, Isaac's involuntary writing senses the dog's true condition long before the symptoms appear. In both cases, Hebrew is assumed to be unlike any other language; it carries with it the power to divine or transform the true essence of things. Isaac is bearing the consequences of the rupture in the use of the holy tongue. He starts by corrupting the traditional formulaic text through excessive embellishing in vain colors. Hubris then pushes him to break Jewish traditional conventions and become a writer, an author who can mold the world through language.[81] But religious language and secular writing cannot be reconciled. The contradictions within him eventually destroy him, as he falls into the abyss of language. His megalomaniac writing brings about his own effacement, which, as if in a Greek tragedy, is described as a cataclysmic event. Unlike the biblical story of Isaac's sacrifice, here no one intervenes to save the boy. His terrible death is received well by the heavens: after a long drought, the skies open with a downpour.

At stake here are the undesired yet inevitable implications of secularizing the holy tongue. While Zionists sought to make Hebrew into a national language of speech, they also wanted to lend "mythic dimensions to the new culture" by harnessing its evocative power and biblical connotations.[82] The rabid dog-text's biblical name, Balak, can be read as a reference to the Zionist recasting of the Bible as a national mythology, which is taught as a history and geography book rather than holy scripture. Agnon seems to share the misgivings of his close acquaintance Gershom Scholem, the scholar of the Kabbalah, who in 1926 warned against the fallacies of Hebrew Revival.[83] "One believes that language has been secularized, that its apocalyptic thorn has been pulled out. But this is surely not true," wrote Scholem. "If we . . . resuscitate the language of the ancient books so that it can reveal itself anew to them, must then not the religious violence of the language one day break out against those who speak it . . . ? We do live inside this language, above an abyss, almost all of us with the certainty of the blind. . . . No one knows whether the sacrifice of individuals who will be annihilated in this abyss will suffice to close it."[84]

Scholem's argument here is that Hebrew's meaning is embedded in religious mythology and centuries of Jewish textual practice. A secular avant-garde could not erase the deep and rich religious resonances of the language. The Zionists wished to rearticulate Jewish redemption in nationalist and colonial terms, channeling the language's messianic impulse into a modernist remaking of a people and land. But the social and cultural forces they unleashed were beyond their control. Hebrew was "pregnant with catastrophes." Scholem's melodramatic warning proved prescient, with Zionism's later shift toward an explicitly religious discourse. After the 1967 war, religious settlers claimed the language of Zionism and reinvested the national language with sanctity, as they spearheaded the colonization of the Occupied Territories. The secular-Zionist attempt to channel the messianic impulse of Hebrew into a project of "normalization" was overcome from within by those who continued the colonizing mission but read the divine promise not as metaphor but as manifest destiny.

But there is another way to read the infection of the dog: as partly, or wholly, accidental. In this case, which Agnon is careful not to exclude, the act of writing is what it seems: a practical joke of a bored painter. Perhaps the label imposed itself on the dog, as frightened Jews chased him out of the city, where he was infected with rabies: an example of how modern labels, however arbitrary, ruthlessly force themselves upon people. Or alternatively, the writing bears no causal relation to the condition of the dog and becomes true only by pure accident, and a fatal twist of irony. In this interpretation there is no meaning in Isaac's "sacrifice." His death is not a tragedy but a grotesque.[85] The text on the dog's back is read not as a transgression of a divine law of writing but rather as a treacherous node in a human textual economy. The story remains one of text and its failure to convey meaning, but it is the human fallacious reliance on labels that explains the ending, in a tragicomedy of readings. Shortly before the fatal bite, Isaac encounters Balak in the Orthodox quarter of Meah Sheʿarim. By now Balak is clearly rabid: "His mouth gapes open and his saliva drools and his ears droop and his tail is between his legs and his eyes are bloodshot and he barks and his voice isn't heard."[86] Yet faced with the usual panic caused by the dog, Isaac is dismissive. "Who says he's crazy? Said they, Isn't that what's written explicitly? Said Isaac, And if it is written, so what? Are we obligated to believe everything that's written? But I'll tell you, I myself wrote on his skin, and I know that he's a healthy dog, for if he were mad, would I have bothered him at all."[87] Isaac's belief in the falsity of the label prevents him from seeing the clear danger in front of his eyes. His behavior is based on the idea that language bears no relation to the truth within. The crowd accepts this explanation and loses all fear of the dog, which now bites its sign maker. The new lax attitude toward the dog relies on the separation between signifier and signified, and the understanding that writing is always potentially arbitrary and false. Yet as a false label it identifies the dog as non-rabid, despite the clear signs to the contrary. While acutely aware of the unbridgeable gap between signifier and signified, between labels and objects, Isaac and other characters in the book never stop trying to stabilize the world around them by anchoring meaning—true or false—in text. Their attempts only destabilize meaning further: a modern condition for which there is no recourse.

While Agnon's tale was fictional and fantastic, the crisis of Hebrew was a very real one, as Grayevsky's compendium reveals. In the late 1920s, as Grayevsky was collecting inscriptions throughout Jerusalem, this writing culture already belonged to the past. This could explain why he described recently placed inscriptions as "ancient." It was the very medium of inscription that had become "ancient." Grayevsky attempted to ensure an honorable place for this heritage, and to write the inscriptions and their patrons into the project of Zionism. He failed; nothing can testify to this better than the fact that his huge, erratic, and fascinating corpus was left unused by Israeli historians of Jerusalem.

The crisis of stone inscriptions manifested itself differently in Islamic and Jewish monumental writing. But in both cases, a once dominant form of writing lost its immediate meaning in the face of challenges that reconstituted the role of language. This transition was paralleled in the most widely circulating textual artifacts: money. Gold and silver coins represented for centuries the main form of money. Jerusalem's complicated currency arrangements provided opportunities for many alphabets and languages to circulate from hand to hand. But like stone inscriptions, the embedded materiality of gold coins was facing challenges from increasingly dematerialized textual artifacts, most notably paper money.

3 GOLD

Text and Value

> It is difficult to imagine a more chaotic state of affairs in currency matters than obtained in Palestine as part of the Turkish Empire before the war. . . . It seems a wonder, even to a postwar generation with experience of currency restrictions and inflations, that any business should have been done at all under such conditions.
>
> *Anglo-Palestine Bank, Report on "Currencies in Palestine Pre-war and post war," 1934*[1]

IT IS HARD TO ARGUE WITH THIS DESCRIPTION OF THE MONETARY situation in late-Ottoman Palestine. The picture is indeed baffling.[2] The Ottoman monetary system was based on the piaster, a fictitious unit originating from a silver coin long withdrawn from circulation. Exchange rates regularly fluctuated, not only between Ottoman and foreign currencies but also between Ottoman coins of different denominations, with considerable divergence between official and trade rates and between cities in the same province, such as Jaffa and Jerusalem.[3] Alongside Ottoman coins, a wide array of European coins circulated as means of payment, from Russian rubles to British sovereigns, with the effect that prices were habitually quoted in more than one currency and payments were often made combining several currencies. Small change was always in short supply, and the sudden arrival of a caravan of trading Bedouins to a town was sufficient to create a devastating currency crisis.[4]

However, defining the monetary situation in terms of "chaos" obscures the far-reaching rearrangement of Palestine's monetary regime in the late nineteenth and early twentieth centuries. With growing commodification of land and labor, social relations in Jerusalem were increasingly monetized. This monetization relied on what could be termed the textualization of the economy: the development of textual technologies to express and manage proprietorship and commercial obligations, transactions and transfers, credit and debt, savings and investments. Coins and banknotes circulated as mobile, legible nodes in an economy that was increasingly complex, abstract, and text-based.

Money has long been a textual artifact, perhaps the most widely circulating of all textual artifacts. It is inscribed with words and numbers, it is passed on from hand to hand, and in each transaction money is appraised, examined, and read. Of all the textual artifacts discussed in this book, money was the one whose daily reading by Jerusalemites was not in question. Pedestrians in Jerusalem could—and did—ignore official street names, signs on buildings, or pilgrims' graffiti without much consequence to their daily lives; but ignoring the writing on money involved a real, and literal, price. In order to identify a fake bill, to discern a coin that would not be accepted by shopkeepers, or to distinguish between coins of ten and twenty French francs—money had to be read.

The manner in which money was read was related to the manner in which money was used and understood by its users. In the late nineteenth century, dominant monetary theory viewed as self-evident the link between money and precious metals, namely silver and gold. It was gold coins' substantial quality as precious metals—not the wording on their face—which ultimately determined their value and use. Not only European economic thinkers but also laypeople in Jerusalem saw this "metalistic" nature of money as necessary and inevitable. However, this self-evident truth came under doubt in the early twentieth century as financial systems increasingly relied on textual artifacts and technologies. With the dematerialization of money, economic theorists started to rethink the link between money and gold.

MONEY IN LATE-OTTOMAN JERUSALEM

Palestine of the 1850s was an overwhelmingly rural country, and agriculture was mostly oriented toward subsistence farming. Money was certainly not unheard of in Palestine's villages, and moneylending from the urban centers to their rural hinterland was growing from the early nineteenth century on.[5] Yet debts and taxes were still paid in kind, mainly in grain and olive oil.[6] This corresponded to what Karl Marx termed the "Asiatic mode of production": a preindustrial economy, dominated by the state and still embedded in the natural rhythms of nature and the yearly harvest cycle. In Marx's view, the collection of taxes in kind was the secret behind the Ottoman Empire's longevity, protecting it from the encroachment of capitalist relations.[7]

Money was more prevalent in urban centers such as Jerusalem. Though never an important center for trade, Jerusalem was a hub of economic activity as a provincial capital and a pilgrimage destination for Muslims, Jews, and Christians. Merchants, craftsmen, moneychangers, and lenders dealt with cash. But even here, much economic interaction was conducted in kind, and wage labor was unusual. In the local soap industry, workers were often paid in soap.[8] When in 1863 the Ashkenazi trader Yehoshua Yellin ran into a property dispute with the fearsome sheikh of Abu Ghosh, the British consul in Jerusalem advised him to bribe the sheikh, "for in Turkey money is the answer to everything." Yellin thanked the consul for his good advice and sent the sheikh not money, but sacks of coffee and sugar.[9] In diaries, memoirs, and autobiographies of Jerusalemites one comes across elaborate systems of barter, pervading most aspects of daily life and making the use of money unnecessary. Teachers receiving their payment in free lodging and food;[10] villagers paying with eggs for lodging in caravanserais;[11] a Muslim gatekeeper turning out the fire on the Sabbath day for an Ashkenazi family in return for cinnamon pastries[12]—are but a few examples of the barter exchange that remained a feature of economic life until the early decades of the twentieth century. In addition, the welfare system of religious communities, providing the poor with education, medication, fuel, and food, reduced the need to use money on a daily basis.

Money was not the standard by which the power of the local notable elite was measured. The notables' status depended on their lineage, connecting them with the Arab conquerors of Palestine, and on their reputation as men of Islamic learning. As mediators between the Ottoman authorities and the local population, and as arbitrators in clan feuds in the district, their influence was widely acknowledged. But even for the most powerful among notable families, wealth in gold was secondary to social capital and political influence.[13]

Yet this state of affairs was changing as the Ottoman Empire underwent rapid economic transformation, characterized by growing monetization and the emergence of a capitalist class. In the last decades of Ottoman rule money appeared more and more in physical form as part of daily life, expanding in circulation and assuming new roles. This development was driven by Ottoman reforms as well as Palestine's growing integration into European spheres of influence, commerce, and tourism. Money was ever present in urban centers such as Jerusalem—and increasingly in the shape of European currencies. Already in the 1850s European coins were circulating in Jerusalem alongside Ottoman coins. J. Murray's Palestine handbook advised travelers that "the gold and silver of nearly every nation in Europe is now current in Syria."[14] When the British consul's wife Elizabeth Finn purchased the land of Artas, a farm near Jerusalem, the payment was made in British coins, not in Ottoman money. The transaction took place in the office of the British Consulate in Jerusalem, where "ten of the fiercest and wildest looking Arabs" assembled. "One hundred and fifty sovereigns were counted slowly into the hand of the Sheik [*sic*]."[15]

The Ottoman monetary system suffered from shortages of coinage and a complicated and confusing array of coins with shifting values. Ottoman gold coins were rare; the main Ottoman coins in circulation were silver, nickel, and copper ones, of medium and low value: *para*, *metlik*, *altilik*, *beshlik*, *majidi*, and others. These coins were commonly used in everyday transactions. Large payments were conducted in European currencies, whose circulation increased greatly in the years leading up to World War I. French gold coins became the standard currency for major transactions; second in popularity were British gold sovereigns.[16] Russian, German, Austrian, and other European coins were also used, but to a lesser degree. These foreign coins were used by ordinary residents of Jerusalem and served to stipulate prices of commodities, rents, houses, and wages. Even the Ottoman authorities used foreign coins at times.[17] "The 'Napoleon' [twenty-franc gold coins] and the Pound Sterling, the Franc and the Shilling, the Krone, the Dollar and the Rouble, all these are current in our city in constant and large amounts," wrote an influential public figure in 1914.[18] It was an extraordinarily heterogeneous system in which coins of many shapes and languages circulated side by side and were routinely exchanged for one another. This diversity, and the constant fluctuation in exchange rates, no doubt made the monetary system confusing, and yet it functioned effectively enough to enable the rapid development of Palestine during this period.

FIGURE 19. Ottoman silver coin of 5 *kuruş* (*piastre*), minted 1909–10, with the *tughra* of Sultan Mehmed V. The denomination and value are not inscribed on the coin.

Sources: (top) Ottoman Empire Mehmed V, by Raimond Spekking, is licensed under CC BY-SA 4.0, https://commons.wikimedia.org/wiki/File:5_Piastres_Mehmed_V._1327_(Rs)-8476.jpg; (bottom) Ottoman Empire Mehmed V, by Raimond Spekking, is licensed under CC BY-SA 4.0, https://commons.wiki media.org/wiki/File:5_Piastres_Mehmed_V._1327_(Vs)-8475.jpg.

FIGURE 20. European coins in circulation in Jerusalem: British gold sovereign featuring Queen Victoria; French 20 franc gold coin, also known as "Napoleon" (1896).
Sources: (top) Original Scanned Gold Coin Souvereign Victoria 1871 Aners. Wikimedia, https://upload.wikimedia.org/wikipedia/commons/2/2c/Sovereign-victoria-avers.jpg; (bottom) Wikicommons.

European currencies circulated throughout the Ottoman Empire, and especially in the Levant, but in Jerusalem they were particularly prevalent. The city was a dynamic place of encounter between imperial European power and capital and local elites and communities. European coins arrived with European diplomats and missionaries, who sponsored schools, hospitals, orphanages, churches, and monasteries; through inflows of charity and commerce of Jewish congregations; and from tourism and pilgrimage. The improvement of train and sea routes made Palestine more accessible to European and North American tourists. Agricultural trade expanded considerably with Palestine's integration into the world economy. Export revenues in British and French currencies flowed into Palestine, and the main benefactors were landlords and traders in the main cities.

The happy circulation of coins of competing European powers alongside Ottoman coinage could be seen as an excellent proof of the political neutrality of money. According to prevalent monetary theory of the day, the value of money was rooted in the value of gold and silver as precious commodities. As pieces of gold and silver, it did not matter which state minted the coins; all that mattered was their metallic substance. Classical economists of the nineteenth century believed that money was, by nature, a commodity.[19] This approach maintained that money's historical origins were in the barter economy of the marketplace. Barter transactions were complicated and inefficient; money developed as a mechanism to make commerce more efficient and cut costs. Out of multiplicities of transactions, one type of commodity emerged as exchangeable for all others. Gold and silver became the "universal equivalent," the commodity through which the value of all other commodities was expressed. Regardless if it was called a thaler or a *beshlik*, money was ultimately a piece of precious metal, and its value was determined by the quantity of gold or silver in the coin. Moneychangers in Palestine would most likely agree with this observation, as they routinely melted silver coins into metal bars and sent them to London banks in exchange for gold coins.[20] "The only difference . . . between coin and bullion, is one of shape, and gold can at any time pass from one form to the other," wrote Karl Marx in *Capital*.[21] For classical economists of the day, money was a binding agent, a lubricant, or a tool for communication between buyers and sellers. Money objectified economic interaction and obscured it, but it was ultimately a neutral instrument.

TEXT ON COINS

Ottoman and European coins used a radically dissimilar visual vernacular, differing in every possible aspect: alphabet, language, imagery, numerals, and calendar. On Ottoman coins, text in Arabic was the dominant feature, in line with a long tradition of Islamic coinage going back to the seventh century.[22] One face of the coin showed the sultan's monogram—the *tughra*; the other face indicated the place of the mint, sometimes below the line *ʿazza nasruhu*—"may his victory be glorious"—in Arabic, rather than in Ottoman Turkish. The Islamic *hijri* year of the sultan's ascension appeared in Eastern Arabic numerals, conveying the official status of the Islamic calendar, which determined not only most official holidays and celebrations but also the economic calendar in Jerusalem.[23] Property leases, for example, were terminated and renewed annually in the month of Muharram, the first month of the Islamic year. Each Muharram brought with it the sight of hundreds of families, Muslim and non-Muslim alike, moving around Jerusalem to their new abodes.[24]

European gold coins, in contrast, were iconographic. One side of the coin typically depicted a human face, usually the monarch or emperor; the other side showed a national icon such as the coat of arms. Text appeared on the margins, inscribed on the perimeter or the bottom rather than at the center. The aniconic tradition of Islam and Judaism did not cause local Muslim and Jewish merchants any hesitation in dealing with European coins carrying human figures. French coins carried the name of the French Republic; British sovereigns displayed the Latin title of the monarch. A common feature was the Christian year, in Latin or Western Arabic numerals. Whatever text the coin carried in Latin, French, Russian, or other languages was illegible for the massive majority of the population, a fact that may explain why they were called not by their official names but rather by colloquial nicknames. French twenty-franc coins were called *lira Faransawiyya* (French lira) in Arabic and *Napolyon* (Napoleon) by Jews. British sovereigns were referred to as "Queen" or "King" according to whose head they featured, and sometimes "horse rider," after the image of Saint George on the back of the coin.[25]

Most coins, European and Ottoman alike, did not display in writing the name of the coin, or its nominal value. One could not find the word *sovereign* on British gold coins, or the term *beshlik* on the Ottoman silver coin by that name. Coins were distinguished by shape, layout, and size, not by explicit naming. Denomination was communicated in speech and sight, and not through inscriptions on the face of the metal. The text and iconography did not declare value but provided coins with imperial endorsement. These symbols placed them within a political order and made them legal tender. Even on coins which were marked by their nominal value (such as French gold coins) the marking was understood to reflect the intrinsic value of the coin rather than to define it.

But on some coins, the inscriptions mattered more. Token coins, the small change with which most daily payments were made, carried very little precious metal, and their nominal value far exceeded their "intrinsic" metallic value. This was especially pronounced in the case of Ottoman silver and base-metal coins. Always in shortage, the coins were black and heavily worn, and "not excelling in beauty" according to a contemporary Jerusalem resident.[26] What determined their convertibility was not their weight but their writing. Small coins were accepted by traders if and only if the *tughra* on them was clearly discernible. If the *tughra* was somehow rubbed off, the coin was likely to be refused, and it was a challenge to dispose of such a coin. Children regularly tried to pass on worn coins to grocers with poor eyesight "during the hours of dusk."[27] The fetishization of the *tughra* as the source of coins' value was not the product of a state edict. In fact, the authorities tried to force the public to use worn coins, owing to the scarcity of small change. The Jerusalem municipality repeatedly warned traders not to reject such coins and reassured the public that they were legal tender as long as the writing was somewhat legible.[28] This seems to have had little success.

Monetary theorists grappled with the question of token coins and their value. Their response was that coins with symbolic (rather than intrinsic) value depended on the enforcement of the state. Token coins could play a role in small-change transactions domestically but could have no value in international trade—which reflected raw economic relations. In Marx's words: "When money leaves the home sphere of circulation, it strips off the local garbs which it there assumes . . . and returns to its original form of bullion."[29]

In Marx's *Capital* we find a lucid articulation of money as camouflage, masking the real social relations behind several layers of disguise. Texts, images, and emblems on coins, wrote Marx, were nothing but "different national uniforms, which are worn at home and doffed again in the market of the world."[30] Gold, the money-commodity, was the source of the coins' value, but gold was also a camouflage, masking the social relations of ownership and labor exploitation. At the bottom level, money, like all other commodities, was an incarnation of exploited human labor, and the text of money was merely the most visible layer of commodity fetishism.

The circulation of a multiplicity of coins in many alphabets in Jerusalem appeared to confirm Marx's assertion that whatever appeared on the face of gold coins was merely a disguise. But European gold coins did not take off their "uniforms" in Jerusalem, and their circulation was the most visible expression of the growing influence of European colonial powers. Ottoman attempts to ban foreign coins from circulation within the empire failed miserably.[31] The local population viewed the heterogeneous monetary system as significant and meaningful. It was symptomatic of the overlapping and competing sovereignties in Jerusalem, of which they were all too aware. "Jerusalem's internationalism is very well expressed in the internationalism of its coins," wrote an influential Jerusalemite in 1914.[32] European hegemony over Ottoman monetary and financial infrastructure came hand in hand with the extraterritorial rights enjoyed by European diplomatic missions and citizens in Jerusalem. European investments, trade, and finance transformed the political economy of Palestine, integrating it into the sphere of European domination. Even the Ottoman Imperial Bank was in fact owned by French and British interests.[33]

HEBREW COINS

Hebrew had no official status in late-Ottoman Jerusalem, but it played an important role in the economic life of the Jewish population. The Ashkenazi communities operated a textual economy of paper, dominating all spheres of life: from rabbinic notices posted in the streets, through an abundance of paper merchandise produced in the print shops and exported to Europe, to credit bills that sustained the communities financially. Hebrew was the written language of account books, receipts, and contracts, and there were unofficial forms of Jewish token money carrying Hebrew letters.

The Ashkenazi communities developed an elaborate system of credit bills in Hebrew based on anticipated Diaspora donations. The credit bills were vital to the life of the community, despite the fact that this was an unreliable system which often resulted in bankruptcy when anticipated donations failed to arrive in time.[34] Ashkenazi economic connections with the European Diaspora led to the development of an industry of writing and publishing in Hebrew in Jerusalem. Calendars, greeting cards, and other textual merchandise were the main Ashkenazi products. These, together with appeals for charity, were sent to Diaspora congregations and potential benefactors each year, mostly before the Jewish High Holidays. Hebrew newspapers published in Jerusalem had overseas subscribers, and Hebrew newspapers in Eastern Europe employed correspondents in Jerusalem. On the eve of World War I there were at least six Jewish print shops in the city and five Hebrew newspapers. It is no accident that the first documented strike in Jerusalem was of Jewish print laborers, bringing together Ashkenazi and Sephardic laborers with Zionist socialist agitators.[35]

Because Ottoman small change was in chronic scarcity, and in order to provide alms for charity, the welfare institutions of Jewish communities improvised "Jewish money": Ashkenazi paper tokens for soup kitchens and charcoal, and Sephardic nickel coins. Both were clearly marked in Hebrew lettering.[36] The Palestinian writer Ishak Musa al-Husayni recalled that when he once found such a "Jewish coin," he went to the Street of the Jews and bought with it "Jewish sweets."[37] Clearly, Hebrew coins were seen as an internal Jewish instrument of payment, associated closely with Jewish spaces, folklore, and products. But the fact that Husayni found the coin outside the Street of the Jews illustrates that these tokens were circulating throughout the city, as proved also by notices of the municipality prohibiting their use in the city markets.[38] By the turn of the century Jews lived and traded in many parts of the walled city and beyond. The appearance of shop signs and advertisements in Hebrew in the new urban center of Jerusalem, Jaffa Gate, also shows that Hebrew and Jewish economic life were no longer contained within the Jewish areas of the town.

The ban on Hebrew token coins did not reflect a general policy against the Hebrew language. The Ottoman post office branch on the Street of the Jews displayed a large trilingual sign where the Hebrew name of the institution was shown below the Ottoman Turkish and above the French. The post office branch was managed by the enterprising Hasidic activist and entrepreneur Eliyahu Honig, also known as Elias Effendi, whose aim was to increase the use of the Ottoman post among Jews. In 1896 Honig obtained approval from the post office director to introduce a trilingual cancellation mark, marking the name of Jerusalem in Ottoman Turkish and in French, as well as in Hebrew as "Yerushalem." The Hebrew label was received enthusiastically among Jewish customers: it provided considerable added value to items they were sending to their Diaspora networks. But this semiofficial use of Hebrew raised suspicions. Honig was accused of being a propagandist for Zionism, and orders came from Istanbul to destroy the cancellation mark. However, Honig insisted that there was nothing political about his initiative, and it was merely a marketing instrument to attract business from the more popular Austrian postal services. His clients, after all, were primarily Orthodox Jews, not Zionists. This argument won the support of the post office manager and the Ottoman governor of Jerusalem, and the Hebrew cancellation mark remained in use until 1906.[39] But it was becoming difficult to disassociate Hebrew from Zionism. In the Zionist colonies, Hebrew stamps were issued by the Jewish National Fund for internal communication and as instruments of fundraising. For Arab nationalists, this reflected the subversive nature of the Zionist movement as a "state within a state." [40] During the war the Ottomans banned "Zionist flags, stamps, and money," and anyone caught with them could be shot dead.[41] But there was no ban on the use of Hebrew in public space. Indeed, during the war the Ottoman authorities published public notices in Hebrew and even a military biweekly newspaper in that language.[42]

THE EXPERIENCE OF MONEY

Money has often been depicted as an anonymous and faceless object which nullifies social differences. "Money, with its colourlessness and its indifferent quality . . . becomes the frightful leveler—it hollows out the core of things, their peculiarities, their specific values and their uniqueness," wrote sociologist Georg Simmel in 1903.[43] But the actual practices of money are in fact far from homogenized.[44] In Jerusalem the experience of money varied considerably according to gender, ethnicity, and class.

Urban women were generally excluded from dealing with money as means of payment or exchange. Before the First World War, very few urban women worked outside their homes. In Muslim, Christian, and Jewish Sephardic households shopping was reserved for men, and women did not visit the markets. Ashkenazi women, in contrast, shopped in the markets, where

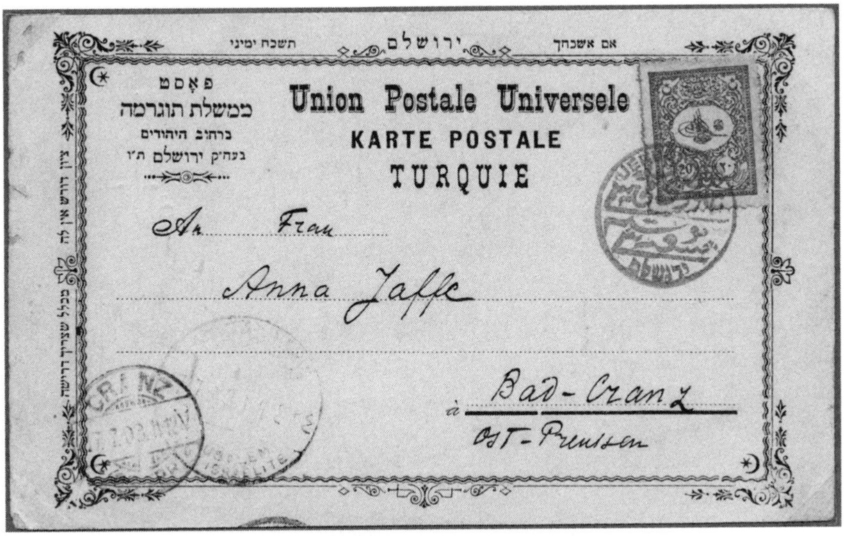

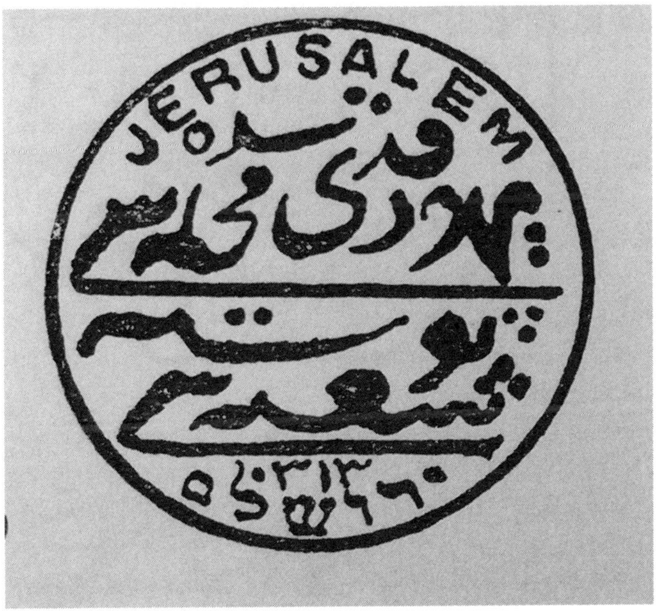

FIGURE 21. Use of Hebrew alongside Turkish and French in the Ottoman post office in Jerusalem, introduced by Hasidic post office manager Eliyahu (Elias) Honig: (top) postcard issued by the post office branch in the Street of the Jews; (bottom) cancellation stamp in Turkish, French, and Hebrew.

Sources: (top) Alexander Collection, Eretz Israel Museum; (bottom) Holy Land Philatelist, 1954.

their uncovered faces evoked fascination. They sometimes even ran shops.[45] Yet Ashkenazi women's control over family income and spending was limited. For an Ashkenazi woman of a well-to-do family, to have savings of one gold coin at her discretion was a rare experience, to be cherished.[46]

It was far more common for urban women of all communities to come in contact with gold coins as jewelry. Headdresses and necklaces of perforated gold coins were popular wedding gifts for all creeds.[47] Silver-coin necklaces were popular among peasant women from Jerusalem's hinterland, who would come to sell fruit and vegetables in the Jerusalem market. Peasant women, who were less socially restricted than urban women, had active experience of money, and they used their necklaces as savings accounts:

> When the villager earns some money through her labor, she quickly exchanges it . . . for perforated coins that are legal tender, threading them on a string one by one . . . until they become a complete necklace, which she then wears on her head as an item of jewelry. In times of hardship, she takes her property off her head one coin after the other and uses it for her subsistence.[48]

The appeal of coin necklaces had little to do with the aesthetics of the inscriptions on the coins. It was the allure of gold and silver, and, more important, their value as coins that made them into desirable items of jewelry.

Contact with gold as means of payment or exchange was generally reserved for men. The frequency of actual use of gold money depended on class and profession; most men used gold coins only on special occasions. Rents were paid annually, and households bought food supplies for many months. For traders and businessmen, however, dealing with gold was almost an everyday necessity, especially since the use of paper money remained limited in Palestine until 1914. Making payments in large sums required the physical transfer and storage of large amounts of gold, and this was cumbersome and risky. Trade between cities was especially unsafe because of highway robberies. The entrepreneur Yosef Chelouche recalls in his memoirs the anxiety involved in a night journey from Jaffa to Gaza on a carriage loaded with gold coins, to pay for barley that was destined for export to Europe. On the other hand, the physicality of money also proved a burden for thieves, who had to escape the police while carrying sacks of heavy coins, and relied on a handful of banks and moneychangers to exchange highly conspicuous banknotes.[49] Money, in late-Ottoman Jerusalem, was not a fungible commodity that could easily disappear without a trace.

In large transactions, the materiality of money imposed itself on its users in sheer volume and weight: one finds repeated mentions of heavy boxes and sacks of gold, illustrating the difficulties involved in the physical circulation of precious metals. Money was cumbersome and awkward, so much so that some members of the elite preferred their servants to carry it for them on trips in the countryside.[50] In Europe and North America such difficulties were overcome with the substitution for gold coins by gold-backed paper money; in the Ottoman Empire up until the war, and especially in the Levant, banknotes were rare, and gold continued to appear in full body.[51]

MONEY, TEXT, AND URBAN SPACE

While money very rarely appeared in the form of banknotes, the monetary economy depended on new textual practices involving paper documents. One such form was the new land-registration certificate. The Ottoman Land Code of 1858 created a new state land registry which recorded transactions and ownership. Land sales had customarily been recorded in the Islamic court, but ownership was not always registered in writing. The 1858 land code did not have much effect on the legal structure of land ownership, but the requirement to register land and receive state-approved deeds of standard form and appearance created much upheaval. The reform gave the local aristocracy an opportunity to expand their land holdings dramatically and also benefited urban merchants of all creeds, turning many of them into land dealers and property developers.[52] The code facilitated the transformation of land into an alienable asset which could more easily be sold and purchased, establishing the conditions for an accelerated expansion of private ownership. Claims to land, once anchored in a common cultural memory and historical rights, were now reduced to a secular document of standard form. The development of a centralized and uniform system of land registry homogenized space, in Jerusalem as in other parts of the world, turning tracts of land into "interchangeable units of space, distinct from one another only in terms of size and relative location."[53] The commodification of land relied critically on its abstraction into a textual artifact, a matter of writing, of words and numbers. Among Jewish communities, new housing units and small house plots were now called *nomer* (number in Yiddish), a term that was also used for bond certificates. The conflation of financial instruments, land, and property under one term manifested the textualization of the economy.[54]

No less important was the introduction of modern systems of finance and communication, operating through a range of artifacts such as personal checks, paper-money transfers, postal stamps, and telegrams. These paper artifacts provided the basis on which trade, purchases, and investments were made. Payments in metal coins were therefore only one aspect of an economic system that increasingly depended on textual encoding. The new institutions of banking and postal services were mostly located in Jerusalem's new commercial center of Jaffa Gate. In addition to the Ottoman post office, five postal services were represented in Jaffa Gate and its vicinity—Austrian, French, German, Italian, and Russian—reflecting the European eagerness to establish a presence in the Holy Land. Foreign post offices were used by the local population and were vital to the economic growth of Jerusalem. The regular, reliable, and quick delivery of letters, parcels, and money transfers facilitated business and trade.[55]

Even more revolutionary were telegraph services, which bound Jerusalem into a global network of instant communication. The Ottoman Empire had one of the largest telegraph networks in the world at the time, extending over more than seventeen thousand miles.[56] Imperial authorities saw it as a tool to advance reforms and to consolidate the sultan's rule over the provinces, but the telegraph was widely used by the general population. The telegraph facility, located in the central Ottoman post office on Jaffa Road, was a considerable attraction to contemporary Jerusalemites. It provided news, information, and also an exciting experience of sound and colors. "While we waited to collect the post, we would entertain ourselves with the clicking sounds of the Morse machine, and the sight of long, colorful ribbons rushing out of the telegraph machine," wrote a Jerusalemite contemporary.[57] Telegrams were the main source of regional and world news for the local press. The telegraph allowed a mother in Jerusalem to receive news of the exam results of her student son in Beirut;[58] Jerusalemite Ashkenazim to book their lunch in a Hebron hotel on the annual pilgrimage to the Tombs of the Patriarchs;[59] the English bishop to check on his bank-account balance in London; and a Russian pilgrim to send business instructions to a small town in Russia.[60] The telegraph inspired local intellectuals such as Khalil Sakakini, who, as discussed above, saw its potential not only to transform communication but also to revolutionize language.

Major banks were also located in Jaffa Gate, close to the post offices. "Our city is the biggest exchange center in our land," boasted an influential local politician in 1914. "[Jerusalem] is richer with small and large banks, with private financiers and bankers, than large cities such as Beirut, Damascus, and Aleppo."[61] This may have been an exaggeration, but there were four major banks in Palestine at this point: Credit Lyonnais, the Deutsche Palästina-Bank, the British-French-owned Banque Impériale Ottomane, and the Zionist Anglo-Palestine Company. These banks ran their accounts in French gold francs, but most of their daily business involved documents such as checks, credit bills, and banknotes. These were hubs of writing and paper, and children sometimes rummaged in the trash outside banks to find broken fountain pens.[62] A fine handwriting and command of the French language were basic requirements for bank clerks, and only graduates of European schools such as the Collège de Frères could hope to get jobs in these prestigious institutions. One bank clerk in turn-of-the-century Jerusalem is described preparing for signing a check as if it were a holy task, solemnly practicing his signature in the air several times before committing it to paper.[63] These banking practices anticipated the twentieth-century transition to bank money which is held primarily in textual form, in account books, and later in digitized systems.

The textual saturation of Jaffa Gate stood in contrast to the paucity of commercial signs in the historical markets within the walls, where (judging by photographs and written accounts) signs announcing the vendor's name or his trade were rare. There the main form of advertisement remained the cries of the merchants and peddlers, announcing their merchandise in various languages. "God is a healer, carob!" cried the carob-syrup seller in the market near Bab al-ʿAmud (Damascus Gate).[64] "Here and there some Koranic text or religious motto, in curiously interlaced ornamental Arabic characters, and placed inside a frame under glass, advertises the piety of the shop owner," reported a traveler in 1910.[65] These glass-framed invocations continued the tradition of pietistic Islamic inscriptions. Whether intended for purposes of self-promotion, good luck, or divine protection, this form of Arabic text invested the market stalls with a religious aura.

FIGURE 22. Commercial signs in Jaffa Road in German, French, Greek, Hebrew, and Arabic [1911-1914].
Source: Library of Congress, Matson Collection, American Colony photographers.

The new signage, on the other hand, solicited the attention of passersby and proclaimed the name of the business. The sign attracted shoppers with its allure, just as trademarks, which started to appear in advertisements and on packaging, promised authenticity and quality. Advertisements in the local press encouraged consumers to look for labels as guarantees of originality, in what was in effect education of the consumer. "Beware of fake [products]," warned the Koronil brothers of shop no. 41 in the New Market, "the only authorized sellers for Gregory Beer in Jerusalem." "Our dear customers are advised to examine the ribbon of the [beer] bottle and the sticker."[66] And yet how reliable was a sticker or a sign, which could easily be replaced?

Some commercial signs were painted directly on facades. Most were painted on boards that hung above the shop fronts, like the Khalidiyya library sign. These signs could easily be removed, amended, or replaced altogether, and such occurrences were not uncommon. Changes can be traced through the many photographs of the city center. No two photographs are alike, with commercial signs appearing and disappearing. The material medium of relatively inexpensive wooden boards, external to the structure, simple to put down or up, no doubt contributed to this state of flux. Yet more significantly, it was the signs' role as signifiers which invited these changes. Most signs proclaimed names of proprietors and the type of business, such as Eilender (hardware shop), Cohen (tailor), Krikorian (photographer), Faraji (solicitor), Gaitanopolous (pharmacist).[67] When businesses moved, closed, opened, or changed ownership, this was reflected in signs. Changing the sign also gave owners the opportunity to reinvent themselves or their business, to shake off a negative reputation or to solicit new clientele with a new name.

The rapid development of Jaffa Gate illustrates that the "chaotic" monetary situation did not impede the accelerated transition toward capitalism. In this site, Jerusalemites of all creeds experienced in their everyday life the effects of European economic influence and Ottoman political and administrative reforms. It was a site rich with signs, texts, and modern institutions of writing; a site marked by flow, movement, and trade, open to foreigners and locals, members of all faiths, but dominated by new Ottoman civic government, the local bourgeoisie, and the presence and influence of European money and power.

THE DEMATERIALIZATION OF MONEY

The embeddedness of money in increasingly complicated systems of finance and communication was observed by sociologist Georg Simmel. In his *Philosophy of Money*, published in 1905, Simmel argued that the development of society inevitably required the abstraction and dematerialization of money.[68] In the modern age, characterized by intellectual complexity and abstract thought, money was losing its material substance and becoming a mere symbol. Dematerialization was epitomized in the transition from coins of precious metal to paper money, that is, to an artifact of pure writing with no intrinsic value.

The use of paper money developed in the nineteenth century in North America and Europe. Bills were initially issued by private banks, and later by central banks, giving them the status of legal tender. Banknotes were a convenient instrument which gradually replaced the use of gold for large transactions, and later for smaller ones. Banknotes were understood as a representation of gold, and could be redeemed in real gold upon request. Hence the pledge, which anachronistically still appears on British pound sterling banknotes in the name of the governor of the Bank of England, "to pay the bearer on demand the sum of. . . ." The value of paper money was widely understood to be dependent on the deposits of gold in the vaults of the central bank. Banknotes acted, in Marx's terms, as "shadows" of gold.[69] But Georg Simmel believed that it was wrong to think of paper money as a signifier of "real money." True, paper money was a pledge for convertibility into gold; but gold's value was similarly symbolic rather than intrinsic. The value of gold derived from social and political conventions, and was upheld by state authorities. In other words, both paper money and gold coins were no more and no less than symbols.[70]

The transformation of money into text was an ambiguous and confusing process for monetary theorists, who could not agree on its meaning. It would appear to be no accident that the textualization of money coincided with a profound transformation of language theory. The Swiss linguist Ferdinand de Saussure, in his formative *Course in General Linguistics* (1915), compared language to money as parallel systems of representation, in which there was a pronounced gap between signifier and signified. Words, like coins, were elements in a system of exchange, which assigned value to things outside it—ideas or commodities. Both systems were based on a degree of arbitrariness. Saussure did not believe that the value of money stemmed from its precious metal. "It is not the metal in a piece of money that fixes its value," he explained, as "a coin nominally worth five francs may contain less than half its worth of silver."[71] The value of the coin is determined by the amount stamped upon it, as well as by its backing by the state. This was even truer in the case of linguistic signifiers, whose bond to the signified was arbitrary. The signifier was a phoneme, an arrangement of sounds with no intrinsic connection to the idea which they represented. The unbridgeable chasm between signifier and signified appeared to be the condition on which human civilization was built. Such ideas stood in contrast to Muslim and Jewish traditions according to which the world was created through the holy tongues of Arabic and Hebrew, respectively. But for Saussure, arbitrariness and profanity were exactly the features that allowed language to become the most sophisticated and universal of all human systems of expression.

In a similar manner, the dematerialization of money, and its transformation into symbolic and textual artifacts, was acquiring a moral meaning as a sign of human progress. This stood in contrast to widespread suspicion toward paper money in the nineteenth century, which persisted well into the twentieth century. In Goethe's *Faust* (*Part Two*) (1832), unsecured paper money is the invention of the devil, who lures the royal court to pay for its profligate spending by issuing notes backed not by gold deposits but by promises of future gold finds. The skeptical emperor soon sacrifices all prudence and succumbs to ever greater extravagance, paid for by dubious banknotes. As a product of fantasy, paper money naturally leads its users to debauchery. In the words of Mephistopheles:

> Paper like this in place of pearls and gold
> Is handy. You know what your hands hold.
> No need to haggle or swap coin before
> You lose your mind in loving or liquor.[72]

But with the advance of capitalism such attachment to the secured solidity of gold was becoming a sign of backwardness. Western observers in Palestine routinely condemned locals for what they saw as a primitive attachment to gold. The peasantry "greedily grasp the coin . . . and then hide it in the ground often dying without revelation of their secret," reported the British consul Finn in Jerusalem in 1857. Peasants had "accumulated an unprecedented degree of wealth, but they bury the coin in holes, they purchase arms, and they decorate their women."[73] Commentators despaired of money-hoarding practices, such as wearing gold-coin necklaces, when the gold could have been used "productively" as capital to invest in land, machinery, or skills. Racist statements about Arab desire to collect metal coins echoed antisemitic references to Jewish adoration of precious metals. We find descriptions of "Arabs" scrambling for coins thrown on the floor, or devouring gold with their "hawk-like eyes."[74] A Zionist journalist lambasted "the savagery of the Arab peasant, who buries his gold and silver in clay pots in the ground and does not trust the British government and its paper notes."[75] Buried in the ground or carried on the head, gold sat idle and brought no profit to its owners.

It was not new for money to have negative connotations. As "filthy lucre," it has long been associated with sinful gains, greed, usury, and avarice. But here was something different. The problem with hoarding gold was not that it was driven by greed, but that it was greed of the wrong kind: the greed of the miser, who holds tight to his gold, compared to the praiseworthy greed of the capitalist, who constantly throws money into circulation in order to expand its value. What distinguished capital from money was its ever-readiness to metamorphose into goods and services, only to be converted back into money: a never-ending cycle whose sole purpose was to accumulate profit. As Marx astutely discerned, it was this perpetual cycle of money → commodity → money, of which money is the starting and end point, which distinguished capitalism from earlier systems of exchange. The insatiable desire to accumulate pure surplus value through constant metamorphosis was what made capitalism into an unstoppable force, turning, in Marx and Engels's dictum, "all that is solid into air."

Marx's commodity fetishism was not the base adoration of gold but rather the worship of the totalizing quality of the commodity form, of which money was the utmost manifestation. Money could mutate into all possible concrete commodities, and had the power to convert everything into its opposite. Marx observed this process with hostile fascination, but for liberals, capitalism's striving toward abstraction had a redeeming quality. As money shed its material skin, it was cleansed of its filthy origins and achieved transcendence and purification. This is why for Simmel, the pleasure of accumulating money was "one of the most abstract enjoyments . . . most remote from sensual immediacy since it is exclusively experienced through a process of thought and fantasy."[76] The textualization of money was a form of ascendance which was built on a disavowal of material sensuality. Simmel viewed money as the quintessential Platonic ideal, as an abstract conceptual system that reflects the world in truest form. Money unified the world's fragmentary and dissimilar material phenomena by assigning them comparable values within a single and universal field. No other system of concepts was as comprehensive and totalizing. The dematerialization of money enabled it to enhance and develop its abstracting role and to penetrate all realms of life.

When the economist John Maynard Keynes proposed, in his 1923 polemic *Tract on Monetary Reform*, to delink money from gold, he famously called gold a "barbarous relic."[77] Keynes's savages were not the Arab peasants of Palestine, hoarding coins in jars, but British bankers and policymakers who were insisting on the gold standard, the system in which the value of the sterling was backed by a fixed measure of gold. These "worshippers of the Calf" were unwilling to let go of a primitive attachment to the precious metal. Keynes's rhetoric not only identified gold-money as a thing of the past, in a narrative of human developmental progress; it also consigned it to the vulgarity of savage practice, a fetishism born out of a crude desire for glittering metal. The rational economic arguments put forward by Keynes about the faults of the gold standard, compelling as they were, were reinforced with a modernist gesture of abjection and disgust at the materiality of money. The stage was set for the transformation of money into pure text, and for the state to assume a far more assertive role in the monetary system. Gold coins were about to disappear from the shops and streets of Jerusalem, and to be replaced with paper banknotes. This development was not the result of financial and monetary reform but rather the dramatic outcome of war and colonial occupation.

4 PAPER

Banknotes and the Colonial Dictionary

IN AUGUST 1914, SHORTLY AFTER THE OUTBREAK OF WAR IN EUROPE, the Jerusalem newspaper *Ha-Herut* notified its readers of the imminent introduction of banknotes of the value of a single "Turkish pound."[1] The authorities announced that the new banknotes would replace all Ottoman coins, from small change to gold coins.[2] The martial imposition of paper currency aimed to strengthen Ottoman sovereignty by moving away from a plural currency regime. The banknotes were headed with a *tughra* and featured no vignettes of places or people, only text in Ottoman Turkish along with the name of the currency in French and geometric ornamentation.

The wartime transition to paper money had global dimensions. During the war and in its aftermath, the gold standard—the fixed link between money and gold—was suspended, and banknotes were no longer convertible to gold. The value of paper money was now wholly dependent on the state and relied crucially on popular trust. But such trust was in short supply in Jerusalem. Official notices were posted guaranteeing that banknotes were as good as gold, pledging that the new paper money was backed by sufficient gold deposits held in German banks. Yet the public received these assurances with widespread skepticism.[3] Suspicions were confirmed when Ottoman officials themselves refused the notes and insisted on payment in precious metal or in wheat for taxes and military exemption.[4] Corrupt Ottoman officers used the banknotes as a means to extract gold from the population, by paying with paper bills and demanding change in foreign gold.[5] Less than two years after their abrupt wartime introduction, the banknotes had lost a third of their value. Paper money was the target of growing popular ridicule. In February 1916 the court in Jerusalem heard the case against an Arab Christian pharmacist from Haifa who was charged with contempt of state money. Nassar, the brother of the Arab-nationalist publisher of the paper *Al-Karmil*, had sent a payment of three Ottoman pounds in banknotes to the Solomon and Levin medical-supplies shop. Well acquainted with Ashkenazim, Nassar attached to the banknotes a whimsical note: "I am sending you three pieces of *asher yatsar* [toilet paper in Yiddish] to settle my account." When rumors of this Arab-Yiddish joke became known to the local Ottoman commandant, Nassar was promptly arrested and sent to Jerusalem to stand trial.[6]

When merchants stopped accepting the notes altogether, the authorities turned to intimidation, blaming the depreciation on urban speculators and "senseless Bedouins."[7] Anyone refusing the notes risked imprisonment and exile. But state coercion was insufficient to uphold the value of paper money, which dropped to as little as a quarter of its initial value by 1917.[8] The urban population of Palestine viewed Ottoman paper money as one of the instruments of oppression brought by the war, along with conscription, the destruction of Palestine's forests, the execution of local leadership, and the deportation of activists and even entire cities and villages.[9]

The war had a dramatic effect on Jerusalem's commercial center. With the Ottoman entry into the war, European extraterritorial rights were terminated. Banks and postal services that belonged to the Allied countries were closed down. These steps coincided with Ottoman policies that sought to control and regulate text in the public sphere in an unprecedented manner. For the first time in Jerusalem, the posting of notices was banned, except on authorized notice boards. Shoe-shiners and carriages were ordered to display their license numbers. Taxes were imposed on commercial signs—which led to their disappearance from the streets: "People began taking down the signs, and by midday the streets, buildings and fences were completely bare of all signs," observed Khalil Sakakini in his diary.[10] Subsequently the Ottoman police issued a detailed order requiring all new signs to be painted in the national colors of the Ottoman flag, red and white. The name had to appear first in the "official languages"—Ottoman Turkish or Arabic—and only then in other languages such as Hebrew or German. "Enemy languages" such as English, French, and Italian were banned and could not appear on signs in Jerusalem.[11] The economy of signage was, after all, a political economy. Before the war, the proud signs in European languages on banks and post offices, much like European gold coins, manifested not only European commercial power but also imperial encroachment. The brutal wartime experience was an Ottoman attempt to assert control over money, population, and space. The battle over textual control lasted until the end of Ottoman rule. On the night of 8 December 1917, as British forces were advancing on the city, the last Ottoman governor of Jerusalem, Izzat Bey, went to the post office and personally smashed the telegraph machine with a hammer, shortly before leaving the city with his troops.[12]

Upon British occupation of the city, the situation dramatically reversed. Now it was German that became an enemy language. Shop owners were quick to realize that signs in German were putting them at risk. Re'uven Zilberstein owned a shop on Jaffa Road, with a large sign in Hebrew and in German. After the occupation, Zilberstein noticed that British soldiers passing by were looking at the sign and shouting "Fucking Germans!"; his German friend who owned the shop on the other side of the street had already been arrested and deported to Egypt. Zilberstein understood that he needed to make a new sign. The sign maker worked all night, and by the next day, to save the owners any problems, "Gebrüder R. und V. Zilberstein" became "R. and V. Silverstein Bros." "This is how I adjusted myself to the new rulers. English soldiers soon started visiting the shop."[13] The malleable and removable format of signage not only enabled but also called for such transformations.

Given such political and textual uncertainty, it is no surprise that when British forces introduced Egyptian and British banknotes as legal tender, the new paper money was initially met with suspicion. Coins were preferred and notes were exchanged at 20 percent below their nominal value.[14] The Jerusalem municipal council, concerned about currency speculators, requested the British to take strong measures to enforce the value of the banknotes. But the authorities replied that there was no need for such measures, as the resumption of commerce would soon have its effects.[15] Indeed, within two years the banknotes gained public trust and were traded at face value—despite

FIGURE 23. Removal of French postal boxes in Jerusalem after the Ottoman Empire joined the war, signaling the end of the capitulations, 1914.
Source: Library of Congress, Matson Collection, American Colony photographers.

the fact that they, like Ottoman war money, were paper bills which could not be redeemed in gold. In 1921 the Egyptian pound was declared the sole legal tender, except for British gold sovereign coins. Other European coins were no longer permitted for trade and banking. Palestine's age of plural metal currencies came to an end.[16] The circulation of European monarchs' portraits alongside the Ottoman *tughra*, which expressed the competing sovereignties in Palestine, was now a thing of the past. The struggle between European imperial powers over Jerusalem was won decidedly by the British. The arrival of a stable paper-currency regime was also the moment of transition from Ottoman rule to direct colonial domination.

Unlike in Europe and North America, where the transition from gold to paper bills was gradual, and banknotes were already in widespread use in the second part of the nineteenth century, in Palestine their arrival was dramatic. The transition from gold to paper corresponded to an assertive redefinition of the state. The brutal remaking of the Ottoman Empire was followed by European colonial rule, introducing a new kind of political framework, technologies of governance, and discourse of legitimacy—all articulated succinctly through new colonial currency notes. British interest in the currency regime went far beyond monetary considerations. High-ranking British officials started planning the new Palestine currency as early as 1919, well before the formal approval of the Palestine Mandate. The new money was not designed to serve economic exigencies but rather as an instrument to promote British and Zionist political agendas. It was, first and foremost, a vehicle of colonial propaganda, intended to communicate Palestine's new status as a separate territory, designated for Jewish settlement as a "Jewish National Home" in accordance with the 1917 Balfour Declaration. This message was communicated in the writing on the new Palestine pound, in Arabic, English, and most important, in Hebrew. When the currency was finally introduced, in 1927, Arabs and Jews read it as a political statement to which they responded in strikingly different ways.

The use of money as a colonial tool relied on a bold new theoretical approach to monetary economy. The new approach, which emerged in the early twentieth century, saw money not as a commodity but as a symbolic instrument of power, whose origin was the state. It rejected the supposed essential link between money and gold. In practical terms, it opened the way to the transformation of money into pure text, allowing the state unprecedented freedom in creating and managing currencies.

John Maynard Keynes played a key role in this monetary revolution, as a grand theorist and as a policymaker. He used British colonial experience to develop his monetary thinking, which he then promoted in public advocacy. Keynes took an active role in shaping British, imperial, and global monetary systems, including in Palestine. He was the only non-Jewish member of a Zionist advisory committee on financial and monetary matters in Palestine, whose report was presented at the 1919 Paris Peace Conference.[17] Keynes's rewriting of monetary theory called upon the state to assume a much bigger role in the management of the economy. In Palestine such intervention had profound political implications for the future of the country.

KEYNES AND THE STATE THEORY OF MONEY

Keynes began his investigations into money and macro-economics during his time as an official in the colonial India Office in London. His first book, *Indian Currency and Finance* (1913), highlighted the fact that the Indian rupee was not shackled to the gold standard and thus enjoyed elasticity in terms of money supply, which was of considerable economic advantage. This elasticity allowed the treasury to respond to market demand and expand the volume of money in circulation, thus preventing money hoarding and currency crises. After World War I, Keynes argued strongly against the dominant calls for the reestablishment of the gold standard. In his polemic *Tract on Monetary Reform* (1923), Keynes advocated for a radical and permanent break with gold. He called for allowing the British Treasury to issue sterling currency notes without restrictions on their volume, in "a more scientific standard" consistent with the spirit and the requirements of the age.[18] In his suggestion to sever the umbilical cord between gold and money, Keynes was advancing a vision of a global monetary system of symbolic currencies, unbacked by precious metals, a system he later helped to create in the 1944 Breton Woods Agreement.

This was a radical and innovatory approach, as according to economic orthodoxy the value of money was necessarily anchored in a real commodity. While it was generally accepted that token money could replace gold in national markets, international trade relied on the solidity of gold as a precious commodity. How could paper notes, of no intrinsic value and with no gold backing, function as money? Keynes now turned to investigating the ancient history of money. In the 1920s, in what he termed his "Babylonian madness," he spent six years studying metrology and numismatics in search of the origins of money in the ancient Near East. Based on these investigations and influenced by the German economist Georg Friedrich Knapp's state theory of money, Keynes came to the conclusion that money did not originate from barter and commodity exchange as classical economists believed.[19] Rather, it developed as a state technology—a legally binding standard for fulfillment of social obligations. Money was an instrument to measure and meet liabilities such as taxes, contracts, credit, and debt. The social nature of these obligations required a framework of laws and customs for negotiations and enforcement. Thus, money could be meaningful only within the social structures of a political community. The role of the state was crucial, not only as the minter of money but also as its very creator.[20] Comparing money to language, Keynes argued that the state was the author of the "dictionary" of money and not merely its enforcer.[21]

It is this view of money as a social technology in the service of political power that prompted Keynes to break with the view of money as a "veil" or a neutral medium. According to the dominant monetary thinking of his day, money expressed and masked—but did not fundamentally affect—the real economic factors of supply and demand. Yet through his research into monetary theory, Keynes reversed the classical perception of money as a symbolic reflection of real economic forces. The "symbol economy," in fact, shaped the real economy. Currency management was not a technical operation but rather a primary tool through which the state could influence market forces. The active management of the volume of money in circulation, currency exchange rates, and interest rates, as well as fiscal deficit and surplus—all these had a profound effect on employment and prices.

Keynes's argument was not technical or mathematical but rather social constructivist. A key observation was that economic dynamics depended crucially on public sentiments about the future, whether optimistic or pessimistic.[22] But knowledge of the future was by definition fluctuating and uncertain. Any economic decision was a step into the unknown. "Human decisions affecting the future, whether personal or political or economic, cannot depend on strict mathematical expectation, since the basis of such calculations does not exist."[23] Keynes was now writing in the wake of the 1929 stock market crash and the Great Depression, and his readers were well aware of the potentially devastating effects of "whim and sentiment," "nerve and hysteria." While many believed that the link between money and gold provided a guarantee for monetary certainty, Keynes's earlier work refuted such ideas, as the security of the precious metal was merely an illusion. Radical uncertainty was not a product of war or a severe crisis but rather an existential condition of modern life, a condition which had to be accepted and could not be overcome.

Keynes's emphasis on the role of perceptions and expectations stood in contrast not only to the neoclassical model but also to the Marxian model, which drew a sharp distinction between the mystifying appearances of the capitalist economy and its objective social realities, a distinction manifest in the schism between money's metallic substance and its deceptive form ("uniforms" which could be worn and taken off). But if one followed Keynes, it was impossible to tell where appearances ended and economic realities began. In the face of radical uncertainty, self-fulfilling public trust was rooted in social and political legitimacy, and that legitimacy could not be seen as contrived. It had to appear as natural and immutable. The ideological naturalization of state legitimacy and its money had to go hand in hand.

Keynes's innovative monetary ideas had a direct impact on Palestine through his advisory role. The introduction of the paper currency of the Palestine pound was geared exactly toward shaping public expectations for the future. The motivation, however, was not to stabilize economic conditions but to determine the political shape of the country.

A PALESTINE CURRENCY

The man behind the establishment of the Palestine pound was Herbert Samuel, a leading British Liberal politician.[24] A British Jew and a dedicated Zionist, Samuel's efforts prepared the ground for the Balfour Declaration, and for this reason he was nominated as High Commissioner of Palestine by Prime Minister David Lloyd George. In June 1919 Samuel assembled a small advisory group on financial policy in Palestine. He invited J. M. Keynes to advise on the question of "banking facilities . . . for the new Palestine." Keynes was the only non-Jewish member.[25] The Advisory Committee to the Palestine Office, Zionist Organisation, met six times between November 1919 and January 1920 at Samuel's house in Bayswater, London. Their main concern was how to transform the Jewish Colonial Trust and the Anglo-Palestine Company into Palestine's de facto central bank, with the aim of providing the best conditions for Zionist colonization. But the group also devoted considerable time to formulating a proposal for a Palestine currency as one of the first priorities for British rule. In the group's discussion, Keynes assertively stressed the benefits of a nonconvertible paper currency for Palestine and argued against a "metallic currency."[26] The proposed currency was modeled after an ad hoc paper currency designed by Keynes in 1918 for North Russia, as part of Allied involvement in the Russian civil war.[27] Keynes's interest in the scheme may have been motivated not only by his Zionist sympathies but also by seeking a trial ground for "managed currencies" that would not be backed by gold.

Samuel's visit to Palestine in early 1920 added a sense of urgency to this plan. The two-month reconnaissance visit, shortly before his official appointment as High Commissioner, was ostensibly intended to survey the country's economic and financial conditions. But the visit's real aim was to examine the political situation. During his stay in Jerusalem, Samuel was taken aback by the zeal of Arab nationalism and the emerging opposition to British policies. He witnessed the large Arab demonstrations in the town center before these were banned by the British military. "Arab Nationalist and Anti-Zionist feeling is a very real thing," he wrote to his son.[28] Local activists rejected the Balfour Declaration and aligned themselves with nationalists in Damascus, where a semi-independent Arab administration was set up by Emir Faysal. "Syria shall not be divided," cried the protest banners in the streets. Arab Palestinian nationalists started referring to Palestine as "Southern Syria," and a weekly Arab-nationalist newspaper was established in Jerusalem with that name. In the Syrian Congress in Damascus in March 1920, Emir Faysal was crowned by Arab delegates as the king of Syria and Palestine.[29]

Two years after the end of the war, the political future of the Middle East was not yet settled. Borders, states, and kingdoms were still being contemplated and negotiated. Many in the British military administration in Jerusalem were hostile to the idea of the Jewish National Home, and they warned London of the dangers of pursuing this policy. They refused to translate the Balfour Declaration into actual policies as long as the country's political status and its borders were not formally defined. They had even gone so far as to recommend recognizing Faysal as king of Palestine—or else, they warned, Palestine could face immediate unrest.[30]

Samuel believed that the inclusion of Palestine in a Syrian kingdom would spell the end of the Zionist project, and he moved quickly to counter these suggestions. The officers in Jerusalem, he wrote, "have regarded rather more seriously than they deserved the anti-Zionist manifestations which had taken place." It was possible to overcome Arab opposition, he argued, by communicating assertively that the future of Palestine was, in his words, a "chose jugée" and that continued agitation would be without result.[31] Not only Palestine's

Arab population but also Britain's international allies and British officers in Jerusalem and London had to be told in clear terms that the British plans were irreversible. Palestine was to be ruled by the British as a separate polity, designated for Jewish settlement as a Jewish National Home, and nothing the Arabs would do could change this. Samuel's chosen medium to communicate this message was a paper currency:

> In determining the form of the future currency of Palestine, political considerations must be a deciding factor. It is assumed in this memorandum that the settlement of the status of Palestine will constitute it as a country with characteristics of its own, developing on independent lines. A distinct currency is one of the principal marks of a distinct State. It is necessary, therefore, that Palestine should have a currency of its own.[32]

In using banknotes and instruments of colonial propaganda, Samuel was in line with British wartime efforts in the Middle East, which paid great attention to the design of stamps and a flag for the Arab Revolt against the Ottomans.[33] The message encoded in the proposed currency was not, as one scholar suggested, a vague pledge for future Palestinian independence, designed to placate local Arab public opinion.[34] Quite the opposite: the currency was meant to deal a blow to Arab aspirations. The quicker the existence of Palestine imprinted itself on public imagination, the less chance there was that the Jewish National Home policy would be reversed. The currency would create symbolic and economic barriers between British-ruled Palestine and French-ruled Syria, furthering the consolidation of Palestine as a separate entity. By issuing a local currency Samuel hoped to "write the dictionary"—not only the monetary dictionary but also the geopolitical one, articulating the colonial vision for Palestine. The notes, which would circulate throughout the entire country, would state in unambiguous manner that Palestine was a separate polity under British rule, divorced from Syria; and Britain's unshakable commitment to Zionism would be demonstrated through the appearance of Hebrew as one of the three official languages. Samuel mentioned this explicitly in his memorandum: "If the Mandate embodies the principle of the Jewish National Home, the Hebrew names of the coins should have reference to the historical Jewish coinage; other names might perhaps be adopted in Arabic." Soon after submitting his memorandum, Samuel wrote to the Zionist leader Chaim Weizmann, asking for suggestions for Hebrew names for the coins as well as emblems to be adopted on the coins and stamps. Prudently, he added that using emblems with a distinctively Jewish political significance, such as the Star of David, would be "premature."[35] No similar consultation with representatives of the Arab majority is recorded.

PALESTINE BY ANY OTHER NAME

It soon emerged that Samuel's plans for an ad hoc introduction of a currency were unrealistic, as it could not be issued before the formal approval of the British Mandate over Palestine. Colonial financial officials were far from enthusiastic about the plans for a local currency. Palestine was still recovering from the ravages of the war. The population's adoption of the Egyptian pound was a remarkable success, which contributed to economic recovery. Introducing a new local paper currency could create mistrust and undermine British achievements.[36]

As the currency had to wait, Samuel searched for other means to communicate the irreversibility of British rule over Palestine and its commitment to the Jewish National Home. He seized on postage stamps to carry this message. Provisional stamps, printed in English and Arabic, had been issued by the military authorities. In June 1920, within days of his arrival in the country, Samuel ordered a reprint of the stamps on the grounds that Hebrew, by now one of the three official languages, was missing. The stamps were overprinted by the Orthodox printing press in Jerusalem with the name of the territory in English, Arabic, and Hebrew.[37]

But what was the name of the territory? Samuel believed that there was no controversy over the English (Palestine) and the Arabic (Filastin). But the Hebrew term was "a point of great delicacy."[38] The Hebrew translation of Samuel's first proclamation used the term Erets Yisra'el (Land of Israel), the most common Hebrew name for the country. But Samuel feared that such an unambiguous term could have severe repercussions. April 1920 saw the first anti-Zionist riots in Jerusalem, and Samuel was concerned that a controversial choice of name could lead to more violence. Consulting neither the local population nor the British Foreign Office, Samuel decided on a compromise. In a handwritten note he instructed the postmaster general that the name of the country in Hebrew would be Palestina followed by the acronym Aleph

FIGURE 24. Temporary military stamps of the Egyptian Expeditionary Force (EEF), printed over with the name Palestine in English, Arabic, and Hebrew (with E.Y), on the orders of Herbert Samuel, 1920.
Source: British Library's Philatelic Collections, FCO Collection, vol. 2.

Yod for Erets Yisra'el.[39] "Palestina" was not Samuel's invention: it was a phonetic transliteration of the German and Russian term for Palestine, which had gained currency in Hebrew writing in Central and Eastern Europe in the late nineteenth century, including in Zionist writing. But it did not carry the emotional and religious resonance of Erets Yisra'el. The term Palestina (E.Y) was therefore resented by Zionists, who saw the term as a game of "hide-and-seek."[40] "Instead of writing . . . 'Eretz Israel' they just write the two Hebrew letters for E. I. Why? What is the meaning of it?" the right-wing Zionist leader Vladimir Jabotinsky asked indignantly in his 1937 testimony before the Royal Commission of Inquiry. "If the country is to be called Eretz Israel, Land of Israel, if that is the name avowed, then print it in full; if it is something which cannot be allowed, remove it."[41] Similarly, Arab nationalists were not deluded: Erets Yisra'el, even in acronyms, was a validation of Zionist claims and intentions. Jamal al-Husayni, secretary of the Palestinian Arab Action Committee, petitioned the

High Court in Jerusalem against the use of the Hebrew term on stamps. He argued that Arabs were being forced to use "a document in which their country is described as the Land of Israel." If the reference to "Erets Yisra'el" could not be removed, he demanded that at least the name Filastin be accompanied with the acronym S.J for Suriya al-Janubiyya (Southern Syria) to express the Arab wish to become part of a unified Syria. This petition was rejected by the court as beyond its purview.[42]

The official status of Hebrew received international approval in 1922. The League of Nations Mandate, endorsing the creation of a Jewish National Home in Palestine, stipulated that "English, Arabic and Hebrew shall be the official languages of Palestine. Any statement or inscription in Arabic on stamps or money in Palestine shall be repeated in Hebrew, and any statement or inscription in Hebrew shall be repeated in Arabic."[43] Along with the symbolic recognition of Hebrew, the Mandate also required Great Britain to facilitate Jewish immigration and Zionist land acquisition, and to coordinate its policies with a Jewish agency representing the Zionist movement. The Arab leadership

FIGURE 25. Trilingual mailboxes at Jerusalem's General Post Office [1920-1938]. Source: Library of Congress, Matson Collection, American Colony photographers.

objected to the adoption of Hebrew as a state language as part and parcel of the rejection of the Jewish National Home. Hebrew was now seen as a colonial language, and the Arab press continued to rail against Hebrew's official status throughout the Mandate.[44]

The trilingual format became the standard not only for coins and stamps but also for Mandatory official stationery, signs, ordinances, and public notices. Officially, Hebrew was required only in districts where Jewish inhabitants constituted at least a fifth of the population.[45] To the very end of the British Mandate, despite substantial Jewish immigration, only six out of Palestine's sixteen districts satisfied this demographic criterion.[46] Even in cities with a substantial Jewish population the adoption of Hebrew was slow. The Jerusalem municipality did not issue licenses and receipts in Hebrew even to Jewish business owners.[47] Stamps and money, however, circulated throughout the entire country, bringing Hebrew to areas where hardly any Jews lived.

The official recognition as a state language gave an enormous boost to the transformation of Hebrew into a spoken national language. As one leading Hebrew Revival activist acknowledged, the "imposition of Hebrew on all walks of life" would not have been successful without the backing of state power and institutions.[48] Hebrew newspapers reported excitedly on trilingual "Drive slowly" signs, and on official signage in three languages in police stations, post offices, and courts.[49] Local campaigners for Hebrew Revival realized the significance of state endorsement. Writing to the High Commissioner, Eliezer Ben Yehuda and David Yellin demanded equal rights for Hebrew "in the municipality and in the government offices from the highest to the lowest, in the railways and in the custom houses, in the post and telegraph, the police and the courts, in official orders and government announcements, on ticket stubs and receipts, and on coins and stamps." They called for Hebrew to be used for all official purposes even in places where no Jews lived. "If there are no Jews there today, some will come tomorrow." While keen to make Hebrew visible throughout Palestine, Ben Yehuda's and Yellin's main motivation was the fear that with the influx of Jewish migrants speaking "dozens of Diaspora languages," Hebrew speakers would be overwhelmed. The project of Hebrew Revival could collapse "unless the government comes to the help of our national tongue."[50] The demand for the "imposition" of Hebrew aimed for linguistic colonization—not only of the landscape but also of the multilingual Jewish community.

FIGURE 26. Official signs in three languages, Jerusalem, 1930s.
Source: Ze'ev Aleksandrowicz.

Much of the contestation over the trilingual format focused on the order of the languages. The stamps placed Hebrew at the bottom of the trilingual order, beneath English and Arabic, and the Hebrew Revival activists found this a "national insult"; they suggested arranging the languages horizontally, side by side. Indeed, on the coins and banknotes issued in 1927 the text was mostly arranged in this way, with Hebrew on the left, English at the center, and Arabic on the right; but the linear arrangement also acknowledged the priority of Arabic. Considering that both Arabic and Hebrew are written right to left, the alignment of the text on the right is more natural, and the positioning of Hebrew on the left was less natural and desirable.[51] These details failed to placate Arab outrage. The main point of contestation was the very recognition of Hebrew as an official language; its exact location was of lesser consequence.

THE PALESTINE POUND AND ITS TEXTS

Herbert Samuel continued to promote the Palestine currency throughout his tenure as High Commissioner, from 1920 to 1925. The process was slower than Samuel originally envisaged and included a lengthy consultation with banks and businessmen in Palestine and with the British Treasury. Officials in London continued to doubt the benefit of the currency, yet Samuel succeeded in winning approval for the Currency Act.

The currency was finally issued in 1927, two years after Samuel's departure. The Palestine pound, like currencies in British colonies in Africa on which it was modeled, was pegged to the sterling as part of the "sterling bloc"; this arrangement reinforced the colonies' economic ties with the metropolis by eliminating currency exchange costs.[52] Trilingual notices were posted in Jerusalem and other cities shortly before the introduction of the currency, emphasizing in bold letters that the new currency was backed by the Palestine government and that the "Palestine Pound will . . . always be worth the same as the British Pound Sterling."[53]

The Palestine pound was a token currency in a double sense. First, it consisted of nickel coins and paper money, whose value was manifestly symbolic; no gold coins were minted. And second, it was effectively a representation of the British pound. The Palestine pound was readily convertible to sterling, but it could not be redeemed in gold. The currency was not backed by gold but by sterling securities held in London. The Palestine pound's nature as a token

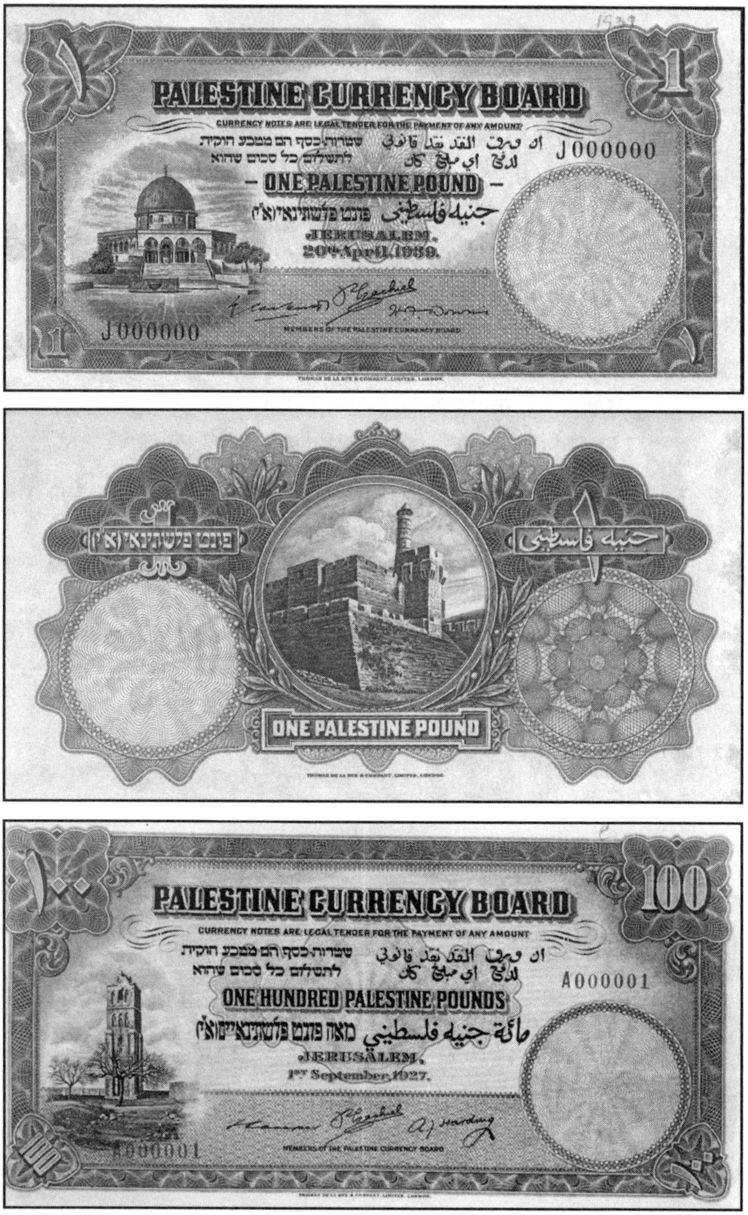

FIGURE 27. Palestine-pound banknotes featuring the Dome of the Rock in Jerusalem (top), the Jerusalem Citadel near Jaffa Gate (middle), and the "Crusader Tower" of Ramleh (bottom).

Sources: (top and bottom) British Library's Philatelic Collections, Crown Agent's Philatelic & Security Printing Archive, Palestine Paper Money Collection; (middle) Jeffrey Douglas, KKL-JNF Photo Archive.

currency found its clearest expression in the wording on the notes, proclaiming in English in small font and in Hebrew and Arabic in much larger letters: "Currency notes are legal tender for the payment of any amount." If British banknotes displayed a pledge "to pay the bearer" (in gold coins), Palestine banknotes did not make such promises. They did away with the pretense that paper money was, in some way, gold, and claimed their status as a matter of legal fact.

Text was the dominant feature of Palestine coins, similarly to Ottoman coins. Text overshadowed the iconographic decorations. But the content and meaning of the text were different. As the state's emblem, the sultan's *tughra* was replaced with the name of Palestine in three languages, imparting legal validity to these artifacts. It was a rather different claim for legitimacy. The Ottoman sultan and European monarchs based their individual claim to power on dynastic lineage, imperial power, and a religious role as protectors of Muslim or Christian faith. The polity of Palestine, on the other hand, was an abstract, modern, and secular entity: a nation-state in the making, in the post–World War I international order. While its name was written in the holy languages of Hebrew and Arabic, it carried no religious meaning. It derived its legitimacy from the territory's colonial rulers, who purported to act as mere custodians.

No less important was the explicit stipulation of the value of money. Palestine coins and banknotes displayed words and numbers indicating the name of the currency unit and its nominal value. The principal unit was called "Palestine pound" (Arabic: *junayh*, Hebrew: *punt*) and it was composed of 1,000 mils. Initial recommendations by committees of Jewish and Arab scholars for more evocative names in Arabic and Hebrew such as *mithqal*, shekel, and dinar were rejected.[54] Unlike coins that circulated in Palestine before the war, which displayed neither their official unit name nor their nominal value, the new Palestine currency declared its value in clearly legible terms, and users were required to read it in order to know how much money they had in their hands. Previously, merchants, buyers, and changers had identified coins primarily according to their shape and size. But the banknotes from £P5 to £P100 notes were identical in size, color, and design; they featured the same vignettes. The single differentiating feature defining value was their text.[55] Money had become pure text, free-floating signifier, written on a blank page. The dematerialization of money was also the dematerialization of text, which was no

FIGURE 28. Palestine 20-mil coin.
Source: Yair Wallach.

longer anchored in gold but rather was seen as external and independent of the material world and had the nominative power to define the world and set its name and value.

The dematerialization went hand in hand with an exponential expansion of the use of money. With Jewish immigration, urbanization, and transition to wage labor, money was ever more present in the daily life of Jerusalemites. Strong growth, increasing monetization of the economy, and wartime inflation during World War II led to money-supply expansion from less than P£1.9 million in 1927 to P£52.6 million in 1948.[56] Paper was replacing coins as the embodiment of money. Coins were still used for daily needs, as the smallest banknote (500 mils) was a considerable amount. But from 1928 to 1947, the share of coins of money in circulation dropped from 10 percent to 2.7 percent.[57]

ICONOGRAPHY OF THE PALESTINE POUND

The design of the new currency had an obvious propagandist role: it expressed the British colonial vision of Palestine. While the currency was introduced to reaffirm British commitment to the Jewish National Home, the iconography did not include any explicit references to Zionism. There were no national Jewish signs or depictions of Jewish "return." Instead, the iconography celebrated Palestine's revered past. The government of Palestine and the Currency Board decided that ancient monuments, primarily those associated with Jerusalem, would best represent Palestine. Human figures were completely absent. Suggestions for a watermark of the head of a Palestinian peasant, or a "patriarchal prototype," common to Jews and Arabs, were rejected because of expected Muslim and Jewish objections to the portrayal of human figures (although Jews and Muslims showed no such reservations when using European coins before the war).[58] The design of the currency presented Palestine as an ancient land, rich with holy sites but empty of people: empty of its Arab majority; empty of its rapidly growing Jewish minority. The banknotes were clearly inspired by early photographs and postcards of Palestine, produced for European consumption, which showed the country as a magical land of ruins and holy sites: a deserted country frozen in time.[59]

Three of the four monuments selected for the Palestine banknotes were in Jerusalem and its vicinity. One side of all the notes featured the Citadel of Jerusalem, a historic landmark that was the focus of British conservation efforts. This Ottoman citadel (built on a Roman foundation) conveyed a sense of security and solidity. The officers in charge of the design of the currency explicitly sought designs suggesting "confidence and strength" in order to gain the trust of the population.[60] The other side of the note showed one of three selected monuments: the Dome of the Rock in Jerusalem, Rachel's Tomb in Bethlehem, and what the British called the "Crusader Tower" of Ramlah.[61] The choice of the citadel, the Dome of the Rock, and Rachel's Tomb reflected the centrality of Jerusalem and Bethlehem to the British imaginary of Palestine. This selection aspired to strike a balance between the three faiths, although, as decried by the Arab press, no Christian monument was chosen, as the "Crusader Tower" was in fact a Mamluk minaret.[62]

Through the banknotes' design, the British implicitly portrayed themselves as impartial custodians of a historical and sacred land. The protection of antiquities and the holy places was mentioned at length in the League of Nations Mandate as the duty of the Mandatory power. It was a mission far less contentious than the British commitment to the Jewish National Home. The currency was introduced to bolster the British commitment to Zionism, by making Hebrew a state language. But its coy visual language precluded any iconographic references to the Jewish National Home; instead it chose to depict Palestine through the tropes of the age-old "Holy Land."

Yet the image of Palestine as an unchanging land of the Bible could not have been further from the truth. The citadel, which was featured on the notes as an aloof and lifeless heritage site, in fact overlooked the bustling Jaffa Gate city center, the manifestation of Jerusalem's incorporation into modern networks of trade, politics, and ideas. But Jaffa Road, with its banks and cafés, was not shown on the notes. During the Mandate, the development of the city, and of Palestine more generally, continued unabated, albeit in a more bifurcated manner. Increasing integration into the world economy, large infrastructure projects, and of course British commitment to Zionism brought economic and political upheavals, which were facilitated by the circulation of the banknotes, with their picturesque designs. Yet modern Palestine was wholly absent from the face of the notes. It was no accident that the coins were decorated with a biblical olive branch rather than the orange tree, the pride of both Arabs and Jews in coastal Palestine and the source of Palestine's main export. One British officer proposed designs representing "the modern activities of Palestine" such as a marine airplane landing on the Sea of Galilee or the new Haifa harbor, the largest public-works project carried out by the British in Palestine. But the High Commissioner dismissed these proposals out of hand. The photograph of Haifa would be "indistinguishable from any other similar harbour in the world," he wrote, recommending the image of the historical city of Acre instead: "I do not think its lack of economical significance matters."[63]

The Currency Board in London had the final say on issues of design. High Commissioner Arthur Wauchope, who was keen to make the design of the banknotes "more worthy of the country," found his suggestions rejected one by one by the Currency Board, mainly on the grounds of forgery prevention (which, for paper money, was a real concern). In a bitter note he succumbed:

"I obey the experts. The result is that we shall have an ugly bank note . . . a deplorable fact for Palestine."[64] Neither local businesses and banks nor local colonial administrators had any real influence over the currency or even its design. Appropriately, the name of the Palestine Currency Board appeared in the largest characters at the head of the banknotes, in English only, while the English signatures of the board members appeared at the bottom. In the final account, the Ottoman sultan's place as the source of authority was taken not by the government of Palestine but by the Currency Board members, little-known imperial bureaucrats in London, the city in which the Palestine pound was minted, printed, and managed.

THE RECEPTION OF THE MANDATE MONEY

Following the introduction of the currency, the Palestine Currency Board announced that "the currency was well received by all sections of the community."[65] But as they knew well, this was not the case. The reception of the currency was sharply divided along national lines. Both the Zionist and the Arab press pointed out that the currency was introduced on the tenth anniversary of the Balfour Declaration; they saw the currency as part of British policies to implement the Jewish National Home.[66] Both sides interpreted the currency as an official statement on Palestine's future, which reinforced their hopes and fears.

All Zionist newspapers, from the Revisionist right-wing *Do'ar ha-Yom* to the Zionist socialist *Davar*, expressed the utmost jubilation at the issue of the currency and pronounced it a historical turning point. One example of the outburst of emotion can be found in *Davar*, "the newspaper of the workers of Erets Yisra'el":

> I am not very fond of money, perhaps because I don't have any. I don't have any money, perhaps because I am not very fond of it. I would give my last penny to see the evil of money depart from this world. But today, more than any other day, I want money. I want to stand in the queue to exchange Egyptian money with Erets Yisra'el money. To feel through a coin of my own, the tremor that passes through me, from head to toe, with the first touch of a coin with square letters, Hebrew letters. . . .
>
> And I know well: Palestina is written on the coin in full, and from Erets Yisra'el all that remains is an acronym, and I am familiar with the companions in English and Arabic. And I also heard the petty accounting: Hebrew is at the

> bottom, at the top, and so on and so forth, but all these would not overshadow my joy and would not belittle this fact: internationally recognized legal tender was established in Erets Yisra'el, and Hebrew letters are inscribed on it! . . . today, we have climbed one step of the ladder, and who can tell where its top will reach.[67]

A more sober commentator in the liberal *Ha-Arets* admitted that the Palestine pound was a mere "shadow of a currency," completely reliant on the strength of the British pound, and lamented the absence of a Palestinian central bank. Zionist economic circles deemed the currency arrangements far from satisfactory.[68] Yet this was largely lost in the nationalist jubilation.

In contrast, the Arab press reacted with suspicion and hostility. Most vehement was the Jerusalem-based *Al-Jamiʿa al-ʿArabiyya*, the organ of the dominant faction of Arab Palestinian politics, the Supreme Muslim Council. The newspaper suggested that the new currency was a conspiracy to render Arab Palestinians destitute and to prepare the ground for the government's political plans. The newspaper highlighted the complaints of Jaffa merchants about losses caused by the transition to the new currency. *Al-Jamiʿa al-ʿArabiyya* also pointed to the prominent place of Hebrew, which proved that the new currency was part and parcel of the Jewish National Home policies.[69] In contrast, the Arabic lettering was of poor quality and indicated a lack of respect for the Arab population and its language. Given the central place of calligraphy in Arabic visual culture, design was not only an aesthetic but also a political question. Criticism of the Arabic script on the notes and coins was widespread, and its inferior quality was acknowledged by Mandatory officers.[70]

In an article titled "Mandate or Colonialism?" the influential Jaffa-based *Filastin* questioned the considerations behind the introduction of the currency: "None of us understands who established it, in whose favor, who will issue it, what guarantees it, and where is the gold to be kept against the paper notes that will pass through our hands?"[71] The Hebrew press never raised such doubts about the financial securities guaranteeing the currency. As paper money, the new currency depended on public trust, but unlike Zionist Jews, Arab Palestinians had little faith in the intentions of the British government. The Arab adoption of the currency was out of need, not persuasion: "[The government] makes for us whatever clothes it wishes, and we have to wear them, whether it suits us or not," concluded *Filastin* bitterly. The comparison of banknotes to clothes is reminiscent of Marx's description of the "uniforms" of money. Marx described the design of coins as "different national uniforms, which are worn at home and doffed again in the market of the world."[72] For Marx, these uniforms were of no real consequence. Yet for *Filastin*, the champion of Arab Palestinian nationalism, the choice of clothes was not something to be dismissed.

A confidential report on the popular reception of the new currency, which was prepared for the Currency Board, revealed that the concerns voiced by the Arab press were widespread. In all Arab cities in Palestine, from Acre to Gaza, people expressed mistrust in the new currency regime and its guarantees: they questioned whether the new currency would maintain its value and its parity with British sterling. At the same time, "keen reaction" to the currency was reported among the Jewish population.[73]

As a clerk in the Jerusalem municipality, Wasif Jawhariyyeh was entrusted with the laborious task of exchanging Egyptian currency for Palestine pounds. In his memoirs he lamented that "the Palestinian currency . . . had the phrase 'the land of Israel' written on it in Hebrew. Despite this hint, we accepted it, and the Arabs of Palestine dealt in it in what was almost an acknowledgment that Palestine was the land of Israel."[74]

THE POWER OF DISGUISE

The Palestine pound was an instrument of disguise. Masquerading as local money, it was in effect pound sterling dressed up in the Palestinian garb of olive branches and historic monuments. As a "shadow of a currency" it had no value of its own, but was wholly dependent on the backing of the British Empire. It was a token currency whose coins and banknotes represented not gold but British pounds, which, after the 1932 abolition of the gold standard, were free-floating symbols of value.

The design of the currency presented additional layers of disguise. The trilingual format, suggesting pluralist unity, concealed a settler colonial enterprise of establishing a Jewish National Home against the wishes of the local population. Palestine was depicted on the banknotes and coins as an ageless heritage site, but the commodifying logic of money-based exchange, increasingly applied to labor and land, was eroding unique features of local society and landscape. It served not only the accelerated integration of Palestine into global markets and the transition from subsistence farming to waged labor, but also Zionist land purchase and colonization, and the peasant dispossession it entailed.

Viewing the texts and images of money as camouflage may seem consistent with the Marxian approach to money as a thin veil behind which real social relations reign. Yet the importance attached by the British, Arabs, and Zionists to the text and images of the currency indicates that these had power of their own. Circulating textual artifacts were a tool to present the British vision of Palestine as a deep-rooted reality, as illustrated by Herbert Samuel's rush to issue stamps before the future of the territory or even its official name had been decided. Most important of all, by promoting Zionist hopes for Jewish self-determination, the Palestine pound had a real effect on the future of the country. In its transition from gold to paper, the text on money underwent a transformation, from a symbol of authority to a sign of value, from aspect to totality, from materiality to abstraction, from empire to the colonial state. In this process, the ideological inscribing of the currency was an arena where the colonial vision of Palestine was articulated, celebrated, and rejected.

The British vision of Palestine, as a separate country whose identity was built on an imagined history of ancient monuments, took hold not only among Jews but also Arabs. Ironically, in the decades after the 1948 Nakba, the formerly disliked banknotes, coins, and stamps became nostalgic artifacts for Palestinians, a relic of the lost homeland and a proof of their historical existence against denialist narratives that erased the name of Palestine from maps and history books.

British attention to the currency was one element in a broader textual agenda. From the very early months of the British civil administration in Palestine, officials placed significant emphasis on the control and manipulation of textual objects and practices. Through these artifacts, the British formulated a textual strategy that was designed to facilitate their rule in Palestine. By introducing new texts and controlling existing textual practices, the colonial administration sought a radical rewriting of Jerusalem and Palestine. Their interest in text did not stop at money and stamps, or the formulation of an official language policy. This intervention extended into the management of urban textuality: the control of advertisements in public space, the supervision of Islamic cloth banners, and the ban on Hebrew graffiti. All these attracted the close attention of the High Commissioner, the governor of Jerusalem, and other prominent officials. One of Herbert Samuel's first priorities in office was the naming of Jerusalem streets with ceramic nameplates—in an effort that aimed to rewrite the meaning of the city.

5 | CERAMIC

The British Street-Naming Campaign

ON THE MORNING OF THE 30TH OF AUGUST, 1920, A GROUP OF eminent scholars, religious leaders, affluent merchants, and administrators—all men—met in Jerusalem to discuss suggestions for civic improvement. Among them were Ragheb Bey Nashashibi, the Arab mayor of Jerusalem; Eliezer Ben Yehuda, journalist and Hebrew Revival champion; Professor Patrick Geddes, a Scottish biologist and town planner; Charles Ashbee, a leading figure in the English Arts and Crafts movement; and other prominent personalities; some native Jerusalemites; and others who were recent immigrants to the city.[1] The discussion was held in French—the cultured lingua franca of the Orient and the only language all the men had in common.

This distinguished forum was the council of the Pro-Jerusalem Society, founded in September 1918 by the British governor of Jerusalem, Ronald Storrs.[2] The living spirit behind Pro-Jerusalem, Storrs was its head, devoted fundraiser, and tireless promoter. He modeled the society after the British National Trust, and its objectives ambitiously included the provision of parks and gardens, the establishment of museums and art galleries, the encouragement of arts and crafts, and the preservation of antiquities. Storrs considered "Pro-Jerusalem" his finest achievement in Jerusalem, not only because of its noble mission but also because of his success in bringing together members of all creeds to work together for the sake of the Holy City. "The rare and stupendous portent of the assembling of these three mutual, and often venomously hostile, prelates around the same board for a common object," he wrote not long after the founding of the society, "encourages me to believe that a neutral ground may yet be found even in Jerusalem in which the courtesies and amenities of civic life may once more be enjoyed."[3] Expressing this idealized harmony, the society's emblem showed the cross, drawn inside a Star of David, outflanked by a crescent, all intertwined within one circle.

On the agenda, on the morning of the 30th of August, was a request from the recently arrived British High Commissioner, Sir Herbert Samuel, who was also Pro-Jerusalem's honorary president. The High Commissioner, declared Governor Storrs, had expressed his wish to see the streets of Jerusalem named and signposted by the society, according to two guidelines: first, that all "worthy traditions" would be kept unchanged; and second, that modern names would be used as little as possible and would be reserved for completely new streets, in the new parts of Jerusalem.[4] Governor Storrs suggested that the nameplates be made of ceramic tiles, and he showed the members a drawing of a proposed nameplate in the new format of the three official languages: English, Arabic, and Hebrew, in that order. Street names would be selected by a special subcommittee "representative of the three great religions."[5]

While some streets had been signposted under Ottoman rule, this was the first rigorous attempt to map the streets of Jerusalem into a comprehensive list of officially approved names.[6] The introduction of official street names meant a transition from oral geographies existing in memory and spoken traditions to a state-validated street map. Such a transition always involves a power struggle between groups and ideologies.[7] In Jerusalem the naming of the streets also pointed to a departure from existing notions of urban space, expressed in landmarks and localities, to an urban geography in which the street assumed a prominent position and addresses were defined as unique combinations of words (street names) and digits (house numbers). The street-naming campaign represented a new way of understanding the layout of the city for its rulers, residents, and visitors.

The significance attached to this municipal issue by the High Commissioner, weeks after he took office, indicated that street naming was not simply a means of civic improvement. It was a technology of mapping, marking, and organizing to make Jerusalem's space and society legible to colonial eyes.

Such instruments were vital to the British political project in Jerusalem: they allowed the calculated balancing of their commitment to Zionism with steps required to keep in check Arab opposition to the Jewish National Home. The colonial bureaucratic machinery was interested in tools for ground-level management of sectarian relations. But street names were not only a functional tool; naming allowed the British to invest the city with their ideological vision. The chosen names imposed a language of sanctity and historicity on the city, reversing half a century of rampant Ottoman urban development. Street naming was a cornerstone of Governor Storrs's coherent and ambitious program of "protecting" and "preserving" Jerusalem, which in effect spelled the destruction of late-Ottoman Jerusalem and a re-creation of the city to fit British notions of what this ancient, sacred, and eternal city should be.[8]

STREET NAMES AND ADDRESSES IN LATE-OTTOMAN JERUSALEM

Official and popular understanding of urban space in Ottoman Jerusalem, as elsewhere in the region, was based on the neighborhood (*mahalla*). These neighborhoods were typically mixed. Ethno-religious groups were generally more concentrated in some parts of the city, but this was far from rigid residential segregation along confessional lines.[9] Thus, Jews lived not only in the Street of the Jews (Hebrew: Rehov ha-Yehudim; Arabic: Harat al-Yahud) but also in the neighborhoods of Al-Wad and Bab Hitta. The Ottoman layout of the city divided it into seven neighborhoods within the walls (Nasara, Bab al-ʿAmud, Saʿadiyya, Al-Wad, Bab Hitta, Silsila, and Sharaf) and another twenty-five localities outside the walls.[10] There was no official signposting of the localities or maps marking them, but they appeared in Ottoman documentations such as census papers, identity cards, and public notices, and in the press.

In describing addresses, Jerusalemites relied on familiar landmarks, buildings, and sites to indicate exact locations. Wasif Jawhariyyeh describes the address of his great-grandfather: "His house was in the Bab al-ʿAmud neighborhood, east of Salah's flour mill, on Al-Wad road, below the arch and opposite the institution of Jewish endowments."[11] The Jawhariyyeh house, in which Wasif and his brothers had been born, was located "in the Saadiyeh Quarter . . . near the shrine of sheikh Rihan."[12] A term that was common in describing residential addresses was the "courtyard" (*hawsh* in Arabic, *hatser* in Hebrew), referring to small flats arranged around a shared patio. As a result of the influx of poor Jewish immigrants into the city, most Jews lived in such "courtyards," which were typically owned by Muslims and leased by a main Jewish leaseholder.[13]

Street names played a relatively minor role in addresses' descriptions. But streets had names, and often several names, in different languages.[14] Different communities used different names to describe the same physical spaces. *Suq al-Qattanin* (cotton weavers' market) was known in Hebrew as Rehov ha-Hanuyot (Street of the Shops); Tariq Nabi Da'ud (King David Street, leading to David's Tomb) was in Hebrew Rehov Habad (Chabad Street), after the main Hasidic synagogue on that street.[15] Street names manifested the existence of parallel imagined geographies, all corresponding to the same physical space: a palimpsest of mental maps.

In the absence of legible markers, addresses were not easily accessible to strangers and newcomers. Finding one's way demanded local knowledge through social interaction and insiders' familiarity. The lack of signposted street names did not prevent the operation of six different postal services in Jerusalem of around 1900 (Austrian, German, French, Italian, Russian, and Ottoman). Letters were either collected at the post office or delivered by agents familiar with different communities in Jerusalem. Those expecting mail usually gathered outside the post office, waiting patiently until "the Armenian clerk . . . had classified the letters in alphabetical order, opened the upper part of the door, and begun to call out the names of the addressees. The responses were given in many languages and the letters were tossed into the laps of the recipients." The letters which were not claimed on mail day were delivered to the addresses by local agents.[16]

But the Ottoman authorities saw a need for reform and rationalization. In 1858 the reformist governor of Jerusalem, Süreyya Pasha, introduced house numbering to the city, as reported by a British visitor:

> He was a strict Moslem . . . and fostered a spirit of fanaticism. It was acknowledged, however, that he was in many respects a clever ruler, and an energetic and vigilant disciplinarian. It was said that he never took bribes, but caused the taxes to be regularly enforced. . . . To facilitate the taxation of all the citizens of Jerusalem he had caused all the houses to be numbered, and large Arabic numerals now appeared on the doors. . . . Every dwelling, however obscure,

> had its especial mark. Then a careful record was made of the names of the owners and inmates.
>
> This was quite a novelty, and I was told that modern Jerusalem had never before been systematically numbered. The lower classes of Arabs viewed it as unlucky and were strongly prejudiced against it; others spoke of it as a very *tyrannical proceeding*.[17]

Jerusalemites' suspicion of the new house numbers may have had something to do with superstition. But it may have been a correct reading of these as instruments of control and regulation that could result in taxes, conscription, and disciplinary state power. In the second half of the nineteenth century, Ottoman population records became increasingly ambitious in their collection of data. Each resident had to be registered in the population register books with an indication of his or her address, which included locality, sub-locality, and sometimes also street name and house number.[18] As the modern state's obsession with population increased, such documents constituted a technology of surveillance, reified in textual form in census documents, public notices, and papers of identity.[19] After repainting the numbers in 1899, the city council issued a warning: "Anyone painting over or erasing the number above his house or shop, deliberately or by accident, will be punished severely."[20]

As part of Ottoman reforms, the authorities paid growing attention to the street—the site of circulation and trade. The municipality introduced street lighting of main thoroughfares with kerosene lamps, and regular street cleaning. Streets inside the walled city were cleared of vendor stalls, carts, and benches; peasant women, who sold fruits, vegetables, and herbs sitting on the ground in the Jaffa Gate area, were now seen as a nuisance to be pushed elsewhere. For the urban middle class, the peasants' backward presence in the cosmopolitan city center appeared an embarrassment.[21] "Widening of the streets" became a metaphor for progress and modernity, used frequently in the local press. During World War I, the authorities launched grand urban projects in cities in the Arab provinces. In Jerusalem these included the massive expansion of the main street, Jaffa Road, the repaving of several other roads, and the mapping of the city, as well as the establishment of a prestigious state Islamic college.[22] Street naming appears to have been part of these efforts. Street nameplates in a combination of Ottoman Turkish and Arabic were emplaced in main streets. The names were hand-painted on metal plates in the

FIGURE 29. Ottoman street nameplate from Jerusalem, with the name Harat al-nasara Cadesi (Streeet of the Christians).
Source: Imperial War Museum © IWM (FEQ 98).

Ottoman national colors of red and white. These plates were removed by the British military in 1917, and some survived in the collection of the Imperial War Museum in London.[23]

However, the effect of these signposting and regulating efforts remained limited. For locals, the Ottoman numbers were obscure signs that played no meaningful role in the mental maps of ordinary residents of the city.[24] State records on residential addresses were rudimentary. Until its collapse, the empire continued to rely on local intermediaries, heads of religious communities, and the neighborhood *mukhtars* (appointed delegates) in its dealings with individual residents. Tax collection, birth and marriage registration, census reports, and conscription data were all administered by these local delegates, who were closely familiar with the community in which they lived. This partly explains the failure of the authorities to locate army deserters during the war. Desertion remained a significant problem despite brutal measures to combat it.[25]

For Turkish nationalists, the lax attitude toward urban geography manifested the failure of the Ottoman Empire in the Arab provinces. Falih Rıfkı

Atay, who served in Jerusalem during the war as the assistant to Syria's commander Jamal Pasha, called his war memoirs *Zeytindağı*, Mount of Olives, to emphasize this point. "*Olberg* is the German for Mount of Olives. *Jabal al-Zaytun* is the Arabic. And *Zeytindağı*? *Zeytindağı* is just the name I gave to my book. *There never was a Turkish Jerusalem*." The failure to dictate the nomenclature encapsulated the shortcomings of the Ottoman Empire's Turkish leaders. Even after four hundred years of rule, "we are lodgers in Jerusalem," he stated. "We have neither colonized this region nor made it part of our land."[26] Colonization required full control of naming and signposting. This was an approach with which British officials, who occupied Jerusalem in December 1917, agreed entirely.

COLONIAL STREET NAMING: MAPPING (AND CREATING) SEGREGATION

British administrators arrived in Jerusalem with a clear notion of the city's geography, informed by nineteenth-century European travelogues, maps, and guidebooks. This geography differed considerably from the Ottoman geography or the mental maps of the local population. European travelers saw the city within the walls as composed of four segregated ethno-religious quarters. These four quarters—Christian, Muslim, Jewish, and Armenian—were neatly divided in straight lines by the two main arteries cutting the city north-south and east-west. European scholars believed the city was organized by this simple cross shape, which retained Roman Jerusalem's layout. This view reflected European fascination with the Jerusalem of early Christianity and a privileging of the street plan as the key to read the city. Such notions did not correspond to local perceptions of geography. What Europeans saw a single east-west artery which they called "David Street," locals understood as a series of streets: Khatt Da'ud, Suwaykat ʿAlun, Tariq al-Bazar, and Tariq Bab al-Silsila.[27]

British authorities assumed that ethno-religious segregation was natural in Jerusalem, and their role was to police it. Among the first signs emplaced by the military authorities were "Out of Bounds" signs forbidding non-Christians from entering the Holy Sepulchre and non-Muslims from entering the Haram al-Sharif. British military guards questioned visitors about their confessional identity at the entrances to these sites. The Orthodox-Christian Wasif Jawhariyyeh describes how he pretended to be Muslim to be allowed entrance to the Haram for a stroll with his friends.[28]

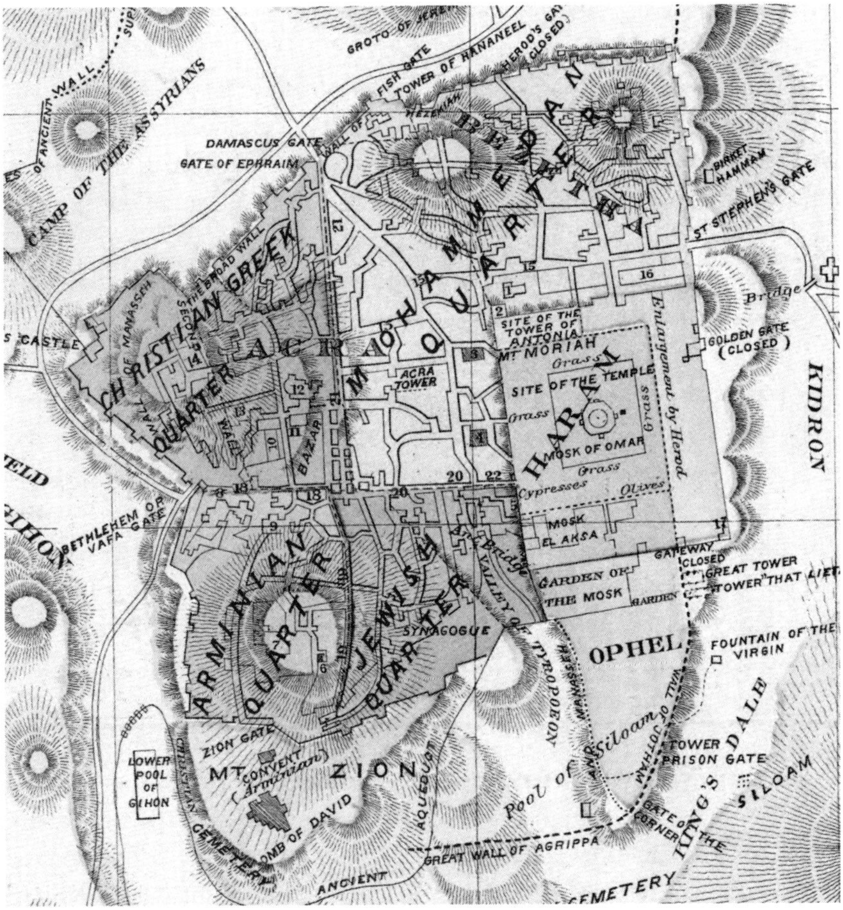

FIGURE 30. Map of Jerusalem, divided into four sectarian quarters in a cross shape. Historical hand-atlas, 1883.
Source: Library of Congress Map Collection.

According to the Balfour Declaration, the Palestine Administration had to facilitate the establishment of a Jewish National Home in Palestine while ensuring no harm was done to the "civic and religious rights" of the "non-Jewish population," that is, the country's overwhelming majority, who increasingly thought of themselves in national terms as Arab Palestinians. Herbert Samuel, a committed Zionist, believed that the interests of the Jewish National Home required a careful balancing act with the rights and needs of the Arab population.[29] To balance what the British termed the "Dual Obligation" toward

Jews and Arabs, the British required instruments of monitoring and control, which were found in bureaucratic and technical tools such as town planning, land registration, and mapping.[30] Samuel saw town planning as a key tool to introduce modern methods of benevolent development to Palestine while enabling the administration to calculate its steps toward the different ethnic and religious groups.[31] Mapping the sectarian layout of the city was an urgent task.

The immediate context for the street-naming campaign was Samuel's preparations for elections for a legislative assembly. The assembly was a central element in Samuel's plans to provide the Palestine Mandate with local legitimacy. The country was to be divided into voting areas in a way that would "secure fair representation of different religious communities."[32] This required a sectarian mapping of Palestine's cities. Yet in Jerusalem the British found to their surprise no clear boundaries between the Jewish, Muslim, and Christian areas. Samuel had hoped to use street names as a key to decipher the religious identity of different parts of the city; selecting street names to reflect the racial and ethnic identity of residents was a familiar colonial practice. But, as he reported to London, there were no such street signs.[33] The street-naming campaign provided the administration with an opportunity to signpost religious identities into new parts of the city. In the walled city, the street-naming committee generally assigned names according to the logic of the cross-shaped "four quarters," despite the mixed nature of the population. Christian, Armenian, Jewish, and Muslim names were chosen to highlight the supposed "Quarter" identity. In the "Christian Quarter," Harat al-Istambuliyya was renamed Casa Nova Street, after the Franciscan pilgrim house by that name; Harat al-Waʿariyya became Latin Street; and Harat al-Mawazina became Coptic Street.[34] The Ottoman neighborhoods of the Old City—Sharaf, Silsilia, Saʿadiyya, Al-Wad—were effectively erased from the map.[35]

British officials involved in the naming campaign indicated that the task was politically sensitive. Harry Luke, the chair of the subcommittee, described it as "the ticklish duty of providing the streets of Jerusalem with names . . . without offending anyone's susceptibilities."[36]As presented in the Pro Jerusalem Records, "here was the scope for not only scholarship but acute political divisions, and the sub-committee had on several occasions to be steered over very dangerous rocks."[37] These political divisions remain unknown, as most protocols of the subcommittee did not survive. Yet the Pro-Jerusalem maps hold some clues to possible differences. It appears that Jewish representatives—quite likely the firebrand Eliezer Ben Yehuda—refused to render names with Christian and Muslim connotations in Hebrew: Via Dolorosa became in Hebrew Rehov ha-Bira (Capital Street), and Al-Buraq (the Muslim name for the Wailing Wall area) became Shvil ha-Barak (Lightening Path), retaining the sound but altering the meaning. Similarly, Rehov ha-Kotel ha-Ma'aravi (Western Wall Street) appears only on the Hebrew map and not on the English and Arabic editions, perhaps owing to rising tensions around this site between Jews and Muslims.[38]

At the same time that the British were inscribing sectarian divides in the city's map, they were also removing congregational autonomy. Unlike the Ottomans, the British preferred, whenever possible, to deal with citizens directly and not through congregational leaders and neighborhood *mukhtars*. Edward Keith-Roach, a senior officer in the administration, described his attempts to register the population for the purpose of food rationing in the early 1920s:

> In some towns registration had been carried out by the heads of the religious communities and I was pressed to implement the same system in Jerusalem. It sounded simple! But few of the streets had names, let alone numbers. There were many religious communities, and mixed marriages were not unknown. . . . In the end I decided that being a spiritually minded bishop, a popular preacher in the mosque, or a devout rabbi did not necessarily make a man a good administrator, or even a tolerable registrar.[39]

The new colonial state, distrustful of local forms of organization and representation, needed to define and signpost the urban geography in clear and definite terms, in order to make subjects visible to its gaze. Residents had to be positioned on a well-defined grid. Using this system, tax collectors, bailiffs, police, postmen, or anyone else in an official position would be able to find any address directly without depending on local knowledge or mediation. In practice, as colonial administrators complained, actual measures of signposting fell far short of the ambition for an exhaustive mapping of the city.[40]

The British reorganization of the official geography and its public display marked a significant step in the project of state centralization and rationalization. It continued the Ottoman drive toward increasing the legibility of land and population, while introducing a new colonial calculus of sectarian segregation as natural and desirable. But it would be wrong to think of street naming only in terms of functional control, reducing tracts of land, houses, and people to a legible and demystified grid. On the contrary, street naming was a project that aimed to remystify urban space and write new mythologies into the city. The seductive power of street naming, as an ideological operation, lay in its ability to connect the concrete everyday experience of navigating the city with historical and mythological narratives. "There is a peculiar voluptuousness in the naming of streets," noted Walter Benjamin as he studied the troubled modern history of Paris's streets and the grand renaming schemes of revolutionaries and monarchists.[41]

> There is the Place du Maroc in Belleville: that desolate heap of stones with its rows of tenements became for me, when I happened on it one Sunday afternoon, not only a Moroccan desert but also, and at the same time, a monument of colonial imperialism; topographic vision was entwined with allegorical meaning in this square, yet not for an instant did it lose its place in the heart of Belleville. But to awaken such a view is something ordinarily reserved for intoxicants. And in such cases, in fact, street names are like intoxicating substances that make our perceptions more stratified and richer in spaces.[42]

Street naming was an opportunity to write new mythologies into the pedestrian experience. Departing from the Ottoman vision of modernity and progress, British nameplates inscribed the city as a biblical phantasmagoria. This vision was best articulated by Ronald Storrs, the new governor of Jerusalem.

RONALD STORRS AND HIS NEW JERUSALEM

Ronald Storrs arrived in Jerusalem with a great sense of history. For him, Jerusalem was not merely another job, one of many in a professional career in the colonial service. "There is no promotion after Jerusalem," he said upon his departure to Cyprus in 1926.[43] Storrs derived much pleasure from the halo of his title as governor of Jerusalem, presenting himself as a successor of Pontius Pilate, and allowing him audiences with the pope and with King George V. During his years as Oriental secretary in Cairo, Storrs had established for himself a reputation as a man of wide cultural horizons and scholarly interests, beyond those expected of a colonial official.[44] The governorship of Jerusalem gave him an opportunity to gratify what he called his "taste for creative foundation," only on a much larger scale. His nine years as governor were decisive for the reinvention of Jerusalem.[45]

Already upon his appointment, when the city was still flooded with refugees and in dire shortage of food and firewood, Storrs was making clear that the British role in Jerusalem did not stop at running the daily affairs of an occupied enemy town. Through a blitz of town-planning decrees and municipal regulations, he declared his responsibility for shaping the character of the city. The future of Palestine was still officially undecided, yet Storrs was staking a claim not only for himself but also for British rule in Jerusalem by articulating a cultural and spiritual mission. This mission had no explicit connection to the Balfour Declaration and the establishment of a Jewish National Home. Rather, it was much more grandiose and universal: the protection and conservation of the Holy City for the benefit of humankind. For this service Storrs hired the abovementioned Charles Ashbee, a leading figure in the English Arts and Crafts movement, as civic adviser in charge of the Pro-Jerusalem Society and town planning. In Ashbee's romantic vision of the ideal modern city, the corrupting effects of modern technology would be minimized and spirituality would be restored through a revival of local crafts. In Jerusalem his cultural "preservation" involved introducing folkloristic crafts that had no tradition in Jerusalem, such as weaving and ceramic tile making.[46] His main mission was the coordination of urban planning, focused not on urban development but on "preserving intact the appearance and atmosphere of Jerusalem."[47]

For the people of Jerusalem, the notion of conservation was largely foreign. The Ottomans restored Islamic monuments and established a local antiquities museum. But the vision of urban development championed by imperial authorities and local elites was one of an aggressive transformation and expansion which took little heed of the city's historical fabric. Jerusalem's mayor in the 1920s, Ragheb Nashashibi, the former Ottoman district engineer and a representative of Jerusalem in the Ottoman parliament, had a vision of modernity based on progress, technology, and new construction. "True, [Nashashibi] wants to make of Jerusalem a city like Paris, a continuous Champs Elysees with abundance of Kiosks," wrote Ashbee in his memoirs, "but I tell him I am no Haussmann and we must agree to differ."[48] Nashashibi promoted the George V Avenue, a major development in the new city.[49] He was exasperated by British intervention in town planning, which had resulted in numerous maps and preservation regulations and left little room for actual development. The British administration also annulled the Ottoman plan for tramlines and electricity provision in Jerusalem. Like early European photography of Palestine, which rendered the country as a biblical theater set, Jerusalem had to abandon its hopes for tramways and electrification and make way for an Orientalist fantasy.

Storrs's campaign to protect Jerusalem's sacred character involved the prohibition of selling alcohol, a ban on cinema and cabaret shows within the Old City, a clampdown on prostitution, the removal of beggars from the Old City streets and from holy sites, the absolute prohibition of advertisements "save on one or two small authorized hoardings in commercial quarters, and out of sight of the walls of Jerusalem"; all these were measures "in keeping with the Holy Land and the Holy City."[50] But these measures were a novelty, as during the final decades of Ottoman rule alcohol could be consumed, prostitution practiced, and cinema films shown.[51] Jerusalem was a holy city, but it was not a very observant one. True, the urban economy depended on pilgrims, tourists, religious trusts, and pious donations. But this did not imply that religion was practiced there more strictly than elsewhere.[52] Under British rule, sanctity became something of a municipal amenity and a matter for zoning regulation. The sacredness of the city applied most strictly within the walled city as a "holy enclosure" (although the walls had no such significance to local Muslims, Jews, and Christians), and to a lesser degree in the new neighborhoods outside the walls.[53]

Storrs's most influential edict was one prescribing that all new buildings in Jerusalem should be stone-clad and banning all other building materials such as stucco, corrugated iron, and roof tiles. In his memoirs Storrs describes the local stone admiringly: "From that rock, cutting soft but drying hard, has for three thousand years been quarried the clear white stone, weathering blue-grey or amber-yellow with time, whose solid walls, barrel vaulting and pointed arches have preserved through the centuries a hallowed and immemorial tradition."[54] It is hard to exaggerate the importance of this decision for modern Jerusalem. By turning a local building tradition into a state regulation, Storrs had set the character of modern Jerusalem far beyond the limits of the walled city. The new Jerusalem, rapidly spreading north, west, and south, was thus modeled after the old one. Stone provided a visual language in which Jerusalem was to be articulated: a language laden with historical and religious meanings; a language through which an overwhelmingly new city could pretend to be ancient; a language through which the holy sites' sanctity could be extended to encompass the city as a whole. Storrs had given Jerusalem the perfect mask behind which claims to eternity and ancientness could be made. This was literally a mask, since the regulation specified that in the new city only the external walls had to be built in stone, while the structure and the inner walls could be built in any possible way.[55] The scholarship on modern Jerusalem has been more than favorable to Storrs on this point. Time and again he is commended for his "vision" that "has helped to preserve the beauty of Jerusalem."[56] Yet it is wrong to take at face value Storrs's claims that this was an act of conservation. Storrs's stone bylaw did not protect the "aesthetic *Status* quo," as he claimed;[57] instead it created it by banning already-in-use modern building materials. Intervening in local social customs, in building practices, and in the built fabric of the city, Storrs and his fellow colonial officials sought to turn a living city into a museum and to position themselves as custodians of a world heritage site. This vision found textual articulation in the naming of the streets. The holiness of the city was, quite literally, to be written onto modern street corners.

DRESSING UP JERUSALEM IN BIBLICAL CLOTHES

In his memoirs, Storrs explained the street-naming campaign in the following manner:

> A discerning conqueror in 1850 could have established the new shops, convents and hotels well away from the Old City and have left the grey ramparts in a setting of grass, olives and cypresses. By 1918 the time was past for seeing Jerusalem adorned as a bride, but it was not too late to determine that for the dumb soul of the City the names at least of her streets in English, Arabic and Hebrew, preserved by tradition or reverently bestowed, should be proclaimed in blue or green tiles glittering against the sober texture of her walls like chrysoprase and lapis lazuli.[58]

Storrs describes street naming in heroic, gendered terms: the feminine soul of Jerusalem is brought to life by a discerning male conqueror. Signposting, for Storrs, is not a simple measure of municipal improvement. Naming is the prerogative of the conqueror; it is an act through which meaning is created and the "dumb" city is given the power of speech. In his memoirs Storrs repeatedly refers to the act of inscribing the urban landscape as a paradigm for enlightened rule, which he contrasts with the childlike writing habits of the native population. He proudly recounts how, on the seventh centenary of Saint Francis's death, he named and unveiled the inscription-tile of Saint Francis Street—"perhaps a worthier commemoration than the posters' 'Evviva il Serafino d'Assisi' with which the gray City walls were then beplastered."[59] Controlling the textual landscape, for Storrs, was key to controlling the local population, the "two and seventy jarring sects."[60] When the German-owned Fast Hotel was confiscated as enemy property, "the Jews wished to rename [it] *'King Solomon'* and the Arabs *'Sultan Sulaiman'* (The Ottoman Soliman [*sic*] the Magnificent), either of which would have excluded half Jerusalem." Storrs's imperial intervention named the hotel *"The Allenby."*[61] Alas, it was not long before the Allenby sign was taken down and replaced. The hotel was renamed twice more before 1948.[62]

It is telling that Storrs describes street naming as a compensation for the impossibility of adorning Jerusalem "as a bride" by drawing a clear separation between the Old City and the new parts. Storrs and other British officials viewed with contempt the Ottoman city center of Jaffa Gate, which hid the walls from sight and blurred considerably the difference between "old" and "new" Jerusalem, creating a contiguous urban sphere of business, leisure, and local politics. The fact that this area was the city's civic and commercial center did not deter British town planners from marking this entire area for demolition in order to create a visual and physical isolation of the Old City. These plans were the most prominent act of British planning in Palestine.[63] The municipality, banks, and shops would be replaced by a park that would leave "the grey ramparts in a setting of grass, olives and cypresses." These plans were largely left unmaterialized under British rule, as they required high compensation to property owners. The British did, however, demolish the Jaffa Gate clock tower, the city's most important late-Ottoman monument.[64] Despite much opposition from the local city council, the clock tower was dismantled in the early 1920s.[65] This was perhaps the most symbolic expression of the British intention to freeze time and send Jerusalem back into the past. In this instance, the project of conservation meant, in fact, destruction and demolition.

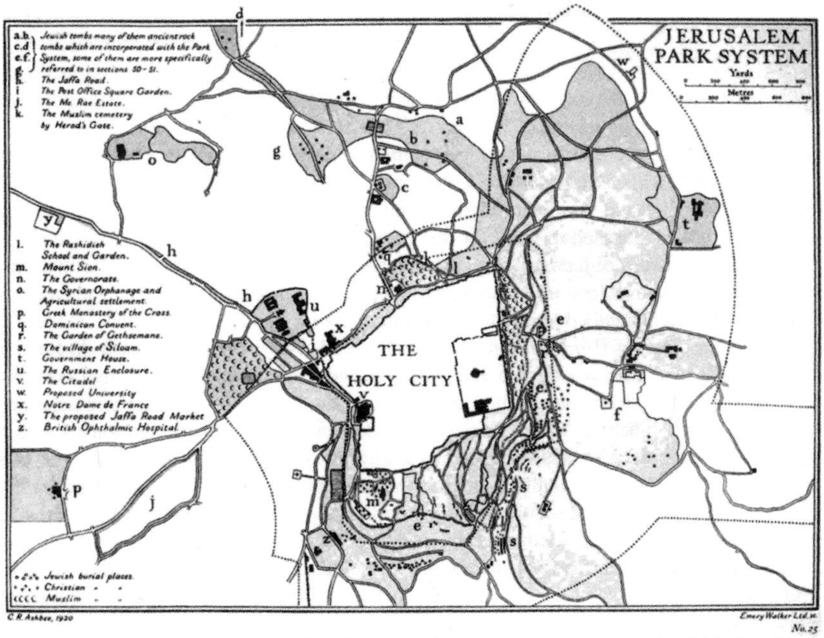

FIGURE 31. Charles Ashbee's plan for Jerusalem, 1920, separating the Old City from the new parts and removing the town center from Jaffa Gate.
Source: Ashbee, *Jerusalem 1918–1920*.

Street naming provided a relatively inexpensive means of urban intervention, which demanded no demolition or construction but could nonetheless reshape the meaning of the city. The choice of the ceramic name tiles was crucial to the symbolic reimagining of the city. The tiles were in the tradition of İznik pottery, which developed in early-modern-period Anatolia. In Jerusalem this distinctively Ottoman craft was represented in the facades of the Dome of the Rock, refurbished by Suleiman the Magnificent in the early sixteenth century. Outside the dome, these tiles were hard to come by and were by no means a typical Jerusalem architectural element. The ceramic industry that was set up by British officials in the 1920s imported Armenian artisans to the city. Central among them was Tavit (David) Ohannessian, a ceramist from the city of Kütahya in Turkey, a historic center of the ceramic industry. Before the war, Mark Sykes had commissioned Ohannessian to tile a "Turkish Room" in his Yorkshire manor. Following the Armenian genocide, Ohannessian became a refugee in Aleppo. After Sykes encountered him there during his visit to Syria, Ohannessian and a number of his apprentices were recruited for the restoration of the tiles of the Dome of the Rock.[66] This project, initiated by the Palestine Administration, was the most ambitious and politically delicate restoration undertaking of its kind.[67] The renovation of the holiest Islamic shrine in Palestine was intended to prove to Muslims in Palestine and beyond—particularly British-ruled India—the sincerity of British intentions. The British were keen to draw propagandist profit from the project.[68] Having the names of the streets "blazoned in the three official languages in coloured and glazed Dome of the Rock tiles" would give further publicity to the restoration. It would also project the sanctity of the dome onto the entire city. The visual language of ceramic signs connoted the historicity of Jerusalem, reverberating well beyond the Old City walls and displayed on modern buildings. The streets of Jerusalem were linked to the Dome of the Rock through a visual code, which implied the city's sacred integrity on the one hand and the British resolve to uphold this integrity on the other.

Ohannessian's workshop produced some of the tiles. A further commission was given to Bezalel, the Zionist School of Arts and Crafts, which produced a somewhat different design.[69] Both types were modest in size, and the designs did not make legibility a top priority. The plates were overburdened with rich colors or decorative motifs. The serifed lettering in English and Hebrew, and the vocalization marks of the Arabic script, made the result delicate, rich, and ornate but not easy to read, especially from afar or from a moving vehicle. The signs were clearly meant for pedestrians who had time to read them carefully and admire their beauty. "The tablets are not conspicuous: perhaps they were not meant to be so, and it is possible that people may yet go on living in a street for long, before knowing what the Committee has decided to call that street," wrote the English newspaper *Palestine Weekly* somewhat disappointedly after the first signs had been posted in December 1922. "We all want to see what are the names of the streets—our own streets among others—and it is not very easy if the only means of satisfying this curiosity is to go up and down the streets of Jerusalem with candles and ladders—like Zechariah (or was it Habakkuk?)."[70]

MAKING THE NEW CITY OLD

The British ideological vision for Jerusalem was articulated most clearly in the naming of the streets outside the walls.[71] These streets were modern and at most three decades old. But the names chosen sought to hide this reality as much as possible. The aim was to purge Jerusalem of its modernity. The names

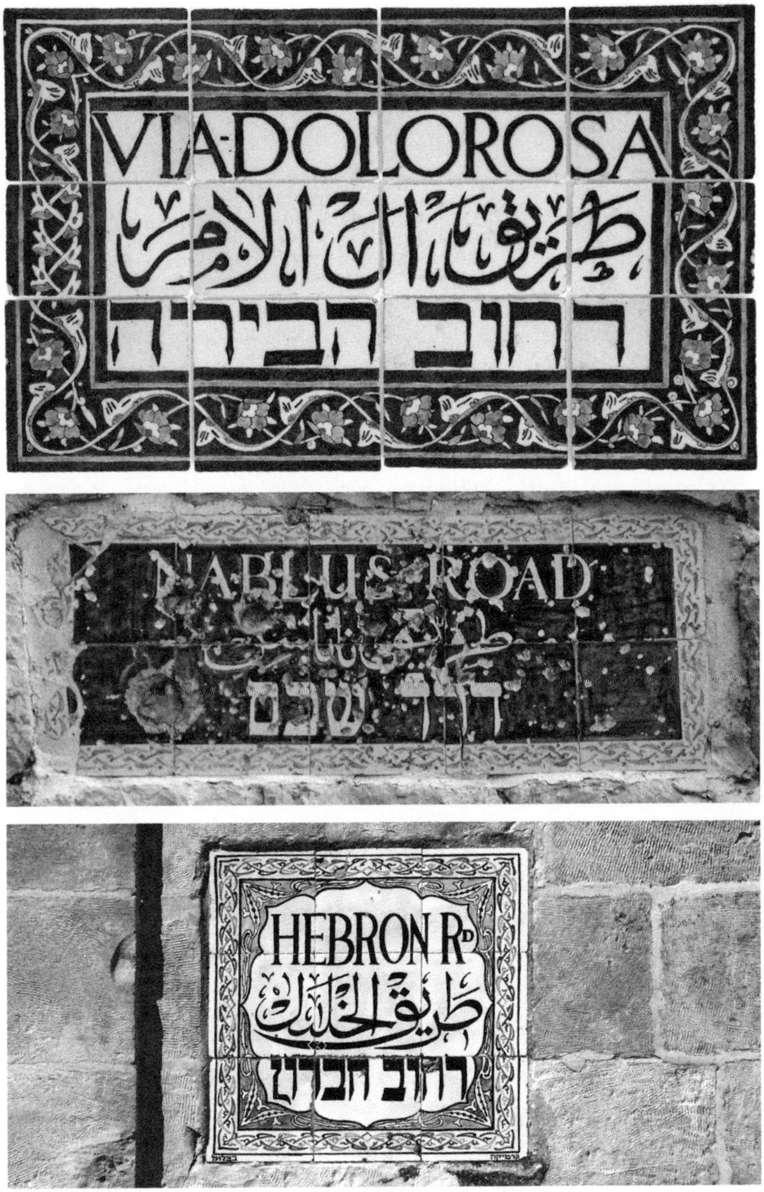

FIGURE 32. Street nameplates as part of the 1920 street-naming campaign: Via Dolorosa in the Old City (top), produced by David Ohannessian; Nablus Road (middle), produced by David Ohannessian; Hebron Road (bottom), produced by Zionist Arts and Crafts School, Bezalel.

Sources: (top) *Feast of Ashes: The Life and Art of David Ohannessian*, by Sato Moughalian, © 2019 by Sato Moughalian, published by Stanford University Press, used by permission; (middle) and (bottom) Yair Wallach.

made no explicit reference to Zionism or Arab nationalism. They also did not make any attempt to articulate an inclusive, civic, Palestinian vision. Instead of suggesting a shared present or future, the names celebrated a revered past.

Unlike in other parts of the British Empire, few streets in Jerusalem were named after British personalities or places.[72] This was in line with the policy to restrict the use of official British symbols in Palestine to a minimum, avoiding references to the Crown on Palestinian stamps, banknotes, and coins. The British flag was very rarely flown.[73] With the exception of red mailboxes and public telephone kiosks, visible icons of British rule were hard to come by in the streets of Jerusalem.

Two-thirds of the streets in the new city were named after individuals, almost all men, and almost all drawn from the ancient past: heroes, prophets, saints, scholars, and kings.[74] Preference for commemorative street names was in evidence in other cities in the British Empire, but Jerusalem was unusual in the fact that most names were drawn from the ancient past. The names chosen made the streets of new Jerusalem resonate with centuries-old history. Pedestrians were reminded on every corner that they were walking in the footsteps of Sultan Suleiman, the prophet Isaiah, and Saint Paul. As the notes in the Pro-Jerusalem Records put it: "The list is so full of history, poetry and folk-lore that it is well-worth a careful study."[75] It was also full of pathos, which was distinctly foreign to the lived geographies of Ottoman Jerusalem.[76]

The list included a large number of biblical and Jewish figures: Bezalel, Amos, Ezra, Nehemiah, Isaiah, and Jeremiah, in addition to the Maccabees, Herod, Agrippa, Josephus, and Moses Maimonides.[77] Striking in their absence were Arab and Muslim names. In the list that appeared in 1922, out of twenty-eight streets named after historical personalities, only two were distinctly Islamic ones: Sultan Suleiman and the geographer Ibn Batuta.[78] There was also a clear bias toward Christian nomenclature. Six names drawn from early Christianity and a further four from the Crusader Kingdom were given to streets in the most prestigious areas of the city. For most of the local population, the Crusades were among the city's darkest periods, remembered for the massacres against Muslims and Jews. But British officials had a sentimental identification with the knights of the Jerusalem Kingdom. The British press sometimes described Allenby and his soldiers in Palestine as modern crusaders.[79] Such a link was also made on the street map, with Tancred Street, named after the knight who led the Crusader attack, leading to General Allenby Square. The street known locally as Faydi al-ʿAlami Street—after the mayor who paved it—was renamed after the first king of the Crusader Kingdom, Godfrey de-Boullion (a name both Arabs and Jews found impossible to pronounce).[80]

One could think of other choices of personalities for commemoration, such as Jerusalemites whose contribution to the city was widely recognized, across confessional groups. Such figures included Jerusalem's first mayor, who was its first representative in the Ottoman parliament, Yusuf Diyaʾ al-Khalidi (1829–1906); the popular mayor Husayn Salim al-Husayni, who died days after British occupation; or the widely respected chief rabbi Yaʿacov Shaʾul Eliachar (1817–1906). Commemorating these local personalities could have suggested a common civic ethos that was based on a shared present.[81] But this was not the consideration guiding the street-naming effort.

The British vision for Jerusalem is best exemplified in the renaming of Jerusalem's most prestigious street. In Arabic the street was known as "the Italian Hospital Street" (ʿAqbat al-Mustashafa al-Itali).[82] In Hebrew it was known as "Consuls Street" (Rehov ha-Konsulim) or "Rothschild Hospital Street" (Rehov Beyt ha-Holim Rotshild).[83] These names highlighted the street's "European" nature. Starting at Damascus Gate, winding westward uphill, and then continuing on the ridge until it joined Jaffa Road, the street was a showcase of Jerusalem's Ottoman modernity. "Here . . . are the finest residences," wrote the U.S. consul E. S. Wallace in 1898. "Many of the Turkish officials and families of high social and financial standing consider this a desirable location. The European population has generally followed, and on the north ridge are the homes of the English and the German, and the few American missionaries, the hospitals and schools, and the consulates of various powers."[84] Along it were located no less than six European hospitals, five European schools, six consulates, and one luxurious hotel.[85] Among the residents were the Ottoman *mutasarrif* (governor) of Jerusalem; members of the notable Nashashibi family; Yoseph Navon Bey, the entrepreneur behind the Jerusalem-Jaffa railway; banker Johannes Frutiger; and architect and scholar Conrad Schick. Zionist leaders and activists such as Ben Yehuda, Arthur Ruppin, and Menachem Ussishkin resided nearby. It was only natural for Governor Storrs to take up residence in this street in 1917. Dispensing with the mundane names of Italian Hospital Street and Consuls Street, the street was rebaptized as Prophets Street. On the new map of Jerusalem, the pan-religious appeal could be read as a code for its mixed ethno-religious character. It is not unlikely that the self-aggrandizing Governor Storrs intervened to name his own street Street of the Prophets.

In his memoirs Wasif Jawhariyyeh recounts how he was hired by Storrs to play the oud (lute) at social function in his residence. On these occasions Storrs insisted that Jawhariyyeh wear the traditional full attire of Arab villagers, including *kufiyya* and *ʿiqal*, which at that time were frowned upon by fez-weaning urbanites.[86] Jawhariyyeh, a modern urban bohemian, was clearly amused by the request. Storrs had previously ordered his servants in Cairo to appear before him only in the national Egyptian *galabiyya*—much to their resentment.[87] He was now dressing up Jerusalem in biblical clothes. As the history of Jerusalem in the twentieth century shows, these clothes proved much more difficult to take off than Jawhariyyeh's villager attire.

LOCAL RESPONSES TO STREET NAMING

In the immediate term, the 1920s street-naming effort had limited impact on the mental maps of Jerusalemites. Many continued to refer to the streets by their previous names. The official new name Suleiman Street, which appeared on nameplates and city maps, did not register with Jerusalemites, who continued to call it ʿAqbat al-Manzil (Headquarters Street, after the Ottoman military headquarters that had been located there).[88]

Moreover, local Jerusalemites—Arabs, Armenians, Greeks, and Jews—continued to think of their urban environment primarily in terms of familiar landmarks and localities and did not embrace the address system of streets and individually numbered houses. In her memoirs, Hala Sakakini explains the lack of street names:

> In pre-1948 Jerusalem, before Palestine was replaced by Israel, our addresses were still simple. Houses had no numbers and streets no names, and yet it was so easy to reach a person by post or in person. People living in the same quarter were like one large family. Everyone knew everyone else. If you happened to come from another town or another quarter and did not know exactly where a person lived in that quarter you only had to ask about him, and of course you were told how to get to his house. Sometimes a passer-by would volunteer to walk with you to the house.[89]

In fact, the entrance to Sakakini's home in Qatamun was marked with a hand-painted number, as can be seen in photographs in her book. And yet this number clearly did not register with her and played no role in her geography. In bourgeois Arab neighborhoods such as Qatamun most streets had no official or unofficial names. These were neighborhoods of doctors, teachers, and businessmen. Some house owners gave their mansions evocative names—Villa Haroun al-Rashid, Vila Deccan, Villa Clermont—that were proudly marked on gates and entrances. Hala's father, Khalil Sakakini, even named the rooms in their house after the grand cities of Arab civilization (Damascus, Cordoba, Sanaa, Baghdad, and Cairo).[90] Yet Sakakini or other residents did not feel the need to signpost their streets in the same manner.

Much attention has been given in recent scholarship to the erasure of Palestinian Arab geography through the replacement of Arab names with Hebrew ones. This Hebrewization of the landscape was a systematic and concerted effort which involved naming, mapping, and signposting.[91] But in her lament for the loss of her childhood Jerusalem, Sakakini refers to a more profound process: not so much the replacement of one street name by another but rather the very introduction of street names as a symptom of alienation. "The atmosphere is totally changed now. Houses have numbers, streets have names, and in addition there are numerous signs and instructions everywhere, but, alas, human relationship is as good as nil. If you dare ask a passer-by a question, you will only get a shrug of the shoulders for an answer."[92] Similar sentiments can be found in the writing of a Jewish Jerusalemite novelist, reminiscing about Jerusalem before 1948.[93] The unmarked space is a sign of a world of social proximity, while signposting is a characteristic of an alienated society retaining neither the intimate knowledge of its geography nor the civilities of neighborly relations. Jerusalemites' decision to ignore new street names and keep with popular names or avoid street names altogether can be seen as a form of resistance against state intervention.

On the other hand, the absence of street names also triggered protests from residents. Some of the complaints reflected everyday difficulties: undelivered mail or visitors who were unable to find the address.[94] However, for recent European Jewish immigrants to the city, this was not merely a practical concern but also a symbolic one. Articles in the Zionist press decried the sorry state of Jerusalem's streets, "full of filth and emitting stench" and impossible to navigate without street names and house numbers.[95] Complaint letters to the municipality from recent Jewish immigrants from Europe expressed exasperation about the lack of street names. The letters betrayed a sense of anxiety that went beyond simple inconvenience. The unmarked streets appeared threatening and backward, like an uncolonized jungle. "If we ask a doctor, a craftsman, a shop owner, or a friend to see us, we are obliged to make a map as for somebody who wants to enter Central Africa," wrote one Jewish resident. The unmarked neighborhood appeared to this resident as a white spot on the map; signposting was a colonial tool to subjugate local geography and make it readable for the enlightened settler. Other letters presented signposting as a basic right of modern citizenship. A Jewish lawyer wondered why "good and law-abiding citizens . . . should be punished" by not being given a house number. Yet another requested his street to be named, since "I am fulfilling always my obligations to the municipality exactly."[96] For these writers, being a citizen meant being able to specify one's address in the "civilized" manner of name and number, as if without these, the residents would have no place in the city. Their marked house number was a reification of their citizenship, a reassuring sign of the colonial state on which they depended.

Street naming was high on the agenda of the local Zionist establishment. The Palestine Land Development Company, a Zionist institution which assisted in the construction of Jewish neighborhoods in the 1920s, encouraged and supervised street naming in these neighborhoods.[97] Dozens of "unofficial street names" were emplaced by Jewish neighborhood committees without intervention by the municipality.[98] Zionist newspapers closely followed official street names. In 1934 they loudly protested against the naming of three streets after the Hashemite kings. "Jerusalem is not an exclusively Arab city!" they emphasized.[99] On another occasion they warned that the Hebrew street names were facing "assassination" with an alleged plot to Arabize all street names in the Old City.[100] The Arab press did not seem to ascribe such importance to the topic. For Zionists, street naming was a national mission, driven by the desire to assert Jewish claims over the city. Zionists approached urban geography as a blank page on which they could write the narratives of Jewish return and national revival.[101] It was an ideological project that bore similarities to the British vision of Jerusalem in drawing heavily on the biblical past, historicizing the city, and ignoring local nomenclature. The aim was not only to take possession of the

FIGURE 33. Unofficial street names from the 1920s and 1930s in the Jewish neighborhood of Rehavia: Ibn Ezra Street (Hebrew, Arabic, and English) (top); Keren Kayemet Street (bottom), named after the Zionist Jewish National Fund (Hebrew and English only).
Source: Yair Wallach.

landscape and its meaning but also to convert Jerusalem's local Jews to Zionism. Some streets celebrated places related to Hebrew history (Masada, Jordan River, Carmel); others were named after Zionist personalities (Menachem Ussishkin, the national poet Bialik) or institutions (the Jewish National Fund).[102]

However, other Jewish neighborhoods chose a less nationalist approach. In the Rehavia neighborhood, established mainly by local Sephardic entrepreneurs, names consisted almost entirely of historical figures from the Jewish

"Golden Age" in Muslim Andalusia. These nameplates were also displayed in Arabic, unlike nonofficial Hebrew street signs in other neighborhoods, and expressed the softer or "inclusive" version of Zionism this milieu represented.[103] In other Jewish neighborhoods, residents chose to commemorate rabbinic figures rather than to embrace the ethos of national revival. Street names in Orthodox neighborhoods continued the practices of commemoration previously inscribed in dedication tablets.[104] When an updated city map was published, the street names in Jewish neighborhoods drew scathing criticism from Zionist writers. "One can hardly find among the streets of the capital any streets named after the founders of the [Jewish] national movement or the creators of Hebrew national literature and thought," protested *Davar* in 1939.[105] Jewish neighborhoods were filled with "petty" names of local rabbis, "Jews whose only claim was that they lived in Jerusalem recently." *Davar*, which claimed to be a secular and socialist newspaper, condemned the "disgusting" mix of sacred and profane. How could these unremarkable local figures be honored alongside "hallowed names in the chronicles of the [Jewish] nation, the names of patriarchs and prophets"?

The Zionist desire to rewrite the landscape of Palestine relied crucially on Hebrew as a tool for appropriation and reinterpretation. Zionist leaders and activists lobbied hard, from the beginning of the Mandate, for Hebrew signs in train stations, government offices, and public services. Their efforts aimed not only to make Hebrew visible in public space but also to claim that space. In the 1920s and 1930s the streets of Jerusalem became saturated with Hebrew of new kinds: commercial signs for shops and advertisements, signs of Zionist institutions, political notices, and street names. This new visibility challenged, and would later displace, Arabic. But it also challenged and reconstituted the Hebrew language itself. Hebrew, the medium of Jewish communality, was remade into a territorial language and a language that could claim territory.

It was at the holiest Jewish site in Jerusalem, the Western Wall, that the Zionist revolution of the twentieth century paradoxically demanded the effacement of Hebrew. Hebrew pilgrims' graffiti, which in the nineteenth century had been a distinguishing feature of the wall, was banned and removed from the face of the stones and from Jewish cultural memory.

6 WALL

Hebrew Graffiti on the Western Wall

THE WESTERN WALL IS A TEXTUAL SITE. ITS VERY SANCTITY RELIES on a rabbinic text according to which the Divine Presence will never depart the Western Wall of the Temple destroyed by the Romans.[1] A section of the western supporting wall of the Temple Mount/Haram compound has been identified, since the sixteenth century, as the rabbinic "Western Wall."[2] Worship at the wall involves not only reading and reciting from prayer books but also, famously, scribbling prayers and wishes on little notes of paper and placing them in the crevices between the huge stones. In the twenty-first century this practice was extended to the internet: a host of websites provide a service by which prayer notes can be sent electronically to the wall, offering an opportunity to "email God."[3]

Yet for many centuries the wall, and other sacred sites in the vicinity of Jerusalem, witnessed another kind of textual production. Jewish pilgrims visiting the site wrote their Hebrew names on the stones in large, bold Hebrew letters, painted in red and black and sometimes chiseled deep into the stones. The Western Wall came under close scrutiny in 1929, when a dispute over Jewish practices at the wall escalated into a large-scale wave of anti-Zionist violence which shook Palestine profoundly, leaving more than two hundred dead. Following the disturbances, the Hebrew graffiti on the wall was perceived as a form of violence and was banned. The British authorities and Muslim and Jewish leaderships, while locked in a bitter conflict over the meaning of the site, agreed that writing on the wall was provocative, unlawful, and sacrilegious. It had to be stopped; pilgrims could not be allowed to leave Hebrew marks on the wall. Jewish, Muslim, and British officials wanted to preserve the wall intact, whether as a national monument, a sacred site, an antiquity, or a disputed ground.

The ban on graffiti was a break with a centuries-old practice. Although some inscriptions are still visible today, most were erased or faded away. They were similarly expunged from Jewish cultural memory: the extensive literature on the wall barely mentions the inscriptions. When the graffiti are mentioned, they are described as the product of a "strange custom" and a form of desecration.[4] The systematic erasure of the inscriptions from the face of the stones and from Jewish cultural memory coincided with the transformation of the Western Wall from a site of popular worship to a national monument and a battleground. Yet on a deeper level, the erasure of the graffiti indicated a shift in attitudes toward writing and materiality. Writing was no longer perceived as a material medium, embedded within its surroundings and objects. Text was increasingly thought of as immaterial in essence: a supplement that is always already detached from its material context, and whose attachment to objects and sites could dangerously transform them. Nowhere, it seems, was this transformation sharper than in attitudes toward graffiti.

THE WALL AND TOMBS: EARLY MENTIONS OF GRAFFITI

The devotional custom of inscribing name graffiti in Hebrew in holy sites dates back to antiquity.[5] Its origins may be related to the Greek practice of *proskynemata*, a form of religious adoration which involved inscribing one's name, alongside formulas of blessing, in holy temples and tombs. Some see the inscriptions as an epigraphic substitute for the worshipper's presence before the god.[6] In the Temple Mount/Haram and its vicinity twelve ancient Hebrew inscriptions of Jewish names were found, engraved or painted in red and black colors. They are believed to date to the early period of Muslim rule (the eighth and ninth centuries) and perhaps earlier.[7] The custom of inscribing names was documented by Benjamin of Tudela, the Jewish traveler from Iberia who visited Jerusalem in the year 1170 and described several sites of Jewish pilgrimage in the vicinity of the Temple Mount, including "the pool used by the priests be-

FIGURE 34. Worshippers and graffiti at the Western Wall, Jerusalem, early twentieth century.
Source: Library of Congress, Matson Collection, American Colony photographers.

fore offering their sacrifices . . . and the Jews coming thither write their names upon the wall."[8] Such graffiti were a common practice of Jewish, Christian, and Muslim pilgrims.[9] Houses of Jerusalemites who went on Hajj pilgrimage were decorated with graffiti, as recorded in 1876: "Poems, proverbs, and verses in Arabic language and script are engraved or painted in many colors on the doors of Ishmaelites who went to Mecca, and there are many such doors."[10]

The inscription of Hebrew names was most commonly practiced as part of the pilgrimage to sacred tombs attributed to biblical and rabbinic figures. These tombs were the primary sites of Jewish sacred geography of the Holy Land. Benjamin of Tudela recounts that close to Bethlehem "is the pillar of Rachel's grave. . . . Upon it is a cupola resting on four columns, and all the Jews that pass by carve their names upon the stones of the pillar."[11] An eighteenth-century Jewish traveler wrote of his visit to Jerusalem and its environs: "And every prophet [tomb] that we visited, we prayed, and read the prophecies

FIGURE 35. A Hebrew name chiseled deep into the wall, and still visible today.
Source: Yair Wallach.

of the prophet, and wrote our name on the stones."[12] Jerusalemite Jews mention in their memoirs that the custom was still practiced in the early decades of the twentieth century at the tombs of Samuel and Rachel near Jerusalem.[13] According to a Zionist geographer, many tombstones were covered with names, some written in pencil or ink and some carved with a chisel.[14]

The extension to the Western Wall of a custom related to sacred tombs is less surprising when the wall is considered as a site of mourning. The wall was perceived by many as a tactile embodiment of the destruction of the Temple. Jewish mourning customs, such as the tearing of men's shirts (customary after the death of an immediate family member) and the lighting of oil lamps, were practiced here regularly.[15] Christian European travelers, who visited the site in the nineteenth century and witnessed the practices of lamentation, dubbed it the "Wailing Wall." The wall functioned within the Jewish sacred geography as a tombstone of a kind, a remnant of the cataclysmic ruin which marked Judaism as a religion of exile: Jews' exile from the Holy Land and God's exile from the world. For some Jewish visitors, it appeared as the tombstone of the Jewish people itself. "A large number of inscriptions cover the wall as if it was a burial stone—only the tombstone of a people could be covered with so many names," wrote a visitor in 1913.[16] It is precisely this notion that would later prove so revolting to Zionists.

NEW VISIBILITY

Until the nineteenth century, the wall was only one of several sacred Jewish sites in Jerusalem and its vicinity. Early modern pilgrims' itineraries included the wall as well as the Mount of Olives and the tombs of Zechariah, Huldah, King David, and other figures.[17] In the nineteenth century, however, the wall attracted growing attention worldwide. "I visited the thing most famous throughout the whole Diaspora, the Western Wall, a memorial for ancient times," wrote a visitor in 1838.[18] The reputation of the site was built not only in written descriptions, published in travel books and in the burgeoning Jewish press, but in visual representations. In the Jewish world the most familiar of these representations was a schematic depiction of the wall and the Temple Mount.[19] Not only was this image stylized in its naive use of straight lines and geometric forms, it was also totally imaginary: no vantage point provided such a frontal view of the wall from top to bottom. The wall was almost entirely hidden from view by the densely built Maghrebi neighborhood nearby. Only when visitors arrived at the alleyway alongside the wall could they see it towering above them. This schematic depiction conveyed the wall's perfection rather than its reality; this is the wall as it essentially "was," not as it was seen.[20] The schematic image was used on a variety of objects, from Sabbath tablecloths to Jewish marriage contracts. With the growth of the global Judaica market in the nineteenth century, the emblem of the wall was found on various devotional objects from Cochin to Algiers and became one of the most recognizable Jewish symbols. The growing Ashkenazi community in Jerusalem contributed to the proliferation of this emblematic motif by using it on a spectrum of textual artifacts that were sent yearly to potential donors overseas, such as postcards, calendars, and yearbooks.[21]

Along with this idealized image, more realistic with representations of the wall started appearing in the second half of the nineteenth century. Growing European interest in Palestine drew photographers and painters to Jerusalem, and the holy sites were the main topics of depiction. The Western Wall was

FIGURE 36. Schematic representations of the Western Wall: on a wine cup (top) (Poland, 1847); challah cover (bottom) (Jerusalem, 1928).
Source: The Gross Family Collection, Tel Aviv.

among the earliest sites to be captured by these European photographers. Taken from the perspective of the dead-end cobbled alley that ran by the wall, these images showed but a stretch of the wall and typically included a staged scene of Jews leaning on the stones, praying and lamenting. Such images were originally intended for Christian viewers, as they resonated with Christian notions of the ruin of the Jewish people and Palestine following the rejection of Christ. But owing to Jewish interest in the site, they became popular as well among Jewish audiences in paintings, photographs, and postcards. By focusing on the stones, emphasizing their immensity compared to human size, the images threw the inscriptions on the stones into sharp relief. Quite suddenly the names on the wall became visible to a wide audience outside Jerusalem and Palestine.

European painters were intrigued with the inscriptions, and they appear in several depictions of the wall. In *A Vow* (1898) the Orientalist painter Théodore Ralli portrayed a group of Jews at the Western Wall, marking an inscription on the stones. The Hebrew inscription, according to Ralli, proclaimed the innocence of Captain Dreyfus, who was fighting his wrongful indictment for treason: "May his innocence be proved."[22] Such an improbable political graffiti on the wall appears to be Ralli's invention: graffiti of protest slogans, in Arabic and in Hebrew, appeared in Jerusalem only in the 1930s. And yet it seems that for Ralli, and for his potential audience, such an explanation was more acceptable than the notion that Jewish pilgrims were inscribing their names in this holy site.

The Jewish-Austrian painter E. M. Lilien was similarly fascinated by the graffiti.[23] Lilien's etchings of the Western Wall (1913) made the inscriptions a striking and dominant feature of the stones, immediately discernible. In his depiction the letters are much more orderly and uniform than what is documented in contemporary photographs of the site. Lilien also decided to "add" his own name to the stones in both his etchings: "Efraim Moshe ben Yaʿakov ha-Cohen Lilyen" (Ephraim Moses son of Jacob Cohen Lilien). This can be read as homage to the inscriptions; had he found the custom sacrilegious, he surely would not have "added" his own name. But it is the location of the name on the bottom row of stones, in the bottom right corner of the etching, which betrays Lilien's intention; his "inscription" is in fact the artist's signature. Here, the textual economy of pilgrims' inscriptions intersects with an economy of artworks.

FIGURE 37. After Théodore Jacques Ralli, *A Vow* (1898). *Jews at the Wailing Wall in Jerusalem*, 1902, lithograph, newspaper print on newsprint, 22.5 × 28.1 cm.
Source: Jewish Museum Berlin, photo: Jens Ziehe.

A signature's function is to bestow upon the work of art an aura of authenticity and uniqueness. It represents a claim for individual authorship, and is intended for an audience who will be able to identify the work as the product of one person, the Artist. Behind the signature lies the modern artist's desire for recognition, which is translated into the exchange value of the artwork. Lilien's name set the value of the etching as a commodity in the art market. Through the signature, masked as inscription, the names on the wall were drawn into a new kind of Hebrew textual economy. Reproduced in the etching, they were torn from their material context and their original meaning, and circulated as fragments of writing in an artwork. In the capitalist art market, the original aura of the Hebrew script as sacred letters within a divine order was replaced by the aura of the individual master-artist and the possibility of converting it into hard cash, that is, commodity fetishism.[24] What had been a devotional inscription, uniquely located on the stones of the wall, became a textual fragment in an artistic composition, on an object made for exchange and reproduction. The growing visibility of Hebrew for commercial, Haskalah,

FIGURE 38. Etching of Jews praying at the wall, E. M. Lilien, 1910. The painter added his "signature" on the stones of the wall.
Source: National Library of Israel.

and later Zionist agendas dislodged the inscriptions from their unique context of pilgrimage practice and threatened their meaning and future. As text became free-flowing and transitory, it also became flattened, two-dimensional, and abstract, a detached referent that can be affixed to real objects.[25]

These paintings captured a crucial transition point for the writings on the wall. The notion of devotional inscription suddenly appeared strange, unusual, and requiring explanation. In the twentieth century the inscriptions were perceived as something which was distinct from the wall and foreign to it; something which was imposed upon the stones; the product of modern subjectivity, inscribing itself on a public holy site, and therefore a form of vandalism, or violence. This was closely connected to new ways of looking at graffiti.

MODERN GRAFFITI

In the late nineteenth century, Jewish pilgrims were not the only people writing their names in ancient sites in the Middle East. As increasing numbers of European tourists traveled to the Mediterranean and the Levant, many of them chose to write their names on the ancient ruins they visited. In the Great Pyramid of Giza and the Temple of Baalbek, one could see hundreds and even thousands of name inscriptions in the Latin alphabet left by European and North American tourists. The custom became an indispensable part of the trip to the region, so much so that in 1892 a guide working for Cook travel agents reassured tourists that when visiting Egyptian temples they would have sufficient time to carve their names.[26] Some wrote their names in charcoal, in pencil, or in paint. Others carved deep into the stone of ancient columns, spending hours and perhaps even days to leave their mark behind. Some reported on the act of writing in their journals or published accounts.

Fascinated with the grand ruins of ancient empires, visitors used graffiti to record their presence at the sites and associate themselves with past grandeur. The Western empires of the time saw themselves as modern-day inheritors of the classical civilizations of Egypt, Greece, and Rome, and they shipped monuments and artifacts of these civilizations to the museums of Paris and London. Individual visitors similarly associated themselves with these celebrated ancient cultures by marking their names on the walls. The French writer and politician Chateaubriand, who only saw the pyramids from afar, instructed a friend "on the first opportunity, to inscribe my name, according to custom, on these prodigious tombs; for I like to fulfil all the little duties of a pious traveller."[27] This was a ritual of a sort in the new religion of Western colonialism. The writing immortalized a sense of "discovery" which constituted the ruins as abandoned and neglected, to be claimed by European visitors. Local people, who lived around and sometimes amid the ruins, were ignored and their connection to these sites denied. Middle Eastern societies were seen as unconnected to the ancient civilizations and unworthy of their grandeur; it was the European writers who had the right to claim them.

In the second half of the nineteenth century, writers started to disapprove of the custom of graffiti. This may have been related to the fact that overseas travel was no longer the privilege of the aristocracy. With the regular steamboats and new rail connections, members of the middle class could afford to see the splendors of the Temple of Baalbek and to visit Jerusalem. With thousands of Western names inscribed on the pyramids, including advertisements for small businesses in Paris, the custom appeared tasteless to critics of high culture. Gustav Flaubert, on his visit to the Orient in 1849–50, was fascinated with the "stupid stupidity" of the graffiti and described them in much detail. Flaubert himself refused to write his name in any of the sites he visited. In Alexandria he encountered the name "Thompson of Sunderland" written in letters six feet tall on Pompey's Pillar. "You cannot see the column without seeing the name of Thompson, and therefore without thinking of Thompson. This idiot has become part of the monument and it is perpetuated with him. . . . Is it not very powerful to compel future travelers to think of you and to remember you? All the idiots are more or less Thompson of Sunderland. . . . When traveling, one meets plenty of them."[28] Flaubert saw the writing of one's name as a vulgar and violent act, similar to leaving "love bites on prostitutes."[29]

It is this view of graffiti as something born in crude instinct, an "impulsive" act, which in the twentieth century would establish it as a forbidden form of writing. Literature on graffiti typically reads it through modern Eurocentric lenses as a raw, unfiltered form of communication which is more truthful and immediate than other forms of text. Graffiti is said to be "driven by emotions and often spontaneously made," conveys intensity and controversy, and challenges hegemony and conventional social relations.[30] As a "dialogical" form of writing, graffiti is seen to invoke the power of the voice of the marginalized. But the notions habitually associated with graffiti—territory marking, transgression, defacement, individual expression—need to be critically examined. As scholars have shown in a variety of contexts, before the twentieth century, graffiti was not only widely practiced but also sanctioned in ways that are foreign and troubling to modern categories of public space and writing.[31]

For Jewish pilgrims, inscribing their name on the stones of the Western Wall and on sacred tombs was a devotional practice which carried a different meaning altogether from the inscription of names by Western tourists in the ruins of the Orient. This becomes apparent when we consider the choice of language, the meaning of names, and the inscriptions' locations. For the pilgrims, Hebrew was first and foremost a sacred language. None of the inscribers used it for everyday speech. Using a Hebrew name was an act meaningful only within the Jewish communal world; people typically used different renderings of their names in dealings with non-Jews. The inscriptions should be seen as a communal praxis rather than individualist affirmation. The product of a socially constituted subjectivity, the Hebrew inscriptions were not an attempt to distinguish the individual from the social context of the congregation but rather to imagine the individual embedded within this context, one name among many others on the stones.

To show the ways in which commemoration for devout Jewish pilgrims differed from contemporary notions, it is worth considering the eerie locations in which pilgrims chose to inscribe their names. Not only were these holy sites, laden with sanctity; for the pilgrims, these were their ancestors' graves. One of the most revered pilgrimage sites in Jerusalem at the turn of the century was the Tomb of Zechariah, below the Mount of Olives and the Jewish cemetery there. The ancient Roman tomb, attributed to the great priest of the First Temple, was surrounded by scores of recent Jewish gravestones, with Hebrew names and Jewish year of expiry engraved on them. There was an uncanny resemblance between the pilgrims' graffiti and the epitaphs. Today, writing one's name in a cemetery would be seen as a strange act of desecration. But for the visitors it was an act of worship. The pilgrims inscribed their names in veneration of the buried saints and prophets, not to disrespect them. Both inscriptions and epitaphs served to write the inscribers into the metaphorical "Book of Life," the heavenly tablets on which the names of the righteous were noted.[32]

ZIONISTS AND THE WALL

"We have been to the Wailing Wall. Any deep emotion is rendered impossible by the hideous, miserable, scrambling beggary pervading the place."[33] In these words Theodor Herzl, the founding figure of the Zionist movement, described his 1898 visit to the wall in his diary. Herzl's comments capture the deep Zionist ambivalence toward the site. By the late nineteenth century, the wall was deemed the holiest Jewish site of worship. Zionists visiting the wall were caught between the obligatory expectations to feel "deep emotion" and the actual sense of alienation from the place and its practices. This alienation, expressed through complaints about the squalor of the site and its miserable-looking visitors, hid a much more profound ideological anxiety. Zionism, as the modern Jewish national movement calling for a return to Zion, wanted to reclaim the wall. Zionist leaders called to "redeem" this site by purchasing the land and houses in its vicinity, paving a plaza for worshippers, and cleansing it of beggars.[34] They sought to transform it into a monument of national revival. But the wall, as a remnant of the destroyed Temple, was a symbol of ruin, and nothing could change that fact. The wall was a constant reminder of God's exile from its people, an exile that no modern "ingathering of the Diasporas" could overcome. Strikingly, the wall is absent from early Zionist iconography and appears (if at all) as a symbol of ruin, contrasted with symbols of Zionist revival such as the Bezalel Art School.[35] Even if Zionists were able to take over the site and shape it for their national agenda, it would still remain a memorial of destruction. This simple and insurmountable contradiction has never ceased to haunt the Zionist engagement with the wall.

Accounts by Zionists of their visits to the wall followed a recurrent pattern.[36] The visitors wander through a maze of Oriental alleyways, dense and dark, full of strange noises and unpleasant smells. The disconcerting journey ends abruptly when the visitors turn a corner and find themselves facing the wall. The giant stones rise up to the sky, towering over them. On the narrow pavement in front of the wall the visitors encounter their "brethren." Ragged and poor, these local Jews are a strange mishmash of clothes, colors, and languages. "Their haggard faces, their outlandish gestures, and their bizarre clothes . . . ," lamented the great Zionist critic Ahad Haʿam in 1891: "These stones are witness to the destruction of our land, and these men—to the destruction of our people."[37] Engrossed in their prayers, immersed in the rituals of reciting, the worshippers cry and wail. Compared to them, Zionist visitors appear awkward and uncomfortable, painfully aware of their own otherness at this strange site, and of their lack of emotions. They express frustration at the beggars, the squalor—and what they perceive as an indulgent ritual of mourning. In some cases the indignation leads to loud arguments, or even to a brawl.[38] The Orientalist descriptions of the site as neglected and the worshippers as primitive and over-emotional justified the desire for a violent appropriation that would not only restore the "dignity" of the wall but change its very essence.

Dr. Yosef Klausner's report on his visit to the wall belongs to this genre. Klausner, a Zionist scholar and writer from Odessa, visited Jerusalem in 1912 as part of his journey in Palestine. In his published travel journal, *The Resurrection of a People and a Land*, he devoted a long section to the wall.

> This is "the Jews' mourning site." A great crowd is gathered here, men and women and children. At first I cannot distinguish between the different types and the colorful attires. My eyes are fixed on the wall: stones immense beyond measure. On the stones names of Hebrew men and women are written in square Hebrew script, and between the stones nails are driven into the stones as "talismans"—a desecration without parallel in the whole world: even the greatest national sanctity is used in our midst as talismans for livelihood and childbearing.[39]

Klausner mentions the graffiti together with the "talismanic" custom of driving nails between the stones, which he condemns as "desecration" of the worst kind. He was not the first to voice disapproval of these popular customs. Already at the turn of the century, modernizing Ashkenazi voices in Jerusalem criticized what they saw as superstitious practices.[40] While their reasoning was rooted in Jewish religious law, for Klausner the issue was a national one. The wall was a site of the "greatest national sanctity": it was a material manifestation of the Jewish people's spiritual essence. The Jewish encounter with the wall, in Klausner's description, represented in crystallized form the union of the people of Israel (spirit) and the Land of Israel (matter). The nails and graffiti, through their unabashed physical interaction with the stones, threatened to corrupt the wall's status as pure substance and thus impinged on the purity of the encounter. Klausner's account is built on a negative dialectic between writing—supplementary and degenerate by nature—and the stones as absolute matter. Interestingly, unlike other Zionist visitors, Klausner was not enraged by the mourning rituals and the role of the wall as metaphoric tombstone; while other commentators expressed outrage and despair toward the unwillingness of the lamenters to rebel against Jewish destiny, he was willing to accept the wailing (albeit temporarily) as befitting a nation awaiting redemption.

> Burning oil lamps are placed between the stones. Nothing else is there. It is precisely because "nothing else is there," because of the plainness of this "wall," because of its "crudeness" so to speak, [that the wall] makes all my heart's veins tremble. This is all there's left—crude and cold stones. . . .
>
> And Jewish men and women stand and kiss these stones, weep and pray in front of these stones. There is no order and no discipline . . . some shout out and others pray in a whisper, some are sobbing and others are watching, as silent as the stones. And it is this disorder—strangely enough—which has a great effect on me. Had this been a sacred place of another people, they would have built a wonderful church or monastery here, and the priests or monks would monitor the worship of God according to fixed regulations and a correct order—and the people would stand respectful but completely passive. Would this become the spirit of the Jews . . . each and every one of them sometimes rabbi, sometimes priest? Crude stones without decorations, and prayers and weeping without order—how becoming a nation exiled and ruined![41]

"Crude stones without decorations," writes Klausner, forgetting the Hebrew inscriptions which he just mentioned. For Klausner, the inscriptions did not belong to the site. He did not see them as a sign of Jewish veneration but as a supplementary layer which disrupted the true essence of the wall, its crude simplicity, its purity.

GENDERED ENCOUNTER

Klausner is confronted at the wall with a powerful experience he is struggling to come to terms with. The unease is palpable here in almost every sentence. The chaotic atmosphere, the tactile and emotional veneration, the crudeness of it all—all these have to be turned on their head, in his account, to be rendered justified and appropriate.

> And Jewish men and women approach the wall, kissing each and every stone. . . . I see this and want to do the same, but on my lips the kisses had frozen. How

can I kiss cold stones? The wall is not really a remnant of the Temple, it is only a remnant of the wall that encircled the Temple. And the Temple itself with its ritual sacrifices—how distant it is from me! Am I a fetishist, kissing stones?

But here I see a young Jew from the Caucasus, dressed in the attire of mountain people, strong-bodied and erect[. He] approaches the wall, bends his erect stature, immerses his head in the hard stones as in a mother's bosom, and sobs in tears.[42]

The most difficult aspect of the experience for Klausner is the direct, "fetishist" contact with the wall. Here, the gendered language he uses is telling.[43] For although Klausner talks throughout about "Jewish men and women," when he comes to describe in detail the people touching the wall they are only men; not a single woman is mentioned, not even his wife, who was at the wall with him. The "strong-bodied" men kiss the wall, caress it, immerse their head in its bosom, and they weep. In front of our very eyes, the wall has become a woman. And when Klausner overcomes his inhibitions, his physical encounter with the wall is described in undisguisable terms:

> The wall is changing in front of my eyes. . . . The stones of the wall are no longer cold, but warm as the tears that poured on them for two thousand years. No, the [stones] are no longer dry, but wet with the blood of a great nation weeping its fate. . . . I pushed my way forcefully through the throngs gathered at the wall, and laid my two hands on the largest two stones I could find . . . and suddenly I felt a great and fresh force flowing from the stones and sweeping into my inner soul. And in that very moment I felt that my abstract belief, that in the past we had a Jewish state, and my abstract hope, that in the future we shall have a Jewish state, become strong as iron. And in that second I realized what great power materiality holds. For the Books of Chronicles, and even the whole Bible itself—they are nothing but scriptures, not substance, not a real object. These stones are a tactile presence, absolute reality and existence, which cannot be doubted. Therefore they are more than dead stones: they are living documents of what had been; and in their tactility they strengthen the hope and faith in what will *be*, what must *be*. No, the people are not wrong in worshipping and adoring these dead stones. Neither dead nor stones are they, but *a living and speaking soul*. The people's soul is embedded in them and speaks from within them—and it is his own soul that he adores and worships in them. . . . Purified and soothed I left the wall.[44]

The male nation of Israel is pouring its soul into the effeminate wall. Through this physical intercourse it regains its own masculinity while breathing life into the wall, turning absolute matter into spirit. This is Klausner's way of validating the popular worship of tactile substance, worship which, so it seems, is born out of a crude and primitive instinct. Klausner's approval of popular customs is qualified and has to be won through argumentation. Throughout one can sense his deep disquiet toward the physicality of the site. The materiality of the wall has to be justified, worked through, and—ultimately—transcended.

Instructive is his contrast between books, which are "nothing but scriptures, not substance, not a real object"—and the stones of the wall. This motif runs through many Zionist accounts of visits to the wall, where the disintegrating Jewish prayer books are compared unfavorably with the wall and its mighty stones.[45] The "immateriality" of scriptures is seen as emblematic of the displaced, transitory, and effeminate Jew. In Zionist discourse, Diaspora Jewish men were described as over-intellectual, bookish, and weak. The reinvention of the Jewish people demanded and depended on the creation of a rooted and invigorated masculinity.[46] From the books, Jews were to return to the soil. In the case of the wall, this demanded putting aside the prayer books and embracing the hard stones. This contrast between books and stones was based on a view of text as abstract, detached, and immaterial. Yet the writing on the wall could not be described in the same way. Its material presence could not be reduced or abstracted, and this is why it caused offense. The modern revulsion at graffiti is rooted in the awareness of its bold material presence. "It is, indeed, the visible placement of modern graffiti that constitutes its scandal as a form of writing that, exceptionally, is understood to be filling space."[47] The writing, like the nails, left an unapologetic mark on the wall, a mark which established the wall's materiality and could not be transcended and discarded—unlike Klausner's encounter with the wall, in which physical intercourse is tolerated only as leading toward a spiritual union.

THE "WAILING WALL RIOTS"

Klausner's visit at the wall left indelible marks on him. In the late 1920s, as tensions built up around Jewish and Muslim practices at the wall and in its vicinity, Klausner returned to the wall to play a part in the escalating conflict over the site. As the number of visitors increased, and practices began to resemble those of an open-air synagogue, Arab Palestinians viewed Jewish presence as a Zionist attempt to take over a strategic location, as a stepping-stone toward the Dome of the Rock. British restrictions on Jewish prayers caused an outcry in the Hebrew press, and Klausner was among the loudest protesters. By now he was professor of Hebrew literature at the Hebrew University and a fellow traveler of the Zionist Revisionist right wing. Outraged by what he saw as the Zionist leadership's weakness in the face of the violation of Jewish rights at the site, in August 1929 Klausner launched the Pro-Western Wall Committee (*Ha-Va'ad le-ma'an ha-Kotel ha-Ma'aravi*). Its first meeting took place during the first nine days of the Jewish month of Av, in which the destruction of the Temple is commemorated. Chapters of the committee were set up throughout Palestine, and public meetings held. The sensational daily newspaper *Do'ar ha-Yom*, edited by militant Revisionists, championed the campaign to "restore" Jewish rights at the wall and published dramatic stories on the Pro-Western Wall Committee and its activities. The committee's public call was posted in Jerusalem's streets and printed on *Do'ar ha-Yom*'s front page.[48] The manifesto invoked Klausner's earlier descriptions of the site: "The Wall had long become the bosom of a compassionate mother, for the sons exiled from the table of their father," it proclaimed. The stoic silence of the sacred stones spoke "more than thousands of books." In 1912, Klausner was primarily occupied with the failure of Jews to embrace the national mission. But this time, the obstacle to purification and transformation of the wall was not internal but external. In 1929, it was the Arab foe who prevented Jews from restoring their ancient greatness. The Arabs had oppressed Jews and "stolen" all the Jewish holy sites. "Almost the entire sacred inheritance has been taken over by strangers." Speaking the language of blood and tears, the manifesto called upon Jews in Palestine not to rest silent until triumph comes and "the entire wall is restored to us." On the eve of the ninth of Av, the fast day commemorating the Temple's destruction, Klausner spoke before thousands in a central synagogue in Jerusalem. He evoked the role of the wall as the chain linking the people of Israel and its land. His talk was followed by a mass procession to the wall, where further speeches were made. The next day, the 15th of August, inspired by this example, hundreds of Revisionist youths marched from the Lämel School to the wall and, for the first time, sang the Zionist anthem at the site.[49] This event, which delighted many Jews and infuriated many Arabs, was widely seen as a crucial moment in the escalation later known as the 1929 Disturbances (*Me'or'aot Tarpat* in Hebrew), the Wailing Wall Riots, or the Buraq Uprising (*Thawrat al-Buraq* in Arabic).

The 1929 events are often described as a watershed in the Zionist-Palestinian conflict. The wave of violence was generally understood as directed against Zionism. But it was non-Zionist Jewish communities, in Hebron, Safed, and elsewhere, that suffered the highest numbers of casualties. In the aftermath of the violence, these local Jewish communities coalesced around the Zionist leadership, leading to the consolidation of the Jewish-Zionist society in Palestine, distinct and separate from the Arab majority society.[50] Among Palestine's Jews, the Zionist interpretation of Jewish identity, history, and geography in Palestine became hegemonic.

From the Arabs' perspective, the 1929 riots were triggered by concerns about Zionist intentions to take over Palestine's Islamic holy sites. The contestation over the Western Wall was seen as the first step in a Zionist plan to rebuild Solomon's Temple on the Haram. Muslim pamphlets reproduced Jewish pictorial representations of the Haram/Temple Mount, which appeared on artifacts such as Jewish New Year's greeting cards and tabernacle decorations. Hebrew captions and biblical verses on these depictions were key evidence of the Zionist desire to transform the Dome of the Rock into a Jewish temple.

These pictorials were discussed at great length at the Shaw Commission, which was appointed by the British to investigate the 1929 "disturbances."[51] As Daniel Monk shows, the commission's deliberations strangely resembled exchanges in art criticism, addressing the question of the meaning of architecture, inscriptions, and representations—much to the bafflement of those involved in the discussions.[52] For Monk, this moment epitomizes the manner in which sacred architecture in Palestine/Israel is mistakenly understood to be self-evident, in what he calls "the cult of the concrete symbol."[53]

A central piece of evidence, Exhibit 69(b), was a *mizrach*, a wall pictorial placed in Jewish homes facing in the direction of Jerusalem to indicate the direction of prayer, produced by the Iranian-born Jerusalemite artist Moshe ben Yitzhak Mizrahi in 1925.[54] The mizrach depicted Isaac's sacrifice, the Western Wall, holy tombs, and at the top, the Dome of the Rock, under the title "Site of the Temple" (*Mekom Mikdash*). What was most ominous about the image was the "replacement" of the Qur'anic inscription on the dome with a Hebrew biblical verse from Isaiah (56:7): "Even them will I bring to my holy mountain, and make them joyful in my house of prayer: their burnt offerings and their sacrifices *shall be* accepted upon mine altar."[55] One Arab witness stated that "the mere existence of the Hebrew inscription in a place where there have always been quotations from the Koran is offensive to Muslim feelings."[56] Hajj Amin al-Husayni, Grand Mufti of Jerusalem and the ascending leader of Arab Palestine, stressed that this image caused "the greatest anxiety and concern. . . . This is a description of what the Zionists intend to do in regard to our Holy Places."[57]

As Monk observes, the underlying question was "In what way does writing signify?"[58] For the Arab side, the Hebrew inscription was a supplement that by "replacing" the Arabic verse had the power to alter the monument's very meaning. Such a reading depended crucially on the fluidity and immateriality of modern text. It was text's abstractness and detachability which made it possible for Hebrew to displace Arabic and, in an almost magical manner, transform a Muslim site into a Jewish one. This response betrayed anxiety about the instability of architectural meaning. It was as if the dome depended on its external Arabic inscriptions to define it. Their embeddedness within the ceramic skin of the building was no reassurance. As text, they were now always in danger of removal and "replacement," even if only symbolically.

The Zionist attorneys were incredulous in the face of such a fetishist interpretation of the image. They argued that the *mizrach*, like other examples brought by the Arab side, were metaphoric representations, to be understood allegorically, not literally. References to the Temple were a millennia-old Jewish tradition—not a Zionist innovation. The *mizrach* in question belonged to a genre of naive Jewish depictions of Jerusalem's holy sites, including the dome, going back to the sixteenth century. As a local "Sephardic" Jew, the artist was not part of the Zionist establishment, and his motivation was commercial. The Hebrew inscription was simply a biblical verse, and its location in the composition was of no significance. Like the Arab reading of the inscription, the Zionist approach also understood text as transitive and immaterial, but it insisted that the artwork was an autonomous ritual object with no political implications regarding the dome itself. The Arab leaders' conspiratorial reading of the image as a literal plot exposed them as either "fanatics" or "liars."[59]

FIGURE 39. Lithograph of Isaac's sacrifice, featuring holy sites in Jerusalem, by Moshe ben Yitzhak Shah Mizrahi, 1925 (top). The Hebrew lettering on the Dome of the Rock (bottom) was discussed by the Shaw Commission investigating the 1929 violence.
Source: The Gross Family Collection, Tel Aviv.

But on cross-examination, the Zionist argument faltered. It became clear that, while there was a long history of Jewish depictions of the dome, prior to the 1920s these had never featured a Hebrew inscription "on" the building, where one would expect Arabic calligraphy. The Zionist witness struggled to explain how this innovation came about.[60] It appeared that the question of placement and replacement was, after all, meaningful.[61] The transitivity of the text, and its power to be written everywhere, was now an assumption which was shared by all: from local Jewish artists to the Arab Executive. And it was this fluidity of the text, on the one hand, and its power to remake space, on the other, which caused anxiety among all parties.

THE WALL UNDER INVESTIGATION

Following the riots, a special commission of the League of Nations was asked to determine the arrangements at the wall. The Jewish claims were submitted to the commission in the form of a lengthy memorandum, rich with historical references proving a Jewish connection to this site. It quoted Benjamin of Tudela's description that "the Jews coming thither write their names upon the wall." The writers of the memorandum elaborated:

> The writing of names on the wall is apparently a very ancient custom and was continued throughout the centuries. The writing was done not only by means of paint and ink, but also by incision on the face of the stones themselves, and there never was any objection, protest or difficulty met in the maintenance of this custom. . . . The fact that the Jews have during the centuries inscribed and incised their names on the stones and fixed these nails between the stones and in the stones is further proof that the Muslim authorities and inhabitants recognised the right of the Jews not only to visit the Western Wall and perform their prayers and devotions there, but also show otherwise the sacred veneration in which they hold it.[62]

For the Jewish attorneys, the writings on the wall had a clear role. They were evidence that the wall was a Jewish sacred site and refuted allegations that it was a holy Muslim site as well. The silence of the Muslim neighbors and authorities in the face of the inscriptions was interpreted as tacit acknowledgment of Jewish rights over the place. "We have never heard . . . of any Moslem, not even of one of those Moslems living close to the place, expressing the slightest offence at this practice," said David Yellin, head of the Jewish National Committee, in his concluding speech for the Jewish side before the commission.[63] While the Jewish side acknowledged that the pavement and the wall were formally owned by Muslims, it was adamant that in practice, the wall was undeniably Jewish. How else could such inscriptions be tolerated? The argument is predicated not just on the identity of the inscribers—Jewish pilgrims—but on the form of writing: "Hebrew inscriptions . . . painted in black and red in very large characters and visible to all."[64] The Hebrew graffiti were territorial marks: external signs that, once attached, defined and confirmed the meaning of the wall. Their content (pilgrims' names) was of little consequence. What mattered was their form—Hebrew script—which determined the nature of the contested site. Yellin mentioned that many of the inscriptions had been removed by means of chemical treatment shortly before the arrival of the commission, insinuating that this was a Muslim attempt to efface this crucial proof and deny Jewish rights at the wall.

However, the subject under discussion was not just ancient inscriptions but a custom that was still, in fact, in practice. And although the Jewish argument relied precisely on this point—that Jews had been marking this place continuously since the Middle Ages, without objection—it was also a source of unease felt by the Jewish attorneys. For if an ancient graffiti could be read as "sacred veneration," a recent one was more likely to be read as vandalism, which could severely undermine the Jewish position. How could Jews violate in such a crude manner their most sacred site? In his concluding speech, Yellin was keen to emphasize that "to our modern taste, such a practice is unseemly in a place held in sacred veneration, and even sixty years ago one of the Jerusalem Rabbis severely condemned it."[65]

The commission's task was to determine the "Status Quo," that is, the "existing" rights and practices of Jewish and Muslim worshippers at the wall. Yet the very concept of a "Status Quo" was dubious. British support for the Jewish National Home was rapidly altering the situation in Palestine in political, economic, and demographic terms, and the cultural meaning of these sacred sites was changing accordingly. Under such conditions, maintaining an "existing" balance between ethnic, national, and religious groups was impossible. In effect, the "Status Quo" was a discursive mechanism through which the British, Muslims, and Jews negotiated over contested sites while pretending to speak in the name of age-old traditions.

The Status Quo was a paradoxical concept: it alluded to a state of affairs which was already there, and therefore could be established (through a juridical, objective inquiry) and protected against change; yet, at the same time, it was something to be constantly produced through active intervention. Nowhere is this paradoxical nature more apparent than in the question of the inscriptions. If a custom of inscription is practiced at the Western Wall, what exactly is to be preserved as it is? The wall in its exact state—or the custom of inscription, which inevitably changed the site's appearance? The question perplexed the deputy district commissioner, Edward Keith-Roach, who eventually decided that any writing on the wall "would appear to violate the Antiquities Ordinance." Could these inscriptions be rubbed out, then? His answer was again in the negative, "because according to the Antiquities Ordinance it is illegal to deface ancient monuments."[66] Locked in the skin of the stones, the pilgrims' inscriptions shifted from defacement in one minute to antiquity in the next. What was clear, in any case, was that physical engagement with the wall, whether through writing or erasure, was against the law.

The final verdict of the League of Nations commission on the issue was unequivocal:

> It shall be held a matter of common interest to Muslims and Jews alike that the Western Wall should not be disfigured by having any engravings or inscriptions placed upon it or by having nails or similar objects driven into it, and also that the Pavement in front of the Wall should be kept clean and be properly respected by Muslims and Jews alike; it is herewith declared to be the Muslims' right and duty to have the Pavement cleaned and repaired if and when that is necessary, upon due notice being given to the Administration.[67]

Keeping the wall free from "disfiguring" engravings was presented as equivalent to keeping the pavement clean. Inscriptions were a form of squalor, and worse: a kind of symbolic violence that constituted a danger to the wall, and more widely to peace and order in Palestine.

BANNED INSCRIPTIONS

Following the recommendations of the commission, a new regime was established at the wall. Police presence, an official Jewish representative, and the attention of Muslim authorities ensured that anything related to the site was closely controlled and regulated. The wall was put under close surveillance; it could be experienced by visitors only through a set of sanctioned practices. Jews resented the prohibitions on prayer benches and blowing the *shofar* (ram's-horn trumpet) on the Jewish High Holidays. But the regulations also banned begging, driving nails into the crevices, and writing names on the stones.

The ban on inscriptions was enforced by the police, and when visitors continued to write their names, they were immediately reproached. In at least four cases pilgrims were arrested for writing on the wall, some of them charged in court. Rabbi Orenstein, who served as the wall's rabbi from 1930 to 1948, documented these incidents in his diary.[68] Orenstein did not object to the inscription ban. On the contrary, when the issue came up in a conversation with a British police officer:

> I explained to him that all the writings were inscribed or written before the wall was put under police and Jewish supervision. Today the police maintain strict control regarding the writing on the wall, and the Jews are even stricter, because Jewish law prohibits writing and inscribing on the wall, which is sacred to us . . . I myself and the *shamash* [attendant] Mr. Meyuhas are very strict and careful with regard to writing on the wall.[69]

A special announcement published by the chief rabbis on proper conduct at the wall listed forms of undesirable behavior, including "any writing and drawing."[70] What had been described a few years earlier, before the League of Nations commission, as a "very ancient custom" which was maintained continuously throughout the centuries without "any objection, protest or difficulty" now appeared to the mainstream Jewish rabbinic authority as disrespectful and sacrilegious, akin to other forms of improper behavior mentioned in the notice: arriving on motorcycles, bringing pets, dressing immodestly, and taking photographs on Jewish holidays. For the chief rabbis, no less than the British policemen or the League of Nations commission, writing on the wall was simply a strange thing to do.

Interestingly, on this point we find rare agreement between all parties to the conflict. The Muslim authorities, represented by the Supreme Muslim Council, were equally hostile to the inscriptions. When the League of Nations commission tried to reach an agreed settlement over the arrangements at the wall, the Grand Mufti of Palestine, Hajj Amin al-Husayni, insisted that "it is a condition of the visit of the Jews that they will not disfigure the Wall by any engravings, signs, figures or inscriptions or notice boards or by nails or similar objects whatsoever."[71]

Rabbi Orenstein notes in his diary that Muslim officials protested several times over what they believed to be "new inscriptions on the Wall." In January 1943, when the head of the Muslim religious endowments noticed what, in his view, were recent inscriptions, he immediately contacted the police.[72] By this stage, any visible writing in Hebrew or Arabic was encroaching on the nature of this contested site. The Hebrew graffiti were cast as Zionist markers—and as such they were a menace. As the conflict escalated, this hermetic identification of Hebrew with Zionism became almost impossible to contest. The 1929 riots pushed non-Zionist Jews in Palestine, such as Rabbi Orenstein, to accept the hegemony of Zionist leadership. Similarly, the appearance of Hebrew language in urban space, and especially at a contested site such as the wall, could only be interpreted as a Zionist statement. Thus the Muslims fiercely objected to the emplacing of a first-aid sign in Hebrew and demanded its removal.[73] Arabic was similarly understood as a territorial stake; Orenstein was alarmed by the writing in Arabic on a gate, in which he thought he recognized "Qurʾanic verses."[74] The wall had become a battleground between two hostile communities, and text was first and foremost a weapon.

THE INSCRIPTIONS AND THE NOTES

A number of factors combined in the ban of the pilgrims' Hebrew inscriptions. The secularization of Hebrew destroyed their sacred aura. The circulation of realist representations of Jerusalem made them suddenly visible and on a global scale. In the new Hebrew textual economy, the inscriptions were inevitably destined to be seen as graffiti in a modern sense: improper self-commemoration, primitive talismans, territory marking, or simple acts of vandalism. This perception was shared by all sides involved in the struggle over the wall: British, Jews, and Muslims. Zionist wishes to make the wall into a national monument of revival, the British self-proclaimed mission in Palestine as custodians of the "Status Quo," and Muslim resolve to prevent the wall from becoming a Jewish-Zionist site all came together in a problematic engagement with the status of the wall as substance. From a site whose worship entailed tactile contact, through touching, inserting nails, and inscribing names, the wall became an architectural abstraction or a "concrete symbol."[75]

FIGURE 40. Police at the Western Wall, 1930s.
Source: Ze'ev Aleksandrowicz.

After the Israeli occupation of East Jerusalem in 1967, the Zionist desire to make the site into a national monument was finally achieved. Within days the entire Maghrebi Quarter was razed to the ground to make room for a huge plaza. Four more rows of stones were excavated in archaeological digs, thus making the wall much higher. The wall came to resemble its image in the schematic nineteenth-century emblem. From a hidden wall, seen only from close proximity, it became a site for state and military ceremonies. But the transformation did not resolve the basic contradictions embedded in the wall, and indeed has only served to accentuate them. Now much more than before, the wall's liminal position as a sharp border between Jews and Muslims, between ruin (the wall) and redemption (the unattainable Temple Mount), is rendered visible. The Temple Mount Faithful movement, calling for Israel to assert Jewish control of the Haram, grew from a fringe group to a mass movement with political backing. There were at least two attempts by militant groups to blow up the Islamic sites on the Haram.

It is interesting to compare the fate of the wall's graffiti with the fortunes of that other writing custom, the prayer notes. This custom was introduced to the wall by East European Jews in the nineteenth century as part of the Ashkenazi paper economy which included credit bills, a flourishing printing industry, and a constant stream of rabbinic notices posted around the city. Sephardic Jews, who did not practice placing notes in the wall, joked with their Muslim neighbors about the Ashkenazi "letters of petition" directed to the Almighty.[76] At the beginning of the twentieth century a modern-Orthodox scholar denounced the prayer notes along with the inscriptions, calling both "superstitious customs" and "a great sin against the sanctity of the place."[77] But by the 1930s the notes had become an established tradition which the Jewish guardians of the wall were resolved to uphold. Rabbi Orenstein recounted a number of incidents in which prayer notes were "desecrated" (thrown to the ground, torn, or burnt) by Muslims. Orenstein lodged a complaint with the police and "explained to the police commander how important the prayer notes are for Jews."[78] This tradition was vigorously reintroduced after 1967 and was firmly established as the Jewish custom of the wall par excellence. It is not difficult to see why the notes were allowed whereas the inscriptions were prohibited. The notes fit well with the perception of text as a supplement that can be attached and detached, but they remain temporary and concealed and hence represent no danger of actual engagement with the wall as substance.

The Hebrew wall graffiti were not the only textual practice of pilgrimage that came under close scrutiny during the British Mandate. Not far from the wall, ancient Islamic banners were guarded by their custodians. Once a year, on the annual pilgrimage to the shrine of Nabi Musa near Jericho, the holy banners were taken out and paraded publicly in mass processions, in what was the most important Islamic festival of the Jerusalem mountain range. After the British occupation of Jerusalem in 1917, colonial hopes and fears fixated on the embroidered banners at the heart of the festival. These velvet artifacts, which featured Arabic inscriptions, woven in gold thread, were sacred forms of text that had to be both respected and controlled. Much like the pilgrims' graffiti on the Western Wall, the inscriptions had become a textual menace, associated with uncontrollable violence; and paradoxically, at the same time, their power as fetish was in decline as Arab Palestinians sought new emblems around which to rally.

7 CLOTH

The Banners of Nabi Musa

THE CELEBRATIONS OF THE MUSLIM NABI MUSA FESTIVAL IN Jerusalem in 1918 were recorded in a short propaganda film titled *With the Crusaders in the Holy Land.*[1] The film shows Ronald Storrs, military governor of Jerusalem, in his headquarters receiving the holy banner of the prophet Musa (Moses), which stood at the center of the celebrations, from the mayor of Jerusalem. Storrs is then seen mounting the banner, embroidered with Arabic writing, onto a long staff. As the uniformed governor unfolds the banner, the writing becomes legible, declaiming, "There is no god but Allah." Storrs, son of a prominent Anglican minister, maintains a solemn face throughout this short ceremony. The camera moves on to what the film's titles describe as the "wild and weird dances . . . held by the natives en route." Yet the "weird" dances do not match the perplexing sight of a Christian official, one of the "Crusaders in the Holy Land," playing a ceremonial role in a Muslim ritual in the third holiest place to Islam.

The film was part of British war propaganda, which sought to capitalize on the occupation of Jerusalem to appeal to diverse global audiences, including Muslims in Algeria and India, whose contribution to the Allied war effort was vital. The ceremony of the banners was designed to illustrate Allied respect for Muslim customs and holy places—a recurrent theme in British propaganda material.[2]

Storrs's successor, Edward Keith-Roach, similarly presided over the ceremony of the banners, "proud as a peacock" as one Arab Jerusalemite recalled.[3] In his memoirs, *The Pasha of Jerusalem*, Keith-Roach described the annual ceremony:

> I was met at the principal entrance to the *Haram*, the "Gate of the Chain," by the *mufti*, the Supreme Muslim Council and the sheikhs of the mosque, surrounded by thousands of worshippers. The proceedings began with prayers, at the conclusion of which we marched in procession to the Muslim law courts. Green, gold, red and silver village banners, embroidered with texts from the Koran in brilliant colours, fluttered in the breeze. Each was followed by its own particular contingent of young and old, arms locked, bodies swaying in a joyous dance. One by one the banners were taken out of their bags, fastened to the great shafts and handed to me to deliver to the bearers. As I handed to each bearer his banner I bade him "to receive it and to bear it with honour and in peace." Then, having concluded our prayers to the one God, the great standard of the Prophet, of green silk embroidered with gold lettering, was ceremoniously presented, held aloft and carried into the mosque for the final prayers before being taken down to the tomb.[4]

Like the Hebrew graffiti on the Western Wall, the Nabi Musa banners were sacred textual objects of a centuries-old tradition. Under colonial rule they were cast in a new role: that of dangerous artifacts which could threaten public order. While the Hebrew graffiti threatened to rewrite the meaning of a contested holy site, the banners were mobile Arabic inscriptions which, by moving through space, rewrote its meaning. The graffiti and the banners became insurgent texts which introduced instability to the urban order by their very presence and therefore had to be regulated, controlled, and eventually, suppressed. In April 1920 the banners stood at the center of the first violent local demonstrations against Zionism and the British. Anxious about the embroidered banners' power to agitate and incite, the British expended considerable effort to monitor the ritual and supervise its banners as part of wider attempts to control the use of text in public space. Under British rule in Jerusalem, increasing limitations were imposed on the banners' display, culminating in the virtual house arrest of the ancient flags. The banners, perhaps more than any other instance of urban writing, were perceived by the

FIGURE 41. Edward Keith-Roach, British district commissioner officer, opening the Nabi Musa festival by handing the main banner to Muslim worshippers at the Gates of the Haram, 1941.
Source: Library of Congress, Matson Collection, American Colony photographers.

British as charged with explosive political-religious power that could easily turn crowds of worshippers into violent mobs.

But British regulation of the festival and its banners was not the only reason for the banners' eventual disappearance as a Palestinian political symbol. Like the inscriptions of Jewish pilgrims on the Western Wall, the decline of the Islamic banners also reflected internal changes in perception of the written word, whose sacred aura was facing challenges. The 1920 riots demonstrated the power of the banners as agitation props, but ironically they also exposed their weakness within the transforming Arab Palestinian society: namely, their inability to articulate the discourse of modern nationalism. In the fateful 1920 procession there appeared, alongside the embroidered banners, new symbols: portraits of modern leaders and the Arab national flag. The enthusiastic adoption of the Arab Flag as the undisputed national Palestinian emblem came at the expense of traditional textual symbols such as the Nabi Musa banners, reflecting the decline in the status of text as a privileged visual register. Here, once more, modernity demanded not only the introduction of new texts—signs, placards, advertisements—but also the suppression or marginalization of old textual forms.

THE PILGRIMAGE

The Nabi Musa pilgrimage (*mawsim*) was the main Muslim festival of the Jerusalem mountain range and one of the biggest religious celebrations in Palestine before 1948. Thousands of pilgrims from Jerusalem, Hebron, and Nablus and their hinterlands set out annually to the Nabi Musa shrine some twenty miles east of Jerusalem and close to Jericho, where, according to a medieval Muslim tradition, the prophet Musa (Moses) was buried. Jerusalem was the festival's official starting and ending point. The festival was established in the twelfth century, shortly after the Muslim recovery of Jerusalem from the Crusaders, to counter the presence of Christian pilgrims in the city during Easter. To coincide with the Easter festivities, the timing of the festival was determined according to the Christian calendar—unlike all other Islamic festivals, which are celebrated according to the lunar year. The festival was richly documented by participants and eyewitnesses, both local and foreign, as well as in films and photographs.[5] There is extensive scholarship dedicated to the pilgrimage, from early Arab Palestinian ethnography through Western accounts to recent critical literature.[6]

The sacred banners stood at the heart of the festival, and its rituals and proceedings were all organized around their movements, as reflected in the festival's terminology. The opening day, "the day of the banner's descent," took place one week before the Christian Good Friday. Notables and officials gathered near the Haram in a house where the Nabi Musa banner was kept. The custodians of the banner were the notable al-Husayni family, who had held prominent religious positions in the city since the eighteenth century and rose to political eminence in the nineteenth and twentieth centuries.[7] On that opening day the Nabi Musa banner was taken out and handed over on a plate to the Mufti. After reciting a prayer he would unfold the banner and fasten it to a long staff with a golden, ornamental metal "crescent" (*hilal*).[8]

The banner would then be paraded through the city on a ceremonial procession to the Haram; there it was joined by the three other most sacred banners of Jerusalem. The two banners of the Haram were taken out of their place of custody in the Dome of the Rock, while the banner of Nabi Da'ud (King

FIGURE 42. Banners in Nabi Musa celebrations: at the Haram al-Sharif, 1919 (top); Mufti Hajj Amin al-Husayni, riding with the banners out of Bab al-Asbat, in the very last festival he attended before fleeing Palestine, 1937 (bottom).
Source: Library of Congress, Matson Collection, American Colony photographers.

David) was carried by the Dajani family, the custodians of David's Tomb. The Haram was filled with crowds and notables from Jerusalem and its neighboring villages, carrying dozens of other banners. After a short ritual the procession would leave the city eastward. The Mufti rode ahead on a white horse, holding high the banner of Nabi Musa. Spectators in large numbers, including Christians and Jews, assembled to watch the procession and attended the lavish reception given by the mayor in a large tent outside the city walls.[9] After the reception the banners were folded, and the procession would continue toward the shrine, mounted or on foot.

At the same time, pilgrims from Nablus and Hebron would prepare to depart toward Jerusalem. Their sacred banners would be taken out of their respective places of custody and displayed in a ceremony termed "the banners' farewell."[10] Having arrived in Jerusalem they would tour the streets in a long procession, singing and dancing. Whimsical sword fights were performed to the amusement of the crowds. The pilgrims would then depart for the desert shrine east of Jerusalem.

When the procession approached the desert shrine of Nabi Musa, the banners would be unfurled and the banner-bearer would walk ahead followed by musicians, dancers, and lancers. Upon arrival at the shrine, the banner would be folded and then carefully placed on the prophet Musa's tomb.[11]

The festivities in the shrine lasted five days, after which the banners of all groups were taken back to Jerusalem. The procession would this time retrace its course into the walled city. The festival ended with a ceremony at the Haram al-Sharif on the Christian Good Friday, or "the Friday of the Banners," when the main banners were wrapped in a silken cloth and returned to their places of custody.[12]

THE BANNERS

The manifold banners of the festival stood for different sites and social groups—whole cities, villages, sacred sites, noble families, and religious groups. Within this great variety there was a clear hierarchy, reflected in their position in the processions and the order of their arrival at the Haram and the shrine. "It is a great honor to carry a banner in the procession," stressed one Hebron merchant who participated in the 1920 procession.[13] The exact position was open for negotiation, as attested by the usual skirmishes between the Nablus and Hebron pilgrims over leading the procession.[14] The leading role of the al-Husaynis, as the custodians of the chief banner, confirmed their ascending importance in the Jerusalem district. The order of flags probably reflected a historical power struggle within the Jerusalem nobility; it could be read as a complex map of the social order of the Ottoman district of Jerusalem.[15]

The rectangular velvet banners varied considerably in appearance and size.[16] The main banners consisted of one predominant color, and the text was inscribed in gold thread.[17] Some banners were centuries old: the Haram banners were made between the sixteenth and the eighteenth century.[18] The banners of villages and their Sufi fraternities were more colorful and consisted of a patchwork of shapes and colors, with inscriptions at their center.

The inscriptions on the banners were brief, of no more than a few lines. Most banners displayed the Muslim creed, abbreviated or with some variation. The main banner quoted the Qur'anic verse "and God spoke to Moses directly."[19] Texts on other banners featured the name of God, Muhammad, caliphs, Sufi saints, and prophets. These were generally short and standard phrases and names, many of which appeared on other artifacts and inscriptions and were familiar to pilgrims. Even those who had not mastered reading could recognize central formulaic elements such as the Islamic creed. Epigraphers referred to such texts somewhat condescendingly as "banal inscriptions," as standard formulas which did not contain information. But it was these simple texts which made the banners into holy relics, around which the entire festival was organized.

The fetishist power of the primary ritual objects of the festival was revealed not only in the terminology of the pilgrimage. Women would attach silk kerchiefs to the banners for brief moments and then cherish them as talismans for healing or good wishes.[20] This was "contact magic"—the belief that the power of the banner would remain in the possession of the believer. A related custom was to cut pieces of the tomb cover of Nabi Musa as a remedy or against the evil eye.[21] The ritualistic use of cloth, threads, and rags in veneration of saints and holy tombs was widespread in the Middle East and was not unique to Islam.[22] Iconographic banners were used by Greek Orthodox pilgrims in the Easter festivities in Jerusalem, to which Nabi Musa corresponded.[23] Jewish women would tie threads around Rachel's Tomb to bring the blessing of childbearing. It was the use of Arabic inscriptions, however, that made the Nabi Musa banners into sacred Islamic artifacts and placed them unmistakably within a Muslim tradition.

In Islamic tradition, banners are associated with the Prophet Muhammad and the banners used in his military campaigns. In the Nabi Musa festival, this military association resonated with the popular attribution of the festival to Saladin, who recovered Jerusalem from the hands of the Crusaders in 1187. The pilgrimage was in many ways an annual reenactment of that reconquest, with the Mufti making a ceremonial return at the end of the festival, mounted on a white horse and holding the banner of the prophet Musa. The Nabi Musa pilgrims' sword games in the streets of Jerusalem, and the gunshots on the departure and return of the procession, helped provide the semblance of a military campaign.

But the meaning of the banners also depended on their place within an Islamic textual economy of sacred shrines and tombs. Until the late nineteenth century, the public display of text in Arabic was most prominent in Islamic places of prayer, study, and worship, and perhaps most conspicuous in holy tombs. Unlike in Jerusalem, in the countryside Islamic inscriptions were rare. But at sacred tombs—the focal points of the rural saints-based religious practice—one could expect to encounter Arabic texts.[24] These took the form of stone inscriptions above the mausoleum's entrance, embroidered banners left by visitors, pilgrims' inscriptions in henna on the tomb's walls and the cenotaph, or woven inscriptions on the cloth tomb cover, the *sitara*, draping the whitewashed cenotaph.[25] These were not merely decorative elements; they signified the sanctity of the site and invested it with the power of the holy language. The banners of Nabi Musa were part of a system of textual artifacts, from stone inscriptions to cloth tomb covers, extending from Al-Haram al-Ibrahimi (the Cave of the Patriarchs) in Hebron, and the tomb of Nabi Yusuf in Nablus, through the Jerusalem Haram to the Nabi Musa shrine itself. The verse embroidered on the Hebron banner, "Abraham is Allah's friend," was also inscribed in stone inside the Gate of Hebron in Jerusalem (Bab al-Khalil, or Jaffa Gate in English)—the gate through which the Hebron pilgrims passed every year upon their arrival in the city. During the annual course of the pilgrimage the banners created a network of tactile connections between unique objects, sites, and communities through movement, display, and touch. Their texts constructed a regional narrative, centered on the Jerusalem mountain range and strongly anchored in the Islamic traditions of the biblical prophets. The main banners of the festival were all related to the "Israelite" prophets revered in the Qur'an: Ibrahim (Abraham), Yusuf (Joseph), Da'ud (David), and of course, Musa (Moses).

NABI MUSA'S POLITICAL SIGNIFICANCE: FROM THE OTTOMANS TO THE BRITISH

During the late-Ottoman period, the festival became an arena for competition between Ottoman officials appointed from Istanbul and the local Arab nobility. In 1911 the festival was the occasion of protests against the Ottoman *mutasarrif* (governor), who had granted secret permission to British archaeologists to survey the Haram in Jerusalem while the pilgrims were in the desert.[26] A political campaign, orchestrated by the Jerusalem nobility and the Jaffa-based (and Christian-owned) newspaper *Filastin*, objected to the sacrilege of European archaeologists digging surreptitiously near the Al-Aqsa Mosque. The campaign led to the removal of the *mutasarrif*. The episode can be seen as an early expression of Arab Palestinian nationalism, mobilizing an alliance which cut across confessional and class differences, and transcended the traditional affiliations of the Jerusalem region to include the coastal areas. Indeed, some scholars have argued that the Nabi Musa pilgrimage provided an early locus for Palestinian national identity.[27] But in the early twentieth century the festival was still firmly tied to its traditional geographic base of the Jerusalem mountain range, binding Jerusalem, Nablus, and Hebron and their rural hinterlands.[28]

During World War I, the Ottoman authorities used Islamic banners to agitate for the war, which was described as a jihad. The banner of the Prophet Muhammad was sent on a tour through the provinces, from Istanbul to Mecca, to rally support. On its arrival in Jerusalem the walled city was lit up and public decorations were hung for the occasion. But the spectacle did not create the hoped-for effects. Jerusalemite Muslim soldier Ihsan al-Turjeman documented the celebrations in his diary in a disillusioned and exasperated tone: "Victory arches were raised on top of Damascus Gate underneath the slogan 'Enter Egypt in Peace with the Will of God'!! The slogan was still hanging yesterday. But today the army decided to remove the banners as a result of public criticism."[29] By that point the Ottoman campaign against Egypt had already proved a dismal disaster.[30] More generally, Turjeman appears disenchanted with the propagandist use of such symbols by the Ottomans.[31] The power of sacred banners to induce fervor was limited. Turjeman's writing evinced a strong sense of civic cross-confessional solidarity, which engaged the young soldier much more than the display of the holy banner. In the same diary entry, he noted his outrage on seeing elderly Jews conscripted to serve as Jerusalem's street cleaners.

For the British who occupied the city in 1917, Nabi Musa soon became a pressing issue: a crossroads at which relations with the Muslim population, and its elite, would be tested and defined. The new governor of Jerusalem, Storrs, did not think too highly of the festival, describing it in his memoirs as "a blameless (if rather pointless) event, consisting of a week's hot sticky holiday by the Dead Sea, with mild feasting, booths of fruit and sweets, and shows ranging from an indelicate version of Punch and Judy to the circumcision of anxious little boys before a gaping assembly of proud relations."[32] Notwithstanding this patronizing view, Storrs was quick to recognize the political potential of the festival. As he noted in his memoirs, Nabi Musa was not only the apex of the Muslim year in Jerusalem; it was also the single occasion on which the city notables, headed by the Mufti and the mayor, were the chief figures in an official ceremony. "Both for them and for us the transition between the Ottoman and the British control of this festival was a delicate matter, for it marked too sharply, unless the Administration was prepared for a little give and take, the passing of thirteen hundred years' Islamic theocracy."[33]

Storrs was certainly ready for more than "a little give and take." In the name of the "Status Quo," he took on what he saw as the Ottoman governor's ceremonial role: receiving the sacred banners in his headquarters and, as shown in the film mentioned earlier, mounting them onto their staffs. He also attended the service on the Haram that opened the festival. To ensure that British participation in the ceremony would resemble the Ottoman legacy, he arranged for twenty-one-gun salutes from army cannons and a British Military Band to accompany the procession. When the British military authorities initially refused the request for a band, Storrs struggled hard to reverse their decision, soliciting a letter of "grave disappointment" from the Mufti of Jerusalem and later recruiting the High Commissioner to his cause.[34] Writing to Secretary of the Colonies Winston Churchill, Herbert Samuel stressed that "the matter is of greater importance than it may at first sight appear."[35] Samuel's argument was that the Ottoman Military Band used to play in these processions, and that continuing this tradition would be beneficial. It should be noted, however, that the Ottoman Military Band was in effect a municipal band, performing regularly in Jerusalem on Saturdays, Sundays, and holidays (including, after 1908, Jewish holidays).[36] Thus its participation in the festival was far less unusual than the odd appearance of the Yorkshire Military Band, which played no such municipal role. The Ottoman "tradition" was exaggerated and manipulated to position British officials at the center of an Islamic ceremony, and to enable them to present themselves as the protectors of the Muslim religion, thereby defusing Arab hostility toward British intentions in Palestine.[37]

But Storrs did not delude himself that the provision of a military band would be sufficient to appease Arab public opinion. The British were eager to reach an understanding with the local elite in order to contain and undermine Arab opposition to Zionism. The festival, led by the local aristocracy, was the perfect ground to negotiate such an alliance. This, in turn, significantly increased the political capital of the festival's main custodians, the al-Husayni family.

HAJJ AMIN AL-HUSAYNI

In April 1920 the festival became the scene of the first violent intercommunal confrontation between Arabs and Jews after the Balfour Declaration. Heated political speeches against the declaration, and the rumor of a Jewish provocation against one of the sacred banners, were followed by an outbreak of anti-Jewish violence. Despite some precautionary measures, the police were unprepared for disturbances of this magnitude. The riots lasted three days and left 5 Jews and 4 Arabs dead, and 216 Jews, 23 Arabs, and 7 British soldiers wounded.[38] The authorities reacted by dismissing the mayor, Musa Kazim al-Husayni, arresting Arab and Jewish "instigators," and appointing a commission of inquiry.

The April 1920 riots marked the earliest public appearance of a young political activist named Hajj Amin al-Husayni, who was to become the leader of the Arab Palestinians. One of the most controversial figures in the history of modern Palestine, Hajj Amin has had his fair share of biographies.[39] The British saw him as one of the prime instigators of the 1920 riots and sentenced him to ten years in prison in absentia. Hajj Amin escaped and was later pardoned by the High Commissioner. Hajj Amin invited Herbert Samuel to his home for a kosher dinner, and pledged his willingness to cooperate with the government.[40] The British concluded that the Husaynis had learned their lesson and could serve as valuable allies. In 1921 the family threw its weight into ensuring that the festival passed without an incident. Heavy British intervention secured the election of Hajj Amin as the Mufti of Jerusalem, elevated to the new role of Palestine's "Grand Mufti." The British also installed him as the lifelong president of the newly established Supreme Muslim Council (SMC), which was to oversee the management of Islamic endowments and courts. The establishment of the SMC reflected the British preference to think of Arabs in Palestine in sectarian terms rather than as a national community. The al-Husaynis, who had been dealt a blow with the loss of the mayorship of Jerusalem, found in the SMC a powerful tool to promote their political agenda within Arab society. By the 1930s Hajj Amin had become the leader of Arab Palestine.

The Nabi Musa festival became a yearly test of the Husaynis' ability to rein in the Palestinian public. They allowed, and no doubt encouraged, the turning of the Muslim festival into a national demonstration, manifesting their leadership of Arab Palestine. Songs celebrating the prophet Moses were replaced with praises to Hajj Amin and messages of defiance against Zionism and British colonialism.[41] Yet the Husaynis were also careful to prevent the festival from turning into a violent demonstration.[42] Despite escalating tensions, riots did not take place again during the festival, not even in the turbulent year of 1929. While Palestinian participants and observers remember the procession as an event of national defiance, the British could view it as an annual proof that their alliance with the Arab elite had successfully contained Arab Palestinian nationalism.[43]

Some historians portray Hajj Amin as an extremist who cleverly manipulated British support to unleash deadly violence against Jews and his Palestinian rivals.[44] Others, however, point to his role in mitigating Palestinian opposition to Zionism and the Mandate between 1921 and 1936. During this time, as the Mufti slowly built up his leadership, he largely refrained from direct confrontation with the Mandatory authorities. As usual with the historiography of Palestine/Israel, the discussion of the Mufti focuses on his role in the large outbreaks of political violence—the 1920 Nabi Musa riots, the 1929 Disturbances, and the 1936–1939 Arab Revolt. But another way to analyze his legacy is through his activities as the SMC president and specifically its flagship project in Jerusalem, the Palace Hotel.

This grand hotel was the largest building project undertaken by the central body of the Arab Palestinian national movement, and the Grand Mufti was closely involved with its construction. The building was located in the commercial heart of the city, bordering on the ancient Muslim cemetery of Mamilla. The project was conceived to serve international conferences planned by the SMC as part of the diplomatic campaign against Zionism. With Arab failure to persuade the British to withdraw their support for the Jewish National Home, the Mufti sought Muslim and Arab support outside the country.[45] The largest among these conferences was the Pan-Islamic Congress in December 1931, with delegations from twenty countries.[46] The Palace Hotel, which was built to host the delegates, was designed by the renowned Turkish architect Mimar Kemalettin. It was one of the last buildings outside Turkey to be built in Ottoman Revivalism style.[47] The hotel was constructed with modern methods of steel skeleton and reinforced concrete, but these were hidden behind a rich historicist ornamentation. The striking symmetrical facade was heavily embellished with Ottoman decorative patterns including balustrades, columns, and arches. The stylistic opulence was also reflected in the chosen name for the hotel, "Palace Hotel," displayed over the main entrance on a fanlike glass-and-iron entrance canopy. Despite being the most prestigious project of the Palestinian national leadership, the name bore no relation to Palestine or to Jerusalem and appeared only in English. Arabic was, however, visible in the large marble inscription crowning the building. It consisted of a quote from an Umayyad poet: "We shall build like our forefathers and act like they did."[48] Emplaced on a commercial building, the inscription was not a mere continuation of centuries-old Islamic writing practices. Rather, it articulated a self-conscious claim about heritage and its use in a contemporary political agenda.

The Palace Hotel, with its architecture and its marble inscription, clearly expressed Hajj Amin's claim to leadership in the language of aristocratic lineage and commitment to the Arab-Islamic legacy. It well captured the elite-led politics that he promoted, which aimed at high-level diplomacy rather than grassroots mobilization. Yet this proud statement of tradition and continuity concealed a very different picture. The Palace Hotel was in fact built by a Jewish contractor, who later installed secret microphones there in the service of the Zionist Hagana militia. The construction involved scandals of desecration of the ancient Arab cemetery nearby, as ancient skeletons were disposed of and the hotel sewage directed to cemetery.[49] The hotel was initially run by

FIGURE 43. Palace Hotel facade (built 1929). The Arabic inscription at the top of the building reads: "We shall build like our forefathers and act like they did."
Sources: (top) Library of Congress, Matson Collection, American Colony photographers; (bottom) Wikicommons.

a Jewish hotel operator who even tried to rename it as the "Allenby Palace Hotel."[50] The building project, which consumed half of the Supreme Muslim Council's budget for 1929 and almost brought it to bankruptcy, was made possible through the financial backing of the colonial government.[51] Rather than the embodiment of Islamic tradition, the SMC was in fact a government agency created by a European power as part of its divide-and-rule calculus.

The Palace Hotel played an important symbolic role in the early 1930s, when it hosted the first and second Arab Exhibitions. These fairs showcased the agricultural and industrial advancements taking place in the Arab world, and promoted a pan-Arab discourse of development that challenged the British and Zionist depictions of Palestine.[52] However, the Palace Hotel itself was a commercial failure and soon ceased operating. It became instead a government office building, and in 1937 it served the Palestine Royal Commission.[53] It was in this very building that the commission formed its plan to partition Palestine—to the complete dismay of Arab Palestinians.

The employment of Islamic traditional writing was an attempt to mask the SMC's uncomfortable reliance on the colonial government through a gesture toward the Islamic past, in a textual format which had already lost its immediacy. At the same time, the holy relics of the Nabi Musa festival were under increasing pressure from Mandatory authorities.

BRITISH CONTROL OF THE FESTIVAL

Following the 1920 riots, as Arab hostility toward the Mandate and Zionism became stronger, British supervision of the festival became increasingly stricter. The banners attracted special attention, as the 1920 riots demonstrated their power to stir the crowds. Police reports reveal the British authorities' anxiety about the banners; speaking of the banners as animated texts, moving around the city on their own, they adopted the fetishist language of the festival itself. The reports discuss the schedule in terms of the arrival and departure of the banners—not that of pilgrims. The British were determined to control the banners' display to the last detail. The exact location of the unfurling of the banners, usually a moment of excitement, had to be approved by the police, who now purported to have authoritative knowledge about the traditions of the festival.[54] Adamant not to allow any violation of the Status Quo, British officers now assumed the role of religious scholars who could decide what was and was not an organic part of the festivities. A request of the villagers of Baytunia to display their banner was refused by the deputy district commissioner on the ground that this was an "innovation."[55] Here once more the discursive mechanism of the Status Quo afforded the British means of political intervention; it gave them the power to shape and control the practice of "tradition."

The British were not only worried about the traditional embroidered flags. In the early years of the Mandate, the medium of words on cloth was adapted to new purposes. Banners painted with slogans emerged as a central medium of Arab political protest against Zionism and British policies. These banners were emplaced in the streets, hung from buildings, displayed at meetings and conferences, and carried by protesters in demonstrations (sometimes affixed to wooden frames). Slogans such as "We demand full independence" and "We oppose Zionism and Jewish immigration" appeared in joint Muslim-Christian protests on Jaffa Road as early as June 1919. These banners marked the emergence of Arabic as a national language, which claimed the streets of Jerusalem for an anticolonial agenda.[56]

By March 1920 the military authorities in Jerusalem banned Arab demonstrations and the display of political slogans.[57] An official notice published before the 1928 Nabi Musa celebrations warned the worshippers that no kind of "notices written on cloth" were to be hung in the city's main streets.[58] Surprisingly, the legal justification for this prohibition was what was known as the Advertisements Ordinance. The absolute prohibition of advertisements "save on one or two small authorized hoardings in commercial quarters, and out of sight of the walls of Jerusalem" was one of Governor Storrs's earliest military orders. This ban was later extended to the entire country in the Advertisements Ordinance, Herbert Samuel's first such edict. One could think of more urgent tasks for the first British High Commissioner for Palestine than the regulation of advertisements, yet in his memoirs Samuel takes great pride in the ordinance: "Palestine has been ever since one of the few countries in the world whose scenery and historic sites and buildings have remained unspoilt by the intrusion of advertisements. . . . I had always felt strongly about this vulgarization of modern life everywhere."[59] The ordinance stated:

> The object of the Ordinance restricting the exhibition of advertisements is to save Palestine, with its historic associations, from the unsightly hoardings and other defacements of the scenery that take away the pleasure of travel in so

FIGURE 44. Cloth banner with the slogan "Long live free Arab Palestine," 1929.
Source: Library of Congress, Matson Collection, American Colony photographers.

> many lands. It is desired to preserve intact the dignity and beauty of the religious and historic sites of the country . . . in order to prevent startling and irritating eye-sores being put up.[60]

The ordinance conjures the image of an exotic, unspoiled historical land whose magic and mystery the British wanted to protect. But this was a myth: the fact was that the advertisements and billboards had been in use in Jerusalem for some decades. Notices, signs, and posters were especially visible in the town center of Jaffa Gate, where they were densely displayed in Hebrew, Arabic, and other languages. These advertisements also introduced magic and mystery into the city, but of a very different kind. They were promises of culture and secular consumption that bound the city into regional and transnational networks. The Bethlehem-born novelist Jabra Ibrahim Jabra, in his recollections of the Nativity Square in the 1920s, tells of how he was enchanted by the posters of Egyptian film and music stars. In Abu-Zaki's hummus restaurant, through the open door, one could see a poster of the famous Egyptian singer Muhammad Abd al-Wahhab titled "The Singer of Kings and Princes" and another one of "The Star of the East," the Egyptian singer, songwriter, and actress Umm Kulthum.[61] These posters connected Bethlehem with the enticing world of modern Arab music, culture, and popular entertainment.

For Herbert Samuel these were the "vulgar" aspects of modernity, from which Jerusalem had to be purified to prevent it from becoming an ordinary modern metropolis. Indeed, in London such commercial encroachment was part of life. When Samuel arranged the letting of his London home, shortly after signing the Advertisements Ordinance, he had no reservations about instructing his wife "to allow one or other, or all of the Agents to put up a board."[62] But what was allowed in London could not be tolerated in Jerusalem. The image of Palestine as an ageless, holy land required actual intervention in the urban landscape to cleanse it from the marks of modernity.

The ordinance represented uncontrolled text as a menace. Whether a threat to the imagined purity of the landscape, a disruption of the projected balance between religious communities, or an inflammatory artifact that could stir crowds, text constituted a danger of unrest and dormant violence. The application of a prohibition on advertisements to outlaw political banners appears not as an improvisation but rather as a logical extension of textual control as a paradigm for British policies in Palestine. By suppressing some forms of text and promoting others, social and political control could be exercised.

The Arab Revolt (1936–1939), which became a full-blown insurgency against British rule, ended the uneasy alliance between the British and the Husaynis. Hajj Amin narrowly escaped arrest and fled the country. The British moved to take control of the Supreme Muslim Council, and the holy embroidered relics became hostages. The festivities were effectively forbidden, and the banners could be displayed within the Haram and the Nabi Musa shrine to only a limited audience. Police orders were clear: "No processions of any kind will be allowed and in no circumstances may any banners be paraded in the streets of the Old or the New city. . . . If it is desired to parade the Nabi Musa banner in the Harem-esh-Sharif it will be necessary for it to be taken privately wrapped up in a packet. No ceremony of any kind may take place while the banner is being transported." The banners could be paraded in the Haram, but upon reaching the gates "they are to be taken off their poles wrapped up and taken through the door and put into the motor car. They may not be unfolded until the arrival at Nebi Musa." [63] Police forces were deployed to prevent the display of banners and to stop processions.[64] The British district commissioner continued to play a ceremonial role in the ritual, as Keith-Roach's memoirs show. By that time the British could no longer entertain any ideas that the ceremony would bolster their prestige in Muslim eyes. Instead their participation was another means of supervision of this risky event.[65]

So far the disappearance of the Nabi Musa banners from the streets of Jerusalem would appear to have resulted from British fears of the fetishized word. Yet this is not the entire story. The change in the status of the banners was also tied to a social process within Arab Palestinian society. The emergence of Arab nationalism called for new symbols that were devoid of any text. To understand this shift, let us return once more to the outbreak of the 1920 riots.

THE 1920 RIOTS AND THE GRAMMAR OF VIOLENCE

The 1920 Nabi Musa riots were the first in a long series of violent mass confrontations during the British Mandate. In the aftermath of violence, the involved parties regularly attempted to control the meaning of these events through constructing competing narratives. There were two main explanatory models of violence: the "pogrom," that is, mass violence instigated by elite incitement; and

FIGURE 45. Nabi Musa procession with the holy banners and the Arab Flag.
Source: Library of Congress, Matson Collection, American Colony photographers.

the "cataclysm," a spontaneous eruption of violence in an emotional and unmediated reaction to an unforeseen "spark."[66] These opposing models of violence have been used throughout the British Mandate and ever since in various parties' attempts to rid themselves of responsibility for the violence and to blame it on other parties. What is denied, in both models, is agency—not only of the victims of violence but also of its perpetrators, who are presented either as pawns in the hand of agitators or as creatures ruled by a violent natural instinct.

In the case of the Nabi Musa riots, different versions of the event used different artifacts to promote their plot: banners, portraits, and flags, whose power is presented as transparent and self-explanatory. Yet a closer look at these artifacts and their changing meanings calls into question the unproblematized immediacy of violence.

In the aftermath of the 1920 riots, an inquiry panel was appointed to determine the causes. The Palin Commission heard testimonies that the violence was triggered by a Jewish insult to the banner of Hebron. Fayyad al-Bakri, who carried the Hebron banner in the procession, testified that while he was standing on Jaffa Street outside the Credit Lyonnais Bank, a red-haired Jew approached him and spat on the banner. As the man was pushed away, other Jewish bystanders started throwing stones at the banner.[67] This version of the event was echoed by at least two other witnesses. A policeman from Hebron, who was walking in front of the banner, had heard a sudden cry "Remember the Hebron banner!" and was told that a Jew had spat on it.[68] In this "cataclysmic" version of the event, violence emerges as an immediate reaction to a real or rumored provocation. Coming from the sacred tomb of Abraham, holding the banner inscribed in his praise, the pilgrims of Hebron arrived in Jerusalem as they had done for centuries through the Hebron Gate (the Arabic name for the Jaffa Gate). When the ancient relic at the center of the pilgrimage came under threat, they rose to defend it.

But the Palin Commission dismissed the incidents relating to the banner as inconsequential. Its report laid the ultimate blame for the riot on Arab frustration with the British commitment to the Balfour Declaration. As for the immediate cause of violence, the report presented a classic example of the "pogrom model":

> The procession halted in the Jaffa road outside the Jaffa Gate to hear speeches delivered by a Sheikh named Aref el Aref. They also halted further up the road to hear more speeches delivered from the balconies of the Municipality and the Nadi el Araby Club by the Mayor and other prominent Moslems. . . . The speeches were of a flagrantly political character, culminating in the exhibition of the portrait of the Emir Feisal, who was greeted as "King of Syria and Palestine." The portrait was later carried in the procession with the flags. The crowd at this point was gradually worked up into a highly inflammatory condition.[69]

The report concluded that although there was evidence to suggest that the attitude of Jewish spectators had been provocative, the outbreak had in all likelihood been caused deliberately by an "agent provocateur raising the cry of an insult to the banner by a Jew."[70] The details of the Nabi Musa pilgrimage were swept aside to make room for a very different scene. Through the eyes of the commission members, the site appears not in its historic role (the Hebron Gate) but rather in its modern form as Jerusalem's commercial and civic center. In the large open plaza, whose buildings house hotels, nationalist clubs, and foreign banks, orators speak from balconies to excited crowds. The inflammatory device in this modernist narrative is not a holy banner but a portrait of a newly crowned king, embodying the promise of Arab nationalism. The man who held up the portrait of King Faysal and reportedly shouted "This is your king!" was Hajj Amin al-Husayni, and it is therefore not surprising that the portrait incident made its way into the historiography of the conflict, where it is typically presented as the dramatic climax of the event and the cue for violence.[71]

Was the real cause of the riot a supposed insult to a holy banner or the display of a king's poster? The event was a moment of ambiguity and transition, which was experienced differently by its participants, and therefore such a question is impossible to answer and is ultimately of little significance. More important is to understand how the dominant narrative of violence has privileged the modernist version and omitted the alleged insult to the holy banners. To present the riot as a reaction to the Balfour Declaration, the nationalist narrative required suitable symbols to promote its plot, and the banners were too traditional and too religious for this purpose. When the two versions are read together, the banners and the portrait appear as equivalent and exchangeable holy objects that had the power to transform a crowd into a mob. The interchangeability of the offended object demonstrates how religious notions of "the sacred" were invested into new national symbols to give them mythical dimensions. One of these new non-textual symbols was the Arab national flag, in one of its earliest appearances in Jerusalem. And in some eyewitness accounts it was the Arab Flag which was the target of attack from a Jewish bystander. In this account, an entirely modern, four-colored flag took the place of the holy banners.[72]

THE ARAB FLAG

Composed of three horizontal strips in green, black, and white and a red chevron, the Arab Flag was first flown in Mecca on June 1917, on the first anniversary of the Arab Revolt against the Ottoman Empire.[73] The flag was designed by British colonial official Mark Sykes (1879–1919). A self-proclaimed expert on the Middle East, Sykes was described by his colleague T. E. Lawrence as "the imaginative advocate of unconvincing world-movements . . . who lacked patience to test his materials before choosing his style of building."[74] Sykes negotiated the notorious Sykes-Picot Agreement, carving up the postwar

Middle East, and was a leading force behind the Balfour Declaration.[75] As he coordinated the Allied invasion of Palestine and Syria, Sykes prepared the propaganda war over hearts and minds. An Arab flag, he believed, would help portray the Allied invasion as a war of liberation rather than a colonial exercise in divide-and-conquer, and allay fears about the French role in the new Middle East. In February 1917 he sketched four possible designs for the "flag of united Arabs."[76] This was not the first time the British intervened to create state symbols for their Sharifian protégé: the Arab Revolt stamps were designed by T. E. Lawrence and Ronald Storrs of the Arab Bureau in Cairo.[77]

The flag fulfilled Sykes's expectations: even before Faysal's arrival in Damascus in September 1918, Arab Flags were flying all across Syria and were enthusiastically received as the flag of liberation—replacing the Ottoman red-and-white flag.[78] "Arab Clubs" in Jerusalem, Jaffa, and Nablus were quick to adopt the Arab Flag, expressing their commitment to a unified Syria and their rejection of the British Mandate.[79] Their hopes were soon dashed. Sykes had a chance to salute the Arab Flag on his visit to Syria in 1919.[80] But shortly afterward French forces landed in Lebanon and Syria, removing Faysal and the flag. The separation between Palestine and Syria became irreversible with the League of Nations approval of the British and French mandates over Palestine and Syria.

Faysal's portrait made a fleeting appearance as a Palestinian symbol. The Arab Flag, however, came to stay. The flag had nothing uniquely Palestinian about it; it was a symbol of the Arab Revolt—in which Palestinians played hardly any part. Nevertheless, the flag was adopted by the Arab Palestinian national movement.[81] In a twist of historical irony, a flag that was designed to serve British colonial interests became an anticolonial symbol. Following the 1920 riots the British banned the display of the Arab Flag, but on religious occasions such as the Nabi Musa festival the flag was tolerated, and it became an integral part of the procession of banners. One witness, who observed the festivities in the 1930s, commented: "Everywhere you could see the Arab Flag with its green, red, white and black colours fluttering high above the heads."[82]

The Arab Flag was very different from the holy banners of Nabi Musa. The banners had no standard shape or color, and their dominating feature was Arabic inscriptions; their social meaning depended on their status as singular and unique material objects held by their noble custodians. In contrast, the modern Arab Flag was a non-textual symbol similar in size and rectangular shape to other national flags. While its colors had resonance in Arab-Islamic visual culture, its schematic and geometric arrangement had nothing Arab or Islamic about it. The flag's ability to represent Arab nationalism depended on its formal resemblance to other national flags in the emerging global system of nation-states. A reproduction by its very essence, the modern national flag was not something that could be possessed by privileged noble families, and therefore could appeal to the nation as an egalitarian community. It was produced in large numbers, sewn by hand by eager Arab youth, nationalist activists who sometimes were not sure about the right order of the colors.[83] Photographs from Mandatory Palestine show that Islamic phrases were sometimes woven into the composition of the flags. These were local appropriations, attempting to integrate textual traditions with the new symbols. The eager adoption of the Arab Flag should tell much about the willingness of Arab nationalists to adopt new ideas and ways of representation. The velvet banners inscribed with sacred text in a gold thread, kept by the noble families of the district, were eclipsed by a geometric pattern of colors that could be patched together by schoolboys.

The disappearance of the Nabi Musa banner from the public stage is also the story of the rise and fall of the notable Palestinian elite. The Husaynis' control over this textual sacred object symbolized their prominent position in Jerusalem during the eighteenth and nineteenth centuries. Ottoman reforms and, furthermore, British colonial occupation gave the Husaynis the opportunity to extend their influence and become the national leadership. Yet for this the banner of Nabi Musa was insufficient, and a modern visual vernacular was developed to express the national aspirations of the Arab Palestinians. The Palestinian catastrophe (Nakba) of 1948 destroyed the Husaynis' power base and led to the emergence of a Palestinian political leadership that no longer relied on noble lineage and clan support. The Husayni family lost its importance as a key institution in Arab Palestine's social and political life, though some of its members continued to be active in Palestinian politics.

Since the 1993 Oslo Agreement, the Nabi Musa pilgrimage has seen a symbolic revival under the auspices of the Palestinian Authority. Because of Israeli restrictions, the festival has been limited to the Nabi Musa shrine. Many Palestinian flags and religious banners are displayed in the festivities, yet the main banner has been missing. The Nabi Musa banner is guarded in

Jerusalem by a member of the Husayni family who has refused to allow its use in the celebrations because, in his view, the revival has nothing to do with the original pilgrimage.[84] But the absence of the festival's most celebrated object did not prevent the Palestinian Authority from staging the revived Nabi Musa festival. The banners that were the festival's raison d'être, around which all its rituals were organized, now became optional items whose material presence could be dispensed with. Locked in a chest in an East Jerusalem mansion and in a display box in the Al-Aqsa Islamic museum, the banners of Nabi Musa have all but disappeared from Palestinian consciousness. The Arab Flag, on the other hand, continues to be raised in Palestine and outside it as a symbol of anticolonial resistance.

The rise of the Arab Flag represented the social transformation of Arab Palestinian society in the late Ottoman and Mandatory periods. New schools, economic development, and greater social mobility gave rise to a new generation of readers and writers. Empowered by rising levels of literacy and growing access to new texts from the Arab world and beyond, modernist intellectuals sought to reinvent themselves and their society. Intellectuals such as Khalil Sakakini and Jabra Ibrahim Jabra wholeheartedly embraced the rupture of modernity and the idea of rewriting their story in new forms and new words. Their political and intellectual project demanded breaking up their culture and society and then reassembling it anew, using the fragmented texts of the streets.

8 CARDBOARD

Visiting Cards and Identification Papers

ONE AFTERNOON IN OCTOBER 1908, AFTER A LONG DAY OF POLITICAL meetings and teaching, Khalil al-Sakakini sat on the balcony of the *Al-Asmaʿi* newspaper offices near Jaffa Gate. As he noted in his diary: "Officer Jalal Effendi, a member of the Committee for Union and Progress [CUP], passed by. He asked that I give him my visiting card. I wrote on the card that I wish to join this association and handed it over to him."[1] The CUP was the new ruling party of the Ottoman Empire: an association of officers and intellectuals that only three months earlier staged the Young Turk Revolution, forcing Sultan Abdülhamid II to reinstate the parliament and constitution. Sakakini had just returned from New York and had high hopes for the revolution. He would soon establish his new, radically modern school and name it the Constitutional School. Like other members of Jerusalem's young intelligentsia, he sought to join the new ruling party.

Sakakini's request to join the CUP was made by sending his visiting card. He did not write a letter of motivation and no interview was required of him. Rather, he sent a brief note on a small piece of cardboard. Sakakini's card acted as a textual proxy of himself, traveling from hand to hand until it reached the local CUP leadership. Some of them knew him in person and would not have required a formal introduction. And yet by producing such a card, Sakakini proved himself a worldly, aspiring, and modern person—a worthy member of a party that sought to revolutionize the empire.

The following evening, Sakakini was invited to a secretive ceremony in which he was admitted to the party. Blindfolded, his right hand on the New Testament and his left on a pistol, he swore that he would defend the constitution and the homeland with his life. The power of the word and the power of the lethal weapon underlined the oath which Sakakini took, instilling a sacred quality in the ceremony. When the blindfold was removed from his eyes, he found himself in front of three officers, their faces and bodies covered. The anonymous functionaries who had read his card had also observed him, in person, as he took the oath blindfolded. They represented the new state machinery: impersonal, ideological, and all-seeing. Under the aegis of the CUP, the revolutionized Ottoman state promised a place to all citizens, regardless of their religion. But it also sought to place them firmly under its gaze.

Sakakini's admission to the party involved two textual artifacts: the visiting card and the New Testament. The visiting card defined him as a worldly and modern individual who was able to write his own future; the holy book marked him as a member of a religious congregation within the multi-faith empire. Both appear as ritual objects, though of radically different kinds. The New Testament was the sacred text, the unchanging source of stability; the visiting card was a door-opener in a modern ritual of secret societies, with text as the medium of mobility and transformation.

FIGURE 46. Khalil Sakakini's visiting card: "A human being, God willing."
Source: Photograph by Salim Tamari, from the collection of the Khalil Sakakini Cultural Center, Ramallah.

Increasingly surrounded by texts of new kinds, urban subjects came to understand and define themselves and their world through what they wrote, and more commonly, through what they read—advertisements, shop signs, nameplates, business cards. New textual media facilitated new modes of subjectivity. In 1908 Jerusalem, this shift took place against an older textual economy which was anchored in divine order. Modern texts unsettled communities and created crisis, displacement, and exile—metaphoric and real—foreshadowing an open-ended process of renaming and redefinition. Some urban subjects, like Sakakini, embraced that opportunity with zeal and enthusiasm. Others, aware of the violence involved in the textual remaking of space and population, were resistant or ambivalent about this transformation. Yet whether they made themselves active participants or not, no one could escape the radical remaking of subjectivity.

VISITING CARD

Emerging in early modern Europe, visiting cards were tools through which one gained access to polite society. As part of upper-class etiquette, cards were left in advance in order to arrange visits and be given interviews. When people were making a social call, they would hand their cards to servants, who would announce the name of the visitor. Etiquette, which comes from the Middle French word for *ticket* or *label*, is about enforcing social roles and boundaries through labeling. Upper-class etiquette was a rigid code of social interaction, prescribing and proscribing the actions of those who moved in high society. Within this system the visiting card was a vital instrument through which one could present oneself to the reading gaze of others. By the early twentieth century, visiting cards had spread beyond their European aristocratic origins, crossing boundaries in terms of class, function, and geography. Visiting cards were no longer primarily an instrument for gaining access to the domestic domain but were increasingly circulated and exchanged in the public realm. For middle-class professionals and businessmen, the card served as a form of advertisement. In many cases visiting cards were used as door openers—a visiting card from an influential person, ideally with their handwritten endorsement, would be presented in the right situations to ensure the card holder a hearing. The cards one received from others were collected carefully, as they provided a textual map of acquaintances, a catalogue of one's social network, influence,

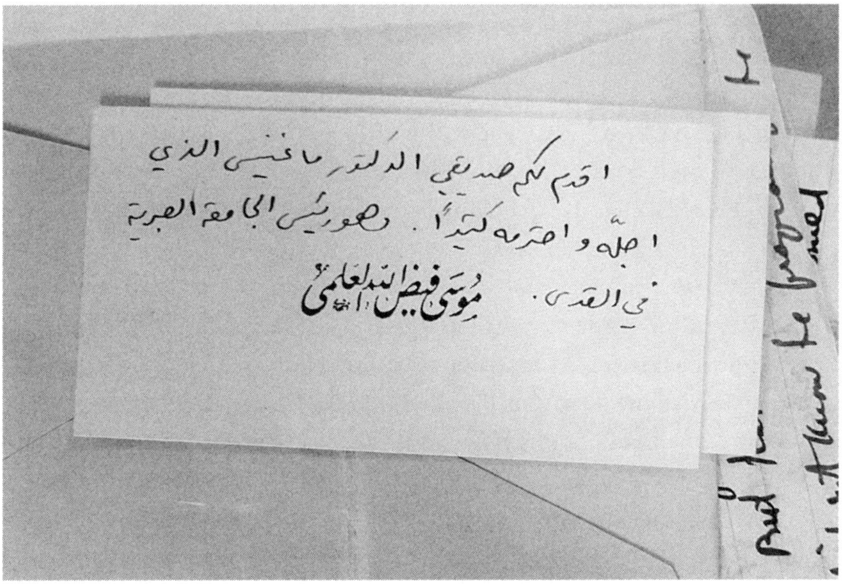

FIGURE 47. Musa al-ʿAlami's visiting card, with his signed statement vouching for Judah Magnes, president of the Hebrew University.
Source: Photograph by Eli Osheroff, from Judah Magnes papers, P3/2426, Central Archive for the History of the Jewish People..

and connections. The text on a visiting card, while brief and "factual," could communicate one's social standing and make one's status readable to a wider public. Without a card, one could not be read by the world, or in other words, one did not exist as an individual of worth. The card was a mask of respectability one would wear in public, more important even than one's clothes.[2]

A contemporary example of the role of visiting cards can be found in E. M. Forster's novel *Howard's End*, published in England in 1910. The novel is occupied with questions of social conventions amid social flux. The Schlegel sisters are cultured, independent women of modest wealth; Leonard Bast is an impoverished clerk. The fateful meeting between them takes place at a Beethoven concert when one of the sisters mistakenly leaves with Bast's umbrella. When the other sister notices this, she offers to return the umbrella and asks for Bast's address. Worried he has fallen prey to an elaborate scam, Bast refuses to give his address to strangers. Faced with people from outside his class, he cannot read their character; their respectable dress and accent offer no guarantees. Margaret Schlegel, who senses his suspicion and pities him, produces her visiting card and invites him to come by. Reading the Schlegels' visiting card, Bast's face brightens: he quickly notices the "W" post code, placing their Wickham Place address in affluent West London, indicating by implication their trustworthy character. In a metropolis of more than seven million people, of huge disparities in income, wealth, and education, London's postal code system did more than facilitate the delivery of mail; it provided an easily legible grid of social status and a reliable mapping of class hierarchies. This information could be presented in the most succinct and "objective" manner on the visiting card, through a single letter.[3] The card allowed its holder to determine her or his own terms of legibility—by choosing words, style, and sometimes photographs—but this choice always operated within, and against, accepted norms.

Sakakini's visiting card was written in the context of Ottomanism, the Nahda, and the possibilities opened by education, print media, and the emergent middle class. Producing one's visiting card was similar to producing one's portrait in a photographer's studio. Visits to the photographer's studio, sometimes with family or friends, were something of a ritual for Sakakini and other middle-class men, an opportunity to reproduce themselves as men of the moment.[4] The photographs and cards allowed such persons to carefully shape their image for circulation. The photographic *carte de visite*, a fashionable artifact of the turn of the century, combined the visiting card and the photograph into one by incorporating a portrait on the back side of the card. The aesthetic of the photographic *carte de visite* captured the ideology of Ottoman modernity, of progress and civilization.[5]

Jerusalem's Franciscan Printing Press was the preferred producer of visiting cards for the city's aristocracy and middle class. A recent study has unearthed a collection of 1,500 calling cards, trade cards, and invitations, printed at the press between 1880 and 1906, demonstrating the prevalence of this custom among Jerusalem's elite. Officials, merchants, and professionals, Muslims, Christians, and Jews, all printed their cards at the Franciscan Press.[6] The rich repository provides a fascinating glimpse into the city's dominant classes and the manner in which they chose to represent themselves. The collection includes cards of leading members of the district and municipal governments, from the *mutasarrif* to council members and dragomen. Photographers, tourist guides, and railway engineers printed their cards there. Almost all the cards were produced by men, with some notable exceptions such as the cards of two midwives. It was a cosmopolitan milieu, in which recent migrants and settlers from Europe had a significant presence alongside Ottoman citizens. Notwithstanding its confessional and ethnic diversity, the Jerusalem elite followed a strikingly similar format in self-presentation. The cards were textual, with little ornamentation, overwhelmingly in Latin characters, especially in French and English, sometimes with the Arabic and Turkish translation. There were cards also in Hebrew, Italian, German, Armenian, Spanish, Greek, and Russian. The purpose of the card was to establish connections rather than provide detailed contact information. Contact details barely featured on the cards: at most they included a loose indication of address, such as "Jaffa Road" or "near the Municipal Hospital," or simply "Jerusalem." Such "addresses" were in keeping with the Ottoman urban geography of the time.

KHALIL SAKAKINI AND HIS CARD

Sakakini's visiting card was famous within his social circle. A century later, its statement still reads as a radical proposition. It stated plainly: "Khalil al-Sakakini. A human being, God willing" (*Insan, insha'Allah*). His students, friends, and acquaintances in Jerusalem were familiar with this motto and understood it as a statement of simplicity, expressing his impatience with social pretense and phony conventions. As his student Wasif Jawhariyyeh wrote: "Those who have known him can testify that it is hard to describe al-Sakakini with words. . . . He was loyal and just and liked everyone to be human in every sense of the word. To this effect, he printed the [aforementioned] statement on his vising card. . . . He mocked those who led a manipulative life, and who were many, in his view."[7] Sakakini prided himself on his honesty, direct manners, and willingness to stand by his principles. Indeed, on numerous occasions he paid a high personal price for his principles, when he confronted the social consensus and those in power. But the statement "A human being, God willing" was also a rejection of social categorization and labeling: not only a rejection of his own confessional identity but a sweeping rejection of nationalism and organized religion in general. As he wrote in 1917 shortly before his arrest by the Ottoman police for sheltering an American Jew:

> Wherever I am, I am simply a human being, nothing else. I don't belong to political parties or religious factions. I consider myself a patriot wherever I am, and strive to improve my surroundings whether they are American, British, Ottoman or African, whether they are Christian, Muslim or pagan. I only work to serve knowledge, and knowledge has no homeland. What is a patriot? If being a patriot means to be sound of body, strong, active, enlightened, moral, affable and kind, then I am a patriot. But if patriotism means favouring one school over another and showing one's brother hostility if he is from a different school or country, then I am no patriot.[8]

Describing himself as a human being was a rejection of the social identities imposed by groups, nations, and creeds. But "a human being" was not the naked truth hiding underneath the social mask; it was a mask in itself, a statement of humility, but also a carefully worded, publicly proclaimed ideological persona. Humanist simplicity was an attestation of Sakakini's commitment to Enlightenment values and his individualistic outlook. "A human being" was not a description but an aspiration, a pledge, a call to arms—as was made clear by the suffix "God willing." Being human was not a given but something to be achieved. The card was part of Sakakini's lifelong project of self-fashioning as a modern individual, much of it inspired by his admiration of Western culture. This self-fashioning involved a strict daily regime of exercises, a cold shower, a vegetarian diet, and obsessive writing in diaries, letters, essays, articles, and books (including a draft of his own eulogy).[9] This was a continuous disciplining of body and soul. Sakakini was a deeply theatrical personality, with a narcissistic streak, and enjoyed performing in front of friends and colleagues. He played many roles in his life: migrant entrepreneur in New York, Ottoman patriot, Arab liberation fighter, Palestinian anticolonial activist, pan-Arab intellectual, always with fervor and great excitement. But the role of the humanist writer and educator was the most important for him, and he played it throughout his adult life.

Sakakini was a deeply embattled and contradictory person. What makes his voice sound so fresh and contemporary is not only his insatiable enthusiasm for modernity, or his penchant for reinventing himself, but also his mercurial personality and the anguished sense of exile that runs through his writing. His individualism came with a profound sense of alienation. He felt estranged and out of place in his hometown Jerusalem, perhaps more than he did in his miserable year in Brooklyn.[10] Frequently plagued by the feeling that he was misunderstood by his social environment, he yearned for intellectual isolation and yet at the same time was always in search of an audience—in classrooms, cafés, street encounters, and in his writing for newspapers and the radio. His calling-card motto expressed this contradiction succinctly. It was a gesture of emancipation from social conventions—performed through a bourgeois social convention.

Although Sakakini was not wealthy and struggled to make ends meet (especially upon his return to Jerusalem), his education and literary skills put him in a relatively privileged position. His visiting card expressed his membership in the new urban middle class and was one instrument with which he wrote his own story. Most Jerusalemites were less fortunate. The urban poor and villagers in Jerusalem and its vicinity did not have such cards. They did not possess the ability to shape in textual terms their public persona, and by implication their future horizons. But in an era of social and political transformation, young Jerusalemites of humble background paid careful attention to the changing textual landscape around them. As signposting and labeling took over the city, poor children used the new texts in the urban environment to rethink their identity and future. Jabra Ibrahim Jabra, the novelist and intellectual, was one such child.

NEW READERS

Jabra Ibrahim Jabra (1920–1994) was "a true renaissance man" whose work included novels, short stories, poetry, and literary and art criticism, as well as translations of Western literary classics from Shakespeare to Samuel Beckett.[11] Jabra was born to a poor family in Bethlehem and moved to Jerusalem at the age of twelve. An extraordinary student, he graduated from the Arab College in Jerusalem and won a scholarship to study English literature at Cambridge. Upon his return to Palestine he taught English in his Jerusalem school. Forced to leave Jerusalem in the 1948 war, he became an exile in Iraq, where he produced most of his work, including his childhood memoirs *The First Well,* which he wrote in the 1980s.[12]

Most of the memoirs, diaries, and autobiographies of Palestinian Arabs from the Mandatory period were written by members of the urban upper and middle classes. Jabra's is one of a few autobiographies written from the viewpoint of a rural and poor family. His father was an unskilled laborer. Bethlehem was at the time a village of five thousand people, and Jerusalem appears as a strange and confusing metropolis through his eyes.

Jabra's childhood stories capture the dramatic transformation of Arab Palestine's reading culture during the British Mandate. Literacy was no longer limited to the urban population and the well-to-do but was spreading to rural areas and to the lower classes. The transformation was powered by the increasing accessibility of schooling for children.[13] Both Jabra's parents were illiterate, but both he and his brother could read and write, and they saved their hard-earned wages to buy books and magazines. For Jabra reading was a means of escape from the dingy one-room family lodging to the world of ancient Arab poets and European adventure tales. Later it would become a real escape, as Jabra's writing skills became his tools of trade.

Jabra first learned to read in Christian Orthodox schools, whose organization and routines were remarkably similar to those in traditional Islamic and Jewish schools. These schools usually consisted of one large classroom. Children sat five or more on long benches, each bench comprising one "class." The teacher was more of an overseer than an instructor, and it was the older children's role to teach the alphabet to the smallest children. During prayer, the choirboys would read hymns from ancient manuscripts; the children would gather in a circle round the lectern and some had to read the text upside down.

> Thus, I learned to read any text in Syriac or Arabic right side up or upside down equally well. . . . It was very rare that any of us understood those texts, or even some of them. We actually prayed in a language which was mostly closed to us, in spite of the fact that we could read it right side up, sideways, or upside down, in the light or in no light at all.[14]

Jabra refrains from direct condemnation of the old world of text, represented by the church school. His descriptions are full of humor and humanity, yet it is impossible to mistake them for nostalgia. The prayer scene appears as a theatrical staging where text is the central actor, in a ritual of reading that means nothing to its participants and locks them into a social order of tradition and deprivation.

For Jabra's father, who had to leave school before he could learn to read and write properly, text had first and foremost a sacred meaning. "I rejoice immensely, and so does this mother of yours, when we see you both reading books," Jabra recalls his father saying. "Why? Because the word is holy. Yes, indeed. The word is from God. Rather, the Word is God, as the Gospel says. The word is the book. Or am I mistaken?"[15]

The uncertain tone in which Jabra chose to end his father's words was not accidental. For Jabra, who grew up reading *Arabian Nights*, *Robinson Crusoe*, and Egyptian magazines of politics and literature, text had a different meaning. Books and journals were not the word of God but a source of adventure stories and news of the unfolding political drama in Palestine. The urban texts documented in Jabra's childhood memories were not religious texts: he mentions signs on buildings and commercial posters, and describes in detail the sign announcing the municipal limits of Bethlehem, which for him marked the dividing line between the familiar and the strange. Beyond the line was Rachel's Tomb, where strange-looking Jews came to pray, and a road leading to Jerusalem, to a world of secrets and mystery. These texts delimited space and defined buildings, but they also defined their readers—a national Arab reading community, a new public of consumers and citizens.

Jabra left the Syriac school in 1929 in favor of the new government school in Bethlehem, which his brother Yusuf had attended the previous year. Through his brother's English textbook Jabra first encountered the tales of *Arabian Nights*; being admitted to the school, he felt, would be equal to obtaining Aladdin's Lamp. The opening day of the school year marked a significant morning in his life. Wearing his only good jacket, unpatched shorts, and uncomfortable new shoes, he made his way to school. Jabra describes his entry to the school as a rite of passage: "The wide iron gate appealed to me. Above it was a large sign written in beautiful calligraphy which proclaimed 'The National School of Bethlehem.' I was instantly filled with a strange pride and felt that the school belonged to me and I to it. I entered the front yard apprehensively."[16]

With subtle irony, Jabra positions one system against the other: text which can be read from all sides but is devoid of social relevance, compared to the modern urban texts he describes so enthusiastically. The text of the hymns, legible but meaningless, in the darkness of the church, stands in contrast to the clear and simple text of the school sign, in broad daylight and in public open space. The modern signs heralded a change of momentous proportions: it involved a breakdown of old social structures and a loss of divine certainty. Yet Jabra had no qualms about forsaking the old text and adopting the new.

NATIONALIZING THE SELF

Having entered the new school, Jabra found himself in a space that was meticulously labeled; on the door to each room was written its name or purpose. He was led to a room labeled "The Principal," and then to "The Third Class" and finally to "The Storeroom." Jabra was struck by the spatial and social organization of his new school. In the National School the children were placed in classrooms according to level and proficiency (but not age, since children started school at different ages). Inside the class the children were seated in twos, all facing the teacher and the blackboard.[17] Thus the signposting of space was part of school standardization, a global revolution which involved "the physical differentiation of rationalized seating arrangements and the development of classrooms as separate walled spaces for the instruction of different levels of students."[18]

Although excited by his admittance to the school, recounts Jabra, he initially felt apprehensive and isolated. He knew none of the boys; he felt he had been "forcibly plunged into a group of strangers."[19] The boys came from many places, also from outside Bethlehem, all speaking different local dialects. Most were Christian (of at least five different churches) and some were Muslim. The teachers were also not local, some coming from Nazareth and Umm al-Fahm in the north of the country. The heterogeneous makeup of the National School stood in contrast to the Christian schools he had previously attended, which served tightly knit religious communities.

Jabra's anxiety soon passed, and it was not long before he became the first in his class. Through interaction with teachers and other students, Jabra felt he was opening up to people of all kinds from whom he had previously been isolated. Going to the state school was "the beginning of my real exposure to life"; his family now seemed to him like "a little cocoon on the margin of everything."[20] The National School provided new possibilities, not only of learning but also of framing oneself in a national vocabulary, that is, becoming an Arab Palestinian. This was the explicit mission of his teachers: to make "a harmonious school" out of this "big human mixture," instilling in them the love of knowledge and learning "so that they might all put these in the service of the idea of Arabism, and especially the Arabism of Palestine."[21] This nationalist ethos, expressed in clear words in the school's gate sign, was the mission of many Arab Palestinian educators who worked under the government's Department of Education. Khalil al-Sakakini, an inspector in the department in the 1930s, believed that education had to be first nationalist and then informative. "If each of us will be a nationalist and will devote all his energy to instilling national consciousness in his students," he said to teachers in Nazareth in 1934, "we will create for the country an army of free, brave, noble and educated people."[22] But using education for an Arab-nationalist agenda was not a simple task, since the administration of the Education Department was in British hands. Arabs were systematically denied participation in decision-making; educational policies and curricula were formulated by British officials. In their mission to instill patriotic feeling in their students, Arab teachers, principals, and inspectors thus had to struggle against a British-designed educational framework.

For these Arab educators, the Arabic language assumed key significance in the creation of national consciousness. In Jabra's rendering of his schoolboy childhood, the classical Arabic poems of bravery and war exploits he was taught in the National School blend into the nationalist poems which swept Arab Palestine in the aftermath of the 1929 riots. More and more people wanted to master reading, not for liturgical purposes but in order to take part in the national struggle. Jabra recalls how he was approached by an illiterate stonecutter to teach him how to read, so that he could follow the dramatic political events by deciphering the headlines of the newspaper *Filastin*. In the 1920s and 1930s, political pamphlets and placards gained wide circulation as means of agitation.[23] During the Arab Revolt of 1936–1939 clandestine placards became a primary medium of communication for the rebels. Typed notices were posted in broad view at the entrance to the Al-Aqsa Mosque in September 1938, when the rebels succeeded in taking control over much of the Old City. By 1945 British intelligence officers stressed that the widespread circulation of political pamphlets in Palestine was "exceptional" compared to other parts of the Middle East.[24]

These headlines, signs, advertisements, placards, and newspapers created an urban scenography of nationalism, which not only defined space as national but also made urban readers into active participants in the national project. Together with other forms, such as slogan banners, political notices, and graffiti, they made Arabic into a national language and claimed the urban space as Arab.

FIGURE 48. Arabs reading rebel proclamations in Jerusalem, Al-Aqsa Mosque, 1938. Source: Library of Congress, Matson Collection, American Colony photographers.

THE SCHOOL GATE: THE HEBREW VERSION

The rapturous experience of leaving a traditional school to enter a modern one was by no means unusual for Jabra's contemporaries in Palestine. For Muslim, Christian, and Jewish boys such a transition was a common experience, especially in the big cities where modern schools were prevalent. Parents seeking a better future for their children transferred them from traditional faith schools to modern institutions, such as the French Catholic Collège de Frères, the Alliance Israélite Universelle, or Khalil Sakakini's Madrasa Dusturiyya. In some cases the demand came from the children themselves, who were attracted to the exciting promise of a new world, often exemplified in Western dress and in modern buildings. Twentieth-century intellectuals who made that transition usually described it, like Jabra, as stepping out of darkness into the light. Traditional schools are often described as dingy and dirty, with outdated methods of instruction and often corporal punishment; most were happy to leave them behind.[25]

The Hebrew writer Ezra Hamenahem, who grew up in Jerusalem in the early twentieth century, presents a more ambivalent voice. Hamenahem's short story "A Different Spirit" described his departure from a Jewish traditional Talmud Torah school and entry to a modern one, and the details of that experience are strikingly reminiscent of Jabra's account.[26] Yet in Hamenahem's story, the transition proves traumatic and offers no emancipation. A Sephardic Jew born in Skopje, Macedonia, Hamenahem came from a humble background. His family immigrated to Jerusalem in 1913, when he was six years old. He left school at a young age to work as a delivery boy in a Zionist bank. Through perseverance and hard work he found his way into literary circles, becoming an editor and a short-story writer.

In his book of autobiographical short stories, Hamenahem remembers fondly his first school, the traditional Talmud Torah. His memories are steeped in nostalgia, yet without embellishment. The Talmud Torah was a dingy and melancholic space, enclosed within metal railings like a prison cell. And yet his teachers, Sephardic and Yemenite Jews, are described affectionately, "wrapped in warm light," their devotion to the students appearing motherly and effeminate.[27] But Hamenahem, like many of his friends, was overtaken by the "folly" of foreign, "European" ways. He felt enticed to find his place in new surroundings. "Outside the walls, amid newly established neighborhoods, stood gallantly the von Lämel School, as was inscribed on its gate, whose sight attracted all gazes. Cleanliness and silence ruled within it, and trees and flowers adorned it."[28]

The Lämel School was a pioneering modern Jewish institution in Jerusalem. Established by the Austrian Jewish doctor Ludwig Frankel in 1858, the school later came under the supervision of Hilfsverein der Deutschen Juden, a German-Jewish philanthropic society which aimed to spread German culture among Jews worldwide. In 1903 the Lämel School moved to new premises designed by the German-Jerusalemite architect Theodor Sandel. David Yellin,

FIGURE 49. The Lämel School (built 1903): the German-Hebrew bilingual school sign (top); the facade, with the sign hidden, after the building was taken over by the ʿEts Hayim Yeshiva (2019) (bottom).
Sources: (top) Wikicommons; (bottom) Yair Wallach.

who taught at the school, described the new building in the Hebrew journal *Ha-Melits* as a "magnificent Temple" whose outer walls of stone were reminiscent of the Western Wall. Above the entrance was an Orientalized engraving of a well and a palm tree, and the silhouette of walled Jerusalem, "a symbol for drawing the water of the Torah and the wisdom of gaining knowledge in the heights of Zion." The name of the school was carved in marble above the entrance, in Hebrew and in German: "*Beyt ha-Sefer le-he-Atsil le-Veyt Lemel* / Edler von Lämel Schule." Above the entrance was a large Star of David and a clock with hours marked in Hebrew characters "informing pupils of the schedule of arrival and departure, the times for learning and the times for rest and play." The Hebrew clock and Hebrew sign both expressed a modern order based on marking, measuring, and labeling.[29]

Hamenahem's parents did not approve of his move to Lämel. They worried that the new school would take him away from sacred ways. The Talmud Torah teachers, well aware of the new trends, sought to dissuade students from leaving the school. Throughout the summer vacation, Hamenahem deliberated between "Lämel with its external splendor, strict and tempting, face to face with the downcast Talmud Torah, its face buried in the ground." His choice of the new school appears almost automatic, robotic, and is belied by the sense of an inevitable catastrophe. As is typical in Hamenahem's stories, the decision to forsake tradition is not a conscious rational choice but almost an involuntary instinct, driven by fate and leading to destruction.[30] On the journey to Lämel on the first day of school he is described as a somnambulist, "walking and dozing, walking and hallucinating." His arrival in the school did not herald any revolutionary emancipation. The gates were locked, and the children gathered for hours on the pavement "as a group of unfortunates in front of a rich man's door," too ashamed to approach each other.[31] After long hours of waiting, the caretaker emerged full of rage, muttering indecipherably and cracking his whip to drive them away. The school was oversubscribed, and Hamenahem was one of the lucky few who were eventually admitted. But his entry through the school gate elicited no magical transformation. Like Jabra, he found himself amid strangers, without friends. But unlike Jabra he did not find his way into the new environment. The children's faces and manners remained foreign and strange. The disciplinarian and severe nature of the school, which was manifested in its somber sign and the school clock, proved profoundly alienating. The teachers were strict, their voices harsh as "cold metal"; their starched collars expressed rigidity. "The Bible rang foreign in their mouth, like mathematical exercises." There was a "stern spirit in the long and narrow corridors."[32] The spotlessness, the children's whispers, and the smell of disinfectant were reminiscent of a hospital and terrified the small child. The new school became a place of exile. But for Hamenahem, who lamented the decision to leave his old teachers, it was too late to turn back.

The Lämel School was established and sponsored by non-Zionist German-Jewish philanthropy, and it accepted Muslim and Christian children. But around the turn of the century it became a primary site of Hebrew-language activism and the place in which local Jews developed modern national awareness and Zionist identity.[33] The disciplinarian ethos of the school also demanded a Europeanized identity and a different kind of masculinity. Many Jewish youths embraced this transformation with enthusiasm, but Hamenahem remained deeply ambivalent about it. For Jabra, on the other hand, the radical reinvention as a national citizen brought with it the promise of freedom and democratization.

DEMOCRATIZING SIGNPOSTS?

By the early 1930s, Arabic signs had become part of the urban landscape of Jerusalem and could be relied on for urban navigation, especially by newcomers to the city—not only Jewish immigrants but also Arabs from Jerusalem's rural hinterland, who migrated to the city in greater numbers. When Jabra moved to Jerusalem, a city which seemed to him strange, busy, and noisy, he was led to his new school by a neighbor—like himself a newcomer to Jerusalem, who had become familiar with the city in his job as a mailman. As they emerged out of the Old City, the mailman pointed across the road and asked: "'Do you see that sign?' On it was written in large letters 'Al-Rashidiyya Secondary School.'"[34] As the city grew, reading skills became vital for finding one's way around, both literally and metaphorically.[35] But the implications of this transformation went far beyond considerations of street navigation. The status of text, its role in society, and attitudes toward it all changed profoundly.

The change was not unique to Jerusalem. It took place in cities all over the world in the nineteenth and twentieth centuries. In his study of urban texts in New York between 1825 and 1865, historian David Henkin charted the dramatic proliferation of commercial signs, the introduction of official warning signs, and early attempts to control graffiti. Henkin argues that urban texts in public space played a significant democratizing role. Text moved out of the closed spaces of bourgeois salons and coffeehouses, where reading had been restricted to an educated minority, and stepped out into the street. Increasingly visible in the urban landscape, shop signs, newspapers, political banners, and banknotes were addressing a widening public. That expansion produced and reinforced a leveling of authority in the city's public life. "Though . . . urban texts did not level incomes, instill ethnic harmony, bridge neighborhoods, or promote political consensus, they bracketed these ruptures within a shared experience of public space by rendering much of the city legible to strangers and facilitating forms of access and interaction that did not require personal acquaintance, face-to-face contact, or recognizable individual authority."[36] Jerusalem was much smaller than the metropolis of New York, and yet urban textuality played a strikingly similar role in these different contexts: it reshaped the urban landscape and urban subjectivity, and created new communities of readers whose experience of street texts was comparable. Textuality appears as a powerful agent of modernity, with far-reaching, global homogenizing effects, producing new collective publics on the one hand and new kinds of individualism on the other. "Streets are the dwelling place of the collective," wrote Walter Benjamin. "The collective is an eternally unquiet, eternally agitated being that—in the space between the building fronts—experiences, learns, understands, and invents as much as individuals do within the privacy of their own four walls. For this collective, glossy enameled shop signs are a wall decoration as good as, if not better than, an oil painting in the drawing room of a bourgeois; walls with their 'Post No Bills' are its writing desk, newspaper stands its libraries, mailboxes its bronze busts, benches its bedroom furniture, and the café terrace is the balcony from which it looks down on its household."[37]

Jabra's affirmation of the liberating qualities of urban reading should be understood against his ideological commitment to Arab nationalism. Through the alienating process of rewriting the self, a new democratic society could emerge, a society in which origin, class, and confessional identity would not be barriers to personal and collective development.[38] Jabra belonged to the generation of mid-twentieth-century Arab intellectuals who invested the Nahda language of Arab rejuvenation with a secular-nationalist zeal. Educated in European schools and universities, they rejected European colonialism but fully accepted the Orientalist view of Arab culture as archaic and ossified.[39] From Arab tradition Jabra suggested "taking what is alive, and leaving what is dead."[40] He saw the Nakba, the devastating defeat of Palestinian society by Zionist society, as the result of a failure to embrace modernity.[41] Like other intellectuals of his generation, Jabra wanted to use the catastrophe as a catalyst for radical transformation.[42] Reminiscing on his early days as a Palestinian refugee and university professor in 1950s Baghdad, Jabra wrote:

> I preached change, unashamedly. We had been cheated and betrayed by a thousand years of decay, I said. We had been the victims of our beautiful inane rhetoric. We lost Palestine, because we had confronted a ruthless modern force with an outmoded tradition. Everything had to change. And change had to begin at the base, with a change of vision. A new way of looking at things. A new way of saying things. A new way of approaching and portraying man and the world.[43]

Here, Jabra articulated explicitly what is described implicitly in *The First Well*: a rejection of Arab cultural "decay" and "outmoded tradition." The school sign became for Jabra a symbol of that necessary change, which was cut short in Palestine by the Nakba: a modernity integrating Western ideas with Arab nationalism. Arab regeneration, as articulated in Jabra's novels, was predicated on an intellectual vanguard who could defy Arab society and show it the road to modernity. Jabra's novels, written in romantic realism, centered on rebel intellectuals and artists. His liberal advocacy of a secular reinvention of Arab society alongside Western principles appealed to a 1950s educated class that was rising against the monarchist colonial regimes. But as decades went by, secular pan-Arabism failed to deliver on its promises. In the decades that followed, Arab secular state nationalism turned increasingly tyrannical and hollow of any promise of renewal, leading to the brutal repression of the Arab revolutions of the twenty-first century.

Jabra saw modern text as an emancipatory tool: employed on paper, signs, and placards, text could be used to empower, rewrite, and reinvent Arab society. Yet modern text was also a tool of state oppression. Textual artifacts and technologies were crucial to the state's increasing control of communities and individuals.

IDENTITY PAPERS

If the visiting card held the promise of defining one's identity in one's own terms, its opposite artifact was the standardized, state-produced personal document.[44] The ID card is "an under-theorized manifestation of a low-tech, visible, physical and tactile means of power."[45] Unlike the visiting card, which remained a middle- and upper-class document, state identity papers were imposed on subjects in a near-universal manner for the purpose of population control. In the Ottoman Empire this took the form of the *nüfus tezkeresi*, the identity card, which was introduced after the 1850s Crimean War, initially only for men. The *tezkeresi* was a mass-printed document, headed with a large *tughra*, on which clerks recorded in handwriting the person's name, date of birth, religion, father's name, and place of abode as well as a physical description. It was compulsory for every male citizen to hold such a certificate.[46] The document was required for all governmental and legal dealings. It had to be produced for buying and selling land, appearing in court, travel within and outside the empire, and interaction with police or municipal authorities. Despite being a personal document, the certificate was not normally obtained directly by the person or his family but through appointed community representatives, the *mukhtars*. It was no surprise, therefore, that it was prone to containing errors of spelling and incorrect details.[47]

The importance of such documents expanded dramatically during World War I, which introduced a revolution in identification practices. The monitoring of soldiers, aliens, and civilians increased markedly, and documents had to be displayed more frequently. Identity papers became something of an "internal passport," used by the Ottoman authorities to regulate and impose checks on movement even within the same district. Travel between Jerusalem and Jaffa was subject to presenting a passage certificate.[48] For soldiers the absence of such a certificate could have grave implications. In June 1916, in order to intimidate the local population, five soldiers without proper papers were hanged as "deserters" (*farar*) at Jaffa Gate on the orders of Jamal Pasha. The "deserters'" main crime was the lack of correct documentation.[49] For users of these documents, they became something like "talismans of status and recognition" which could make the difference between life and death, between safe passage and failed travel.[50] As the war sowed chaos and dislocation, the

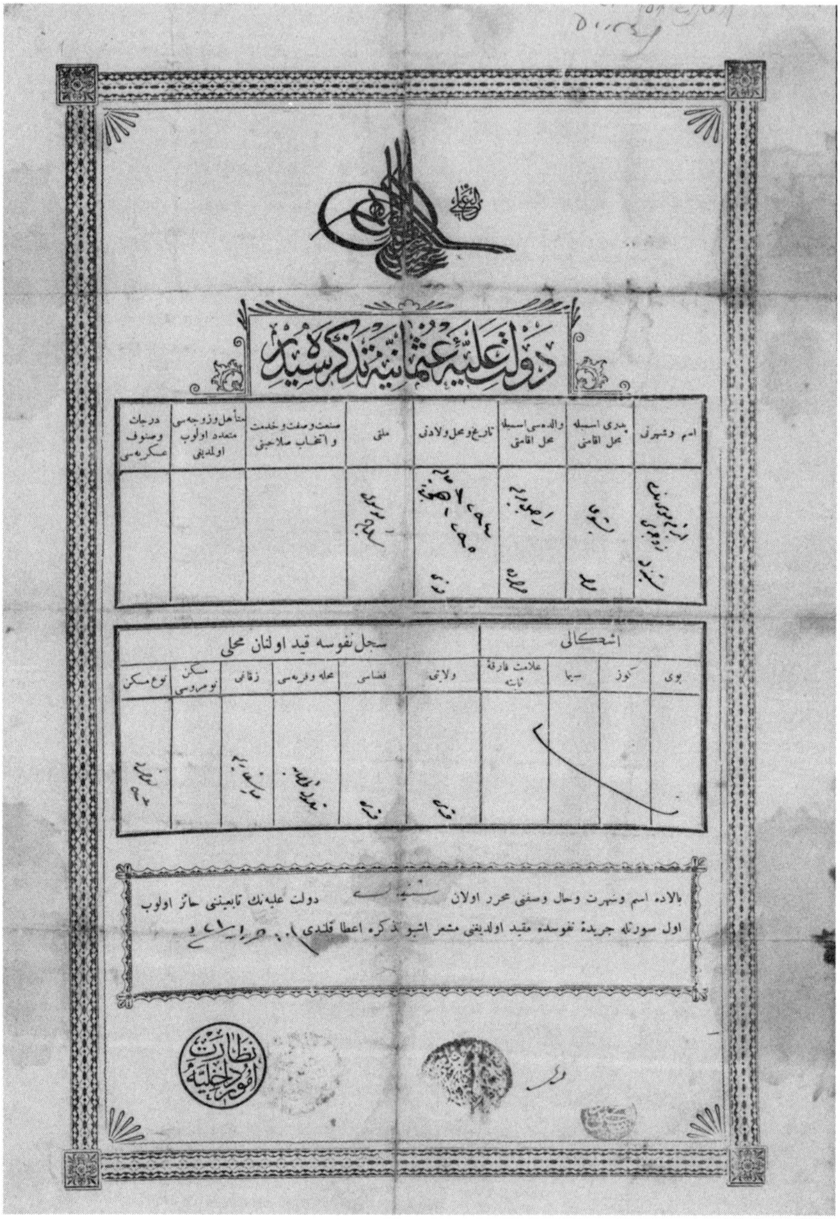

دولت علیهٔ عثمانیه تذکره‌سیدر

اسم وشهرتی	پدری اسمیله محل اقامتی	والده‌سی اسمیله محل اقامتی	تاریخ و محل ولادتی	ملتی	صنعت و صفت و خدمت و انتخاب صلاحیتی	متأهل و زوجه‌سی متعدد اولوب اولمدیغی	درجات و صنوف عسکریه‌سی

اشکالی				سجل نفوسه قید اولنان محلی					
بوی	کوز	سیما	علامت فارقهٔ ثابته	ولایتی	قضاسی	محله و قریه‌سی	زقاقی	مسکن نومروسی	نوع مسکن

بالاده اسم و شهرت و حال و صفتی محرر اولان ... دولت علیه‌نك تابعیتنی حائز اولوب
اول صورتله جریدهٔ نفوسده مقید اولدیغنی مشعر اشبو تذکره اعطا قلندی

نظارت امور داخلیه

FIGURE 50. Ottoman identity papers (*nüfus tezkeresi*) of Abraham Moshe and his wife Schneydel Halfman. Meah Shearim, Jerusalem, 1905.

Source: Yad Ben Zvi, Israel State Archive.

reliance on this document for identification became crucial. Ahmad Shuqayri, the first chairman of the Palestine Liberation Organization, recalls in his memoirs the importance of his *nüfus* during the war. As an eight-year-old orphan, he traveled on his own to distant relatives in Haifa he had never met, and proved his identity to them by showing his *nüfus* paper. Shuqayri recalls his cousin carefully reading the *nüfus*. Without this paper, Shuqayri says, he would have been thrown out as a stranger.[51]

Identity cards were introduced again by colonial authorities as part of the suppression of the Arab Revolt (1936–1939).[52] The leaders of the revolt saw them as surveillance instruments and called on the population not to carry them.[53] These cards, printed in English only, included a photograph of the individual as well as a longer list of details: place of residence, business, occupation, race (defined as Arab or Jewish), height, eye and hair color, build, and "special peculiarities." During the late 1940s, amid the anti-British Zionist insurgency as well as the hostilities between Jews and Arabs, strict restrictions were imposed on movement within the city, especially to the barricaded city centers where British command was located. Special pass permits were issued to regulate individual freedom of mobility within the city.[54]

But it was in the aftermath of the 1948 war that population registration assumed a key place in the architecture of dispossession. The first Israeli census of November 1948 allocated identity numbers to the entire population, serving as the basis of Israeli citizenship.[55] The 700,000 Arab residents who fled or were expelled during the war were termed "absentees;" their return was forbidden, and their property effectively expropriated. In the years following 1948, identity papers became a metonym of the Palestinian condition.[56] At least half the Palestinians were stateless, and others held complicated citizenship arrangements involving several states. Acquiring paper documentation was a challenge in itself. The checkpoint or border crossing, where one had to submit these papers to an official gaze, became an all-too-familiar metaphor for the dispossession of Palestinians of basic civic rights. The denial of entry or exit from one's village, neighborhood, or country by a soldier was and remains a painfully familiar experience to virtually all Palestinians and serves as a constant reminder of their disappearance from history as sovereign subjects. It was a poem on a young Palestinian presenting his identity papers which made the twenty-two-year-old Mahmoud Darwish Palestine's most celebrated poet.

FIGURE 51. British Mandate ID card of Ahmad Said Muhammad Bseisi, an Arab Palestinian resident of Al-Maliha, near Jerusalem. Al-Maliha was occupied in 1948 by Israeli forces and its population was permanently displaced.
Source: Ayah Bseisy.

MAHMOUD DARWISH'S "IDENTITY CARD"

From 1948 to 1965, Palestinians who remained within Israel were placed under the Military Administration and faced severe restrictions and limitations. Identity cards were instrumental in policies of surveillance and control. The new Israeli-issued ID cards closely resembled the Mandatory IDs and included the same categories of information. Citizens were required by law to carry the cards at all times. Their rights of residence, travel, work, welfare, and education depended on the status of their ID. Obtaining a civic ID card was not straightforward; many Palestinians' cards were initially withheld on various grounds.[57] Mahmoud Darwish's family belonged to this group. After fleeing to Lebanon during the 1948 war, they crossed back into Israel and were internal refugees, or in official Israeli terminology "present absentees." Under military rule, all Arab citizens required special written permissions for any travel. "Present absentees" faced additional difficulties and were denied rations, welfare, work, travel, and education. Darwish's poem, presented in part below, describes an interrogatory situation in which the protagonist provides his details to a Jewish-Israeli official;

a situation that originally took place in Hebrew but is rendered in Arabic. Filling the headers of personal details, the narrator provides his ethnicity, number of children, occupation, name, physique, address, and other details. The situation, however, is turned on its head as the narrator subverts the logic of the interrogation. Rather than providing simple factual answers, he dictates a rallying cry of Palestinian defiance. He speaks as a peasant quarry worker, struggling against his dispossession. The narrative is one of the rootedness and steadfastness of an entire people, not a single individual.

Write it down! I'm an Arab
My card number is 50000
My children number eight
And after this summer, a ninth on his way.
Does this make you rage?
...
Write it down!
I am an Arab.
I am a name with no honorific.
Patient in a land
Where everything lives in bursting rage
My roots were planted before time was born
Before history began
Before the cypress and the olive trees
Before grass sprouted
My father is from the plough clan
Not from the noble class
My grandfather was a peasant farmer
Had no pedigree
Taught me the pride of the sun
Before teaching me to read
A shack to guard groves is my home,
Made of branches and reeds
Are you pleased with my status?
I am a name with no honorific.
Write it down!
I am an Arab.[58]

Darwish first delivered the poem in 1964, in front of a packed cinema in Nazareth, and the audience was electrified. The poem, which led to Darwish's house arrest, was immediately read as an act of poetic resistance against Israeli erasure of Palestinian identity. It remained Darwish's most popular poem. But critics have placed it among his early works of political protest, effective yet two-dimensional, before his artistic development in exile.[59] The depiction of the narrator as an earnest villager, a masculine and virile quarry worker, reads as an exercise in socialist realism. This judgment of the poem as immature is confirmed by Darwish's own refusal to recite it in his public appearances after he went into exile in 1970. In one Beirut performance, after persistent calls from the audience—"Write it down! I am an Arab"!—Darwish replied angrily: "Write it down yourself!" In interviews Darwish explained that the poem had meaning in the context of subjugation and resistance; reciting it in other contexts would be self-congratulatory and stultifying.[60] Yet a careful reading suggests that "Identity Card" is far more complex than a straightforward declaration of defiance. Rather, the poem insightfully discerns the intricate dialectics of writing, erasure, and counter-writing which make these operations codependent on each other.

Darwish's strategic choice in the poem is to take over the pen of his oppressor. The identity card at the center of the poem is a state-imposed textual artifact whose aim is the control of population and especially of "dangerous" population. State categorization was employed in order to fragment, dispossess, and erase indigenous existence. In its transformation of the native population into "minorities," the state denied its national existence and historical rights, and sought to fragment it along lines of religion and clans. Darwish is well aware of all this and chooses to use the cataloguing logic of the state against it, to take the oppressor's terms and turn them on their head. That choice is made clear in the very opening of the poem. "I'm an Arab," states the narrator. "An Arab"—and not a Palestinian, repeating the Israeli categorization of Palestinians as mere "Arabs," a term which denies their national identity. That choice is no simple internalization of the oppressor's nomenclature, but rather a conscious attempt to reclaim a derogatory term. The narrator is asked for his identifying details, as they are recorded in his papers. But at every turn he provides answers which are generic, evasive, and mythological. His identity number is the unlikely "50000"; his name has "no honorific" and "no pedigree"; his roots are from "before time was born"; his grandfather was "a peasant farmer"; his physical traits are of a generic Arab villager: brown eyes, black hair, and of course, the *kufiyya* (the villagers' headgear that became a national symbol in the 1930s revolt). These are not the traits of an individual but rather a portrayal of the Palestinian salt of the earth. What may read first as a propaganda poster is in fact a conscious attempt to provoke the oppressor: "Does this make you rage?" he repeatedly asks his interrogator. Indeed, it is unclear which if any of the details here are intended to be read literally. Exposing the operation of categorizing, measuring, and specifying as a technology of oppression, the narrator seeks to empty it from within. Such an approach is reminiscent of what Homi Bhabha has termed "colonial mimicry": instances in which the colonized, through parodic performance that imitates the colonizer, is able to deconstruct the discourse of European hegemony. The ironic appropriation of the rulers' symbolic apparatus produces a displacement that exposes the operation of power and, in turn, empowers the colonized, who is able to reclaim his terms of oppression.[61]

As such, the poem is not merely an articulation of the Palestinian narrative; it is a provocative act of writing that takes place in the language of the oppressor and uses his categories. This choice is particularly intriguing. Why did Darwish choose to assert Palestinian existence through the terms of his interrogators? In the 1980s, scholars seeking to redeem the voice of the oppressed searched for the voice of subaltern groups in the archives of the powerful. The ability to retrieve such voices through hegemonic narratives was questioned in Gayatri Spivak's famous essay "Can the Subaltern Speak?" But in Darwish's case, the subaltern actively chooses to speak through the report of his tormentor. He does not pen his own narrative; instead he dictates it to his interrogator. Why would he speak through his oppressor's voice? Why would he choose his instrument of oppression—the objectifying and dispossessing identity card—as a device through which to tell his story?

Darwish appears to suggest that in the dialectics of domination in Israel/Palestine, the gaze of the Israeli is inescapable and therefore has to be part of the process of emancipation. The pervasive logic of registration and categorization cannot simply be ignored. Rather, it has to be fought and resisted from within, through the very terms of the identity card. The Palestinian writes himself back to the landscape, but he is unable to do so outside the instruments of his oppression.

That ambivalence regarding erasure and writing perhaps become clearest when the author provides his address:

> My address:
> I am from a forgotten abandoned village
> Its streets nameless

The namelessness of the village streets is not surprising. The popular geography of Palestinian villages, like that of Jerusalem, was not organized around a linear grid of streets but rather in relation to landmarks and locales. That namelessness is emblematic of the organic connection between the narrator and his environment, a connection so strong and natural it does not require the naming of people or streets. For Walter Benjamin, nameless city squares were unique places which managed to escape the careful planning of the city's authorities. Avoiding surveillance and scrutiny, they emerged "slowly, sleepily, belatedly" and held a magical sense of resilience and vitality. "In such squares, the trees hold sway; even the smallest afford thick shade . . . their earliest green glow at dusk is the automatic signal for the start of spring in the big city."[62] The nameless streets of Darwish's forgotten and abandoned village could similarly be seen as defying the attempts to bring the villagers under surveillance. After all, modern mapping and naming of villages were conducted as part of attempts to control, subjugate, and colonize. Ottoman census and land registration aimed to extract taxes, conscript men to the empire's wars, and take over "unused" land. British mapping exercises, such as the 1870s Survey of Western Palestine, paved the way for the occupation of Palestine in 1917. Colonial mapping during the British Mandate aimed to facilitate Zionist land acquisition.[63] In the 1940s, Zionist intelligence agencies collected detailed information on Palestinian villages in view of the impending war. Most of these villages were occupied, depopulated, and destroyed in the 1948 war.[64] Remaining forgotten and nameless can be seen as an act of resistance against the colonial imposition of a legible grid on Palestinians. The narrator's determination to withhold these identifying details is perhaps a measure by which to escape the organizing gaze of the colonizing state.

But the namelessness of the streets and the village can also be read differently: not as a choice of resistance but as a sign of their ruin, expressing the destruction of Arab Palestine. After all, the final act in the drama of mapping Palestine's villages was their removal from the Hebrew map. In the early decades of Israel's establishment, the state conducted a grand overhaul of Hebraizing the landscape and removing Palestinian nomenclature from maps and signs.[65] Remote and forgotten, the narrator's village is a relic of a thriving Palestinian society that was overwhelmed in 1948, its lands stolen, its population driven into exile, and its nomenclature removed from books, maps, and memory. In such a reading, namelessness is not a virtue but a weakness. The narrator's project is an attempt to write his village back into existence, even if that means existence in the Israeli state records.

Written more than half a century after Sakakini printed his visiting card, stating simply "A human being," Mahmoud Darwish's "Identity Card" is devoid of the simple optimism that characterized Sakakini's modernist gesture. Unlike Sakakini, Darwish writes himself against his identity papers, an artifact that was produced in order to control and dispossess him. His poem illustrates that any resistance is not a simple act of "rewriting" but rather a complicated dialectic in which the narrator seeks simultaneously to escape the recording gaze and to take ownership of it.

CONCLUSION

SHORTLY AFTER JABRA IBRAHIM JABRA'S FAMILY MOVED TO Jerusalem in the 1930s, Jabra's father was told of a Muslim mystic who had magical powers: "He tells the future, heals neural diseases, reconciles hearts and makes a barren woman give birth to twins!"[1] The father, suffering badly from Parkinson's disease, approached the mystic, who provided him with an amulet in a black leather pouch to be wound tightly around his neck. The father came back home announcing that he would heal in a month or two. Yet Jabra and his brother Yusuf were outraged to learn that their father had fallen victim to a quack, who had charged him the small fortune of three Palestinian pounds. "Three pounds?!" exclaimed Yusuf. "We all work every day and don't earn as much as three pounds in a whole month. Are you crazy?"[2]

The sons convinced the father to demand the money back. They knocked on the mystic's door, above which was a sign as wide as the facade of the house, reading "Noor el-Deen, Astrologer and Spiritualist." An awe-inspiring man wearing a green turban and a black cloak stepped out. After a short exchange, the surprised mystic agreed to return the money. When they were back in their little shack, the disillusioned father took the amulet from around his neck and threw it on the ground in anger and frustration. Jabra recalls:

> I picked it up, tried to open it, but couldn't. I brought a pair of scissors, cut off the end of the amulet, and took from it the magic my father was promised: a

> white, foolscap paper on which squares were drawn, about forty of them. In each square, there was a letter of the alphabet or a star. The letters did not suggest any meaning. I had hoped it might at least be the Throne Verse of the Qur'an. But the astrologer-spiritualist was more clever than to write Qur'anic verses that everyone knew. Letters and stars, however, had a cryptic character and therein lay his magic. If we were to tell him what we had done, he would doubtlessly say that magic would lose its effect if its secret was uncovered.[3]

Eighty years earlier, in the 1850s, such amulets were extremely popular in Jerusalem, as recorded by the Swiss physician Titus Tobler.[4] Muslim mystics complained to Tobler that their amulets were in such high demand that they could not find time for religious studies. The talismanic power of writing cut across religious affiliations. Tobler was witness to a ritual in which a Muslim sheikh attempted to heal a young Jewish man suffering from peritonitis by writing Arabic characters in squares on a piece of paper placed on the patient's forehead.

Jabra, however, lived in another generation. Eschewing the sacred and cryptic text and celebrating the rationalist order of modern signs, he could not see the enigmatic arrangement of letters as anything but a clever ploy. The large commercial sign above the mystic's door was far more familiar to Jabra than the magical sequence of letters that were the sheikh's merchandise.

While Jabra and his brother rejected the divine power of the amulet, they had no similar doubts about the meaning of Palestine-pound banknotes. As capitalist relations encroached on traditional social structures, the Jabra family, like many Arab Palestinians from the rural parts of the country, increasingly depended on wage labor for their daily survival. Jabra himself, although a small child, worked as a shop assistant and a day laborer in a foundry. The talismanic power of the amulet's letters was dubious, but the mystifying power of the colonial state's words and numbers was undeniable. Hard work, books, rent, could all transform into these pieces of paper, printed in English, Arabic, and Hebrew.

The demise of the written language's power to heal, and its newly acquired powers to advertise and to embody value, are aspects of the transformation described in this book. In Jerusalem of the mid-nineteenth century, the appearance of text in Arabic and Hebrew was anchored in the life of religious communities and in the sanctity of the scriptures. The circulation of text was dictated by a strict formulaic logic determining what could be written, where, and in what form. Within these unspoken rules, inscriptions invested sites, objects, and buildings with ideological meaning as well as with heavenly protection. This use of text corresponded to a world in which writing was practiced by few, news was delivered primarily by voice, and urban geography was communicated through oral culture rather than by signs.

Modernity brought new uses and meanings to writing. The religious underpinning of the written language lost ground in a new social order dominated by capitalism, nationalism, and colonialism. Text was encountered more frequently around the city, in signs on buildings and shops, public notices, commercial advertisements, street nameplates, and house numbers. These were hardly unique to Jerusalem. Modernity heralded a growing homogeneity in textual media and technologies, heavily influenced by Western forms and ideas. But the nature of this textual transformation in Jerusalem was inevitably unique and determined by the city's matrix of economies and cultures. Local traditions of writing were abandoned or adapted to fit in with a new age. The sacred quality of Arabic and Hebrew continued to reverberate and was harnessed for secular agendas. The political projects which framed and facilitated the new texts were a product of the specific constellation of Jerusalem in which global, regional, and local networks collided. The *tughras* of Ottomanism, the signs of Arabic Nahda, Ashkenazi placards, Haskalah school signs, British colonial street names, and Zionist signage: this condensed combination was unique to Jerusalem, and it brought together, within a small urban space, a rich set of contexts in which textual modernity was negotiated.

The transformation of urban text was not merely a symptom of social changes but also a potent tool employed to achieve those very changes. Through the introduction of certain texts and the withdrawal of others, new orders were pursued. In this sense, urban text was an important agency of modernity. In a world increasingly transient, fragmented, and in flux, text provided a method of organizing, naming, and defining the urban surroundings. But the successful rewriting of the landscape did not—and could not—amount to full control of the textual landscape. While signposting the urban environment was designed to introduce order and meaning, it also had the opposite effect, creating anxieties and instability. The collapse of the traditional textual economy unleashed text from its secure position and opened possibilities of constant rewriting. The new order harbored inherent disorder, always threatening to erupt. Sacred texts were feared as a dangerous fetish which had power over crowds. A sign that was put up could be taken down; a street could be named and renamed; identities could be redefined. In a world of social instability, text was not only a tool of control but also something to be controlled. While signs attempted to freeze the meaning of a world in flux, their very presence opened an abyss of uncertainty.

TEXT, POWER, MYTHOLOGIES

The modern state relied heavily on the deployment of textuality in tightening its grip over the city. The authorities accumulated information on residents and properties through a textual system of addresses, population and land registers. This required a mammoth and never-ending project of rationalization, documentation, marking, and signposting, which began in Jerusalem during the late-Ottoman period, accelerated during the First World War, and continued with added vigor under British rule. Maps, reports, and statistics organized the world into lists and tabulated columns, striving toward an orderly universe in which space and population were readable. Urban textual forms externalized this form of organization and imposed it on an unprecedented level. Information was not only collected and held in state depositories; it was now marked on houses and in official identity documents held by citizens. The use of such documents reached a peak in times of war and crisis, when identity papers had to be submitted to the gaze of state officials regularly and frequently in ports, police stations, and checkpoints. The absence of "correct" papers could lead to denial of access, imprisonment, and exile, and in some cases even death sentences. These measures coincided with attempts to establish control over urban signage, specifying what could be written, in what languages and where, and what texts could no longer be tolerated. New official forms of public writing were introduced; networks of textual communication, through telegraph and postal services, were expanded; and the monetary economy was reshaped and became thoroughly textualized, especially with the transition to paper money.

Dematerialization and abstraction were the most striking features of the modern transformation of urban texts. Releasing writing from its material grounding was crucial for constructing a new relationship between text and the world. A dichotomy appeared between text and substance, parallel to modern polarities of signifier and signified, content and form. Text was imagined as an external referent, as if it were written on a blank page. The external referentiality enabled the use of text as a signifier, dictating the true meaning of signified artifacts and sites: signs marked the purpose and name of buildings or streets; identity papers defined individuals; banknotes embodied free-flowing exchange value, spelling out amounts in words and numbers. This external position made text a perfect instrument to promote modernity's reorganization of knowledge and social practices through renaming and signposting.

The abstraction of text was tied to a gendered understanding of the operation of writing as a form of masculinity. The dichotomy of text and the material world corresponded to polarities of (masculine) mind and (feminine) body. Imposing textual order on the world, imprinting names into the fabric of the city—these were masculine acts. In Ronald Storrs's words, it was up to the (male) conqueror of dumb Jerusalem to determine the dumb names of "her streets." In instances where writing was disavowed it was seen as an excessive act of penetration. The materiality of graffiti, its unashamed engagement with unauthorized writing surfaces, emerged as a vulgar crime.

For contemporary European thinkers, this abstraction of text was not only useful but also ethically imperative. Simmel viewed abstract capital as the Platonic ideal, and for Saussure the arbitrary nature of signifiers was the source of their power. Keynes saw overcoming the barbaric adoration of shining metal as a sign of human progress. And yet the transformation of text into an abstract signifier enabled new forms of symbolic violence. It opened new possibilities of establishing order and hierarchy through inscription and erasure, on an unprecedented level.

The textualizing gaze of the state met with ground-level resistance. The 1858 numbering of houses was understood by the local population as a "tyrannical" exercise, reflecting popular awareness of the link between public writing and disciplinary power. These marks were erased or painted over by residents, perhaps in an attempt to frustrate the authorities' reading efforts. Residents often refused to give primacy to the written sign in their understanding of local space. They ignored the prominently signposted names on sites and streets, and continued to use their own nomenclature. Whether politically motivated by an anticolonial agenda or not, such steps worked to limit the efficacy of signposting as a means of control.

The shift from traditional textual economies to modern ones was far from abrupt. It was a long process which involved overlapping practices, which saw older forms of texts used alongside newer ones. The banners of Nabi Musa were paraded enthusiastically in the streets well into the 1930s. Jewish pilgrims continued to try to write their name on the Western Wall in the same decade. These customs can be read as resistance to the new age of rational and secular text, by insisting on the devotional role of written language. Colonial repression was instrumental in clamping down on these age-old textual practices. However, Arab Palestinian society and the Jewish Yishuv were active agents in transforming textuality. By the 1930s, both Arabs and Jews, locals and newcomers alike, embraced new symbols and new texts, from political placards to signs on buildings. Traditional textual practices became forms of heritage or were discarded.

But as Walter Benjamin observed, the imposition of the new textual grid could not be described only in terms of rationalization and demystification. Quite the opposite: new texts breathed new mythologies into urban space. The new signs saturating the urban environment not only organized information in functional and readable manner; they also wrote new stories about the meaning of the city, its past, present, and future. The state ideology of Ottomanism blended imperial patriotism, Islamic legitimacy, and fervent belief in progress and development. The authorities renovated historical Islamic inscriptions, but also flooded the city with new signs that expressed the new ideology. The sultan's insignia was employed as a national symbol, appearing on money, official documents, placards, signs, and stone inscriptions on new civic institutions. The *tughra* as text-logo adapted the calligraphy of a medieval cypher into an easily recognizable, mass-produced emblem of sovereignty. Looking over the city from the clock tower in the new city center with the municipality, banks, and cafés, the *tughra* harnessed the supremacy of text as a visual register to promote a modernist vision of civic development. With the Nahda, local intellectuals employed Arabic on signs and newspapers as a modern language of cultural revival, leading, in the aftermath of the Great War, to Arab nationalism. For the fast-growing Jewish communities in turn-of-the-century Jerusalem, Hebrew was a means to express a diversity of ideologies and imagined futures: from Haskalah enlightenment through Orthodox guarding of pious ways to Hebrew national revival and Zionist colonization.

Hebrew Revival activists sought to make Hebrew a secular language of the street while recasting its mythical and messianic power in the service of national redemption.

The British rulers of Jerusalem after 1917 understood the city in strikingly different terms. Jerusalem's Ottoman modernity, with its religious and ethnic pluralism and naive pursuit of technology and progress, was forsaken in favor a historicist remaking. The British imposed a discourse of preservation and conservation on Jerusalem, ensuring that a largely modern city would look like an ancient one. They believed that religious segregation was an essential trait of the city, which they sought to maintain in planning policies. The 1920s street-naming campaign was a means through which the ethos of sanctity, reverence, and historicity was inscribed on street corners. Modern Jerusalem was rewritten with the names of biblical prophets and Crusader kings, emblazoned in tiles reminiscent of the Dome of the Rock. The names carved up the city according to sectarian code, gesturing toward a future of segregation and partition. At the same time, the recognition of Hebrew as an official language confirmed British support for Zionism. The trilingual format in English, Arabic, and Hebrew became the trademark of British-ruled Palestine. The display of Hebrew on official signs, stamps, and money was the most visible affirmation of British commitment to the establishment of a Jewish National Home in Palestine. Endorsed by the colonial state, the Zionist movement invested a different urgency into the language, as a tool to claim and rewrite the land as well as its Jewish communities.

TEXTUAL ANXIETIES, TEXTUAL PROMISES

The power of text to impose order, organize the world, and fix its meaning depended on a disappearance of meaning. As a supplement in the Derridian sense, signage functioned as an addendum which, while external to the "original," becomes inextricably linked to it and is able to determine it. This very ability exposed the deficiency of the original as always incomplete, always unstable, and potentially absent. The weight of meaning shifted from the signified to the signifier, from buildings to the texts they displayed. This led to an economy of detached signifiers, increasingly divorced from the material world, taking on a life of their own. But as meaning was deferred from the subject (the person) or object (city, building, street) to a textual layer, the doubts and uncertainty inherent in such representation came to threaten the truthfulness of the text. The specter of counter-writing loomed, inducing anxiety and fear. And even when counter-writing did not materialize, its very possibility exposed the vulnerability of the new order. The relative ease with which text would now be displayed in the street made it necessary to control and regulate it more closely. The state could now write money into existence, but without the reassurance of gold backing its value could be at risk. Urban geography could be determined top-down through edict and signposting, but that also meant the possibility of counter-naming and rewriting. The anxiety around older forms of text (banners, graffiti) and around unregulated text pointed to the inherent weakness of modern text: it can serve to organize the world, but it can also be removed, rewritten, disrupted.

This anxiety is especially evident in the manner in which the British Mandatory authorities approached the issue of text in urban space. In their attempt to control the textual landscape, the authorities did not stop with determining official languages, naming streets, and issuing stamps and money. They also tried to control—and prevent—the use of Arab protest banners, on the pretext of regulating advertisements. And they feared the menace of the fetishized text, the potent talisman that could undo public order. The special attention to these artifacts, which involved writing "out of control," illustrated the fragility of the new textual matrix. This anxiety went beyond the British. Zionist calls for the "imposition" of the Hebrew language betrayed fears about the fragility of Hebrew Revival. For Arab Jerusalemites, Hebrew script acquired a menacing dimension as indicators of a looming Jewish takeover, and age-old pilgrims' graffiti were now seen as Zionist interventions.

Many in Jerusalem embraced the textual instability and the possibilities for counter-writings that it opened. The saturated signage invited new opportunities for dreams, fantasies, and nightmares. Modernity's enthusiast, Khalil al-Sakakini, believed in the possibility of rewriting himself and his surroundings. The Arabic language was for him a vehicle of emancipation and the promise of a new future. His visiting card, "A human being," remains, a century later, a startlingly radical declaration whose political relevance has in no way diminished. For Sakakini, as for Jabra Ibrahim Jabra, the alienated condition of modernity was an exhilarating opportunity. The very fragmentation and dislocation of texts allowed their radical appropriation.

Through the language of telegrams, signs, and posters, a new world could be constructed. When, in the 1960s, Mahmoud Darwish appropriated the identity card as a weapon of counter-writing, he was building on decades of Palestinian modernist resistance.

However, for those attached to the sacred quality of language, modern signs created an ominous sense of loss, captured in Agnon's novel *Only Yesterday*. Agnon's lamentation of the lost sacred unity of text and meaning did not amount to fantasies of going back. Orthodox attempts to guard the sanctity of Hebrew, by covering the streets of Jerusalem with excommunication notices, only further impelled the fragmentation of language and its removal from sacred immediacy. But at the same time, Agnon warned that the pioneer profane language, which, in a godlike manner, names and conquers, could come back to bite its authors. Agnon's warning materialized toward the end of the century when the messianic language of redemption ousted the Labor Zionists and relegated them to the sidelines of politics. The Golem of nationalized sacrality came back to haunt its creators. The triumph and defeat of Hebrew Revival can be found in the fate of Jerusalem's first modern Jewish school. The Lämel School, established in 1856, was the bastion of local Haskalah and the nemesis of the Ashkenazi Orthodox establishment. When its new building opened in 1903, it was a symbol of German-inspired modernity. During the 1920s it became a stronghold of Zionism. It was from here that Zionist youth marched to the Western Wall in August 1929, triggering the outbreak of riots.[5] But with the changing nature of the neighborhood, the school was taken over in the early twentieth-first century by Jerusalem's oldest Ashkenazi yeshiva 'Ets Hayim. The new proprietors not only wrote the name of the yeshiva in large letters over the elegant facade, they also whitewashed the German and Hebrew sign above the entrance. The hated institution of the Haskalah had been taken over by the Orthodox. And yet they, in turn, fully adopted the logic of Hebrew signposting.

It is often suggested that the clash between Zionism and Arab Palestinian society was an encounter between two radically different civilizations, understood through the polarities of Europe and the Orient, modernity and tradition. Interpretations of these dichotomies differ widely, but what they share is agreement about the incommensurability of the two societies, and their profound cultural differences. Evidently, there were significant differences between the two societies in class structure, political economy, resources, and agency.[6] However, this book suggests that in cultural terms, commonalities may run deeper than is generally acknowledged. There were striking affinities in the ways Arabic and Hebrew texts were used and understood, and between Jewish and Muslim traditions of text, its divine power, and its prominent place in material culture and architecture. There were also parallels in the manner in which Jews, Muslims, and Christians in Palestine adopted new technologies of writing. Clearly, there were also important differences in textual practices. The Ashkenazi economy of paper—in posters, debt certificates, print shops, and wish notes placed in the Western Wall—stood out in comparison to practices of other groups (including Sephardic Jews). The emphasis on the aesthetics of Arabic script, and the political ramifications of calligraphy, did not have a parallel in Hebrew. The most crucial difference between Arabic and Hebrew in early-twentieth-century Jerusalem was the Zionist emphasis on territorialization through language. Street naming and signposting appeared as a high Zionist priority, as instruments of colonization of Hebrew and in Hebrew.

However, when it comes to urban texts, the dichotomy tradition/modernity does not correspond to a dichotomy of Arab/Zionist or colonized/colonizers. Quite the contrary: Arab Palestinian anticolonial resistance was as enthusiastic about new forms of signification as were Zionists; and within Jewish circles we can find voices wary about forsaking ancient ways of writing. Rather than a story of Zionist modernizers (progressive or ruthless, depending on viewpoint) meeting traditional Arab culture, modernity was a challenge and opportunity that Arabic and Hebrew responded to similarly, albeit from different positionings.

MODERNITY AND ERASURE IN JERUSALEM

I started this book in Jerusalem's train station, as it lay in ruins in the 2000s. A year after my trespassing visit the station was torched and suffered considerable damage. Following this incident, the site's commercial potential and its prime location were finally recognized by developers. It was renovated into an open-air shopping center and now hosts a hub of shops and restaurants, dominated by commercial signs and branding logos in English and Hebrew. Texts of consumption rule the space, and the turbulent history of the station was relegated to harmless nostalgic photographs in black and white, placed here and there amid the shops. A small exhibit frames the history of the station as part of European and Zionist interest in the Holy Land, effectively erasing the station's early history: its Ottoman, local, multi-faith beginnings. As I walk among the stalls and the cafés, I look to the Ottoman name of the city which continues to hang above the station, and I can hear the ghosts of 1900, telling different stories.

My journey through the streets of Jerusalem has had an alienating and disorienting effect on me. As I traced obliterated signs and textual artifacts, and as I read the memoirs and diaries of the early twentieth century, the city took an unfamiliar shape. Jerusalem, as I knew it from my childhood, was a city rooted in sanctity, antiquity, and sectarian segregation, a city defined by the clash between its supposed unity and its divided condition: between Israeli Judaization and Palestinian resistance; a city of fragmentation and diversity of communities, which found limited common denominators in religion or national identity. The late-Ottoman city that emerged from my readings was a different and unfamiliar one. It was a city of a nonsectarian civic identity, which was defined in terms of a turbulent present and a promising future. A city whose civic life took place between the train station and the municipal gardens. A diverse and cosmopolitan city with an ethos of progress and aggressive development, mesmerized by the promise of tramways, public libraries, telegrams, and photographer studios. This city survived under the British Mandate in form but not in spirit. Despite the escalating Zionist-Arab conflict, cross-confessional social and business ties persisted well into the 1940s, as did a mixed urban reality. Yet the meaning of the city was being rewritten. The British notion of Jerusalem as an eternally ancient, holy, and segregated city took root. The colonial government left very few monuments in Jerusalem and only a handful of buildings. Yet the self-effacing nature of the British legacy was its greatest success. Jerusalem today, as it is perceived by many within and outside the region, is largely a product of British imagination. The stone-built city, eternally holy and ever divided between its quarreling sects, was the brainchild of Ronald Storrs, Herbert Samuel, and a generation of British administrators, who named its streets after prophets and kings, covered its new buildings with a stone mask, and painted its banknotes with revered monuments.

Early-twentieth-century Jerusalem is today simultaneously present and absent. The Ottoman and post-Ottoman core of the city is still visible and identifiable. But the effects of British planning, the 1948 war and depopulation, the division of the city from 1948 to 1967, and Israeli planning policies since the occupation of East Jerusalem have resulted in a profound reconfiguration of urban space, so much so that the early-twentieth-century city has been rendered invisible.

After the 1948 division of the city, depopulation was followed by the rewriting of the landscape. In the Israeli part of town, streets named after Christian, Crusader, and British personalities were unceremoniously given biblical names instead.[7] Saint Paul became the Tribes of Israel (Shivtey Yisra'el); Princess Mary became Queen Shlomtsion (Salome Alexandra, the last Judean queen). Governor Storrs, the mastermind of Jerusalem's colonial remaking, was not exempt. Storrs Avenue (named such in the late 1930s) was renamed after Koresh (Cyrus). A similar attempt was made to Hebraize the former bourgeois Arab neighborhood, now repopulated with Jewish immigrants. New names were marked on maps and road signs: Ge'ulim for Baq'a; Gonen for Qatamun; Komemiyut for Talbiya; Morasha for Musrara. But these new names failed to take hold. The old Arab names have remained and are still in use. In the Jordanian side of the city, the trilingual street nameplates were replaced with bilingual (Arabic and English) signs; and the Street of the Jews became the Street of the Fighters (Tariq al-Munadilin).

Since the 1967 Israeli occupation of East Jerusalem and its unilateral annexation, planning policies have transformed the city and its hinterland. The expropriation of Palestinian land, establishment of Jewish-Israeli neighborhoods in East Jerusalem, settlements within Palestinian neighborhoods, and severe limits on Palestinian construction have resulted in a deeply segregated and unequal city. The Israeli municipality materialized the British plan to separate the Old City from the new parts by destroying most of the former Ottoman city center near Jaffa Gate.

Such attempts were part of the physical and symbolic erasure of the lived Arab geography of Palestine, whose clearest manifestation was the removal of place names from the map. Since 1948 Israeli naming committees devised thousands of new names for streets, neighborhoods, settlements, mountains, and rivers in an effort to de-Arabize the landscape of the country. They built on the work of nineteenth-century European Christian scholars and explorers, and 1920s British colonial officials, who viewed Palestine and Jerusalem primarily through biblical lenses. Israeli authorities even tried to change the Arabic name of the city from Al-Quds to Urshalim al-Quds. The liturgical Christian name for Jerusalem, Urshalim, was chosen as an official name because of its similarity to the Hebrew Yerushalayim. The Judaizing operation of claiming territory through naming and renaming found material manifestation in road signs, informative boards at historical sites, and in guidebooks and maps. But opposition to Arabic is so deep that some abhor the very presence of Arabic script on signage, regardless of its content. Arabic legends are often vandalized and obliterated.

The Israeli rewriting of the city's geography and history continues to unfold. Resisting the colonial logic of rewriting thus has a political urgency which has in no way decreased.[8] Policies of exclusion and discrimination are legitimized through narratives of denial. The textual traces of Jerusalem before 1948 can be used to write alternative pasts for the city, which in turn may enable alternative futures. Bringing these traces to visibility is a counterpoint to the project of erasure.

And yet terms such as *erasure* and *replacement* unwittingly assume a textual order in which the world is a blank page, and in which texts are signifiers which define and name. A narrative of "writing" in which one nameplate is removed and another one is affixed in its stead implicitly accepts the logic of signposting as immediate and natural. Such understanding of writing as signposting misses the fundamental violence of this operation, its modern quality, and its embeddedness within colonial logic. Signposting arrived in Jerusalem with coloniality and with modern state violence. The active shaping of Jerusalem's landscape and demographics in favor of nationalist and colonialist agendas hinged on the ability to use text as a tool of intervention, in monumental signs and on residents' identification cards. Such interventions were a novelty that often was at odds with local notions of space and textuality. Modernity's obsession with signifiers and labels, and its understanding of the world as a blank page to be written on, were the preconditions of the rewriting exercise and its violent ramifications. The colonial operation of dispossession, appropriation, and rearticulation is not specific to Jerusalem but rather is an essential trait of modernity's reformulation of relations between language and the world.

FIGURE 51. Jerusalem road sign with Arabic erased.
Source: Hagar Goren, Parhesya.

TEXT IN RUIN

In searching for Jerusalem's lost texts, I followed in the footsteps of two epigraphers of the early twentieth century who surveyed Jerusalem's textual landscape. The celebrated Orientalist Max van Berchem carefully documented Jerusalem's Islamic stone inscriptions. The amateur local historian Pinhas Grayevsky collected the city's Hebrew stones of memory, without scientific credentials but with no less enthusiasm. While driven by very different philosophical, scholarly, and political agendas, their missions were similar: salvaging the writings in stone before they crumbled and disappeared. Both were propelled by a sense of urgency. They believed that the inscriptions, and the cultures they embodied, were facing rapid disintegration.

My textual-rag-collecting journey in the streets of Jerusalem could be said to be driven by a similar mission of salvaging. The texts I set out collecting, more eclectic in form and material, were the texts of modernity: the railway sign, the library name, shop signage, Palestine banknotes, street nameplates, visiting cards, and identity papers. Many of these artifacts are slowly transforming into nostalgia items, relics of the twentieth century. These textual media , in their Jerusalem incarnations, were a product of local political crises and opportunities. Their ruin, disappearance, and obliteration had much to do with the city's turbulent modern history. But at the same time, these textual media are in the midst of symbolic disintegration for reasons that are wider than Jerusalem's upheavals.

The modern textual forms of the early twentieth century are ruins in the making. The systems of artifacts and labels which organized the world are losing their footing in today's world. The digital revolution has redefined the manner in which we read and write, the manner in which we are written and are read. In the analogue heyday of the 1970s, it seemed as if writing was receding from many realms of the everyday. Communication and media moved in visual and aural directions. With audiotapes, videotapes, record players, and the omnipresence of television and the telephone, writing was becoming an unusual activity which was reserved for specific professions. But the arrival of the personal computer and the internet have proved the opposite. Text has experienced a renaissance of unprecedented dimensions. Indeed, text became, for the first time, a verb in English, "to text," associated with sending messages on mobile phones. The ubiquity of social media has led to an explosion in readable material and in writing practices. We read and write on smartphones, tablets, computers, and a range of other digital media, at home, at work, during travel or leisure. At the same time, many textual media of the twentieth century are becoming artifacts of heritage and nostalgia. While still in use, their place and future are no longer evident. The printed newspaper makes way for the digital edition. The card index was replaced with a digital catalogue and file system. Holiday postcards are superseded by text messages or emails. Street nameplates are rendered far less necessary with satellite navigation and digital maps. Identity cards are replaced with biometric identification. Visiting cards no longer carry the same usefulness. Banknotes are replaced with plastic cards. Political agitation is conducted less through pamphlets and more through social-media posts.

The new digital media continue the trends of fragmentation, abstraction, and dematerialization of text. Written in binary code, and projected onto flat screens, text is more ephemeral than ever. Twentieth-century textual systems encouraged their readers and writers to think in terms of organization and hierarchy by affixing labels and meanings to people, places, and things. The new digital texts push us away from fantasies of simple truths and clear hierarchies into a world increasingly chaotic and networked, of multiple and competing narratives and webs of information, where text leads in manifold potential directions.

Making sense of this startling expansion of textuality requires understanding the historicity of text and its dependence on context. While there is no denying that globalization has contributed to the homogenizing of textual media, the impact and nature of these transformations can only be appreciated through localized constellations. To understand modern textuality it is vital to look beyond Western scripts and writing cultures. We can see this in the sanctified status of Arabic and Hebrew scripts, which continues to resonate today in Jerusalem. The aura of these scripts cannot compare to what it was two centuries ago. But it would be similarly wrong to believe that these languages have lost their halo. The proliferation in Jerusalem of religious bumper stickers and graffiti, in Arabic and in Hebrew, is a constant reminder that sacred scripts may have transformed but their aura has not disappeared.

To understand the significance of new textual technologies, it is necessary to revisit the moment of their emergence, to investigate how writers and readers perceived the moment of change. Novel texts could only be understood against the background of existing textual economies. Such a study requires an appreciation of the diverse universe of historical textual practices beyond Eurocentric print cultures. It means going back to textual artifacts which to modern observers may appear strange, opaque, or banal, such as holy banners and pilgrims' graffiti. These texts do not evoke the same nostalgia and familiarity as an old advertisement or political poster. But such a sense of alienation is a useful resource if we are to think through textuality, its diverse premises and permutations. In thinking of the texts of today, their potential for human emancipation and as tools of repression, we benefit from remembering that textuality is anything but stable and uniform, and from appreciating how malleable, and how open to change, our world of text is.

Acknowledgments

In writing this book, I have benefited from many colleagues who have shared their knowledge and sharp intellect with me, suggesting sources, links, and ideas, in personal meetings and in correspondence. Annie Coombes followed the project in its initial stages, and her insightful guidance was crucial in the early stages of my career. Salim Tamari, whose work on Jerusalem is a true inspiration, was generous in providing comments and advice. Ami Ayalon, Benjamin Fortna, Emma Aubin-Boltansky, and Ariel Hirschfeld offered advice in the earlier stages of the project. Nirit Shalev Khalifa shared my interest in lost signs in Jerusalem and provided crucial advice on art-historical and urban aspects. Eli Osheroff and Lee Rotbart assisted with aspects of the archival research. My friends and colleagues Karène Summerer-Sanchez, Hannes Baumann, and Najat Abdulhaq were constant sources of support and advice. I am deeply grateful to all of these wonderful scholars. Naturally, the responsibility for the finished book is mine and mine only.

London, rich with history of empire and radical resistance, was and remains a challenging and rewarding context from which to think about modernity and urban space. My initial encounter with this messy metropolis had a determining effect on this book. In South London's radical social centers, such as 56a, I found friendship, solidarity, material help—as well as a unique space for intellectual reflection and political education. I learned the importance of trespassing and scavenging as critical methodologies. These intellectual and urban adventures taught me to call into question the immediacy of dominant social and cultural orders, and to open my eyes to the pain, injustice, beauty, and magic of the streets. I am thankful to the many friends who shared that journey with me.

I was fortunate to have been a research associate in the Conflict in Cities program at the University of Cambridge (2010–11). My work there on "shared space" in Jerusalem allowed me an opportunity to think comparatively about the dynamics of conflict in urban space. I'm thankful to Wendy Pullan, who led the project, as well as to colleagues I met in that context, especially Haim Yacoby, Max Sternberg, and Monika Halkort.

During the research for this book, I found assistance in archives and museums. I would like to thank the staff in those institutions: Berlin's Jewish Museum, Oxford's Middle East Centre Archive, King's College and Pembroke College in Cambridge, the Imperial War Museum in London, and in Jerusalem the Central Zionist Archives, Israel State Archives, Yad Ben Zvi, and the National Library of Israel. The digitization project at the National Library of Israel, bringing online early Hebrew and Arabic newspapers, is a wonderful development that made research for the book much easier.

I am thankful to my colleagues at SOAS, the University of London, who provided a supportive and encouraging environment to think about language and history in Asia and Africa. Research leave in 2014–15 and again in early 2018 made the writing of the book possible.

I have benefited from the opportunity to present segments of this work in conferences and workshops, where I received helpful feedback. These took place at SOAS, the Van Leer Institute, the University of Leiden, the Jewish Studies seminar at the Institute of Historical Research (London), and the European Research Council's Open Jerusalem project, whose 2016 Rethymno conference brought together an outstanding group of scholars working on the social history of Jerusalem.

I am thankful to Kate Wahl, editor-in-chief of Stanford University Press, for supporting this book. Her invaluable editorial feedback, sound advice, and patience made it happen. The anonymous reviewers of the book provided insightful comments and feedback which pushed me to make the book better.

And finally, those closest to me deserve a special word. My parents, Maya and Efi Wallach, helped enormously during research trips to Jerusalem, particularly with looking after our daughters, allowing me to spend long days in the libraries and archives of Jerusalem. I am grateful to my siblings, Shlomit and Avner, for their love and support.

This book is dedicated to Phoebe von Held, my partner and my wisest interlocutor. Phoebe's interest in modernism and its discontents made her an incredibly insightful reader and commentator on this project. She helped me to understand what I wanted to say, and how to say it better. At the same time, her support in shouldering most of the care responsibilities for our daughters during the last stage of this project made the completion of the book possible.

Notes

INTRODUCTION

1. Travis, *On Chariots*.

2. Recent historical scholarship approaches material culture not simply as "evidence" which captures and illustrates social change but rather as embedded agency through which change is produced. In the words of Toufoul Abou-Hodeib, material culture should be seen "not as epiphenomenal . . . but rather as an integral part of the experience of modernity." Abou-Hodeib, *Taste for Home*, 40.

3. Much of Benjamin's writing revolves around cities and urban experience. Among the key texts are "One-Way Street," "Moscow, 1927," and "Berlin Childhood around 1900," all available in Benjamin, *Selected Writings*, as well as Benjamin, *Arcades Project*.

4. In the unfinished *Arcades*, Benjamin set out to chart nineteenth-century Paris as a crossroads of modernity. Starting with defunct shopping arcades, the *Arcades* resembled a mammoth card index or an archive. It explored the reshaping of the urban sphere by the state and capital, not only in utilitarian terms but also by writing myth and desire into daily life.

5. I use the term *urban text* as a flexible category to cover a corpus of diverse textual artifacts, encountered primarily in urban settings. Bierman, *Writing Signs*, studies similar texts in medieval Egypt under the term *public text*. But "public" is a modern category, tied to an understanding of "a public" with corresponding "public spaces." Many texts discussed in this book appeared in congregational and confessional contexts. In Jerusalem, a nonsectarian Ottoman "public" emerged in the second

half of the nineteenth century, but it divided into Jewish and Arab publics during the British Mandate.

6. Derrida, *Of Grammatology*. Textuality and writing are also central to Derrida in *Writing and Difference* and *Dissemination*. For an insightful conceptualization of Derrida's early work on writing, see Fleming, *Cultural Graphology*.

7. Derrida, *Of Grammatology*, 9.

8. Derrida, 158–59.

9. Fleming, *Cultural Graphology*, 24. While Fleming sees the need to ground the inquiry in cultural and material contexts, she argues that Derrida's theorization and investigation of textuality offers considerable strengths, especially in his psychoanalytical line of inquiry. Fleming followed this direction in her study of the material context of writing and book publishing in early modern England. See also Fleming, *Graffiti*.

10. Derrida et al., "Paper or Myself," 1.

11. de Certeau, *Practice of Everyday Life*, 131–53.

12. Scott, *Against the Grain*, 139. Scott, who writes on premodern states, argues that writing, from its very inception, was an instrument of state oppression designed to make its population and resources legible.

13. The importance of urban textuality in Benjamin's work has yet to receive scholarly attention. The most relevant work is his experimental tract "One-Way Street," in Benjamin, *Selected Writings*, vol. 1, 444–88. The *Arcades* also devotes much attention to signage, street naming, house numbering, and commercial advertisements.

14. Benjamin, *Selected Writings*, vol. 1, 456.

15. Benjamin, *Arcades Project*, 423.

16. Benjamin, "Berlin Chronicle," in *Selected Writings*, vol. 2, 598.

17. For a "reading" of a walking itinerary, see de Certeau, *Practice of Everyday Life*.

18. Lefebvre, *Production of Space*, 142–43.

19. For studies of reading, see Boyarin, *The Ethnography of Reading*; Cavallo, Chartier, and Cochrane, *History of Reading in the West*; Fischer, *History of Reading*.

20. Landry and Bourhis, "Linguistic Landscape." While the term *linguistic landscape* covers many of the textual media in this book, it is less suitable for capturing the circulation of mobile textual artifacts such as coins, banknotes, ID cards, or visiting cards, which are also discussed here. Hence my preference to use *urban texts* and *textual economies*.

21. See Suleiman, *War of Words*; Shohamy, *Linguistic Landscape*.

22. Such studies in cultural geography include Azaryahu, *'Al Shem*, on street naming in the Yishuv and in Israel; and Kadman, *Erased from Space and Consciousness*, on the erasure of traces of Palestinian pre-1948 society from Israeli landscapes.

23. I have been inspired by cross-disciplinary studies of the social use of text

beyond the book. Messick, *The Calligraphic State*, an anthropological study of the changing roles of writing, reading, and text in twentieth-century Yemen, uses Foucauldian terms to describe a shift from Islamic practices and structures to modern preoccupations with rational order and social control. Bierman's *Writing Signs* examines the role of inscriptions on architecture, coins, and textiles in legitimizing a Shiite minority's rule over a Sunni society in Fatimid Cairo. Henkin, *City Reading*, investigates the democratizing role of the proliferation of text in the public sphere in nineteenth-century New York. Fleming, *Graffiti*, is a psychoanalytical history of graffiti, tattoo, and other forms of writing in Elizabethan England, drawing on Derrida, Freud, and Lacan.

24. I am drawing on Doreen Massey's conceptualization of space as a product of interrelations and a sphere of coexisting heterogeneity, in which forces of different scales clash and coincide. Massey, *For Space*.

25. Kark and Oren-Nordheim, *Jerusalem and Its Environs*, 28.

26. See Ben-Arieh, *The Old City*; Ben-Arieh, *Emergence of the New City*; Kark and Oren-Nordheim, *Jerusalem and Its Environs*; Gilbert, *Jerusalem in the Twentieth Century*; Goldhill, *Jerusalem*; and Montefiore, *Jerusalem*.

27. As editor of the *Jerusalem Quarterly*, Salim Tamari has revolutionized modern Palestinian social history by publishing memoirs and diaries of ordinary people in late-Ottoman and British-ruled Jerusalem, such as the World War I diary of Ihsan al-Turjeman, an Ottoman soldier (Tamari, *Year of the Locust*), and the memoirs of the Wasif Jawhariyyeh, a Greek-Orthodox Arab who was a well-connected musician and bohemian. Jawhariyyeh's memoirs were published in two volumes in Arabic (*Al-Quds al-ʿUthmaniyya*; *Al-Quds al-Intidabiyya*) and in an abridged English translation, Jawhariyyeh, *Storyteller of Jerusalem*. Tamari has used these sources to rigorously rethink categories of identity, space, and Palestine's conflicted modernity. See Tamari, *Mountain against the Sea*; Tamari, *The Great War*.

28. Recent contributions in this vein include Mazza, *Jerusalem*; Jacobson, *From Empire to Empire*; Campos, *Ottoman Brothers*; Lemire, *Jerusalem 1900*; Büssow, *Hamidian Palestine*; Klein, *Lives in Common*.

29. Mazza, *Jerusalem*, 37.

30. Hanssen, Philipp, and Weber, *Empire in the City*.

31. On the middle class in Palestine and Syria, see Watenpaugh, *Being Modern in the Middle East*; Abou-Hodeib, *Taste for Home*; Seikaly, *Men of Capital*.

32. Sheehi, *Foundations of Modern Arab Identity*.

33. On publishing, literacy, and newspapers, see Ayalon, *Reading Palestine*; Ayalon, *Arabic Print Revolution*.

34. For a careful discussion of the Ottoman census, its use by historians, and its limitations, see Campos, "Placing Jerusalemites." Population estimates made

by European scholars and visitors and Jewish organizations put Jerusalem's total population in 1914 at between 75,000 and 100,000, as elaborated by Mazza, *Jerusalem*, 37. Building on a wide literature survey, Mazza suggests that 80,000 is the most reliable estimate. The population fell during the war due to emigration, disease, and war casualties. The first comprehensive census took place in 1922 under British rule, recording a total population of 62,578 among which 13,413 were Muslims, 14,669 Christians, and 33,971 Jews. One question is the population of Jerusalem's immediate hinterland, which increasingly became part of the city in the twentieth century but was not counted as part of the urban population. According to the British 1922 census, the population of suburbanizing villages such as Silwan and Lifta amounted to 10,719 people, almost all Muslim. For the census figures, see Barron, *Palestine*.

35. As argued by Haj, "The People of Jerusalem Reordered."

36. On relational history in Palestine/Israel, see Lockman, "Railway Workers and Relational History."

37. For a 1908 survey of Jewish houses of prayer and study in Jerusalem, see Luncz, *Luah Erets Yisra'el: Mivhar*, vol. 2, 91–134.

38. The historiography typically refers to Palestine's Jews as a single overarching community or Yishuv, divided between Zionist modernizers (New Yishuv) and traditionalists (Old Yishuv). However, these terms are anachronistic, ideological, and misleading. A single Jewish society emerged in Palestine only in the 1930s. See Wallach, "Rethinking the Yishuv."

39. Estimates from Mazza, *Jerusalem*, 41–42; Ben-Arieh, *The Old City*, 354–63. The Zionist wartime census (1916) found 26,605 Jews in the city, divided almost equally between Ashkenazim and Sephardim, and the Ottoman report of Zaki Bey (1917) reported 31,147 Jews out of a population of 53,410. Many Ashkenazi Jews left Palestine with the outbreak of war, as they were enemy citizens, so it is safe to assume prewar figures were higher.

40. Ben-Gurion, in *Ha-Ahdut*, 7 August 1910. Quoted in Ben-Arieh, *Emergence of the New City*, 443–44.

41. On these differences, see Jacobson, *From Empire to Empire*, 82–116.

42. On European scholarly interest in Palestine as a "recovery," see Abu El-Haj, *Facts on the Ground*; Bar-Yosef, *Holy Land in English Culture*.

43. Quoted in Bar-Yosef, *Holy Land in English Culture*, 7.

44. Ben-Arieh, *The Old City*, 254.

45. Ben-Arieh, *Emergence of the New City*; Kroyanker, *Adrikhalut bi-Yerushalayim*.

46. Tamari, "Confessionalism and Public Space."

47. Alan Cunningham, "Foreword," in Kendall, *Jerusalem: The City Plan*, v.

48. On the legal history of the "Status Quo," see Eordegian, "British and Israeli Maintenance of the Status Quo."

49. Ashbee, *Jerusalem 1918–1920*, 12.

50. Schmelz, *Modern Jerusalem's Demographic Evolution.*

51. As argued in Cohen, *Year Zero.*

52. Ben-Gurion, *Yoman ha-Milhama*, 359, entry of 25 April 1948.

53. Estimated at 75,268 Arab refugees from Jerusalem and its environs. Tamari, *Jerusalem 1948*, 79.

54. It is estimated that 25,000 Jews were displaced in Jerusalem during the war, but most were able to return to their homes. Cohen-*Levinovisky, Plitim Yehudim*, 137.

55. Jawhariyyeh, *Al-Quds al-ʿUthmaniyya*, 9.

56. See Barton, Hamilton, and Ivanič, *Situated Literacies*; Street, *Social Literacies.*

57. The changing meaning of Arabic literacy in modern Palestine is explored in Ayalon, *Reading Palestine.* Parush, *Hahot'im bi-Khtiva*, demonstrates the dramatic transformation of Hebrew writing cultures in the Jewish Ashkenazi world of the Haskalah, with relevance to Jews in Jerusalem.

58. These opposing textual modes, "traditional" and "modern," are hermeneutic constructs. This polarized model is a simplification of a historical process which by its nature was confusing and overlapping, as seen through the eyes of contemporaries involved in the transition as writers, readers, and users of urban texts.

59. Sakakini, *Kadha Ana Ya Dunya*, 282. Sakakini was referring to the use of the term Erets Yisra'el during the opening of the Palestine Broadcasting Service.

60. Genet, *Prisoner of Love*, 269–70.

61. Levy, "The Nahda and the Haskala." On the Nahda-Haskalah Sephardic milieu in Jerusalem, see Noy, *ʿEdim o Mumhim.*

CHAPTER 1

1. Berchem, "Lettre," 306.

2. The inscriptions were documented in their original textual form, in translation, and, in some cases, in photographic documentation; the exact location was noted together with historical, architectural, and philological commentary. The multivolume corpus was published under the title *Matériaux pour un Corpus inscriptionum Arabicarum* (in acronym, MCIA). The relevant volumes on Jerusalem are Berchem, *Jérusalem "Ville,"* and Berchem, *Jérusalem "Haram."* Below I follow the epigraphic convention and refer to specific inscriptions by number (e.g., MCIA *Jerusalem* no. 1).

3. Berchem, *Jérusalem "Haram,"* 240.

4. Gautier-Van Berchem and Ory, *La Jérusalem musulmane*, 20.

5. Berchem, *Egypt*, ix.

6. Walls and Abul-Hajj, *Arabic Inscriptions in Jerusalem*, list sixty-two additional inscriptions documented after van Berchem's survey. Tütüncü, *Turkish Jerusalem*, provides detailed information about all Ottoman inscriptions, including several late-Ottoman inscriptions ignored by van Berchem.

7. E.g., in the account of the eleventh-century Persian traveler Nasir-i Khusraw, *Diary of a Journey through Syria and Palestine*, 27–28.

8. Rogers, *Domestic Life*, 33.

9. Armenian memorial inscriptions were located in and around Saint James Convent. Hebrew inscriptions appeared outside the handful of synagogues and in select sites of pilgrimage. See chap. 2.

10. See Blair, *Islamic Inscriptions*.

11. Only 3 out of the 104 Ottoman stone inscriptions in Jerusalem are in Ottoman Turkish. See Tütüncü, *Turkish Jerusalem*, 243.

12. Moustafa and Sperl, *The Cosmic Script*.

13. Schimmel, *Calligraphy and Islamic Culture*.

14. George, *The Rise of Islamic Calligraphy*, chap. 3.

15. As documented by a Swiss physician, Tobler, *Beitrag zur Medizinischen Topographie von Jerusalem*, 7–8.

16. The removal of the ancient Siloam inscription to the Istanbul Archaeological Museum caused nearby villagers of Silwan great distress, and they blamed it for poor rainfall. Yellin, *Yerushalayim shel Temol*, 181.

17. MCIA *Jerusalem* no. 29.

18. The most famous example of such rewriting was the erasure of the name of the Umayyad caliph ʿAbd al-Malik from the Dome of the Rock's foundation inscription and its replacement with the name of the Abbasid caliph Al-Ma'mun. MCIA *Jerusalem* no. 215; Berchem, *Jérusalem "Haram,"* 228–46.

19. The holy enclosure is referred to as Al-Haram al-Sharif or Al-Aqsa Mosque in Islamic contexts, while Christian and Jewish terminology uses "Temple Mount" (Har ha-Bayit). In this book I use all these terms, depending on contexts and reference.

20. Gautier-van Berchem and Ory, *La Jérusalem musulmane*, 22; Berchem, *Jérusalem "Haram."*

21. The Sarai (the governor's headquarters) was relocated in the 1860s from its historical site northwest of the Haram to the Khaski Sultan complex west of the Haram. Tütüncü, *Turkish Jerusalem*, 34; Jawhariyyeh, *Storyteller of Jerusalem*, 89. The Islamic Court was located near Bab al-Silsila.

22. Cohen, *Economic Life in Ottoman Jerusalem*, 6–8. On public baths, see Ben-Arieh, *The Old City*, 166. The main food markets (Khan al-Zayt, Suq al-Lahhamin) and medicinal herbs (Suq al-ʿAttarin) were not in the Haram's immediate vicinity.

23. For a detailed description of the *sabil*, see Natsheh, "The Architecture of Ottoman Jerusalem, 685–88."

24. MCIA *Jerusalem* no. 112.

25. MCIA *Jerusalem* nos. 39, 80, 87, 105, 112, 175, 182–86; Walls and Abul-Hajj,

Arabic Inscriptions, no. XLVIII. For locations, see Walls and Abul-Hajj, *Arabic Inscriptions*, fig. 2, "Qubbat al-Sakhra."

26. In van Berchem's corpus of 301 inscriptions only 15 mention the name of the place of the inscription, explicitly or obliquely: MCIA *Jerusalem* nos. 70, 95, 100, 101, 125 (inscription in passage), 152, 183, 208, 240, 280, 292, 295–98.

27. Van Berchem, *Jérusalem "Ville,"* 109.

28. Van Berchem, *Jérusalem "Ville,"* 413–15. The style of writing, Ottoman Naskhi, is a cursive script of Arabic typical of the Ottoman dynasty, used for public writing.

29. Blair, *Islamic Inscriptions*, 29. The typical format of such inscriptions is: (1) the invocation of God, (2) a verb indicating what was done, (3) the object of the work, (4) the name and titles of the patron—almost always a man—which typically take up the most space, and (5) the date of construction. Two-thirds of the inscriptions in Jerusalem are dedication inscriptions. Fragmentary inscriptions could also be found in Jerusalem: invocations of the name of God and the Prophet, the name of the ruler, signatures of builders and artisans, or truncated graffiti. But these were relatively rare and far less visible. See Walls and Abul-Hajj, *Arabic Inscriptions*.

30. On Jewish pupils collecting water from Bab al-Silsila, see Lemire, *Jerusalem 1900*, 98–99.

31. The *sabil*s were the monumental termini of an elaborate system laid on Suleiman's orders, addressing Jerusalem's age-old water scarcity by running water in aqueducts from springs near Bethlehem to the heart of the city. The Ottoman waterworks went through cycles of disrepair and restoration. See Lemire, *La soif de Jérusalem*.

32. Blair, *Islamic Inscriptions*, 42.

33. Sapir, *Ha-Levanon*, 6 October 1865. The reporter, Sapir, immigrated to Palestine from Belarus as a child.

34. See note 8 above.

35. MCIA *Jerusalem* no. 188; Van Berchem, *Jérusalem "Haram,"* 161.

36. Ben-Arieh, *Emergence of the New City*, 91–98.

37. Ben-Arieh, *The Old City*, 29–31.

38. Of 115 Ottoman inscriptions emplaced in Palestine between 1520 and 1838, only 12 were in Turkish. In contrast, of the 22 inscriptions emplaced between 1838 and 1918, 10 were in Turkish. Overall, of the 22 Ottoman inscriptions in Turkish, nearly half were emplaced after 1838. Tütüncü, *Turkish Jerusalem*, 240–53.

39. Ottoman "Turkification," in the sense of enforcing a Turkish national identity, targeted only specific minorities in the empire such as the Kurds. Ülker, "Contextualising 'Turkification.'"

40. Kayali, *Arabs and Young Turks*, 93.

41. Photographic evidence shows that signs in Ottoman Turkish were emplaced on the building of the municipality, the Ottoman post office, the commercial court, the military headquarters during World War I, the gendarmerie, and on street nameplates.

42. Musil, *Posthumous Papers*, 62.

43. See Yellin, *Yerushalayim shel Temol*, for mentions of Ottoman flags in celebrations, on the sultan's birthday (9), and in the 1898 inauguration of a Jewish school (187–88).

44. Al-Dusturiyya School, photographer unknown (1908–1915), from the Jawhariyyeh collection, in Khalidi, *Before Their Diaspora*. An 1893 Jewish wedding document, crowned with the crescent and the star, can be seen in *A Local Wedding*, 58.

45. On the *tughra*, see Keten, *The Ottoman Monograms*; and Wittek, "Notes sur la tughra ottomane."

46. Ferguson, *The Proper Order of Things*, 51–53. Ferguson argues that while the *tughra* invoked individual, dynastic power, it was in fact the product of an impersonal bureaucratic machinery which ruled the empire already in the fifteenth century.

47. A list of twenty-one *tughra* engravings in Palestine, mostly dating to the final three decades of Ottoman rule, in Tütüncü, *Turkish Palestine*, 295.

48. Deringil, *The Well-Protected Domains*, 26–35.

49. Lemke, "Ottoman Photography."

50. Sheehi, *Foundations of Modern Arab Identity*.

51. As Hala Auji shows, the Arabic printing revolution did not consist merely of importing Western technology; it involved the refashioning and localizing of printing products. As printers developed a new typographic and visual language of printing in Arabic, they drew on earlier scribal practices from manuscripts, as evinced by the use of motifs such as *tughras* and diagonal alignment of texts. Auji, *Printing Arab Modernity*.

52. On the library, see Ayalon, *Reading Palestine*, who situates the Khalidiyya within the changing patterns of reading in Palestine, paying attention to the library's use of modern signage. Conrad, "Khalidi Library," views the Khalidiyya through the reformist agenda of the Khalidis.

53. The four inscriptions on the mausoleum are documented in Berchem, *Jérusalem "Ville,"* 188; MCIA *Jerusalem* nos. 59–63.

54. On Yusuf Diya' al-Khalidi and Ruhi al-Khalidi, see Khalidi, *Palestinian Identity*, 63–88.

55. Ayalon, *Arabic Print Revolution*, 32.

56. Conrad, "Khalidi Library," 202. Similar organizational reforms took place in other libraries in the Arab world, e.g., in Yemen. See Messick, *The Calligraphic State*, 119–22.

57. On Hananya, see Tamari, *The Great War*, 97–104; Ayalon, *Arabic Print Revolution*, 52–57.

58. The Franciscan Monastery printshop (1846) was the first in the city to print in Arabic. It was followed by printshops of other Christian church associations; their output was primarily religious. Ayalon, *Arabic Print Revolution*, 27, 52.

59. Hananya supported the Young Turks, ruling party, the Committee for Union and Progress (CUP), as well as the Greek-speaking Orthodox establishment against challenges from the Arabic-speaking laity. See Tamari, *The Great War*, 97–104.

60. Ayalon, *Arabic Print Revolution*, 53, 55.

61. Ayalon, 86–87.

62. Ayalon, 86. The Ottoman authorities and the municipality posted public notices in Arabic in Jerusalem.

63. Ayalon, 53.

64. Chelouche, *Parashat Hayay*, 25.

65. On the emergence of the late-Ottoman city center, see Wallach, "Jerusalem's Lost Heart."

66. See chap. 3 below.

67. Mehmed Tevfik Bey, quoted in Lemire, *Jerusalem 1900*, 91.

68. Lemire, 91.

69. On the clock tower of Beirut, see Hanssen, *Fin de Siècle Beirut*, 243–47. On clock towers in the empire and in Jerusalem, see Wishnitzer, *Reading Clocks, Alla Turca.*

70. Dimitriadis, "Tramway Concession of Jerusalem."

71. On Sakakini, see Tamari, *Mountain against the Sea*, chaps. 7 and 11.

72. On the Vagabonds and café culture in Jerusalem, see Tamari, chap. 11.

73. Simmel, "Metropolis," 109.

74. Sakakini, *Yawmiyat*, vol. 2, 97, diary entry of 2 September 1914.

75. Sakakini, *Yawmiyat*, vol. 1, 96, 20 January 1908. For an analysis of Sakakini's dreams as indications of Jerusalem's intersection with regional and global networks, see Schayegh, *Middle East*, 28–33. For an attentive reading of Sakakini's turbulent personality and his time in New York, see Tamari, *Mountain against the Sea*, chap. 7.

76. The Arab Club was on Jaffa Road, close to the gate, above Credit Lyonnais. The Arab Literary Club was nearby in Mamilla. Oskotski, *Kol Yerushalayim*, 85.

77. Sakakini, *Kadha Ana Ya Dunya*, 186, 15 June 1919. The occasion was the arrival of the King-Crane Commission.

78. These slogans were recorded in reports on the demonstrations in *Jerusalem News*, 28 February 1920, 9 March 1920; and in photographs in LOC Matson collection, American Colony photographers, of the demonstrations on 27 February 1920 (00129u) and 8 March 1920 (00133u, 00132v).

79. M. D. Eder, *Jerusalem News*, 13 March 1920.

80. *Lisan al-'Arab*, quoted in Hebrew in *Ha-Arets*, 15 July 1921, 2.

CHAPTER 2

1. Agnon, *Only Yesterday*, 285.

2. In the rich commentary on *Only Yesterday*, most relevant are works that focused on questions of language, writing, and signification. Hochman, *Fiction of S. Y. Agnon*, perceptively identified the primary rupture of the novel as the collapse of the ancestral system of reference and the failure of secular alternatives to replace it. Hoffman, "Mad Dog," offers a Derridean reading of *Only Yesterday* as a world of writing out of control, with the madness inherent in writing, although her main interest is an oedipal analysis of the novel. Haddad, *Mi She'oseh Siman*, is a semiotic reading of the novel which focuses on the broken relation between signifier and signified. Hasak-Lowy, "A Mad Dog's Attack on Secularized Hebrew," contributes by locating this crisis in the context of Hebrew Revival and the transformation of Hebrew into an everyday national language. Pardes, *Agnon's Moonstruck Lovers*, sees the novel as a critique of Zionist nationalizing of the Bible and its language. More prevalent but less relevant to my discussion are readings of *Only Yesterday* as an oedipal struggle, e.g., Arbel, *Katuv 'al 'Oro Shel Ha-Kelev*, and Arpaly, *Rav-Roman*, who also provides a valuable and detailed literature review.

3. Of the aforementioned critics, Haddad is the only one to discuss the memorial tablet and its juxtaposition with the dog. She notes that the tablet is not "indexical" writing, that is, its function is different from that of the sign on the dog. However, the difference is not only in function but also in the order and philosophy of language.

4. Characters and events in *Only Yesterday* are largely based on Agnon's own experiences in Jaffa and Jerusalem and on historical events. Holz, "Hitbonenut," 178–221.

5. On Agnon's contribution to the Hebrew Revival, see Bar-Adon, *Shay 'Agnon u-Tehiyat ha-Lashon ha-'Ivrit*. Bar-Adon's ideological commitment to Hebrew Revival stops him from seeing the complexity and ambivalence in *Only Yesterday*.

6. *Ha-Arets*, 29 August 1946.

7. As argued by Hasak-Lowy, "A Mad Dog's Attack on Secularized Hebrew"; Pardes, *Agnon's Moonstruck Lovers*. Hagbi, *Language*, shows that the question of the Hebrew language, its status as the divine language of creation, and its modern corruption are crucial to Agnon's writing. Parush, *Hahot'im bi-Khtiva*, uses Agnon to demonstrate the Haskalah transition from a readerly culture of rabbinic texts to a writerly culture of individual creation. Hagbi and Parush do not discuss *Only Yesterday* but rather other works by Agnon.

8. Grayevsky, *Sefer Avney Zikaron*, vol. 1, unnumbered opening page.

9. Grayevsky's prolific legacy has yet to receive a dedicated study. For a brief discussion of Grayevsky and his social and intellectual context, see Caplan, "Shki'a," 355–57.

10. Gafni, "Zikhron," explores the value of memorial tablets in Jerusalem's synagogues as historical sources. Gafni mentions Grayevsky's corpus but does not examine it closely.

11. Luncz, *Luah Erets Yisra'el: Mivhar*, vol. 2, 91–94. The oldest surviving inscription in the Ben Zakai Sephardic synagogues dated to 1802; three more inscriptions were placed in the 1830s. See Grayevsky, *Sefer Avney Zikaron*, vol. 1, 1.

12. The oldest operating synagogue in Jerusalem was a small Karaite house of prayer dating to the tenth century. The heterodox Karaite community operated separately from rabbinic Jewish congregations. The oldest surviving inscription in the synagogue was from 1710. See Pinkerfeld, "Beyt ha-Kneset le-ʿAdat ha-Kara'im." The Ha-Hurva Synagogue was the first Ashkenazi synagogue to operate with permission; its inscription dated to 1836. Grayevsky, *Sefer Avney Zikaron*, vol. 1, 3.

13. On Jewish immigration from Eastern and Central Europe to Palestine during the late-Ottoman period, see Alroey, *An Unpromising Land.*

14. Luncz, *Luah Erets Yisra'el*, vol. 2, 91–134.

15. Ben-Arieh, *The Old City*, 354–63.

16. On the early modern development of transnational Jewish networks of charity for the upkeep of Jerusalem communities, see Lehmann, *Emissaries.*

17. Friedman, *Hevra be-Mashber.*

18. Agnon, *Only Yesterday*, 282–83.

19. Yechiel Michel Tucazinsky, quoted in Hacohen, "Le-Toldot Beyt ha-Kneset ha-Hurva," 13–15.

20. Hacohen, 15.

21. Unlike Islamic inscriptions, Hebrew inscriptions sometimes used geometric arrangement of the text, such as an arch-shaped head verse. Some inscriptions also highlighted in slightly bigger letters the name of patrons.

22. Assyrian script (*Ktav Ashuri*), also known as square script (*Merubaʿ*), is based on Aramaic script and was adopted in the Roman period. Before the Haskalah, square script was usually reserved for official, sacred, and ritual purposes. An embellished square script, *Ktav Stam*, was reserved for copying Torah scrolls and scrolls emplaced in *mezuzot* (affixed to Jewish gates and doorways) and *tefillin* (black leather boxes worn during prayer). Semi-cursive and cursive scripts in Hebrew did not carry the same sanctity. These cursive scripts varied considerably between Sephardi and Ashkenazi congregations. See the richly detailed Yardeni, *Book of Hebrew Script.*

23. On Hebrew language in mystical traditions, see Idel, "Reification of Language."

24. The *Genizah* was collected in the cellars of the Istambuli Sephardic synagogue. Luncz, *Luah Erets Yisra'el*, vol. 2, 29–30.

25. For the development of these legends, see Idel, *Golem.* In Idel's interpretation, the parable was an instrument for legitimizing the status of the Jewish learned elite.

26. Rabbi Kalonymus considered himself a sinner and ordered the people of Jerusalem not to mark his tomb with an epitaph but instead to throw stones at it each time they passed by. See Alexander, "Ha-Agada."

27. Frumkin, *Derekh Shofet*, 89.

28. Wallach, "Rethinking the Yishuv."

29. There were instances of cross-ethnic support and charity, such as the Ashkenazi Ha-Hurva synagogue funded by a Baghdadi donor; but these were the exception.

30. On Finn as part of British interest in Palestine, see Moscrop, *Measuring Jerusalem*, 37–41.

31. In 1871 missionaries posted proselytizing placards in Hebrew in the Street of the Jews, sparking outrage. *Havatselet*, 17 November 1871. Hebrew verses were inscribed above the entrance to the English Mission Hospital for Jews (built 1896); see Ben-Arieh, *Emergence of the New City*, 319–25.

32. Nur Masalha sees Finn's Abraham's Vineyard as a precursor of Israel's project of erasing Arab geography. Masalha, *The Zionist Bible*, 82–84. For further details on Abraham's Vineyard, see Ben-Arieh, *Emergence of the New City*, 62–64.

33. Abu El-Haj, *Facts on the Ground*, 22–44.

34. See Abu El-Haj; Moscrop, *Measuring Jerusalem*.

35. Kroyanker, *Adrikhalut bi-Yerushalayim*.

36. Ben-Arieh, *Emergence of the New City*, 133.

37. *Ha-Tsvi*, 1 June 1909.

38. Yellin, *Zikhronot*, 37.

39. Levy, "The Nahda and the Haskala."

40. Parush, *Hahot'im be-Khtiva*.

41. Parush, 173.

42. Lehmann, *Emissaries*.

43. Ben-Arieh, *Emergence of the New City*, 263–65.

44. The first Hebrew journal printed in Jerusalem, *Ha-Levanon*, was Orthodoxy's mouthpiece. See Be'er-Marx, *'Al Homot ha-Niyar.*

45. These were the Orthodox papers *Havatselet* (Hasidic) and *Moriya* (Perushi) and the Zionist papers *Ha-Herut* (Sephardic), *Ha-'or* (published by Eliezer Ben Yehuda, appearing also under *Ha-Tsvi* and *Hashkafa*), and *Ha-Ahdut* (socialist).

46. Yellin, *Yerushalayim shel Temol*, 30–31.

47. *Hadashot me-ha-Arets*, 12 July 1918, 4.

48. On the Ashkenazi use of public notices, often anonymous, see Friedman, "Pashekevilim." Kluger, *Min ha-Makor*, is a five-volume collection of hundreds of Jewish placards posted in Palestine between 1840 and 1940, mostly from Jerusalem and almost entirely in Hebrew.

49. *Ha-Po'el ha-Tsa'ir*, 12 October 1907.

50. *Ha-Tsvi*, 20 April 1910.

51. Zaydan, *Al-Rihlat al-Thalath*, 276.

52. On the transformation of Hebrew into a spoken language in Palestine, see Harshav, *Language in Time of Revolution*; Saposnik, *Becoming Hebrew*, 65–92.

53. On "Ottoman Zionism" in Palestine, see Campos, *Ottoman Brothers*, 197–223; Jacobson, *From Empire to Empire*, 82–116.

54. *Ha-Po'el ha-Tsa'ir*, 21 November 1913.

55. Shor, *Gdud Maginey ha-Safa*, 33. On the continued use of "foreign" languages among Jews in Palestine during the Mandate, see Halperin, *Babel in Zion*.

56. One example is Brisk, *Sefer Helkat Mehokek*, published in 1900, which mapped and recorded burial inscriptions in the Mount of Olives Jewish cemetery in Jerusalem.

57. See Grayevsky, *Sefer Avney Zikaron*, vol. 3, for communications and endorsements by the Ashkenazi chief rabbi; Muhamad Ja'far, *Hebron*, vol. 4 (inscription 727); the Syriac bishop in Jerusalem, the Canon of Saint George Cathedral in Jerusalem, Samaritan chief priest, vol. 5.

58. Grayevsky, *Sefer Avney Zikaron*, vols. 1, opening page.

59. Agnon, *Only Yesterday*, 282–83.

60. Writing in gold appears elsewhere in Agnon's work, e.g., in the short story "'Ad Hena" (Thus far) as a symptom of excess and a corruption of the simplicity of the divine word: "a violence imposed on language, on its letters, a violence that colors words in gold." Hagbi, *Language*, 45.

61. Agnon, *Only Yesterday*, 303.

62. Hoffman, "Mad Dog," 59.

63. Hoffman, 59.

64. See Arbel, *Katuv 'al 'Oro shel Ha-Kelev*. The dog has also been read as a representation of Arab Palestinians, who are almost completely absent in the novel. Hilu, "Sipuro shel Kelev Shahid."

65. Agnon, *Only Yesterday*, 325.

66. Agnon, 331.

67. Agnon, 425.

68. As noted by Amos Oz, *The Silence of Heaven*, 165.

69. Agnon, *Only Yesterday*, 630.

70. Derrida, *Of Grammatology*, 127.

71. In Derrida's reading of Lévi-Strauss's "Writing Lesson," Derrida, 112.

72. In Hoffman's reading of *Only Yesterday* madness is always inherent in writing, and therefore attempts to inscribe stable meaning are ultimately doomed. Hoffman, "Mad Dog."

73. In his review of Foucault's *Madness and Civilization*, Derrida questions Foucault's argument on the historicity of madness as an early modern invention and

instead argues that the construction of madness is inimical to language. "Cogito and the History of Madness," in Derrida, *Writing and Difference.*

74. For examples, see Arpaly, *Rav-Roman*, 75.

75. Hoffman, "Mad Dog."

76. Such practices are documented, e.g., in an early-twentieth-century public notice warning against the desecration of printed Hebrew material in square script by discarding it "in main roads... in filthy places." Levintahl, "Lo Tehalelu," in Kluger, *Min ha-Makor*, vol. 5, 135.

77. Agnon, *Only Yesterday*, 524.

78. Hoffman, "Mad Dog," 50.

79. Hochman, *Fiction of S. Y. Agnon*, 156.

80. Hasak-Lowy, "A Mad Dog's Attack on Secularized Hebrew."

81. My reading is indebted to Parush's interpretation of Agnon's short story "The Legend of the Scribe," where a scribe who copies the Torah loses his mind as he ventures into creative writing. Parush, *Ha-hot'im bi-Khtiva*, 400–406.

82. Saposnik, *Becoming Hebrew*, 89–90; Pardes, *Agnon's Moonstruck Lovers*, 12–14.

83. On Scholem and Agnon, and the affinity between their views on Hebrew secularization, see Hasak-Lowy, "A Mad Dog's Attack on Secularized Hebrew"; Pardes, *Agnon's Moonstruck Lovers.*

84. Gershom Scholem to Franz Rosenzweig, 1926, in Derrida and Anidjar, *Acts of Religion*, 226–27.

85. As argued by Hirschfeld, "Ha-Sekhel ha-Enoshi"; Oz, *The Silence of Heaven*, 186–91; Hochman, *Fiction of S. Y. Agnon.*

86. Agnon, *Only Yesterday*, 618.

87. Agnon, 624.

CHAPTER 3

1. CZA, L51/424, Anglo-Palestine Bank folder.

2. On coinage in late-Ottoman Palestine, see Rubinshtayn, *Matbe'ot.* See also Pamuk, *Monetary History*; Eldem, *History of the Ottoman Bank.*

3. On the official exchange rate (*sagh*) vs. the trade rate (*shurk*), see the memoirs of Ashkenazi businessman Yellin, *Zikhronot*, 18.

4. Chelouche, *Parashat Hayay*, 27–30.

5. Doumani, *Rediscovering Palestine*, 179.

6. Cohen, *Economic Life in Ottoman Jerusalem*, 80.

7. Marx, *Capital*, vol. 1, 140.

8. Doumani, *Rediscovering Palestine*, 200.

9. Yellin, *Zikhronot*, 40–41.

10. On barter payments in Jewish traditional schools, see Yellin, *Le-Tse'etsa'ay*, vol. 2, 48–49; in traditional Christian schools, Jabra, *First Well*, 35.

11. Yellin, *Le-Tse'etsa'ay*, vol. 2, 69.

12. Frumkin, *Derekh Shofet*, 23.

13. Pappe, *Rise and Fall*, 81.

14. *A Handbook for Travellers in Syria and Palestine*, lix.

15. Rogers, *Domestic Life*, 316.

16. See Rubinshtayn, *Matbe'ot*, 26, 32.

17. In the correspondence of the Ottoman *mutasarrif* of Jerusalem from 1906 to 1908, money is usually stipulated in Ottoman denominations but occasionally also in French francs. Kushner, *To Be Governor of Jerusalem*.

18. Albert Antebi, *Ha-Tsvi*, 14 September 1914.

19. Ingham, *The Nature of Money*.

20. Chelouche, *Parashat Hayay*, 29.

21. Marx, *Capital*, vol. 1, 126.

22. Early Islamic coins included iconographic elements, but these were soon abandoned in favor of a purist textual design. On Islamic coinage, see Bosworth, Darley-Doran, and Freeman-Greenville, "Sikka."

23. Eastern Arabic numerals were used in the Levant and the Ottoman Empire—to be distinguished from "Western Arabic numerals," which are the numerals commonly used in the West.

24. Yellin, *Yerushalayim shel Temol*, 53–56.

25. Rubinshtayn, *Matbe'ot*, 33. According to Rubinshtayn, British sovereigns with the image of Queen Victoria were exchanged for 2 percent less than those carrying King Edward VII's portrait, reflecting merchants' prejudices against a woman ruler.

26. Yehoshua, *Yerushalayim*, vol. 2, 26–29.

27. Yehoshua, vol. 2, 26–29.

28. Yehoshua, vol. 2, 26–29; Chelouche, *Parashat Hayay*, 100–101; *Havatselet*, 11 September 1903; municipal decree, 2 April 1895, JMA OttomanRegisters/Vol3/p16a/item112.

29. Marx, *Capital*, vol. 1, 141.

30. Marx, vol. 1, 125.

31. Eldem, *History of the Ottoman Bank*, 207.

32. Albert Antebi, *Ha-Tsvi*, 14 September 1914.

33. Eldem, *History of the Ottoman Bank*.

34. Yellin, *Yerushalayim shel Temol*, 55. For examples of such credit notes, see Meshorer, *Sixty Economic Documents*, 30–33.

35. On these workers' mobilizations, see Olitski, *Omanut ha-Dfus*, 71–92.

36. Frumkin, *Derekh Shofet*, 13, 27, 83; Yehoshua, *Yerushalayim*, vol. 2, 30–31. Some

of the coins were in fact worn Ottoman coins rebranded in Hebrew "charity for the poor" (*tsdaka la-ʿaniyim*).

37. As quoted in Yehoshua, *Yerushalayim*, vol. 2, 30–31.

38. Yehoshua, vol. 2, 30–31. Municipal decrees prohibiting Jewish nickel coins, 9 January 1907, OttomanRegisters/Vol12/p3b/item20; prohibition on Jewish paper tokens, 23 August 1910, JMA OttomanRegisters/Vol16/p31b/item236.

39. On the Hebrew cancellation mark, and more generally on Eliyahu Honig, see Lavi, *Elias Effendi*, 218–34.

40. Zaydan, *Al-Rihlat al-Thalath*, 275.

41. Sakakini, *Yawmiyat*, vol. 2, 148, 12 January 1915; Kaiser, "The Ottoman Government." See 1914 public notice by Jaffa Qaymaqam, Bahaʾ al-Din, 1914, in Kluger, *Min ha-Makor*, vol. 1, 150.

42. For Ottoman wartime notices in Hebrew, see Kluger, *Min ha-Makor*, vol. 1, 31–34, 132, 136, 150, 156. A notice by Jerusalem's police chief explicitly allowed the use of Hebrew on signage (below the Turkish), *Ha-Herut*, 15 October 1915, 2. On the Ottoman Hebrew biweekly *Ha-Midbar*, issued in 1917, see Gross, *Yerushalayim 5678 1917/19*, 113–15.

43. Simmel, "Metropolis," 106.

44. Zelizer, *Social Meaning of Money*.

45. Rogers, *Domestic Life*, 8; Yehoshua, *Sipuro shel ha-Bayit ha-Sefaradi*, 23–24.

46. Yellin, *Le-Tseʾetsaʾay*, vol. 2, 39.

47. Yellin, vol. 2, 51–52; Yehoshua, *Yerushalayim*, vol. 2, 27–28. On coin-adorned headdresses as wedding gifts from the groom's family to the bride in Christian and Muslim villages near Jerusalem, see Weir, "A Bridal Headdress from Southern Palestine."

48. Yellin, *Yerushalayim shel Temol*, 22.

49. For stories of theft, see Tamari, *Year of the Locust*, 92–93; Yehoshua, *Yerushalayim*, vol. 2, 113. On a thief caught when trying to exchange a twenty-five-ruble banknote, see Yellin, *Le-Tseʾetsaʾay*, vol. 1, 83–84.

50. Jawhariyyeh, *Al-Quds al-Intidabiyya*, 291.

51. Gold made up more than half of the empire's money supply in 1914; currency notes accounted for a fifth but did not circulate much beyond Constantinople. Pamuk, *Monetary History*, 219–20.

52. Schölch, *Palestine in Transformation*, 110–16.

53. Henkin, *City Reading*, 36. Henkin discusses the effects of land registration in early-nineteenth-century New York.

54. *Nomer* appeared in a range of meanings: as a plot of land on which to build a housing unit (advertisement in *Moriya*, 21 June 1912); a flat (Yellin, *Le-Tseʾetsaʾay*, vol.

2, 1); the numbered address of a flat or a shop (*Hashkafa*, 3 May 1907, 6); or as financial certificates such as lottery bonds (*Ha-Herut*, 12 September 1913, 1).

55. On the postal services, see Jawhariyyeh, *Storyteller of Jerusalem*, 93–94; Persoff, *The Running Stag*.

56. Bektas, "The Sultan's Messenger."

57. Frumkin, *Derekh Shofet*, 112–13.

58. Tannus, *The Palestinians*, 27.

59. Frumkin, *Derekh Shofet*, 70.

60. Blyth, *When We Lived in Jerusalem*, 85; Graham, *With the Russian Pilgrims to Jerusalem*, 129.

61. Albert Antebi, *Ha-Tsvi*, 14 September 1914, 1.

62. Hamenahem, *Mi-Sipurey Na'ar Yerushalmi*, 66.

63. Yehoshua, *Yerushalayim*, vol. 2, 139.

64. Jawhariyyeh, *Storyteller of Jerusalem*, 60.

65. This description of the silversmiths' market is found in Hanauer, *Walks about Jerusalem*, 89–91.

66. *Ha-Tsvi*, 10 February 1911.

67. These names can be seen in photographs of Jaffa Road from 1898 to 1919. LOC American Colony photographers, 00815u, 000129u, 04611u, 06541v.

68. Simmel, *Philosophy of Money*.

69. Marx, *Contribution to the Critique of Political Economy*, 252.

70. Simmel, *Philosophy of Money*, 129–203.

71. Saussure, *Course in General Linguistics*, 116.

72. Goethe, *Faust*, lines 6119–22, 258.

73. British Consular reports, quoted in Schölch, *Palestine in Transformation*, 105–6.

74. Rogers, *Domestic Life*, 316.

75. Hacohen, *Milhemet ha-'Amim*, vol. 4, 156.

76. Simmel, *Philosophy of Money*, 330.

77. Keynes, *Tract on Monetary Reform*, 138.

CHAPTER 4

1. *Ha-Herut*, 28 August 1914.

2. The French- and British-owned Ottoman Imperial Bank issued gold-backed banknotes before the First World War, but their circulation was largely restricted to Constantinople. See Pamuk, *Monetary History*, 209–24.

3. The notes were issued by the Ottoman Treasury rather than the Imperial Ottoman Bank. The initial issue was, in fact, backed by sufficient gold reserves, but subsequent issues were not. Eldem, *History of the Ottoman Bank*, chaps. 13–14.

4. Chelouche, *Parashat Hayay*, 225–27.

5. Chelouche, 215–16.

6. Hacohen, *Milhemet ha-ʿAmim*, vol. 2, 34–36. Nassar was saved from Ottoman prison after the Jewish shop owner testified that the mentioned toilet paper referred to merchandise, not banknotes.

7. NLI, v. 2131, Fu'ad Shihab, Qaymaqam of Jaffa, public notice regarding banknotes (1914–1916). On Ottoman attempts to uphold the value of the currency in the provinces, see Eldem, *History of the Ottoman Bank*, 342–45.

8. Eldem, *History of the Ottoman Bank*, 346.

9. As explored in Tamari, *Year of the Locust.*

10. Sakakini, *Yawmiyat*, vol. 2, 118, 5 October 1914.

11. *Ha-Herut*, 24 August, 15 October, 18 December 1915. In Tel Aviv, the authorities ordered the removal of shop signs and street nameplates in Hebrew (Hacohen, *Milhemet ha-ʿAmim*, vol. 1, 19, 64–65). But this appears to have been due to the absence of Turkish on these signs rather than a ban on Hebrew. The Ottomans continued to publish public notices in Hebrew.

12. *Hadashot me-ha-Arets ha-Kdosha*, 4 April 1918, 3.

13. Re'uven Zilberstein, quoted in Gross, *Yerushalayim 5678 1917/19*, 207.

14. CZA, L51/424, Anglo-Palestine Bank folder, *Currencies in Palestine Pre-War and Post War*, 1934; Hacohen, *Milhemet ha-ʿAmim*, vol. 4, 156.

15. Shiryon, *Zikhronot*, 198–99. See also Rubinshtayn, *Matbeʿot*, 77–90.

16. Rubinshtayn, *Matbeʿot*, 101.

17. Weizmann, *Trial and Error*, 303. Keynes, who held anti-Jewish prejudices, was a supporter of Zionism and the Balfour Declaration. Paulovicova, "Immoral Moral Scientist."

18. Keynes, *Tract on Monetary Reform*, 164, 195–96.

19. Ingham, "Babylonian Madness."

20. Keynes, *Treatise on Money*, vol. 1, 3–22.

21. Keynes, vol. 1, 5.

22. Keynes, *General Theory*, chap 12.

23. Keynes, *General Theory*, 163.

24. On Samuel, see Wasserstein, *Herbert Samuel*. A critical review of Samuel's Palestine policy is found in Huneidi, *Broken Trust*.

25. CZA, Z4/402228, Keynes to Samuel, 27 June 1919. Other members included a representative of the Zionist bank Anglo-Palestine Company and the Liberal politician and Zionist sympathizer James de Rothschild. Keynes, however, did not wish to become a public advocate for Zionism, declining an invitation to speak for Zionism at the London School of Economics. CZA, Z4/41905, Keynes to Zionist Organisation, 8 June 1921.

26. CZA, Z4/41162, "Report of the Sub-Committee on Finance to the Advisory Committee on the Economic Development of Palestine," [January 1920], 6.

27. CZA, S25/557, Minutes of the First Meeting of Financial Committee, 20 November 1919, 5–7. On the North Russian currency, see Ponsot, "Keynes."

28. 22 February 1920, quoted in Wasserstein, *Herbert Samuel*, 243.

29. On the "South Syrian" option, see Khalidi, *Palestinian Identity*, 162–76.

30. Wasserstein, *The British in Palestine*, 38–41.

31. Wasserstein, *Herbert Samuel*, 241.

32. PRO, F152/1 6/620-30/10/24121/Finance/2451(F.I), Herbert Samuel, Currency Memorandum [2nd April 1920].

33. See Wallach, "Creating a Country through Currency and Stamps."

34. Smith, *Roots of Separatism*, 27.

35. CZA, L51/425, Samuel to Weizmann, 28 May 1920. Samuel also consulted with the former chief rabbi of Jerusalem, Yaacov Meir, on ancient Hebrew coins. Elmaleh, *Ha-Rishonim le-Tsiyon*, 357.

36. The economic rationale for a new currency was weak; Smith, *Roots of Separatism*, 28. Dabbah, *Currency Notes*, 21, suggests that seigniorage revenues were the primary motivation for the establishment of the Palestine currency. Yet he notes with puzzlement that the seigniorage consideration was not mentioned even once in the lengthy discussions prior to the currency issue in 1927.

37. Persoff, *The Running Stag*, 18.

38. PRO, FO 371/5124, Samuel to Foreign Office, 25 November 1920, in Ingrams, *Palestine Papers*, 113–14.

39. Herbert Samuel to Major Hudson, 14 July 1920, reproduced in Resnik, "Eretz Israel on Palestine Stamps." The decision was received with surprise by the Foreign Office, as shown in Huneidi, *Broken Trust*, 122. See also Storrs, *Orientations*, 383–84.

40. Frumkin, *Derekh Shofet*, 237–38.

41. Jabotinsky, *Evidence*, 19.

42. Persoff, *The Running Stag*, 16. See Friedman, "H.C No.55/25 Jammal Eff. Husseini vs. The Government of Palestine," in *Collection of Judgments*.

43. Mandate for Palestine, 1922, Article 22.

44. See, e.g., *Al-Jami'a al-'Arabiyya*, 3 November 1927.

45. Suleiman, *War of Words*, 145.

46. McCarthy, *The Population of Palestine*, 69.

47. As documented in 1920s complaint letters. Shor, *Gdud Maginey ha-Safa*, 32.

48. Lipschütz, *Ktavim*, vol. 2, 260.

49. *Do'ar ha-Yom*, 12 August 1920, 2.

50. Ben Yehuda and Yellin, "Tazkir [1922]."

51. Suleiman, *War of Words*, 189.

52. Dabbah, *Currency Notes*, 66–67.

53. CZA, KH4/3766, S. S. Davies, Currency Officer, "Notice: Palestine Currency," 1 October 1927.

54. Dabbah, *Currency Notes*, 55–57.

55. £P 5, 10, 50, and 100 notes were in equal size; 500 mils and £P 1 notes were smaller. For detailed specification, see Berlin, *Coins and Banknotes of Palestine*, 55–76.

56. BEA OV7/11 Palestine Currency Board Reports, years 1928, 1948.

57. BEA, OV7/11, Palestine Currency Board Reports, years 1928, 1948.

58. ISA, F/30/31, Palestine Currency Officer to Chief Secretary, 1 March 1931.

59. See Nassar, *European Portrayals of Jerusalem*.

60. ISA, F/30/31, unsigned typescript to Chief Secretary, 6 February 1932.

61. On the Ramlah Tower, its Islamic history and its rebranding as a "Crusader Tower," see Halevy, "Ottoman Ruins Captured."

62. The absence of Christian monuments was criticized in *Al-Jami'a al-'Arabiyya*, 28 November 1927, 4. An issue of notes with the image of the Holy Sepulchre was later planned but never took place. ISA, F30/31, A. M. Young to Secretary of State for the Colonies, 21 October 1931.

63. ISA, F/30/31, Arthur G. Wauchope, High Commissioner of Palestine, handwritten note, 15 September 1931.

64. ISA, F/30/31, Arthur G. Wauchope, handwritten note, 17 December 1934.

65. BEA, OV7/11, "Report of the Palestine Currency Board for the Period Ended 31st March 1928," p. 4.

66. *Ha-Arets*, 1 November 1927.

67. "Le-Yom ha-Matbe'a," *Davar*, 1 November 1927.

68. Smith, *Roots of Separatism*, 31.

69. *Al-Jami'a al-'Arabiyya*, 24 November 1927, 1; 28 November 1927, 4.

70. ISA, F/30/31, Currency Officer to Chief Secretary, 9 February 1931.

71. *Filastin*, 18 October 1927. The only Arab newspaper to report favorably on the introduction of the currency was the pro-British *Mir'at al-Sharq*.

72. Marx, *Capital*, vol. 1, 125.

73. PRO, File F.152/2, Currency Officer Davis to Palestine Currency Board, 23 December 1927 (no. 87).

74. Jawhariyyeh, *Storyteller of Jerusalem*, 195.

CHAPTER 5

1. KCC, Ashbee Papers, fol. 45, "Pro-Jerusalem Council Minutes," 30 August 1920. Minutes in French.

2. Pro-Jerusalem published two biannual reports on its activities: Ashbee, *Jerusalem 1918–1920*; Ashbee, *Jerusalem, 1920–1922*. Storrs discusses Pro-Jerusalem in great detail in his memoirs; Storrs, *Orientations*. Ashbee published a semi-fictional account of his sojourn in Palestine; Ashbee, *A Palestine Notebook*. For scholarly analysis of Pro-Jerusalem, see below.

3. PCC, Storrs Papers III/4, undated typescript [1918].

4. KCC, Ashbee Papers, fol. 45, "Pro-Jerusalem Council minutes," 30 August 1920.

5. Storrs, "Preface" in Ashbee, *Jerusalem, 1920–1922*, vi.

6. My analysis is focused on the early-1920s street-naming campaign. The municipality resumed street naming in the late 1930s and 1940s, with a rather different emphasis. British administrators were less ideologically involved, and the city was seen as de facto divided in national (rather than religious) terms between Jews and Arabs. These efforts were discontinued because of escalating tensions in the 1940s. Graves, *Experiment in Anarchy*, 39–42; Azaryahu, *'Al Shem*, 116–30.

7. On street naming as class struggle in late-nineteenth-century Stockholm, see Pred, *Lost Words and Lost Worlds*.

8. Jerusalem's colonial street naming is discussed in Azaryahu and Cook, "Mapping the Nation"; Azaryahu, *'Al Shem*, 116–30. While recognizing the colonial nature of the campaign and the historical character of the chosen names, these studies repeat uncritically the British discourse of respect and impartiality. Tom Segev, less reverent, speaks of Storrs's pomp and presumption, yet does not question the motivation behind the street-naming campaign. Segev, *One Palestine, Complete*, 161.

9. Tamari, *Mountain against the Sea*, 81–83.

10. The neighborhoods of Nabi Da'ud and Bab al-Khalil encompassed areas both within and outside the walls. Arnon, "The Quarters of Jerusalem in the Ottoman Period."

11. Jawhariyyeh, *Al-Quds al-ʿUthmaniyya*, 9. Jawhariyyeh refers to addresses by the term *house* (*ʿamara* or *dar*), a building that typically housed several families on separate floors.

12. Jawhariyyeh, *Storyteller of Jerusalem*, 6. The preference for describing addresses in terms of landmarks and localities, rather than streets, is deeply rooted in the region and remains prevalent even in its metropolises. In Amman, a large-scale 2007 project of street naming and house numbering met with limited success. Residents continue to give directions using "restaurants, pharmacies, mosques or even the number of speed bumps on a road" rather than street names and numbers. Maʿayeh, "Amman Addresses Its Street Name Problem."

13. Yehoshua, *Sipuro shel ha-Bayit ha-Sefaradi*, 15–23.

14. Arabic street names in popular use were recorded in Charles Wilson's 1865 map of Jerusalem. The names were collected by Dr. Carl Sandreczki, a German missionary living in Jerusalem. Assisted by the "well-known resident of Jerusalem" Yaʿqub al-Saʿati, Sandreczki conducted a ten-day survey of street names and compiled a report on it. Sandreczki, "Namen der Plätze." A shorter English version was published in facsimile in Wilson, *Ordnance Survey of Jerusalem*.

15. Jewish (and particularly Ashkenazi) toponyms of the Old City are captured wonderfully in the memoirs of Frumkin, *Derekh Shoftet.*

16. Cohen-Reiss, *Mi-Zikhronot*, 265–66.

17. Rogers, *Domestic Life*, 385, italics in the original. In the rejection of house numbering Rogers finds echoes of the prophet Isaiah's reproach (22:10) "Ye have numbered the houses of Jerusalem."

18. Pagis, *Mifkadey ha-Ukhlusin*, 115.

19. These bureaucratic methods of population control are what Michel Foucault termed the modern "technologies of the individual"; Foucault, *Discipline and Punish.*

20. Luncz, *Luah Erets Yisra'el Year 4*, 157; house numbering mentioned again in 1907, Ben-Arieh, *Emergence of the New City*, 356.

21. *Ha-Herut*, 18 February 1916.

22. On the planned expansion of Jaffa Road, see *Ha-Herut*, 12 March 1916. On Jamal Pasha's development policies in Syria, see Tamari, *Year of the Locust.*

23. Ottoman nameplates in the Imperial War Museum, London are of Harat al-Nasara Caddesi (Street of the Christians), Bab al-Asbat Caddesi (Asbat Gate Street), Dir al-Siryan Caddesi (Syrian Monastery Street), and Sharaf Cadsusi (Sharaf Bazaar). The names are a combination of Arabic (the proper name) and Turkish (the word *street* or *bazaar*). The scope, rationale, and dates of these nameplates remain unknown. I have not been able to find reference to the Ottoman street naming in archives or published records.

24. In the 1865 street-name survey, Sandreczki and his Arab helper Saʿati found that numbering started at Jaffa Gate, but they could not discern the logic of the system. Sandreczki, "Namen der Plätze," 46. Shops in some modern commercial developments were numbered, and the number was used in advertising. In Jewish social housing, flat numbers were inscribed, and these were used by residents, as can be seen in the 1921 address book, Oskotski, *Kol Yerushalayim.*

25. Jacobson, *From Empire to Empire*, 28–29.

26. Falih Rıfkı [Atay], *Zeytindaği* (1932), quoted in Tamari, *Year of the Locust*, 48–50.

27. See names on the map, Wilson, "Ordnance Survey of Jerusalem 1864–5."

28. Jawhariyyeh, *Storyteller of Jerusalem*, 107.

29. Smith, *Roots of Separatism*, 7.

30. On town planning as a tool of containment and cultural reinvention in the British Empire, see Home, *Of Planting and Planning.*

31. Town planning was the first item on Samuel's agenda of the first meeting of the Advisory Council (a short-lived appointed assembly of British officials, Arabs, and Jews which Samuel planned to transform into a Palestine legislature). Town planning was discussed in the three subsequent meetings of the Advisory Council. Hyman, "British Planners in Palestine," 408, 702.

32. PRO, CO 733/27, "Samuel to the Duke of Devonshire, Dispatch no. 895," 17 November 1922.

33. Ibid.

34. See the original Arab names in Wilson, "Ordnance Survey of Jerusalem 1864–5."

35. The *haras*, the main thoroughfares running through the heart of the localities, were demoted to ordinary streets. This is evident in the English translations, where Harat al-Sharaf became "Honour Lane" and Harat al-Sa'adiyya "Saadiah Steps."

36. Luke, *Prophets, Priests and Patriarchs*, 3.

37. Ashbee, *Jerusalem, 1920–1922*, 26.

38. "General Map of Jerusalem," compare English, Arabic, and Hebrew versions.

39. Keith-Roach, *Pasha of Jerusalem*, 111–12.

40. Graves, *Experiment in Anarchy*, 39.

41. Benjamin, *Arcades Project*, 517.

42. Benjamin, 518.

43. Storrs, *Orientations*, 440.

44. In Cairo, Storrs was a member of the Comité pour la Conservation des Monuments Arabes and was involved in the establishment of the Coptic Museum. He was also an opera critic for the *Egyptian Gazette*. Storrs, *Orientations*, 94–96.

45. For an overview of Storrs's legacy in Jerusalem, see Shalev-Kalifa, *The First Governor*.

46. Gitler, "Ashbee's Jerusalem Years."

47. PCC, Storrs Papers, September 1918. Ronald Storrs, Typescript , III/1. On British town planning in Jerusalem, see Hyman, "British Planners in Palestine"; Hysler-Rubin, "Arts & Crafts and the Great City"; Hysler-Rubin, "Geography, Colonialism and Town Planning."

48. Ashbee, *A Palestine Notebook*, 158.

49. Hyman, "British Planners in Palestine," 394.

50. See Storrs, *Orientations*, 294 (beggars), 310 (annulment of tramlines concession, advertisements), 394 (alcohol), 432 (prostitution).

51. Prostitution was widespread in Jerusalem during World War I. See Tamari, *Year of the Locust*.

52. Tamari, *Mountain against the Sea*, 90. The strictly Orthodox Jewish Ashkenazi congregations were an exception in this sense. See Friedman, *Hevra be-Mashber*.

53. On the creation of the Old City as a separate and symbolically charged area, see Pullan and Sternberg, "The Making of Jerusalem's 'Holy Basin.'"

54. Storrs, *Orientations*, 310.

55. Weizman, *Hollow Land*, 30–31.

56. Armstrong, *A History of Jerusalem*, 374. For other positive evaluations, see

Gilbert, *Jerusalem in the Twentieth Century*, 71; Benvenisti, *City of Stone*, 137. Weizman, *Hollow Land*, provides a somewhat more critical assessment of Storrs's bylaw, though he mainly focuses on its use by Israeli planners.

57. Storrs, *Orientations*, 310.

58. Storrs, 315.

59. Storrs, 315.

60. Storrs, 273.

61. Storrs, 317.

62. In the 1930s the hotel reverted back to German ownership and to the name "Fast," only to be confiscated again after 1939 and turned into "Australian Soldiers Club."

63. Wallach, "Jerusalem's Lost Heart"; Hyman, "British Planners in Palestine," 699.

64. Fuchs and Herbert, "A Colonial Portrait of Jerusalem," 93.

65. On Jerusalemites' attachment to the clock, see Yehoshua, *Yerushalayim*, vol. 1, 24–25; Jawhariyyeh, *Storyteller of Jerusalem*, 139–40.

66. Moughalian, *Feast of Ashes*, 147.

67. On the restoration of the Dome of the Rock, see Monk, *Aesthetic Occupation*, 45–72.

68. Herbert Samuel suggested that the new Palestine stamps would be decorated with geometric patterns from the tiles of the dome. Persoff, *The Running Stag*, 17.

69. JMA folder 829, 1921–1923, "Jerusalem Town Planning Committee minutes no. 22," 22 December 1922.

70. *Palestine Weekly*, 29 December 1921.

71. A list of the official street names appeared in Ashbee, *Jerusalem, 1920–1922*, 26, with accompanying notes written most likely by Storrs. In 1924 Pro-Jerusalem published three official street maps of the city in English, Arabic, and Hebrew, "General Map of Jerusalem." A few street names on the maps differ from the original list.

72. In British-ruled Singapore, e.g., most streets named after individuals commemorated European personalities. Yeoh, "Street Names."

73. Storrs, *Orientations*, 299.

74. Only two streets were named after women: Princess Mary Street, after the British Princess Royal (1897–1965); and Queen Melisande's Way, after the Crusader queen (1105–1161).

75. Ashbee, *Jerusalem, 1920–1922*, 26.

76. Of ten streets which retained their names, eight had historical or religious connotations: Mamilla Road, after the ancient Muslim cemetery of Mamilla; Abyssinian Street, after the Abyssinian church; and the biblical roads leading to Jericho, Hebron, Bethlehem, Gaza, Jaffa, and Nablus.

77. Ashbee, *Jerusalem 1918–1920*, 26–27.

78. Ashbee, 27. The 1924 "General Map of Jerusalem" also included a main street named after Saladin.

79. Bar-Yosef, *Holy Land in English Culture*, chap. 5.

80. Al-ʿAlami's name is mentioned in Jawhariyyeh, *Storyteller of Jerusalem*, 42. On local dissatisfaction with the name Godfrey de-Boullion, see Azaryahu, *ʿAl Shem*, 122.

81. Only one street was named after a recent resident of Jerusalem—Ben Yehuda Street—and this exception was probably due to the fact that Eliezer Ben Yehuda was a member of the Street-Naming Committee until his death.

82. Jawhariyyeh, *Al-Quds al-Intidabiyya*, 310, 428, 459.

83. Oskotski, *Kol Yerushalayim*.

84. Wallace, *Jerusalem the Holy*, 94.

85. Kroyanker, *Rehov ha-Nevi'im*.

86. Jawhariyyeh, *Al-Quds al-Intidabiyya*, 311.

87. Storrs, *Orientations*, 92.

88. Salim Tamari, private communication.

89. Sakakini, *Jerusalem and I*, 105.

90. Sakakini, *Kadha Ana Ya Dunya*, 296. Hala Sakakini's map of her neighborhood Qatamun, drawn in exile in Cairo shortly after her family was forced to leave Jerusalem, shows names of families and businesses but no street names. Sakakini, *Jerusalem and I*, 105.

91. Kadman, *Erased from Space and Consciousness*.

92. Sakakini, *Jerusalem and I*, 105.

93. David Shahar recounts that in his childhood only major streets had names, and addresses were described by familiar landmarks. "Since the founding of Israel every alleyway has a name and every house has a number, and yet often no one has any idea where it is." Shahar, *ʿAl ha-Halomot*, 42–43.

94. On a petition from an Arab doctor, see Graves, *Experiment in Anarchy*, 39–40.

95. *Do'ar ha-Yom*, 6 December 1922, 2. The style and content suggest that this anonymous piece was written by Yosef Klausner (see chap. 6).

96. JMA, 840, J. Isaac to Municipality, 22 July 1945; David Elstein to Municipality, 27 October 1942; Mr. Rosenstein to Municipality, 6 February 1940.

97. *Davar*, 2 August 1931, 4.

98. On naming the streets of Rehavia, *Do'ar ha-Yom*, 10 November 1925, 4; Talpiyot neighborhood, *Do'ar ha-Yom*, 5 February 1926, 8; Shaʿarey Hesed, *Do'ar ha-Yom*, 29 January 1933, 4.

99. *Do'ar ha-Yom*, 23 October 1934, 1.

100. *Davar*, 19 March 1946; Azaryahu, *ʿAl Shem*, 126.

101. In Tel Aviv street names were decided before they were laid, and the names

were hotly debated in the earliest residents' meetings. Bar-Gal, "Shemot la-Rehovot be-Tel Aviv."

102. A list of "unofficial street names" is found in JMA 840, "Schedule showing the names of streets within the Municipal area of Jerusalem where street-naming plates are fixed thereupon and not approved by the Council," 21 October 1945. Some of these names, while unofficial, appeared on the 1937 Survey of Palestine map of the city, "Jerusalem Compiled, Drawn & Printed." Out of seventy-six "unofficial names," seventy-one were Hebrew names of Jewish initiative and a further five were emplaced by the Mandatory authorities without a proper process of approval. There seem to have been no Arab unofficial street names. The Municipal Street-Naming Committee in the 1940s planned to rename some of these streets.

103. On Sephardic Zionism during the Mandate, see Jacobson and Naor, *Oriental Neighbors*.

104. The first streets to be named after Jewish benefactors were in the Yemin Moshe neighborhood, built 1892–1894: Yehudit Street, after Judith Montefiore, for Sephardi residents; Natan Street, after Rabbi Nathan Adler, for Ashkenazi residents. Lavi, *Elias Effendi*, 206.

105. Y. Shuchman, *Davar*, 3 January 1939.

CHAPTER 6

1. Shemot Raba 2.2.

2. For an introduction to the wall, its history and customs, see Ben-Dov, Naor, and Anner, *Ha-Kotel*.

3. IOL News, "Now You Can Email God."

4. Ben-Dov, Naor, and Anner, *Ha-Kotel*, 91.

5. On Jewish devotional graffiti in the Roman Levant, see Stern, *Writing on the Wall*.

6. Rosenmeyer, *The Language of Ruins*, chap. 3.

7. Six Hebrew names were found inscribed on the supporting boundary walls of the Mount/Haram, Ben-Dov, "Ktovot 'Ivriyot." A further six medieval inscriptions were found within the Mount/Haram, e.g., in the inner space of the Golden Gate, Gera, "Ha-Ktovot." Muslim pilgrims left similar graffiti in Arabic in the same locations. See Walls and Abul-Hajj, *Arabic Inscriptions in Jerusalem*, inscription XLI.

8. Tudela, *Itinerary*, 23.

9. On Arabic graffiti in Islamic shrines, see Grehan, *Twilight of the Saints*, 166.

10. Luncz, *Netivot Tsion vi-Yerushalayim*, 1876, 18. The practice of Hajj decorations is still prevalent in Jerusalem, although graffiti is sometimes replaced with posters.

11. Tudela, *Itinerary*, 25.

12. A 1785 account of a Karaite Jew, quoted in Bahat, *Yerushalayim: Osef Mekorot*, 253.

13. The custom is noted by Sephardic and Ashkenazi writers alike. See Yehoshua, *Yerushalayim*, vol. 3, 59; Frumkin, *Derekh Shofet*, 69.

14. Vilnay, *Matsevot Kodesh*, 34–35.

15. On the tearing of men's shirts, see Ish, *Sefer Masa'ot Yerushalayim*, 16. On oil lamps, see Ben-Dov, Naor, and Anner, *Ha-Kotel*, 78.

16. *Ha-Tsfira*, 12 May 1913, 1.

17. As captured in pilgrimage itineraries, pilgrims' travelogues, lists of holy places, and illustration-maps. See Reiner, "Traditions of Holy Places," 9–19.

18. Louis Loewe (Eliezer ha-Levi), quoted in Ben-Dov, Naor and Anner, *Ha-Kotel*, 66.

19. The schematic representation of the wall first appeared in eighteenth-century Jewish-Italian illustrations, and became popular after it was reproduced by Yoseph Schwarz in 1837. See Sarfati, "The Illustrations of Yihus ha-Avot"; Sabar, "Ha-Kotel ha-Ma'aravi."

20. As suggested by Poseq, "The 'New Jerusalem.'"

21. Genachowsky, "Pictures of Holy Places as Fundraising Aid."

22. Katsanake, *Theodore Ralli*, 204–6.

23. An early Zionist enthusiast, Lilien became something of an official artist and photographer of the nascent Zionist movement, and his art nouveau work celebrated the prospects of Jewish revival in Palestine. His depictions of the Western Wall, however, lack Zionist symbolism and anticipate his later turn toward commercial Judaica. Stanislawski, *Zionism and the Fin-de-Siècle*, 102.

24. The aura, as defined by Walter Benjamin, is the experience of distance even when in close proximity, derived from a sense of sacredness. Benjamin, "The Work of Art in the Age of Its Technological Reproducibility: Third Version," *Selected Writings*, vol. 4, 251–83.

25. Lilien painted some inscriptions as meaningless sequences of letters which do not add up to Hebrew names, perhaps trying to retain their mystical aura.

26. Dord-Crouslé, "Inscrire la mémoire," 326. My account here is based on Dord-Crouslé's superb analysis of graffiti by European travelers in the Middle East and its reflection in French memoirs and travel writing.

27. Chateaubriand, *Travels*, 412.

28. 6 October 1850, Flaubert, *Correspondance*, vol. 1, 689.

29. Quoted in Dord-Crouslé, "Inscrire la mémoire," 332.

30. Lovata and Olton, "Introduction," *Understanding Graffiti*.

31. Fleming, *Graffiti*, 29.

32. On the "Book of Life" in early Jewish and Christian traditions, see Baynes, *Heavenly Book Motif.*

33. Herzl diaries, 31 October 1898, quoted in Gilbert, *Jerusalem in the Twentieth Century*, 227.

34. On Zionist attempts to "redeem" the wall, see Segev, *One Palestine, Complete*, 71–72.

35. Saposnik, "Wailing Walls and Iron Walls."

36. See in Ben-Dov, Naor, and Aner, *Ha-Kotel*, the visit accounts by historian A. S. Hirschberg, educator Rachel Yanait Ben-Tsvi, and novelist Yehudit Harari.

37. Ahad Ha'am, "Truth from Eretz Yisrael," quoted in Dowty, "Much Ado about Little," 178–79.

38. On such a clash between worshippers and Zionist students from Bezalel Art School, see *Moriya*, 19 August 1910.

39. Klausner, *'Am va-Erets*, vol. 1, 75.

40. Avraham Luncz condemned several "superstitious" customs related to the wall; Luncz, "Kotel ha-Ma'aravi,", 152. The Hasidic weekly *Havatselet*, 30 October 1896, published a reproachful description of the inscriptions, calling for them to be banned. Luncz and *Havatselet* were modernizing voices in the local Ashkenazi Orthodox community.

41. Klausner, *'Am va-Erets*, vol. 1, 76.

42. Klausner, 76.

43. The encounter between Klausner and the stones is already gendered as male-female, as "stone" (*even*) is in the feminine in Hebrew.

44. Klausner, *'Am va-Erets*, vol. 1, 77–78. Emphasis in the original.

45. See accounts by Rachel Yanait Ben-Tsvi and by Yehudit Harari in Ben-Dov, Naor, and Aner, *Ha-Kotel*, 217.

46. On Zionist masculinity, see Mayer, "From Zero to Hero."

47. Fleming, *Graffiti*, 33–34.

48. Yosef Klausner and the Pro-Western Wall Central Committee, *Do'ar ha-Yom*, 12 August 1929, 1. For a copy of the printed notice, see Kluger, *Min ha-Makor*, vol. 1, 59.

49. *Do'ar ha-Yom*, 16 August 1929.

50. As argued compellingly in Cohen, *Year Zero.*

51. For the minutes of the Shaw Commission, see Colonial Office, *Palestine Commission*. Daniel Monk's detailed and insightful analysis of the commission's discussion formed the basis of my analysis here. Monk, *Aesthetic Occupation*, 100–126.

52. Monk, 110.

53. Monk, 126.

54. On Mizrahi and this image, see Sabar, "'Akedat Yitshak."

55. *King James Bible*, Isaiah 56:7.

56. Colonial Office, *Palestine Commission*, 425.

57. Colonial Office, 496.

58. Monk, *Aesthetic Occupation*, 110.

59. Monk, 107.

60. Monk, 112–14. As Monk shows, a complete disaster for the Zionist side was averted by its solicitor's argument that the dome itself should be considered a supplement of a sort, as the real signified object was not the architecture but the holy rock at its core. Thus he portrayed the Jewish pictorial representation and the dome as similar (rather than conflicting) expressions of devotion to the sacred rock.

61. Did Mizrahi's 1925 *mizrach* express a desire to transform the dome into a Jewish temple? A prominent member of the contemporary Temple movement in Israel does not believe so. Yehuda ʿEtsion, the Jewish right-wing militant who was convicted in 1984 for plotting to blow up the dome, wrote a treatise on Zionist and Muslim discourses on the dome/Temple around 1929. ʿEtsion examines the *mizrach* closely and concludes reluctantly that it was a naive depiction and not a claim for possession or Jewish takeover: "The bleak conclusion is that Moshe Mizrahi is still mired in the swamp of diasporic mentality and has not opened up to redemption." ʿEtsion, *ʿAlilot*, 55.

62. Adler, *Memorandum on the Western Wall*, 27–28.

63. CZA, L59/160, Commission on the Western Wall, Jerusalem, "Closing Speech by Mr. David Yellin," 17 July 1930.

64. "Closing Speech by Mr. David Yellin."

65. "Closing Speech by Mr. David Yellin."

66. CZA, S25/2931, Wailing Wall Commission, Minutes, Jerusalem Session 18 Meeting, 16 July 1930, 58–61.

67. International Commission for the Wailing Wall, "Report of the Commission," December 1930.

68. Orenstein, *Yoman*, 183, 184, 187, 190, 262.

69. Orenstein, 262.

70. Kluger, *Min ha-Makor*, vol. 5, 131, no date [1939–1947].

71. PRO, FO 371/14488, President of the Moslem Council to Chief Secretary of the Palestine Government, 15 October 1930.

72. Orenstein, *Yoman*, 261–62.

73. Orenstein, 317.

74. Orenstein, 96.

75. Monk, *Aesthetic Occupation*, 119, 126.

76. Yehoshua, *Yerushalayim*, vol. 3, 116.

77. Luncz, "Kotel ha-Maʿaravi," 152.

78. Orenstein, *Yoman*, 118.

CHAPTER 7

1. IWM film collection, 45. *The NEBI-NUSA* [*sic*] *FESTIVALS: Scenes and incidents en route*. Jury's Imperial Pictures, 1919.

2. On Jerusalem in British propaganda, see Bar-Yosef, *Holy Land in English Culture*, 260–69.

3. Jawhariyyeh, *Storyteller of Jerusalem*, 192.

4. Keith-Roach, *Pasha of Jerusalem*, 160.

5. For a comprehensive bibliography in Arabic, see ʿAsali, *Mawsim al-Nabi Musa*, 153–204. For an 1896 detailed description of the festival for an East European Jewish readership, see Yellin, *Yerushalayim shel Temol*, 36–39. Shami, *Nikmat ha-Avot* is a 1927 Hebrew novel revolving around the pilgrimage, written by a Sephardic-Arab Jew from Hebron. On Shami and his novel, see Tamari, *Mountain against the Sea*, 150–66.

6. An early ethnographic account was written by Palestinian scholar Canaan, *Mohammedan Saints*. On Canaan, see Tamari, *Mountain against the Sea*, 93–112. Recent contributions are ʿAsali, *Mawsim al-Nabi Musa*; Halabi, "The Nabi Musa Festival"; Halabi, "Symbols of Hegemony and Resistance"; Aubin-Boltanski, *Pèlerinages*. The Nabi Musa banners and their embroidery were studied by artist and scholar Vera Tamari, "Nabi Musa Banners."

7. On the Husayni family, see Pappe, *Rise and Fall*.

8. Some crescents were ornamented with short inscriptions such as the Islamic creed, "There is no god but Allah," or simply the name of God or the Prophet. Canaan, *Mohammedan Saints*, 203–5.

9. Yehoshua, *Yerushalayim*, vol. 2, 70–71.

10. Shami, *Nikmat ha-Avot*, 39–56.

11. Aubin-Boltanski, *Pèlerinages*, 215.

12. Canaan, *Mohammedan Saints*, 213–14.

13. "ʿEdut 19," *Ha-Arets*, 13 May 1920.

14. "ʿEdut 42," *Ha-Arets*, 28 May 1920. See also Shami, *Nikmat ha-Avot*, 96.

15. Tamari, "Nabi Musa Banners," 318.

16. The Nabi Musa banner measured 200 × 140 cm, and the Haram banners 120 × 100 cm. Tamari, "Nabi Musa Banners," 319.

17. Tamari, 320.

18. Tamari, 320. The Nabi Musa banner was embroidered with the number 1391, suggesting it was restored in that Hijri year (1891). Canaan, *Mohammedan Saints*, 201.

19. Qur'an 4:164; Canaan, *Mohammedan Saints*, 201–3.

20. Tamari, "Nabi Musa Banners," 319; Aubin-Boltanski, *Pèlerinages*, 281.

21. Canaan, *Mohammedan Saints*, 113.

22. On rags and cloths in holy tombs and trees, see Canaan, 103–6; Grehan,

Twilight of the Saints, 169–70. On Jewish talismanic use of threads in Rachel's Tomb, see Frumkin, *Derekh Shofet*, 69.

23. Tamari, "Nabi Musa Banners," 317.

24. On the saints-centered popular religion in Greater Syria as "agrarian religion," see Grehan, *Twilight of the Saints*.

25. See Canaan, *Mohammedan Saints*, 14, 21–22, 50, on banners elsewhere in Palestine; stone inscriptions, 19–20; henna inscriptions, 14, 25; cloth covers, 29–30.

26. Fishman, "1911 Haram al-Sharif incident."

27. Schölch, *Palestine in Transformation, 1856–1882*, 16; Khalidi, *Palestinian Identity*, 151.

28. Official representation of towns of Palestine's coastal plain such as Jaffa, Ramlah, and Lyd began in 1929, when the festival emerged as a national festival of Arab Palestine. *Al-Jami'a al-'Arabiyya*, 2 May 1929, quoted in 'Asali, *Mawsim al-Nabi Musa*, 127.

29. Tamari, *Year of the Locust*, 63.

30. See Sakakini, *Yawmiyat*, vol. 2, 12, 141–42, entries of 19–20 December 1914, for a skeptical account doubting the enthusiasm of the celebrations.

31. Turjeman also describes a debauched party of high officers with alcohol and prostitutes, where (he notes with dismay) the gate was decorated with signs saluting the sultan. Tamari, *Year of the Locust*, 72.

32. Storrs, *Orientations*, 386.

33. Storrs, 385–86.

34. PCC, Storrs papers, reel 7, "Mufti Kamel Huesseini to Governor Storrs," undated typescript [1919–1920], and also Storrs, 386.

35. PRO, CO 733/20/19426, Samuel to Winston Churchill, Secretary of State for the Colonies, 30 April 1922, quoted in Halabi, "The Nabi Musa Festival."

36. See Yehoshua, *Yerushalayim*, vol. 2, 34.

37. Halabi, "The Nabi Musa Festival."

38. Segev, *One Palestine, Complete*, 127–41.

39. See Pappe, *Rise and Fall*; Elpeleg, *The Grand Mufti*; Mattar, *Mufti of Jerusalem*.

40. Pappe, *Rise and Fall*, 217.

41. 'Asali, *Mawsim al-Nabi Musa*, 131, 175–176, 191.

42. Halabi, "The Nabi Musa Festival."

43. For perspectives of Palestinian contemporaries, see Sakakini, *Jerusalem and I*, 49; 'Asali, *Mawsim al-Nabi Musa*, 153–204.

44. Elpeleg, *The Grand Mufti*.

45. Mattar, *Mufti of Jerusalem*, 50–64.

46. Pappe, *Rise and Fall*, 255.

47. Yavuz, "Influence of Late Ottoman Architecture."

48. Al-Mutawakkil al-Laythi, stanza 890, in Salih, *Abu Thamam*, 586–87.

49. Katinka, *Me-ʾaz ve-ʿad Hena*, 257–63, 285–86.

50. The operator was George Barsky, who also managed the nearby Allenby Hotel; Segev, *One Palestine, Complete*, 229. The name Allenby Palace was displayed on a small sign next to the entrance. Yavuz, "Influence of Late Ottoman Architecture."

51. Kupferschmidt, *Supreme Muslim Council*, 179.

52. On the 1933 and 1934 Arab Exhibitions, see Abusaada, "Self-Portrait of a Nation."

53. See cover image.

54. ISA B30/31, "Report on Nebi Musa and Easter Ceremonies, 1931," undated typescript, 2. Villagers from ʿAyn Karim were told that unfurling their banner on Jaffa Road could not be tolerated; a less central location was chosen.

55. ISA, B30/31, "Report on Nebi Musa and Easter Ceremonies, 1931," undated typescript, 2. For detail, see Halabi, "Symbols of Hegemony and Resistance."

56. Cf. chap. 1.

57. *Jerusalem News*, 15 March 1920.

58. Notice on behalf of the municipality, *Al-Jamiʿa al-ʿArabiyya*, 16 April 1928, 2.

59. Samuel, *Memoirs*, 164.

60. ISA, CS/125, Civil Secretary to District Governors of Palestine, "Note on the Advertisement Ordinance," 13 August 1920.

61. Jabra, *First Well*, 106.

62. ISA, 651/41, Herbert Samuel to Lady Samuel, undated typescript [September 1920].

63. ISA, 6958/44, Government of Palestine, Department of Health Festivals—Nabi Mousa. No. 99/26/JD, "Police Orders for the Year 1940," 17 April 1940, 1.

64. ISA, 6958/44, "Police Orders for the Year 1940," 1–5.

65. Shepherd, *Ploughing Sand*, 42.

66. This insightful typology was suggested by Monk, *Aesthetic Occupation*, 80–83.

67. "ʿEdut 44," *Ha-Arets*, 28 May 1920, 4.

68. *Ha-Arets*, 3 June 1920, 4. Another Hebron merchant testified that he had heard of a Jewish plan to attack the banners at Jaffa Gate. *Ha-Arets*, 13 May 1920, 4.

69. PRO, WO 32/9614, "Report of the Court of Inquiry convened by order of H.E. the High Commissioner and Commander in Chief, dated the 12th day of April 1920. The Riots in Jerusalem [Palin Commission Report]." The report was suppressed by Samuel because of its criticism of the Jewish National Home policy.

70. PRO, WO 32/9614, "Report of the Court of Inquiry," 30–31.

71. Mattar, *Mufti of Jerusalem*, 17.

72. Qasimiyya, *Al-ʿAlam al-Filastini*, 23. Another eyewitness recounted that the riot started when young Jewish men spat and threw stones at Faysal's portrait. French

Consul in Jerusalem to French High Commissioner of Syria, 8 April 1920, quoted in Laurens, *La question de Palestine*, vol. 1, 508.

73. Qasimiyya, *Al-ʿAlam al-Filastini*, 13. According to Qasimiyya and ʿAbd al-Hadi, *Tatawwur al-ʿAlam al-ʿArabi*, the flag originated from a three-colored emblem in green, white, and black, adopted by Arab nationalists in 1914.

74. Lawrence, *Seven Pillars of Wisdom*, 57.

75. Leslie, *Mark Sykes*. Sykes also staged General Allenby's ceremonial entry to Jerusalem on December 1917. Bar-Yosef, *Holy Land in English Culture*, 260–65.

76. Kedourie, *In the Anglo-Arab Labyrinth*, 198–99. For Sykes's original sketches, see PRO FO 882/16 SP/17/5, Mark Sykes to Sir Reginald Wingate, 22 February 1917.

77. Wallach, "Creating a Country through Currency and Stamps."

78. Gelvin, *Divided Loyalties*, 244–45.

79. Qasimiyya, *Al-ʿAlam al-Filastini*, 22. The color order was changed in 1928, when white was placed at the center rather than at the bottom. Qasimiyya, 27.

80. Leslie, *Mark Sykes*, 280.

81. In 1929 the Jaffa-based newspaper *Filastin* launched a readers' competition for designs for a unique and local Palestinian flag. All suggestions were based, in one way or another, on the Arab Flag, and none contained any text. Sorek, "The Orange and the 'Cross in the Crescent.'"

82. Sakakini, *Jerusalem and I*, 49.

83. Qasimiyya, *Al-ʿAlam al-Filastini*, 27.

84. Aubin-Boltanski, *Pèlerinages*, 212.

CHAPTER 8

1. Sakakini, *Yawmiyat*, vol. 1, 320–21.

2. On the role of visiting cards in the downfall of Oscar Wilde, see Hernen, "Names Are Everything."

3. Forster, *Howards End*, 30.

4. Tamari, *The Great War*, 160.

5. Sheehi, "Portrait Paths."

6. Rioli, "Introducing Jerusalem."

7. Jawhariyyeh, *Storyteller of Jerusalem*, 152.

8. Sakakini, 3 December 1917, in Tamari, "Khalil Sakakini's Ottoman Prison Diaries."

9. Sakakini, *Kadha Ana Ya Dunya*, 336–38.

10. Sakakini's mercurial personality is explored beautifully in Bawalsa, "Sakakini Defrocked."

11. Boullata, "Living with the Tigress," 214. On Jabra as a modernist, see Abu-Manneh, *The Palestinian Novel*; Boullata, *Nafidha ʿala al-Hadatha*. See Halabi, *Unmaking of the Arab Intellectual*, on Jabra as an intellectual exile.

12. Jabra, *First Well.*

13. Ayalon, *Reading Palestine*, 22–26, 93.

14. Jabra, *First Well*, 40. Syriac is a liturgical language similar to Aramaic, used in the Eastern Jacobite Church.

15. Jabra, 117.

16. Jabra, 103.

17. On the transformation of Qur'anic schools into state schools, see Messick, *The Calligraphic State*, 99–114.

18. Messick, 104.

19. Jabra, *First Well*, 114.

20. Jabra, 109.

21. Jabra, 107.

22. Sakakini, *Kadha Ana Ya Dunya*, 265.

23. Ayalon, *Reading Palestine*, 75–78. Among the earliest recorded instances of Arabic clandestine political notices in Jerusalem were the anti-Zionist notices posted in 1921 as part of a campaign in favor of Hajj Amin al-Husayni's appointment as Mufti. Pappe, *Rise and Fall*, 215.

24. Quoted in Ayalon, *Reading Palestine*, 76.

25. Messick, *The Calligraphic State*, 99–114.

26. Hamenahem, "Ruah Aheret," *Mi-Sipurey Na'ar Yerushalmi*, 22–28.

27. Hamenahem, "Ba-Ulpana," *Mi-Sipurey Na'ar Yerushalmi*, 7.

28. Hamenahem, "Ruah Aheret," *Mi-Sipurey Na'ar Yerushalmi*, 22.

29. David Yellin, "Mikhtavim mi-Yerushalayim" (Letters from Jerusalem), *Hamelits*, 7 September 1903.

30. On Hamenahem's troubled engagement with modernity, see Govrin, *Kri'at ha-Dorot*, vol. 1, 443–61.

31. Hamenahem, "Ruah Aheret," *Mi-Sipurey Na'ar Yerushalmi*, 25.

32. Hamenahem, 25.

33. In 1913 teachers in Lämel and other Hilfsverein schools in Palestine demanded to teach more of the curriculum in Hebrew. On the "Language War," see Saposnik, *Becoming Hebrew*, 213–36.

34. Jabra, *First Well*, 157.

35. Ayalon, *Reading Palestine*, 78.

36. Henkin, *City Reading*, 14.

37. Benjamin, *Arcades Project*, 423.

38. Jabra's embrace of alienation as a radical tool of transformation also led him to articulate the productive qualities of exile. As Zeina Halabi argued, Jabra saw the Palestinian experience of exile as a catalyst for change. "By virtue of their education

and their displacement . . . Palestinian intellectuals emerged as archetypical modern and humanist subjects." Halabi, *Unmaking of the Arab Intellectual*, 84.

39. Stephen Sheehi argues that this intellectual project was undermined by the colonial formation of subjectivity of these intellectuals. The West's domineering presence made it impossible to formulate a sense of self that was separate from Western hegemony. Sheehi, *Foundations of Modern Arab Identity*, 10.

40. Boullata, *Nafidha ʿala al-Hadatha*, 6.

41. Boullata, 8–9.

42. See also Alami, "The Lesson of Palestine."

43. Jabra, "The Palestinian Exile as Writer." As Bashir Abu Manneh shows, Jabra's early literary writing before 1948 was in English because he believed Arabic was "too wordy, too flowery." However, the Nakba propelled him to embrace Arabic as "the vehicle of our revolutionary thinking and expression." Abu-Manneh, *The Palestinian Novel*, 39.

44. For a global history of modern identification papers, see Caplan and Torpey, *Documenting Individual Identity*. On travel documents used by travelers in the Middle East and North Africa, see Hanley, "Papers for Going, Papers for Staying."

45. Tawil-Souri, "Orange, Green and Blue," 220.

46. Shaw, "The Ottoman Census System and Population, 1831–1914."

47. Frumkin, *Derekh Shofet*, 106. Frumkin's first name, Gad, was spelled "Kadak" in his *nüfus* papers.

48. On the necessity for travel documents during World War I, see Yellin, *Zikhronot*, 192–202.

49. Shiryon, *Zikhronot*, 191.

50. Hanley, "Papers for Going, Papers for Staying," 194.

51. al-Shuqayri, *Arbaʿun ʿAma*, 37–38.

52. According to Lauren Banko, who is currently researching the topic, the government issued the cards on a voluntary basis in 1938. Government employees and workers in key sectors were likely to carry such cards, but most of the population did not have them. Personal correspondence.

53. Cohen, "The Matrix of Surveillance," 101.

54. Such a "Resident's Pass" is reproduced in Sakakini, *Jerusalem and I*.

55. Robinson, *Citizen Strangers*, chap. 3.

56. See Tawil-Souri, "Orange, Green and Blue." Rashid Khalidi's book *Palestinian Identity* opens with a scene involving border control.

57. Robinson, *Citizen Strangers*, chap. 3.

58. Mahmoud Darwish, "Bitakat Hawiyya" (1964). Translated by Salman Masalha and Vivian Eden, "ID Card," *Ha-Arets*, 21 July 2016.

59. Nassar and Rahman, *Mahmoud Darwish, Exile's Poet*, 275.

60. Mattawa, *How Long Have You Been With Us?*, 49–51.

61. Bhabha, *Location of Culture*, 121–32.

62. Benjamin, *Arcades Project*, 516–17.

63. Gavish, *Survey of Palestine*.

64. Benvenisti, *Sacred Landscape*, 70–78.

65. Benvenisti.

CONCLUSION

1. Jabra, *First Well*, 176.

2. Jabra, 177.

3. Jabra, 178.

4. Tobler, *Beitrag zur medizinischen Topographie von Jerusalem*, 7–8.

5. *Do'ar ha-Yom*, 16 August 1929.

6. For a nuanced account along these lines, see Khalidi, *The Iron Cage*, 9–22.

7. Azaryahu, *'Al Shem*, 132–36.

8. A prominent example of colonial rewriting is the state-backed settler effort to transform the Palestinian neighborhood of Silwan into the "City of David" through house demolitions, eviction, and dispossession, conjoined with archaeological excavations and the creation of a biblical tourist attraction. See Pullan and Gwiazda, "Designing the Biblical Present."

Bibliography

HISTORICAL PRESS

Arabic

Al-Jami'a al-'Arabiyya

Al-Quds

Filastin

Mir' at al- Sharq

English

Jerusalem News

Palestine Weekly

Hebrew

Davar

Do'ar ha-Yom

Ha-Arets

Hadshot me-ha-Arets ha-Kdosha

Ha-Herut

Ha-Levanon

Hapo'el Ha-Tsa'ir

Hashkafa

Ha-Tsfira

Ha-Tsvi
Havatselet

ARCHIVES

BEA	Bank of England Archive, London
BLMC	British Library Map Collection, London
CZA	Central Zionist Archives, Jerusalem
IWM	Imperial War Museum, London
ISA	Israel State Archive, Jerusalem
JMA	Jerusalem Municipal Archives, Jerusalem
KCC	King's College, Cambridge
LOC	Library of Congress, Prints and Photographs Division, Washington DC
NLI	National Library of Israel, Jerusalem,
PCC	Pembroke College, Cambridge
PRO	Public Record Office, Kew

PUBLISHED SOURCES

ʿAbd al-Hadi, Mahdi. *Tatawwur al-ʿAlam al-ʿArabi min al-Fath al-Islami hatta al-Qurn al-ʿIshrun.* Amman, 1986.

Abou-Hodeib, Toufoul. *A Taste for Home: The Modern Middle Class in Ottoman Beirut.* Stanford, CA: Stanford University Press, 2017.

Abu El-Haj, Nadia. *Facts on the Ground: Archaeological Practice and Territorial Self-Fashioning in Israeli Society.* Chicago: University of Chicago Press, 2001.

Abu-Manneh, Bashir. *The Palestinian Novel: From 1948 to the Present.* Cambridge: Cambridge University Press, 2016.

Abusaada, Nadi. "Self-Portrait of a Nation: The Arab Exhibition in Mandate Jerusalem, 1931–1934." *Jerusalem Quarterly* 77 (2019): 122–35.

Ada Yardeni. *The Book of Hebrew Script: History, Palaeography, Script Styles, Calligraphy & Design.* Jerusalem: Carta, 1997.

Adler, Cyrus. *Memorandum on the Western Wall: Prepared for the Special Commission of the League of Nations on Behalf of the Jewish Agency for Palestine.* Philadelphia, 1930.

Agnon, Shmuel Yosef. *Only Yesterday.* Translated by Barbara Harashav. Princeton, NJ: Princeton University Press, 2000.

Alami, Musa. "The Lesson of Palestine." *Middle East Journal* 3, no. 4 (1949): 373–405.

Alexander, Tamar. "Ha-Agada ha-Sefaradit-Yehudit ʿal Rabenu Kalonimus bi-Yerushalayim." *Jerusalem Studies in Jewish Folklore,* nos. 5–6 (1984): 122–85.

Alroey, Gur. *An Unpromising Land: Jewish Migration to Palestine in the Early Twentieth Century*. Stanford, CA: Stanford University Press, 2014.

Arbel, Michal. *Katuv ʿal ʿOro shel ha-Kelev: ʿAl Tefisat ha-Yetsirah etsel Shay ʿAgnon*. Jerusalem: Keter, 2006.

Armstrong, Karen. *A History of Jerusalem*. London: HarperCollins, 1996.

Arnon, Adar. "The Quarters of Jerusalem in the Ottoman Period." *Middle Eastern Studies* 28, no. 1 (1992): 1–65.

Arpaly, Boaz. *Rav-Roman: Hamisha Maʾamarim ʿal Temol Shilshom le-Shay ʿAgnon*. Bnei Brak: Ha-Kibuts ha-Meʾuhad, 1998.

ʿAsali, Kamil J. *Mawsim al-Nabi Musa fi Filastin: Taʾrikh al-Mawsim wal-Maqam*. Amman: Manshurat al-Jamiʿa al-Urduniyya, 1990.

Ashbee, C. R. *A Palestine Notebook: 1918–1923*. London: William Heinemann, 1923.

———, ed. *Jerusalem 1918–1920: Being the Records of the Pro-Jerusalem Council during the Period of the British Military Administration*. London: John Murray, 1921.

———, ed. *Jerusalem, 1920–1922: Being the Records of the Pro-Jerusalem Council during the First Two Years of the Civil Administration*. London: J. Murray, 1924.

Aubin-Boltanski, Emma. *Pèlerinages et nationalisme en Palestine: Prophètes, héros, et ancêtres*. EHESS, 2007.

Auji, Hala. *Printing Arab Modernity*. Leiden: Brill, 2016.

Ayalon, Ami. *Reading Palestine: Printing and Literacy, 1900–1948*. Austin: University of Texas Press, 2005.

———. *The Arabic Print Revolution*. Cambridge: Cambridge University Press, 2016.

Azaryahu, Maoz. *ʿAl Shem: Historya u-Politika shel Shemot Rehovot be-Yisraʾel*. Jerusalem: Karmel, 2012.

Azaryahu, Maoz, and Rebecca Cook. "Mapping the Nation: Street-Naming and Arab-Palestinian Identity: Three Case Studies." *Nations and Nationalism* 2, no. 8 (2003): 195–213.

Bahat, Dan. *Yerushalayim: Osef Mekorot*. Jerusalem: Ariel, 1999.

Bar-Adon, Aharon. *Shay ʿAgnon u-Tehiyat ha-Lashon ha-ʿIvrit*. Jerusalem: Mosad Byalik, 1977.

Bar-Gal, Yoram. "Shemot la-Rehovot be-Tel Aviv: Perek be-Historya Tarbutit ʿIronit (1909–1933)." *Cathedra* 47 (1988): 118–32.

Barron, J. B. *Palestine: Report and General Abstracts of the Census of 1922 Taken on the 23rd of October 1922*. Jerusalem: Green Convent Press, 1923.

Barton, David, Mary Hamilton, and Roz Ivanič, eds. *Situated Literacies: Reading and Writing in Context*. London: Routledge, 2000.

Bar-Yosef, Eitan. *The Holy Land in English Culture 1799–1917: Palestine and the Question of Orientalism*. Oxford: Clarendon Press, 2005.

Bawalsa, Nadim. "Sakakini Defrocked." *Jerusalem Quarterly*, no. 42 (Summer 2010): 5–25.

Baynes, Leslie. *The Heavenly Book Motif in Judeo-Christian Apocalypses 200 BCE–200 CE*. Leiden: Brill, 2012.

Be'er-Marks, Roni. *'Al Homot ha-Niyar: 'Iton ha-Levanon ve-ha-Ortodoksia*. Jerusalem: Zalman Shazar, 2017.

Bektas, Yakup. "The Sultan's Messenger: Cultural Constructions of Ottoman Telegraphy, 1847–1880." *Technology and Culture* 41, no. 4 (2000): 669–96.

Ben Yehuda, Eliezer, and David Yellin. "Tazkir [1922]." *Zikhronot Va'ad ha-Lashon* 6 (1928): 73–75.

Ben-Arieh, Yehoshua. *Jerusalem in the Nineteenth Century: The Old City*. New York: St. Martin's, 1984.

———. *Jerusalem in the Nineteenth Century: Emergence of the New City*. New York: St. Martin's, 1986.

Ben-Dov, Me'ir. "Ktovot 'Ivriyot Hakukot ba-Even be-Har ha-Bayit u-Sevivato." *Kathedra* 40 (1986): 3–30.

Ben-Dov, Me'ir, Mordechay Naor, and Ze'ev Anner. *Ha-Kotel*. Tel Aviv: Misrad ha-Bitahon , 1981.

Ben-Gurion, David. *Yoman ha-Milhama: Milhemet ha-'Atsma'ut*. Tel Aviv: Misrad ha-Bitahon, 1982.

Benjamin, Walter. *Selected Writings*. Edited by Marcus Paul Bullock, Michael William Jennings, Howard Eiland, and Gary Smith. Cambridge, MA: Belknap Press, 1996.

———. *The Arcades Project*. Edited by Kevin McLaughlin; translated by Howard Eiland. Cambridge, MA: Belknap Press, 1999.

Benvenisti, Meron. *City of Stone: The Hidden History of Jerusalem*. Berkeley: University of California Press, 1996.

———. *Sacred Landscape: The Buried History of the Holy Land since 1948*. Berkeley: University of California Press, 2000.

Berchem, Max van. "Lettre a M. Barbier de Meynard sur le projet d'un corpus inscriptionum Arabicarum." *Journal Asiatique* 20 (November 1892): 305–17.

———. *Egypt*. Matériaux pour un corpus inscriptionum Arabicarum. Cairo: Institut français d'archéologie orientale, 1903.

———. *Syrie Du Sud, Tome 1, Jérusalem "Ville."* Matériaux pour un Corpus inscriptionum Arabicarum. Cairo: Institut français d'archéologie orientale, 1922.

———. *Syrie Du Sud, Tome 2, Jérusalem "Haram."* Matériaux pour un Corpus inscriptionum Arabicarum. Cairo: Institut français d'archéologie orientale, 1927.

Berlin, Howard M. *The Coins and Banknotes of Palestine under the British Mandate, 1927–1947*. Jefferson, NC: McFarland, 2001.

Bhabha, Homi K. *The Location of Culture*. London: Routledge, 1994.

Bierman, Irene A. *Writing Signs: The Fatimid Public Text*. Berkeley: University of California Press, 1998.

Blair, Sheila. *Islamic Inscriptions*. Edinburgh: Edinburgh University Press, 1998.

Blyth, Estelle. *When We Lived in Jerusalem*. London: J. Murray, 1927.

Bosworth, C. E., R. E. Darley-Doran, and G. S. P. Freeman-Greenville. *Encyclopaedia of Islam*, 2nd ed., s.v. "Sikka." Leiden: Brill, 2012. http://dx.doi.org/10.1163/1573-3912_islam_COM_1076 (Accessed 7 October 2019).

Boullata, Issa J. "Living with the Tigress and the Muses: An Essay on Jabra Ibrahim Jabra." *World Literature Today* 75, no. 2 (2001): 214–23.

———. *Nafidha ʿala al-Hadatha: Dirasat fi Adab Jabra Ibrahim Jabra*. Beirut: Al-Mu'assasa al-ʿArabiyya lil-Dirasat wal-Nashr, 2002.

Boyarin, Jonathan. *The Ethnography of Reading*. Berkeley: University of California Press, 1993.

Brisk, Asher Leib. *Sefer Helkat Mehokek*. Jerusalem: Zuckerman, 1900.

Büssow, Johann. *Hamidian Palestine: Politics and Society in the District of Jerusalem 1872–1908*. Leiden: Brill, 2011.

Campos, Michelle. *Ottoman Brothers: Muslims, Christians, and Jews in Early Twentieth-Century Palestine*. Stanford, CA: Stanford University Press, 2010.

———. "Placing Jerusalemites in the History of Jerusalem: The Ottoman Census (Sicil-i Nüfûs) as a Historical Source." In *Ordinary Jerusalem, 1840–1940*, edited by Angelos Dalachanis and Vincent Lemire, 15–28. Leiden: Brill, 2018.

Canaan, Taufik. *Mohammedan Saints and Sanctuaries in Palestine*. London: Luzac, 1927.

Caplan, Jane, and John Torpey. *Documenting Individual Identity: The Development of State Practices in the Modern World*. Princeton, NJ: Princeton University Press, 2002.

Caplan, Kimmy. "Shkiʿa, Priha ve-ʿInyan: Megamot u-Me'afyenim be-Heker ha-Ortodokosia." *Zion* 74 (2009): 353–72.

Cavallo, Guglielmo, Roger Chartier, and Lydia G. Cochrane. *A History of Reading in the West*. Oxford: Polity Press, 1999.

Certeau, Michel de. *The Practice of Everyday Life*. Berkeley: University of California Press, 1984.

Chateaubriand, François-René. *Travels in Greece, Palestine, Egypt, and Barbary, during the Years 1806 and 1807*. New York: Van Winkle & Wiley, 1814.

Chelouche, Yosef Eliyahu. *Parashat Hayay 1870–1930*. Tel Aviv: Babel, 2005.

Cohen, Amnon. *Economic Life in Ottoman Jerusalem*. Cambridge: Cambridge University Press, 1989.

Cohen, Hillel. "The Matrix of Surveillance in Times of National Conflict: The Israeli-Palestinian Case." In *Surveillance and Control in Israel/Palestine: Population, Territory and Power*, edited by Elia Zureik, David Lyon, and Yasmeen Abu-Laban, 99–127. London: Routledge, 2011.

———. *Year Zero of the Arab-Israeli Conflict 1929*. Translated by Haim Watzman. Waltham, MA: Brandeis University Press, 2015.

Cohen-Levinovisky, Nurit. *Plitim Yehudim be-Milhemet ha-'Atsma'ut*. Tel Aviv: Am Oved, 2014.

Cohen-Reiss, Ephraim. *Mi-Zikhronot Ish Yerushalayim*. Jerusalem: Sifriyat ha-Yishuv, 1967.

Collection of Judgments of the Courts of Palestine 1919–1933, vol. 4, 1483–86. Tel Aviv: L. M. Rothenberg Law Publisher, 1937.

Colonial Office. *Palestine Commission on the Disturbances of August, 1929*. Vol. 2, *Evidence Heard during the 30th to 47th Sittings, and a Selection from the Exhibits*. Colonial 48. London: HMSO, 1930.

Conrad, Lawrence. "The Khalidi Library." In *Ottoman Jerusalem: The Living City, 1517–1917*, edited by Sylvia Auld and Robert Hillenbrand, 191–209. London: Altajir World of Islam Trust, 2000.

Dabbah, Raphael. *Currency Notes of the Palestine Currency Board*. Jerusalem: R. Dabbah, 2005.

Deringil, Selim. *The Well-Protected Domains: Ideology and the Legitimation of Power in the Ottoman Empire 1876–1909*. London: I. B. Tauris, 1998.

Derrida, Jacques. *Of Grammatology*. Translated by Gayatri Chakravorty Spivak. Baltimore: Johns Hopkins University Press, 1997.

———. *Writing and Difference*. Translated by Alan Bass. London: Routledge, 2001.

———. *Dissemination*. Translated by Barbara Johnson. London: Continuum, 2004.

Derrida, Jacques, and Gil Anidjar. *Acts of Religion*. New York: Routledge, 2002.

Derrida, Jacques, Marc Guillaume, Daniel Bougnoux, and Keith Reader. "Paper or Myself, You Know . . . (New Speculations on a Luxury of the Poor)." *Paragraph* 21, no. 1 (1998): 1–27.

Dimitriadis, Sotirios. "The Tramway Concession of Jerusalem, 1908–1914: Elite Citizenship, Urban Infrastructure, and the Abortive Modernization of a Late Ottoman City." In *Ordinary Jerusalem 1840–1940*, edited by Angelos Dalachanis and Vincent Lemire, 475–89. Leiden: Brill, 2018.

Dord-Crouslé, Stéphanie. "Inscrire la mémoire de soi dans les lieux visités: Pratique et réception des graffitis par les voyageurs du XIXe siècle." In *Le voyage et la mémoire au XIXe siècle*, edited by Moussa Sarga and Sylvain Venayre, 321–37. Paris: Créaphis Éditions, 2011.

Doumani, Beshara. *Rediscovering Palestine: Merchants and Peasants in Jabal Nablus, 1700–1900*. Berkeley: University of California Press, 1995.

Dowty, Alan. "Much Ado about Little: Ahad Ha'am's 'Truth from Eretz Yisrael,' Zionism, and the Arabs." *Israel Studies* 5, no. 2 (2000): 154–81.

Eldem, Edhem. *A History of the Ottoman Bank*. Beyoğlu, Istanbul: Ottoman Bank Historical Research Center, 1999.

Elmaleh, Abraham. *Ha-Rishonim le-Tsiyon*. Jerusalem: Rubin Mass, 1970.

Elpeleg, Zvi. *The Grand Mufti: Hajj Amin Al-Hussaini, Founder of the Palestinian National Movement*. London: Frank Cass, 1993.

Eordegian, Marlen. "British and Israeli Maintenance of the Status Quo in the Holy Places of Christendom." *International Journal of Middle East Studies* 35 (2003): 307–28.

ʿEtsion, Yehuda. *ʿAlilot ha-Mufti ve-ha-Doktor: Ha-Siakh ha-Tsioni-Muslemi be-Nose Har ha-Bayit ve-Hamikdash ʿal Rekaʿ Praʿot Tarpat*. Jerusalem: Sifriyat Bet El, 2014.

Ferguson, Heather L. *The Proper Order of Things: Language, Power, and Law in Ottoman Administrative Discourses*. Stanford, CA: Stanford University Press, 2018.

Fischer, Steven R. *A History of Reading*. London: Reaktion, 2003.

Fishman, Louis. 2005. "The 1911 Haram al-Sharif Incident: Palestinian Notables versus the Ottoman Administration." *Journal of Palestine Studies* 34 (3): 6–22.

Flaubert, Gustave. *Correspondance*. Vol. 1. Paris: Gallimard, 1973.

Fleming, Juliet. *Graffiti and the Writing Arts of Early Modern England*. London: Reaktion, 2001.

———. *Cultural Graphology: Writing after Derrida*. Chicago: University of Chicago Press, 2016.

Forster, E. M. *Howards End*. New York: Penguin, 2000.

Foucault, Michel. *Discipline and Punish: The Birth of the Prison*. Harmondsworth, UK: Penguin, 1975.

Friedman, Menachem. *Hevra be-Mashber Legitimitsya: Ha-Yishuv ha-Ashkenazi ha-Yashan 1900–1917*. Jerusalem: Mosad Byalik, 2001.

———. "Pashekevilim u-Modaʿot Kir ba-Hevra ha-Haredit." In *Pashekevilim*, edited by Genya Dolev. Tel Aviv: Eretz Israel Museum, Yad Ben Zvi, 2005.

Frumkin, Gad. *Derekh Shofet bi-Yerushalayim*. Tel Aviv: Dvir, 1954.

Fuchs, Ron, and Gilbert Herbert. "A Colonial Portrait of Jerusalem: British Architecture in Jerusalem of the Mandate 1917–48." In *Hybrid Urbanism: On the Identity Discourse and the Built Environment*, edited by Nezar AlSayyad, 81–108. Westport, CT: Praeger, 2001.

Gafni, Reuven. "Zikhron ha-Yahid ve-Todaʿat ha-Tsibur: Luhot Zikaron ve-Luhot Hantsaha be-Batey Kneset." *ʿAl Atar* 16 (2011): 83–103.

Gautier-van Berchem, Marguerite, and Solange Ory. *La Jérusalem musulmane dans l'oeuvre de Max van Berchem*. Lausanne: Éditions des Trois Continents, 1978.

Gavish, Dov. *A Survey of Palestine under the British Mandate, 1920–1948*. London: Routledge, 2005.

Gelvin, James L. *Divided Loyalties: Nationalism and Mass Politics in Syria at the Close of Empire*. Berkeley: University of California Press, 1998.

Genachowsky, Dov. "Pictures of Holy Places as Fundraising Aid." In *Offerings from*

Jerusalem: Portrayals of Holy Places by Jewish Artists, edited by Rachel Sarfati, 31–35. Jerusalem: Israel Museum, 2002.

"General Map of Jerusalem. Approx. Scale, 1:5,000." El-Giza: Survey of Egypt, 1924. British Library Map Collection [versions in English, Arabic, and Hebrew].

Genet, Jean. *Prisoner of Love*. London: Picador, 1989.

George, Alain. *The Rise of Islamic Calligraphy*. London: Saqi Books, 2010.

Gera, Shulamit. "Ha-Ktovot be-Otiyot ʿIvriyot be-Shaʿar ha-Rahamim." *Kathedra* 61 (1991): 176–81.

Gilbert, Martin. *Jerusalem in the Twentieth Century*. London: Chatto & Windus, 1996.

Gitler, Inbal Ben-Asher. "C. R. Ashbee's Jerusalem Years: Arts and Crafts, Orientalism and British Regionalism." *Assaph: Studies in Art History* 5 (2000): 29–52.

Goethe, Johann Wolfgang von. *Faust: The Second Part of the Tragedy*. Translated by David Constantine. Cambridge: Penguin, 2009.

Goldhill, Simon. *Jerusalem: City of Longing*. Cambridge: Belknap Press of Harvard University Press, 2008.

Govrin, Nurit. *Kri'at ha-Dorot: Sifrut ʿIvrit be-Maʿagaleha*. Vol. 1. Jerusalem: Karmel, 2002.

Graham, Stephen. *With the Russian Pilgrims to Jerusalem*. London: Thomas Nelson and Sons, 1918.

Graves, Richard. *Experiment in Anarchy*. London: Gollancz, 1949.

Grayevsky, Pinhas M. Ben Tzvi. *Sefer Avney Zikaron: Avney Kodesh bi-Yerushalayim*. 15 vols. Jerusalem: Tzukerman, 1928–1932.

Grehan, James. *Twilight of the Saints: Everyday Religion in Ottoman Syria and Palestine*. New York: Oxford University Press, 2016.

Gross, Yaʿacov. *Yerushalayim 5678 1917/19 Hurban Nes u-Ge'ulah*. Jerusalem: Koresh, 1992.

Hacohen, Mordechai ben-Hillel. *Milhemet ha-ʿAmim: Yoman*. 4 vols. Jerusalem: Mitspe, 1929–1930.

Hacohen, Mordekhai. "Le-Toldot Beyt ha-Kneset ha-Hurva." In *Ha-Hurva be-Binyana*, 7–21. Jerusalem: Misrad ha-Hinukh ve-ha-Tarbut, 1970.

Haddad, Shirah. *Mi she-ʿoseh Siman: Keri'a Semyotit bi-"Temol Shilshom," me-et Shay ʿAgnon*. Jerusalem: Mosad Byalik, 2011.

Hagbi, Yaniv. *Language, Absence, Play: Judaism and Superstructuralism in the Poetics of S. Y. Agnon*. Syracuse, NY: Syracuse University Press, 2009.

Haj, Samira. "The People of Jerusalem Reordered." In *The Next Jerusalem: Sharing the Divided City*, edited by Michael Sorkin, 188–201. New York: Monacelli, 2002.

Halabi, Awad. "The Nabi Musa Festival under British-Ruled Palestine." *ISIM: International Institute for the Study of Islam in the Modern World*, no. 10 (2002): 27.

———. "Symbols of Hegemony and Resistance: Banners and Flags in British-Ruled Palestine." *Jerusalem Quarterly*, no. 36 (2009).

Halabi, Zeina G. *The Unmaking of the Arab Intellectual: Prophecy, Exile and the Nation.* Edinburgh: Edinburgh University Press, 2017.

Halevy, Dotan. "Ottoman Ruins Captured: Antiquities, Preservation, and Waqf in Mandatory Palestine." *Journal of the Ottoman and Turkish Studies Association* 5, no. 1 (2018): 91–114.

Halperin, Liora R. *Babel in Zion: Jews, Nationalism, and Language Diversity in Palestine, 1920–1948.* New Haven, CT: Yale University Press, 2014.

Hamenahem, ʿEzra. *Mi-Sipurey Naʿar Yerushalmi.* Tel Aviv: Eked, 1988.

Hanauer, J. E. *Walks about Jerusalem.* London: London Society for Promoting Christianity amongst the Jews, 1910.

A Handbook for Travellers in Syria and Palestine. London: John Murray, 1858.

Hanley, William. "Papers for Going, Papers for Staying: Identification and Subject Formation in the Eastern Mediterranean." In *A Global Middle East: Mobility, Materiality and Culture in the Modern Age, 1880–1940*, edited by Avner Wishnitzer, Liat Kozma, and Cyrus Schayegh, 177–200. London: I. B. Tauris, 2014.

Hanssen, Jens. *Fin de Siécle Beirut: The Making of an Ottoman Provincial Capital.* Oxford: Clarendon Press, 2005.

Hanssen, Jens-Peter, Thomas Philipp, and Stefan Weber. *The Empire in the City: Arab Provincial Capitals in the Late Ottoman Empire.* Beirut: Wurzburg Ergon Verlag, 2002.

Harshav, Benjamin. *Language in Time of Revolution.* Stanford, CA: Stanford University Press, 1993.

Hasak-Lowy, Todd. "A Mad Dog's Attack on Secularized Hebrew: Rethinking Agnon's *Temol shilshom.*" *Prooftexts* 24, no. 2 (2004): 167–98.

Henkin, David M. *City Reading: Written Words and Public Spaces in Antebellum New York.* New York: Columbia University Press, 1998.

Hernen, Elaine. "Names Are Everything: For Oscar Wilde, Posing as a Letter and Visiting Card." *MLA VIDES* 1 (March 2013): 219–28.

Hilu, Alon. "Sipuro shel Kelev Shahid: Kri'a *Postkolonialit* be-Temol Shilshom me-et Shay ʿAgnon." *Ho! Ktav Et le-Sifrut* 4 (2006): 54–66.

Hirschfeld, Ariel. "Ha-Sekhel ha-Enoshi ve-Sekhel ha-Maʿasim: Ha-Kelev u-Merhava shel Yerushalayim ba-Roman Temol Shilshom shel ʿAgnon." *Yerushalayim* 15, no. 2 (1981): 56–67.

Hochman, Baruch. *The Fiction of S. Y. Agnon.* Ithaca, NY: Cornell University Press, 1970.

Hoffman, Anne Golomb. "'Mad Dog' and Denouncement in Temol Shilshom." In *Tradition and Trauma: Studies in the Fiction of S. J. Agnon*, edited by David Patterson and Glenda Abramson, 45–64. Boulder, CO: Westview Press, 1994.

Holz, Avraham. "Hitbonenut be-Pirtey Temol Shilshom." In *Kovets 'Agnon*, edited by Emunah Yaron, vol. 1, 178–221. Jerusalem: Magnes, 1994.

Home, Robert K. *Of Planting and Planning: The Making of British Colonial Cities*. London: Spon, 1997.

Huneidi, Sahar. *Broken Trust: Herbert Samuel, Zionism and the Palestinians, 1920–1925*. London: I. B. Tauris, 2001.

Hyman, Benjamin. "British Planners in Palestine, 1918–1936." PhD diss., London School of Economics, 1994.

Hysler-Rubin, Noah. "Arts & Crafts and the Great City: Charles Robert Ashbee in Jerusalem." *Planning Perspectives* 21, no. 4 (2006): 347–68.

———. "Geography, Colonialism and Town Planning: Patrick Geddes' Plan for Mandatory Jerusalem." *Cultural Geographies* 18, no. 2 (2011): 231–48.

Idel, Moshe. *Golem: Jewish Magical and Mystical Traditions on the Artificial Anthropoid*. Albany: State University of New York Press, 1990.

———. "Reification of Language in Jewish Mysticism." In *Mysticism and Language*, edited by Steven Katz, 42–79. New York: Oxford University Press, 1992.

Ingham, Geoffrey. "'Babylonian Madness': On the Historical and Sociological Origins of Money." In *What Is Money?*, edited by John Smithin, 16–41. London: Routledge, 2012.

———. *The Nature of Money*. London: John Wiley & Sons, 2013.

Ingrams, Doreen. *Palestine Papers, 1917–1922: Seeds of Conflict*. London: John Murray, 1972.

International Commission for the Wailing Wall. *Report of the Commission Appointed by His Majesty's Government in the United Kingdom of Great Britain and Northern Ireland: With the Approval of the Council of the League of Nations, to Determine the Rights and Claims of Moslems and Jews in Connection with the Western or Wailing Wall at Jerusalem, December, 1930*. London: H. M. Stationery Off., 1931.

IOL News, "Now You Can Email God." Accessed 21 January 2020. https://www.iol.co.za/news/eish/now-you-can-email-god-206171

Ish, Hayut. *Sefer Masa'ot Yerushalayim*. Munkacs, 1931.

Jabotinsky, Vladimir. *Evidence Submitted to the Palestine Royal Commission, House of Lords: February 11th, 1937*. London: New Zionist Press, 1937.

Jabra, Jabra Ibrahim. "The Palestinian Exile as Writer." *Journal of Palestine Studies* 8, no. 2 (1979): 77–87.

———. *The First Well: A Bethlehem Boyhood*. Fayetteville: University of Arkansas Press, 1995.

Jacobson, Abigail. *From Empire to Empire: Jerusalem between Ottoman and British Rule*. Syracuse, NY: Syracuse University Press, 2011.

Jacobson, Abigail, and Moshe Naor. *Oriental Neighbors: Middle Eastern Jews and Arabs in Mandatory Palestine*. Waltham, MA: Brandeis University Press, 2016.

Jawhariyyeh, Wasif. *Al-Quds al-'Uthmaniyya fi al-Muddhakkirat al-Jawhariyya:*

Al-Kitab al-Awal min Mudhakkirat al-Musiqi Wasif Jawhariyya, 1904–1917. Edited by Salim Tamari and Issam Nassar. Beirut: Mu'assasat al-Dirasat al-Filastiniyya, 2003.

———. *Al-Quds al-Intidabiyya fi al-Mudhakkirat al-Jawhariyya: Al-Kitab al-Thani min Mudhakkirat al-Musiqi Wasif Jawhariyya, 1918–1948*. Edited by Salim Tamari and Issam Nassar. Jerusalem: Institute of Jerusalem Studies, 2005.

———. *The Storyteller of Jerusalem: The Life and Times of Wasif Jawhariyyeh, 1904–1948*. Edited by Salim Tamari and Issam Nassar. Translated by Nada Elzeer. Northampton, MA: Interlink, 2013.

Kadman, Noga. *Erased from Space and Consciousness: Israel and the Depopulated Palestinian Villages of 1948*. Bloomington: Indiana University Press, 2015.

Kaiser, Hilmar. "The Ottoman Government and the Zionist Movement during the First Months of World War I." In *Syria in World War I: Politics, Economy, and Society*, edited by M. Talha Çiçek, 107–29. London: Routledge, 2015.

Kark, Ruth, and Michal Oren-Nordheim. *Jerusalem and Its Environs: Quarters, Neighborhoods, Villages, 1800–1948*. Jerusalem: Magnes, 2001.

Katinka, Baruch. *Me-'az ve-'ad Hena*. Jerusalem: Kiryat Sefer, 1964.

Katsanake, Maria. *Theodore Ralli*. Athens: A. G. Leventis Foundation, A. G. Leventis Gallery, 2018.

Kayali, Hasan. *Arabs and Young Turks: Ottomanism, Arabism and Islamism in the Ottoman Empire, 1908–1918*. Berkeley: University of California Press, 1997.

Kedourie, Elie. *In the Anglo-Arab Labyrinth: The McMahon-Husayn Correspondence and Its Interpretations, 1914–1939*. Cambridge: Cambridge University Press, 1976.

Keith-Roach, Edward. *Pasha of Jerusalem: Memoirs of a District Commissioner under the British Mandate*. London: Radcliffe Press, 1994.

Kendall, Henry. *Jerusalem: The City Plan, Preservation and Development during the British Mandate, 1918–1948*. London: H.M.S.O., 1948.

Keten, Ismet. *The Ottoman Monograms: Tughra*. Ankara: I. Keten, 2002.

Keynes, John Maynard. *A Tract on Monetary Reform*. London: Macmillan, 1923.

———. *A Treatise on Money*. 2 vols. London: Macmillan, 1930.

———. *General Theory of Employment, Interest and Money*. London: Macmillan, 1936.

Khalidi, Rashid. *Palestinian Identity: The Construction of Modern National Consciousness*. New York: Columbia University Press, 1997.

———. *The Iron Cage: The Story of the Palestinian Struggle for Statehood*. Boston: Beacon Press, 2006.

Khalidi, Walid, ed. *Before Their Diaspora: A Photographic History of the Palestinians, 1876–1948*. Washington, DC: Institute for Palestine Studies, 1984.

The King James Study Bible: King James Version. Nashville: Thomas Nelson, 2008.

Klausner, Joseph. *'Am va-Erets Kamim li-Thiya: Rishmey Masa' be-Erets Yisra'el.* 2nd ed. 2 vols. Tel Aviv: Yavneh, 1943.

Klein, Menachem. *Lives in Common: Arabs and Jews in Jerusalem, Jaffa, and Hebron.* New York: Oxford University Press, 2014.

Kluger, Binyamin. *Min ha-Makor: Ha-Yishuv ha-Yashan 'al Luah ha-Modaot.* 5 vols. Jerusalem, 1978.

Kroyanker, David. *Adrikhalut bi-Yerushalayim.* Vol. 3, *Ha-Bniya ha-Eropit Notsrit mi-huts la-Homot, 1855–1918.* Jerusalem: Keter, 1987.

———. *Rehov ha-Nevi'im, Shkhunat ha-Habashim ve-Shkhunat Musrara: Sipuro shel Makom, Dyokana shel 'Ir, Yerushalayim 1850–2000.* Jerusalem: Keter, 2000.

Kupferschmidt, Uri M. *The Supreme Muslim Council: Islam under the British Mandate for Palestine.* Leiden: Brill, 1987.

Kushner, David. *To Be Governor of Jerusalem: The City and District during the Time of Ali Ekrem Bey, 1906–1908.* Istanbul: Isis Press, 2005.

Landry, Rodrigue, and Richard Y. Bourhis. "Linguistic Landscape and Ethnolinguistic Vitality: An Empirical Study." *Journal of Language and Social Psychology* 16, no. 1 (1997): 23–49.

Laurens, Henry. *La question de Palestine.* Vol. 1, *L'invention de La Terre Sainte 1799–1921.* Paris: Fayard, 1999.

Lavi, Shay. *Elias Effendi: Eliahu Honig of Jerusalem, His Era, Communal Activities and Family, 1860–1924.* Tel Mond: Honig Family Foundation, 2012.

Lawrence, T. E. *Seven Pillars of Wisdom.* Harmondsworth, UK: Penguin, 1962.

Lefebvre, Henri. *The Production of Space.* Oxford: Blackwell, 1991.

Lehmann, Matthias. *Emissaries from the Holy Land: The Sephardic Diaspora and the Practice of Pan-Judaism in the Eighteenth Century.* Stanford, CA: Stanford University Press, 2014.

Lemire, Vincent. *La soif de Jérusalem: Essai d'hydrohistoire, 1840–1948.* Paris: Publications de la Sorbonne, 2010.

———. *Jerusalem 1900: The Holy City in the Age of Possibilities.* Chicago: University of Chicago Press, 2017.

Lemke, Wolf-Dieter. "Ottoman Photography: Recording and Contributing to Modernity." In *The Empire in the City: Arab Provincial Capitals in the Late Ottoman Empire,* edited by Jens-Peter Hanssen, Thomas Philipp, and Stefan Weber, 237–49. Beirut: Wurzburg Ergon Verlag, 2002.

Leslie, Shane. *Mark Sykes: His Life and Letters.* London: Cassel, 1923.

Levy, Lital. "The Nahda and the Haskala: A Comparative Reading of 'Revival' and 'Reform.'" *Middle Eastern Literatures* 16, no. 3 (2013): 300–316.

Lipschütz, Eliezer Meir. *Ktavim.* Vol. 2. Jerusalem: Mosad ha-Rav Kook, 1949.

A Local Wedding: Ketubbot from Eretz Israel 1800–1960. Tel Aviv: Eretz Israel Museum, 2005.

Lockman, Zachary. "Railway Workers and Relational History: Arabs and Jews in British-Ruled Palestine." *Comparative Studies in Society and History* 35, no. 3 (1993): 601–27.

Lovata, Troy R., and Elizabeth Olton. *Understanding Graffiti: Multidisciplinary Studies from Prehistory to the Present*. London: Routledge, 2016.

Luke, Harry Charles. *Prophets, Priests and Patriarchs: Sketches of the Sects of Palestine and Syria*. London: Faith Press, 1927.

Luncz, Abraham Moses. "Ha-Kotel ha-Ma'aravi" (1911), in *Netivot Tsion vi-Yerushalayim*. Edited by G. Kressel. Jerusalem: Mosad ha-Rav Kook, 1971.

———. *Luah Erets Yisra'el Year 4*. Jerusalem: A. M. Luncz, 1899.

———. *Netivot Tsion vi-Yerusahalaim*, Jerusalem: Y. D. Frumkin, 1876.

———. *Luah Erets Yisra'el: Mivhar Ma'amarim*. Edited by Eli Schiller. 3 vols. Jerusalem: Ariel, 1980.

Ma'ayeh, Suha Philip. "Amman Addresses Its Street Name Problem." *The National*, accessed 26 January 2019. https://www.thenational.ae/world/mena/amman-addresses-its-street-name-problem-1.497220.

Marx, Karl. *Capital: A Critique of Political Economy*. Vol. 1. London: Lawrence & Wishart, 1954.

———. *A Contribution to the Critique of Political Economy*. Moscow: Progress Publishers, 1970.

Masalha, Nur. *The Zionist Bible: Biblical Precedent, Colonialism and the Erasure of Memory*. Durham, NC: Acumen, 2013.

Massey, Doreen. *For Space*. London: Sage, 2005.

Mattar, Philip. *The Mufti of Jerusalem: Al-Hajj Amin Al-Husayni and the Palestinian National Movement*. New York: Columbia University Press, 1992.

Mattawa, Khaled. *How Long Have You Been with Us? Essays on Poetry*. Ann Arbor: University of Michigan Press, 2016.

Mayer, Tamar. "From Zero to Hero: Masculinity in Jewish Nationalism." In *Gender Ironies of Nationalism: Sexing the Nation*, edited by Tamar Mayer, 283–307. London: Routledge, 2000.

Mazza, Roberto. *Jerusalem: From the Ottomans to the British*. London: I. B. Tauris, 2009.

McCarthy, Justin. *The Population of Palestine: Population History and Statistics of the Late Ottoman Period and the Mandate*. New York: Columbia University Press, 1990.

Meshorer, Yaakov. *Sixty Economic Documents of Eretz Israel, 1870–1944: The Sidney Olson Collection in the Israel Museum, Jerusalem*. Jerusalem: Israel Museum, 2001.

Messick, Brinkley Morris. *The Calligraphic State: Textual Domination and History in a Muslim Society*. Berkeley: University of California Press, 1993.

Monk, Daniel Bertrand. *An Aesthetic Occupation: The Immediacy of Architecture and the Palestine Conflict*. Durham, NC: Duke University Press, 2002.

Montefiore, Simon Sebag. *Jerusalem: The Biography*. London: Phoenix, 2012.

Moscrop, John James. *Measuring Jerusalem: The Palestine Exploration Fund and British Interests in the Holy Land*. London: Leicester University Press, 2000.

Moughalian, Sato. 2019. *Feast of Ashes: The Life and Art of David Ohannessian*. Stanford, CA: Redwood Press.

Moustafa, Ahmed, and Stefan Sperl. *The Cosmic Script: Sacred Geometry and the Science of Arabic Penmanship*. London: Thames & Hudson, 2014.

Musil, Robert. *Posthumous Papers of a Living Author*. London: Penguin, 1995.

Nasir-i Khusraw. *Diary of a Journey through Syria and Palestine*. Translated by Guy Le Strange. London: Palestine Pilgrims' Text Society, 1888.

Nassar, Hala Khamis, and Najat Rahman. *Mahmoud Darwish, Exile's Poet: Critical Essays*. Northampton, MA: Olive Branch Press, 2008.

Nassar, Issam. *European Portrayals of Jerusalem: Religious Fascinations and Colonialist Imaginations*. Lewiston, NY: Edwin Mellen Press, 2006.

Natsheh, Yusuf. "The Architecture of Ottoman Jerusalem." In *Ottoman Jerusalem: The Living City, 1517–1917*, edited by Sylvia Auld and Robert Hillenbrand, 583–655. London: Altajir World of Islam Trust, 2000.

Noy, Amos. *'Edim o Mumhim: Yehudim Maskilim Bney Yerushalayim ve-ha-Mizrah bi-Thilat ha-Me'a ha-'Esrim*. Tel Aviv: Resling, 2017.

Olitski, Yosef. *Omanut ha-Dfus: 400 Shanim le-Omanut ha-Dfus be-Erets Yisra'el*. Safed: Ha-Muze'on le-Omanut ha-Dfus, 1973.

Orenstein, Yitshak Avigdor. *Yoman ha-Kotel ha-Ma'aravi*. Jerusalem: Bet Orenstein, 1968.

Oskotski, Avraham. *Kol Yerushalayim le-Shnat Tarpa-b (1921): Sefer Shimushi, Sefer Yedi'ot, Sefer Adrese'ot*. Jerusalem: Dfus Levi, 1921.

Oz, Amos. *The Silence of Heaven: Agnon's Fear of God*. Princeton, NJ: Princeton University Press, 2000.

Pagis, Jonathan. *Mifkadey ha-Ukhlusin ha-Othmaniyim be-Erets Yisra'el, 1875–1918*. Jerusalem: Israel State Archive, 1997.

Pamuk, Sevket. *A Monetary History of the Ottoman Empire*. Cambridge: Cambridge University Press, 2000.

Pappe, Ilan. *The Rise and Fall of a Palestinian Dynasty: The Husaynis, 1700–1948*. London: Saqi Books, 2010.

Pardes, Ilana. *Agnon's Moonstruck Lovers: The Song of Songs in Israeli Culture*. Seattle: University of Washington Press, 2013.

Parush, Iris. *Hahot'im bi-Khtiva: Mahapekhat ha-Ktiva ba-Hevra ha-Yehudit ba-Me'a ha-Tsha-'esre*. Jerusalem: Karmel, 2017.

Paulovicova, Nina. "The Immoral Moral Scientist: John Maynard Keynes." *Past Imperfect* 13 (24 March 2008).

Persoff, Meir. *The Running Stag: The Stamps and Postal History of Israel.* London: R. Lowe, 1973.

Pinkerfeld, Jacob. "Beyt ha-Kneset le-ʿAdat ha-Karaʾim bi-Yerushalayim." *Kovets ha-Hevra ha-ʿIvrit le-Hakirat Erets Yisraʾel*, no. 2 (1928).

Ponsot, Jean-François. "Keynes and the 'National Emission Caisse' of North Russia: 1918–1920." *History of Political Economy* 34, no. 1 (2002): 177–206.

Poseq, Avigdor. "The 'New Jerusalem,' the Star of Zion and the Mandala." In *The Real and Ideal Jerusalem in Jewish, Christian, and Islamic Art*, edited by Bianca Kühnel, 325–40. Jerusalem: Center for Jewish Art, Hebrew University of Jerusalem, 1998.

Pred, Allan. *Lost Words and Lost Worlds: Modernity and the Language of Everyday Life in Late Nineteenth-Century Stockholm.* Cambridge: Cambridge University Press, 1990.

Pullan, Wendy, and Maximilian Gwiazda. "Designing the Biblical Present: Jerusalem's 'City of David.'" In *Memory Culture and the Contemporary City: Building Sites*, edited by Andrew Webber, Uta Staiger, and Henriette Steiner, 106–25. London: Palgrave Macmillan, 2009.

Pullan, Wendy, and Maximillian Sternberg. "The Making of Jerusalem's 'Holy Basin.'" *Planning Perspectives* 27, no. 2 (2012): 225–48.

Qasimiyya, Khayriyya. *Al-ʿAlam al-Filastini.* Beirut: PLO Research Center, 1970.

Reiner, Elchanan. "Traditions of Holy Places in Medieval Palestine—Oral versus Written." In *Offerings from Jerusalem: Portrayals of Holy Places by Jewish Artists*, edited by Rachel Sarfati, 9–19. Jerusalem: Israel Museum, 2002.

Resnik, S. "Eretz Israel on Palestine Stamps: Herbert Samuel's Historic Decision." *Holy Land Philatelist* 1, no. 3 (1955): 12–14.

Rioli, Maria Chiara. "Introducing Jerusalem: Visiting Cards, Advertisements and Urban Identities at the Turn of the 20th Century." In *Ordinary Jerusalem, 1840–1940*, edited by Angelos Dalachanis and Vincent Lemire, 29–49. Leiden: Brill, 2018.

Robinson, Shira. *Citizen Strangers: Palestinians and the Birth of Israel's Liberal Settler State.* Stanford, CA: Stanford University Press, 2013.

Rogers, Mary Eliza. *Domestic Life in Palestine.* London, 1862.

Rosenmeyer, Patricia A. *The Language of Ruins: Greek and Latin Inscriptions on the Memnon Colossus.* New York: Oxford University Press, 2018.

Rubinshtayn, Shimʿon. *Matbeʿot, Midot u-Mishkolot, mi-Reshit ha-Meʾa ha-19 ve-ʿad li-Tkufat ha-Maʿavar me-ha-Shilton ha-Turki la-Briti be-Erets Yisraʾel.* Jerusalem: Rubinshtayn, 1997.

Sabar, Shalom. "ʿAkedat Yitshak be-ʿAvodotav shel Moshe Shah Mizrahi: Mi-Halutsey ha-Omanut ha-ʿAmamit be-Erets Yisraʾel." In *Minha le-Menahem: Kovets*

Ma'amarim Likhvod ha-Rav Menahem ha-Cohen, edited by Hayim Be'er, Hana Amit, and Aviad Hacohen. Bney Brak: Ha-Kibuts ha-Me'uhad, 2007.

———. "Ha-Kotel ha-Ma'aravi be-Omanut Yehudit be-Mahalakh ha-Dorot." *Ariel* 180–81 (2007): 78–104.

Sakakini, Hala. *Jerusalem and I: A Personal Record*. Amman: Economic Press, 1990.

Sakakini, Khalil. *Kadha Ana Ya Dunya*. 2nd ed. Beirut: Al-Ittihad al-'Amm lil-Kuttab wal-Suhufiyin al-Filastiniyin, 1982.

———. *Yawmiyat Khalil al-Sakakini*. Edited by Akram Musallam. Vol. 1, *Nyu Yurk, Sultana, al-Quds 1907–1912*. Ramallah: Khalil Sakakini Cultural Center, Institute of Jerusalem Studies, 2003.

———. *Yawmiyat Khalil al-Sakakini*. Edited by Akram Musallam. Vol. 2, *Al-Nahda al-Urthuduksiyya, al-Harb al-'Uzma, al-Nafi ila Dimashq*. Ramallah: Khalil Sakakini Cultural Center, Institute of Jerusalem Studies, 2004.

Salih, 'Abd al-Mun'im Ahmad. *Abu Thamam Diwan al-Hamasa*. Baghdad: Dar al-Rashid, 1980.

Samuel, Herbert. *Memoirs*. London: Cresset Press, 1945.

Sandreczki, S. "Die Namen der Plätze, Strassen, Gassen u. s. w des jetzigen Jerusalem." In *Zeitschrift des Deutschen Palaestina-Vereins*. Leipzig, 1882.

Saposnik, Arieh Bruce. *Becoming Hebrew: The Creation of a Jewish National Culture in Palestine before the First World War*. New York: Oxford University Press, 2008.

———. "Wailing Walls and Iron Walls: The Western Wall as Sacred Symbol in Zionist National Iconography." *American Historical Review* 120, no. 5 (2015): 1653–81.

Sarfati, Rachel. "The Illustrations of Yihus ha-Avot." In *Offerings from Jerusalem: Portrayals of Holy Places by Jewish Artists*, edited by Rachel Sarfati, 21–29. Jerusalem: Israel Museum, 2002.

Saussure, Ferdinand de. *Course in General Linguistics*. New York: McGraw-Hill, 1966.

Schayegh, Cyrus. *The Middle East and the Making of the Modern World*. Cambridge: Harvard University Press, 2017.

Schimmel, Annemarie. *Calligraphy and Islamic Culture*. New York: NYU Press, 1984.

Schmelz, Uriel. *Modern Jerusalem's Demographic Evolution*. Institute of Contemporary Jewry, Hebrew University of Jerusalem, 1987.

Schölch, Alexander. *Palestine in Transformation, 1856–1882*. Washington, DC: Institute for Palestine Studies, 2006.

Scott, James. *Against the Grain: A Deep History of the Earliest States*. New Haven, CT: Yale University Press, 2017.

Segev, Tom. *One Palestine, Complete: Jews and Arabs under the British Mandate*. London: Little, Brown, 2000.

Seikaly, Sherene. *Men of Capital: Scarcity and Economy in Mandate Palestine*. Stanford, CA: Stanford University Press, 2016.

Shahar, David. *'Al ha-Halomot*. Tel Aviv: Am Oved, 1955.

Shalev-Kalifa, Nirit, ed. *The First Governor: Sir Ronald Storrs, Governor of Jerusalem, 1918–1926*. Tel Aviv: Eretz Israel Museum, Yad Ben Zvi, 2010.

Shami, Yitshak. *Nikmat ha-Avot*. Tel Aviv: Yahdav, 1975.

Shaw, Stanford J. "The Ottoman Census System and Population, 1831–1914." *International Journal of Middle East Studies* 9, no. 3 (1978): 325–38.

Sheehi, Stephen. *Foundations of Modern Arab Identity*. Gainesville: University Press of Florida, 2004.

———. "Portrait Paths: Studio Photography in Ottoman Palestine." *Jerusalem Quarterly*, no. 61 (2015): 23.

Shepherd, Naomi. *Ploughing Sand: British Rule in Palestine, 1917–1948*. London: John Murray, 1999.

Shiryon, Yitshak. *Zikhronot*. Jerusalem, 1943.

Shohamy, Elana. *Linguistic Landscape in the City*. Bristol, UK: Multilingual Matters, 2010.

Shor, Shimon. *Gdud Maginey ha-Safa be-Erets Yisra'el 1923–1936*. Merkaz Hertsl le-Heker ha-Tsiyonut, Haifa: University of Haifa, 2000.

Shuqayri, Ahmad. *Arba'un 'Ama fi al-Hayat al-'Arabiyya wal-Dawliyya*. Beirut: Dar al-Awda, 1973.

Simmel, Georg. "The Metropolis and Mental Life (1903)." In *The Blackwell City Reader*, edited by Gary Bridge and Sophie Watson. Oxford: Blackwell, 2002.

———. *The Philosophy of Money*. London: Taylor & Francis, 2011.

Smith, Barbara J. *Roots of Separatism in Palestine: British Economic Policy, 1920–1929*. London: I. B. Tauris, 1993.

Sorek, Tamir. "The Orange and the 'Cross in the Crescent': Imagining Palestine in 1929." *Nations and Nationalism* 10, no. 3 (2004): 269–91.

Stanislawski, Michael. *Zionism and the Fin-de-Siècle: Cosmopolitanism and Nationalism from Nordau to Jabotinsky*. Berkeley: University of California Press, 2001.

Stern, Karen B. *Writing on the Wall: Graffiti and the Forgotten Jews of Late Antiquity*. Princeton, NJ: Princeton University Press, 2018.

Storrs, Ronald. *Orientations*. London: Nicholson & Watson, 1943.

Street, Brian V. *Social Literacies: Critical Approaches to Literacy in Development, Ethnography and Education*. London: Longman, 1995.

Suleiman, Yasir. *A War of Words: Language and Conflict in the Middle East*. Cambridge: Cambridge University Press, 2004.

Survey of Palestine. "Jerusalem Compiled, Drawn & Printed under the Direction of F. J. Salmon, Commissioner for Lands & Surveys, Palestine" [map, BLMC]. Survey of Palestine, 1937.

Tamari, Salim. *Jerusalem 1948: The Arab Neighbourhoods and Their Fate in the War.* Jerusalem: Institute of Jerusalem Studies, 1999.

———. "Khalil Sakakini's Ottoman Prison Diaries." *Jerusalem Quarterly File*, no. 20 (2004): 7–23.

———. *Mountain against the Sea: Essays on Palestinian Society and Culture.* Berkeley: University of California Press, 2009.

———. "Confessionalism and Public Space in Ottoman and Colonial Jerusalem." In *Cities and Sovereignty: Identity Politics in Urban Spaces*, edited by Diane E. Davis and Nora Libertun de Duren, 59–82. Bloomington: Indiana University Press, 2011.

———. *Year of the Locust: A Soldier's Diary and the Erasure of Palestine's Ottoman Past.* Berkeley: University of California Press, 2011.

———. *The Great War and the Remaking of Palestine.* Berkeley: University of California Press, 2017.

Tamari, Vera. "Nabi Musa Banners." In *Ottoman Jerusalem: The Living City, 1517–1917*, edited by Sylvia Auld and Robert Hillenbrand, 310–30. London: Altajir World of Islam Trust, 2000.

Tannus, Izzat. *The Palestinians: A Detailed Documented Eyewitness History of Palestine under British Mandate.* New York: I.G.T., 1988.

Tawil-Souri, Helga. "Orange, Green and Blue: Color-Coded Paperwork for Palestinian Population Control." In *Surveillance and Control in Israel/Palestine: Population, Territory and Power*, edited by Elia Zureik, David Lyon, and Yasmeen Abu-Laban, 219–38. London: Routledge, 2011.

Tobler, Titus. *Beitrag zur medizinischen Topographie von Jerusalem.* Berlin: G. Reimer, 1855.

Travis, Anthony S. *On Chariots with Horses of Fire and Iron: The Excursionists and the Narrow Gauge Railroad from Jaffa to Jerusalem.* Jerusalem: Magnes, 2008.

Tudela, Benjamin of. *The Itinerary of Benjamin of Tudela.* London: Henry Frowde OUP, 1907.

Tütüncü, Mehmet. *Turkish Jerusalem (1516–1917): Ottoman Inscriptions from Jerusalem and Other Palestinian Cities.* Haarlem: SOTA, 2006.

———. *Turkish Palestine (1069–1917): Inscriptions from Al-Khalil (Hebron), Nebi Musa and Other Palestinian Cities under Turkish Rule.* Haarlem: SOTA, 2008.

Ülker, Erol. "Contextualising 'Turkification': Nation-Building in the Late Ottoman Empire, 1908–18." *Nations and Nationalism* 11, no. 4 (2005): 613–36.

Vilnay, Zev. *Matsevot Kodesh be-Erets-Yisra'el: Te'ur ha-Kvarim ha-Kdoshim be-Livyat Tsiyurim u-Tmunot.* Jerusalem: Ahi-ever, 1985.

Wallace, Edwin Sherman. *Jerusalem the Holy: A Brief History of Ancient Jerusalem; with an Account of the Modern City.* New York: Oliphant, 1898.

Wallach, Yair. "Creating a Country through Currency and Stamps: State Symbols and

Nation-Building in British-Ruled Palestine." *Nations and Nationalism* 17, no. 1 (2011): 129–47.

———. "Rethinking the Yishuv: Late-Ottoman Palestine's Jewish Communities Revisited." *Journal of Modern Jewish Studies* 16, no. 2 (2017): 275–94.

———. "Jerusalem's Lost Heart: The Rise and Fall of the Late-Ottoman City Centre." In *Urban Neighbourhood Formations*, edited by Hilal Alkan and Nazan Maksudyan, 138–58. London: Routledge, 2020.

Walls, Archibald G., and Amal Abul-Hajj. *Arabic Inscriptions in Jerusalem: A Handlist and Maps*. London: World of Islam Trust, 1980.

Wasserstein, Bernard. *The British in Palestine: The Mandatory Government and the Arab-Jewish Conflict, 1917–1929*. Cambridge: Blackwell, 1991.

———. *Herbert Samuel: A Political Life*. Oxford: Clarendon Press, 1992.

Watenpaugh, Keith David. *Being Modern in the Middle East: Revolution, Nationalism, Colonialism, and the Arab Middle Class*. Princeton, NJ: Princeton University Press, 2006.

Weir, Shelagh. "A Bridal Headdress from Southern Palestine." *Palestine Exploration Quarterly* 105, no. 1 (1973): 101–9.

Weizman, Eyal. *Hollow Land: Israel's Architecture of Occupation*. London: Verso, 2007.

Weizmann, Chaim. *Trial and Error: The Autobiography of Chaim Weizmann*. London: Hamish Hamilton, 1949.

Wilson, Charles W. "Ordnance Survey of Jerusalem 1864–5" [map, BLMC]. Southampton, UK: Ordnance Survey, 1865.

———. Ordnance Survey of Jerusalem. Southampton, UK: Ordnance Survey Office, 1865.

Wishnitzer, Avner. *Reading Clocks, Alla Turca: Time and Society in the Late Ottoman Empire*. Chicago: University of Chicago Press, 2015.

Wittek, Paul. "Notes sur la Tughra ottomane (I et II)." *Byzantion* 18 (1948): 311–34; 20 (1950): 267–93.

Yavuz, Yildim. "The Influence of Late-Ottoman Architecture in the Arab Provinces: The Case of the Palace Hotel in Jerusalem." *Electronic Journal of Oriental Studies* 4, no. 44 (2001): 1–22.

Yehoshua, Ya'akov. *Sipuro shel ha-Bayit ha-Sefaradi ba-Rova' ha-Yehudi ba-'Ir ha-'Atika shel Yerushalayim*. Jerusalem: Rubin Mass, 1979.

———. *Yerushalayim Temol Shilshom: Pirkey Havai*. 3 vols. Jerusalem: Rubin Mass, 1977–1981.

Yellin, David. *Yerushalayim shel Temol*. Jerusalem: Rubin Mass, 1972.

Yellin, Ita. *Le-Tse'etsa'ay*. 2 vols. Jerusalem: Dfus ha-Ma'arav, 1941.

Yellin, Yehoshua. *Zikhronot le-Ven Yerushalayim*. Jerusalem: Dfus Tsion, 1924.

Yeoh, Brenda S. A. "Street Names in Colonial Singapore." *Geographical Review* 82, no. 3 (1992): 312–22.

Zaydan, Jurji. *Al-Rihlat al-Thalath: Al-Astana—Uruba—Filastin*. Beirut: Arab Center for Research and Policy Studies, 2017.

Zelizer, Viviana. *The Social Meaning of Money*. Princeton, NJ: Princeton University Press, 1997.

Index

Note: Figures are designated by f following the page number.